AMERICA'S MUSICAL LANDSCAPE

FOURTH EDITION

AMERICA'S MUSICAL LANDSCAPE

JEAN FERRIS

ARIZONA STATE
UNIVERSITY

Boston   Burr Ridge, IL   Dubuque, IA   Madison, WI   New York   San Francisco   St. Louis
Bangkok   Bogotá   Caracas   Kuala Lumpur   Lisbon   London   Madrid   Mexico City
Milan   Montreal   New Delhi   Santiago   Seoul   Singapore   Sydney   Taipei   Toronto

McGraw-Hill Higher Education

*A Division of The **McGraw-Hill** Companies*

AMERICA'S MUSICAL LANDSCAPE

Published by McGraw-Hill, an imprint of The McGraw-Hill Companies, Inc. 1221 Avenue of the Americas, New York, NY, 10020. Copyright © 2002, 1998, 1993, 1990 by The McGraw-Hill Companies, Inc. All rights reserved. No part of this publication may be reproduced or distributed in any form or by any means, or stored in a data base or retrieval system, without the prior written consent of The McGraw-Hill Companies, Inc., including, but not limited to, in any network or other electronic storage or transmission, or broadcast for distance learning. Some ancillaries, including electronic and print components, may not be available to customers outside the United States.

This book is printed on acid-free paper.

1 2 3 4 5 6 7 8 9 0 DOC/DOC 0 9 8 7 6 5 4 3 2 1

ISBN 0-07-241426-X

Editorial director: *Phillip A. Butcher*
Executive sponsoring editor: *Christopher Freitag*
Developmental editor: *Nadia Bidwell*
Senior marketing manager: *David Patterson*
Project manager: *Rebecca Nordbrock*
Senior production supervisor: *Lori Koetters*
Producer, media technology: *Todd Vaccaro*
Coordinator freelance design: *Mary E. Kazak*
Associate supplement producer: *Joyce J. Chappetto*
Photo research coordinator: *David A. Tietz*
Photo researcher: *Connie Gardner*
Cover illustration and design: *Lawrence Didona*
Stock images: *© PhotoDisc*
Typeface: *10/12 Times Roman*
Compositor: *Shepherd Incorporated*
Printer: *R. R. Donnelley & Sons Company*

Library of Congress Cataloging-in-Publication Data

Ferris, Jean.
  America's musical landscape / Jean Ferris.—4th ed.
    p. cm
  Includes discographies and index.
  ISBN 0-07-241426-X (acid-free paper)
    1. Music—United States—History and criticism. I. Title.
ML200 .F47 2002
780'.973—dc21
                                                   2001034506

www.mhhe.com

With a song in my heart for
Christopher Andrew, Larissa Renee, Noah Ives—
and all our other grand children (space intended).

Contents

PRELUDE

The Elements of Musical Sound xxi

PART 1

Music in Early North America 2

1

North American Indian Music 10

2

Folk Music 18

3
The Colonial, Revolutionary, and Federal Periods   25

PART 2
The Nineteenth Century   50

4
Populist Music of the Nineteenth Century   58

5
Early Concert Music   86

6
American Concert Music Comes of Age   98

The Growth of Vernacular Traditions   110

7
The Rise of Popular Culture   114

8
Country-Western and Urban Folk Music   127

9
The Jazz Age   151

10
Jazz 1930–1960   171

11
Jazz since 1960   188

12
Latin Popular Musics   202

13
Rock and Roll   214

14
Popular Music since 1970   233

PART 4
Music for Theater and Film   246

15
Musical Theater   249

16
Music for Films   274

19

Mainstream Concert Music: Evolution   326

20

The Avant-Garde after 1950   337

21

American Concert Music since 1950   349

Listening Examples

Preface

The survey course for which this text is designed affords the same broad coverage of musics—classical and popular, secular and religious, vocal and instrumental—as does the traditional music appreciation course predominantly featuring European examples. Here we tackle the happy task of introducing basic musical terms and concepts using selected examples of outstanding American music.

As suggested in the title of the text, I have consistently related music to other arts, finding such comparisons to have pedagogical as well as aesthetic value for nonmusicians, often more familiar with visual and literary than with aural experience. Asher B. Durand's stunning landscape painting *Kindred Spirits* (Figure 38), an eloquent portrayal of American poet William Cullen Bryant and American painter Thomas Cole sharing reverent admiration for their country's natural splendors, in fact inspired this text, which seeks to capture some of that painting's expression of the interdependence uniting American arts and artists.

The musical landscape this text explores is that of the regions stretching from the Pacific Ocean to the Atlantic, and from Canada to Mexico, the areas comprising today's continental United States. Influences abound from above and below the northern and southern borders upon this "American" music experience, and each of the many cultures of North America, Mexico, and Central and South America—and, of course, Hawaii—has a rich musical landscape of its own. But time constrains most "American music" courses to cover only some of the music, of only certain regions, within these limited borders of the United States. Regret for what we cannot cover here must only enhance our enthusiasm for the rich landscape we shall explore, and encourage us to extend our exploration as soon and as far as possible throughout all of the Americas' musical landscapes.

This fourth edition includes up-to-date information on each of the areas of music, popular and classical, covered in the text. The vernacular genres have been extended to include new chapters on folk music, recent jazz, and pop since 1970, and the historical and current situation of women in popular as well as in classical music is addressed. A third CD added to the package, for a total of 225 minutes of music, greatly increases the students' listening opportunities. Further, I have reorganized the text, in response to the valuable suggestions of users and reviewers: Parts 1 and 2 cover music in early North America through the nineteenth century. Parts 3, 4, and 5, all primarily concerned with music of the twentieth century, reflect the significance afforded genre distinctions less relevant in earlier periods. Thus Part 3 concerns the rise of popular culture, from the years of ragtime and Tin Pan Alley through country-western, jazz, Latin pop, rock, and a variety of recent popular music; Part 4 covers music for theater and film; and Part 5 concerns the concert music, traditional and experimental, of recent periods up to today. Relevant social and cultural information, formerly placed throughout the text, now appears before each section in part openers, and the Prelude has been extended to include most of the technical information concerning texture, form, and notation, rendering the flow of the narrative smoother than in earlier editions. I hope all these changes will prove advantageous to students and professors alike, and I hope those who have suggestions for further improvements to the text will freely share them with me.

I particularly wish to thank Professor Warren Gauguin of Warren Wilson College and Professor Wallace Rave of Arizona State University for their expert advice concerning the jazz chapters in this new edition. Further, I am more than grateful to the following prepublication reviewers, whose recommendations on matters throughout the text proved invaluable: Laurie Blunsom, Northeastern University; Joseph Estock, James Madison University; Peter Lefferts, University of Nebraska, Lincoln; Cristina Magaldi, Towson University; James Phillips, University of Notre Dame.

I remain in awe of the expertise and diligence of the McGraw-Hill book team who put this book together, and I express to all of them my most profound thanks.

Jean Ferris

Introduction

Most Americans today would find it difficult, perhaps impossible, to experience a day without music, so pervasive is the sound of music in our everyday lives. Music enhances many of our social, religious, and work-related experiences. Music sets rhythms for us to dance or exercise to, keeps us company at work or play, enhances our concentration and our emotional response when viewing a film or a musical, accompanies some religious services, helps us go to sleep at night, and makes it easier to wake up in the morning and to prepare for another day filled with the sounds we individually enjoy.

From the wide field of *popular* musics, we generally develop preferences for certain kinds, or styles, over others. That is, from the incredibly rich menu of sounds available today we might choose most often to hear rap, jazz, rock, country, pop—or something else. Some of us enjoy instrumental music; others prefer song. Our tastes change over long periods of time, and our preferences may differ from one moment to another, depending on our mood or circumstance at a given time.

The great world of *classical* music, as it is often called, also encompasses a tremendous range of sounds. Unfortunately, none of the terms generally used to distinguish between the music we call popular and the music we call classical is truly descriptive of the differences we recognize between them. We can agree that music that serves no functional purpose, but simply expresses an abstract concept a composer thought worth sharing—music that requires intense concentration and sometimes a measure of learning and experience on the part of the listener—differs from music that exists primarily as a means of entertainment. It is difficult, however, to describe differences between these two kinds of music without implying unintended and inappropriate judgments of value. Commonly we speak of music that requires extensive training on the part of composers and performers, and that may assume some guided experience on the part of the listener, as *classical, art, concert,* or *serious* music; but none of those terms properly distinguishes between this music and much of the music played by deejays on popular radio sites. No one is more *serious* about music than outstanding singer/songwriters in the popular fields. Many great American songs have survived beyond their days of initial popularity to become *classics* in their own right. *Concerts* are among the most important venues for experiencing so-called popular music of many kinds. And *art* suggests simply a creative means of expression, with no inherent requirement that it be simple or complex or even good or bad. Further confusing the issue, many so-called classical pieces have become so familiar and well-loved that today they are performed in concerts we refer to as *pops*.

The terms italicized above, however, have become inherent parts of the language of music. We will hear and read them in formal and informal discussions of music, and we will use them here, in this text, although with sensitivity to the unintended connotations they have acquired. Words, after all, serve only to broaden our ideas *about* music and our knowledge of its history. No words can substitute for the glorious experience of hearing, and understanding, the great and beautiful music of America.

The more we understand about musical forms and the elements that constitute the building materials of music, the better we are prepared to enjoy music of all kinds. Recognition of the historical context in which music was conceived, and an awareness of the relationships between music and the other arts of a given period, enhance our understanding and pleasure. It is my personal wish that your delight in listening to all kinds of music will increase immeasurably as you discover the many and varied aspects of America's musical landscape.

Prelude
The Elements of Musical Sound

Music, an art of organized sounds, is virtually limitless in variety and in the power to enchant and challenge our ears. However, because it never holds still, and we can neither see nor touch it, understanding music can be an elusive thing, and some of the world's greatest music may challenge the unprepared listener's ears. The more we understand the qualities of music, the elements of which it is constructed, the historical/social setting in which a given piece evolved, the intent of the composer, and the performer(s)' contributions, the greater will be our intellectual, emotional, and aesthetic rewards for listening to any kind of music.

Musicians generally recognize four **elements of music**—rhythm, melody, harmony, and timbre—as the fundamental materials of which music is composed. As we listen to music, any one of the elements—a memorable tune, a driving rhythm, the unusual sound of an exotic musical instrument—may attract our attention, but more often we respond to the combination of two or more of the elements of music without methodically analyzing the name and proportions of each. Understanding these building blocks of music enhances our listening and provides a vocabulary with which to discuss a piece in some detail; and of course the more we are *aware* of what we hear, the greater is our capacity to enjoy all kinds of music.

Rhythm

Because music consists of arrangements of long and short sounds and silences, **rhythm,** having to do with time relationships in music, is the most basic of the elements. The system of music notation used in the Western world indicates the rhythm of music by giving the *proportional* length of each sound and silence; that is, written music dictates the duration of each sound or silence only in relation to other sounds and silences in the piece.

Rhythmic values are expressed in the familiar terminology of fractions (Table 1), the value of a *half note,* for example, equal to half the value of a *whole note.* But the specific duration of a half note depends upon the *tempo,* or rate of speed, at which the music is performed.

Tempo, which means time, is one of many Italian words adopted into a virtually universal music language during the sixteenth and seventeenth centuries, when Italians dominated music in the Western world. Foreign musicians studying in Italy absorbed the techniques and much of the terminology of their Italian masters, which they shared with their own students and patrons

Table 1   Rhythmic Notation

This table assumes the quarter note equals one beat. Any other note may equal one beat instead, and the other note values then change proportionately.

Notated Symbol	Name	Rest	Number of Beats per Note	Number of Notes Equal to 4 Beats
○	Whole note	–	4	1
♩	Half note	–	2	2
♩	Quarter note	⸜	1	4
♪	Eighth note	⸜	½	8
♪	Sixteenth note	⸜	¼	16

Table 2   Common Tempo Indications

Largo	Slow; "broad"
Adagio	Slow; "at ease"
Andante	Moderately slow; "walking" tempo
Moderato	Moderate
Allegro	Fast; cheerful
Presto	Very fast
Vivace	Lively
Molto	Very (*allegro molto* = very fast)
Non troppo	Not too much (*allegro non troppo* = not too fast)
Con brio	With spirit

upon returning to their homelands. Since then, many Italian music terms have been used all over the world, remaining in common use today.

Music listeners quickly become familiar with the most common Italian words for tempos, shown in Table 2, which regularly appear in printed concert programs and often in newspaper concert and recording reviews as well.

Meter   Just as language is formed of irregularly occurring accented and unaccented syllables, musical sounds, too, may occur without specific rhythmic organization. If, however, musical sounds are arranged in rhythmic patterns, similar to those of poetry as opposed to prose, we say the music is metered.

Meter organizes rhythm into units called *measures,* each containing a particular number of pulses or beats. The common meters are *duple* (two beats per measure), *triple* (three beats per measure), and *quadruple* (four beats per measure). In Western practice, the first beat of each measure is normally accented, or stressed, and if there are four or more beats per measure, there is at

Duple meter

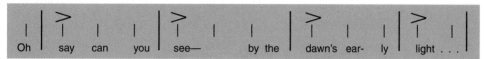

Triple meter

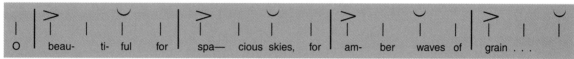

Quadruple meter

least one secondary accent as well. For example, in quadruple meter (Figure 1), the secondary accent falls on the third beat.

Figure 1
Common meters, showing accents.

Melody

Musical sounds, called **tones,** are caused by something vibrating at a particular frequency, or rate of speed. Tones are said to be relatively high or low in **pitch,** depending upon the rate of vibration of the medium producing the sound: The faster a string on a violin or the column of air in a trumpet vibrates, the higher the level of pitch. Much as a sentence is a meaningful succession of words, a **melody** is a meaningful succession of tones of various levels of pitch.

Tones have *letter* names, A through G. The **interval,** or distance, between tones is named according to the *number* of tones it includes; for example, from A to B is a *second,* from A to C, a *third,* and so on (Figure 2). The most basic interval is the *eighth,* called an **octave.** The two tones of an octave share the same letter name and sound nearly alike, because the higher vibrates at exactly twice the rate of the lower tone and the simple relationship of their frequencies (the ratio 2:1) causes little tension between them.

All keys on a keyboard that bear the same letter name *look* the same as well, because they occupy the same position relative to other keys. For example, if we start at the left of the keyboard and move up, we see that the last white key before the third of the three black keys is always an A (Figure 2), D is always the white note between the two black notes, and so on.

Scales Melodies are based on stepwise rising or descending patterns of pitches within the range of an octave called **scales.** By the seventeenth century, two particular seven-note patterns—the **major** and **minor scales**—

Figure 2

A piano keyboard.

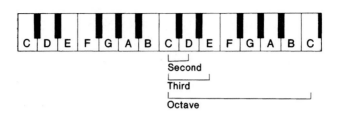

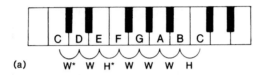

Figure 3

The major and minor scales. (*a*) The white notes of the octave from C to C on the keyboard correspond to the pattern of the major scale. (*b*) The white notes of the octave from A to A on the keyboard correspond to the pattern of the minor scale.

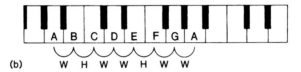

had been accepted as those that best served European composers of concert music, and they continue to prevail in Western music today.

The major and minor scales each include two **half steps** (the closest distance between two keys on a keyboard) and five **whole steps** (the equivalent of two half steps). The white notes of the octave from C to C on the keyboard correspond to the pattern of the *major* scale, while the white notes of the octave from A to A correspond to the pattern of the *minor* scale.

Music based on the major scale sounds very different from music that is minor, because of the different order in which the half and whole steps occur (Figure 3). If you can play a keyboard instrument, you might play the first three notes of "Doe, a Deer" from *The Sound of Music,* beginning on C. These are the first three notes of the major scale. Now *lower* the third tone by a half step, or begin playing on A and use all white keys, and you will hear how the melody would begin if it were based on a minor scale.

Other scales we will encounter in our survey of American music include the **modes**—seven-note patterns whose arrangements of half and whole steps differ from those of either the major or minor scale. If you start on any white key of a keyboard *other* than C or A, and play up or down an octave using white keys only, you will have played a mode different from the major or minor scale. Notice that although each mode, or scale, has five whole and two half steps, the different order in which they occur strongly affects the "flavor" of the sound. Another popular scale, on which many children's songs and much folk music is based, is the simple **pentatonic** (five-note) pattern, represented by the five black keys on a keyboard. If you can play "by ear," you will find many tunes can be played using those five tones only.

(a) Smooth melody line   (b) Angular melody line

Figure 4
Melodic contours.

Further Characteristics of Melody
Melodies of course have rhythm, the tones of a melody occurring in some order of long and/or short sounds. If a melody, such as a children's song or folk song, is particularly singable and memorable and seems complete in itself, we call it a **tune.** A different kind of melody is a brief, fragmentary melodic idea or **motive,** recurring throughout a piece, particularly in instrumental music. Probably the most famous motive in Western music is the four-note "knocking" pattern that begins Beethoven's Symphony no. 5, identified at least as readily by its rhythm as by its melodic characteristics.

Because we may draw a line up or down from one note of a melody to the next, we think of a melody as a *linear* concept and identify its contour as angular (with large leaps between the tones), smooth (with the tones closely connected), or some combination of these. Figure 4 compares, for example, the smooth contour of "Merrily We Roll Along" with the angular shape of "Westminster Chimes." Other familiar tunes that might further clarify this distinction are "My Country, 'Tis of Thee" (smooth) and "The Star Spangled Banner" (sharply angular in contour).

Harmony

The melodies of European and American music generally are accompanied by vertical combinations of sounds called **harmony,** defined as the simultaneous sounding of two or more different tones in a logical or meaningful (not necessarily beautiful) manner. The system of harmony that has governed Western music for nearly four hundred years, based upon the major and minor scales, is called **tonality** or the **tonal system.**

Purposeful combinations of *three or more* different tones constitute **chords,** which enrich the sounds of Western music and please Western ears much as linear perspective adds depth and pleases the eyes of lovers of Western art. Indeed, chordal harmony, like linear perspective is a peculiarly Western concept; both the aural and visual concepts were developed during the Western Renaissance, and neither has become characteristic of non-Western arts. As shown in Figure 5, the tones of a chord are notated in *vertical* fashion, above and beneath each other.

Consonant and Dissonant Sounds
Certain combinations of musical sounds, which we call **consonant,** have the effect of being passive, or at rest. Other harmonies, sounding relatively tense or active, we call **dissonant.** It is important to understand that dissonance and consonance have nothing to do

Figure 5

Triads on each note of the C major scale.

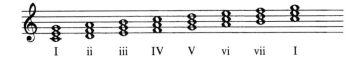

I   ii   iii   IV   V   vi   vii   I

with "good" or "bad" sounds (composers are hardly likely to choose "bad" sounds for their music), but refer only to the relative degree of activity or tension the composer intends or the listener perceives.

Of course, these concepts are entirely subjective, differing widely from one time, culture, or individual to another. Generally, though, dissonance and consonance work together to provide variety and stability in musical compositions, dissonant sounds creating tension that may (or may not) resolve to consonant harmony, much as a dancer expressively tenses and then relaxes muscles.

Tonal Harmony   The first tone of a major or minor scale, called the **tonic,** represents a kind of home base, from which a piece of music in the Western tradition is likely to begin and on which it is even more likely to end. The tonic names the **key** of a composition; for example, we say a piece is in the key of A major, meaning that the tonic note is A and most of the tones are those of the major scale. For another example, a piece based on the D minor scale is said to be in the key of D minor.

Each of the tones in a major or minor scale bears a specific relationship, relatively distant or close, to the tonic. The fifth step of the scale, called the **dominant,** is the tone most closely related to tonic. It is heard frequently during a piece, and it seems to bear almost a gravitational pull back to tonic, or home base. The second-closest tone to tonic is the fourth step above (or the fifth below) tonic, called the **subdominant.**

The most basic chord in the tonal system, consisting of three alternate tones (or a third piled on top of a third), is called a **triad** (Figure 5). Triads may be built on any tone of the major or minor scale and bear the same relationship to tonic and to each other as the tones upon which they are built. Thus the strongest relationship is between the tonic triad (often represented by the Roman numeral I) and the triad built upon the fifth note of the scale, or the dominant (V). The next-closest chord to tonic is the triad built upon the fourth, or subdominant, step of the scale, which provides a somewhat weaker drive toward tonic.

The I, IV, and V chords, then, provide the cornerstones of tonal harmony. Many simple melodies are effectively accompanied by just these three closely related chords.

Timbre

The quality or **timbre** of a musical sound depends on characteristics of the medium producing it. Thus musical instruments have distinctive timbres ac-

Table 3 Dynamic Levels		
Levels of Volume		
Italian Term	*Abbreviation*	*English Meaning*
Pianissimo	pp	Very soft
Piano	p	Soft
Mezzopiano	mp	Moderately soft
Mezzoforte	mf	Moderately loud
Forte	f	Loud
Fortissimo	ff	Very loud

cording to their size, the material of which they are made, and the manner in which they are played. For example, the timbre or "color" of the sound produced by a violin differs from that of a flute, and the sound produced by plucking the string of a violin is unlike the sound made when the same string is bowed.

Pitch also affects the timbre of musical sound: Notice how the high tones of a piano differ in timbre as well as pitch from the very low tones of the instrument, and how men's and women's voices are distinguished in terms of timbre as well as the range of their pitches.

Another factor affecting the timbre of a voice or instrument is the loudness or softness of the sound, called its **dynamic level.** Composers often vary the dynamic level within a piece for many reasons: to achieve emotional effects, to illustrate events described in the text of a song, or to achieve extramusical effects in descriptive instrumental music. The Italian words **piano** and **forte,** respectively meaning soft and loud, are among the commonly used dynamic terms included with their abbreviations in Table 3.

Texture

Much as we describe the texture of a piece of fabric according to the way in which its threads are interwoven, so we describe the **texture** of music in terms of its "threads," or melodic lines. Music consisting only of one line of melody—a Native American song or flute piece, or an ancient folk tune, for example—we call **monophonic** in texture, the prefix "mono" indicating the sounding of *one* line of music. No matter the number of voices or instruments performing the same melody in **unison**—that is, all sounding the same pitches (not necessarily in the same octave) at the same time—the texture of the music remains monophonic.

A piece such as a **round,** involving melody in more than one line simultaneously, is **polyphonic** in texture, the prefix *poly* indicating more than one of something occurring at the same time. In a round, all the voices perform the same melody, entering however at different times and therefore sounding

Figure 6

Texture in music.

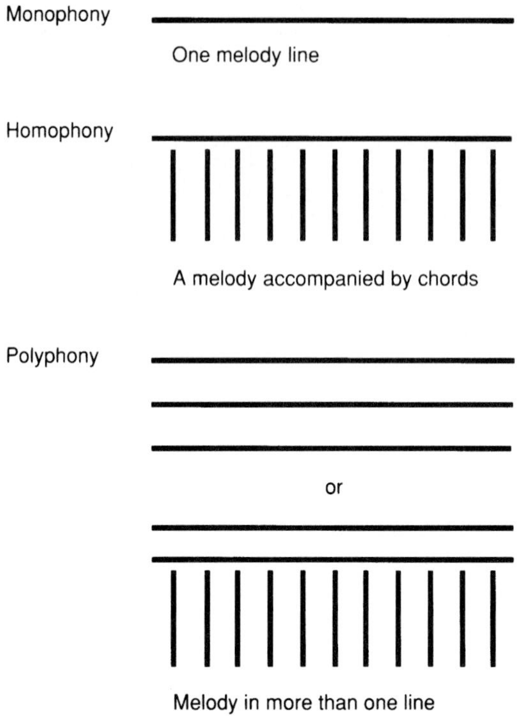

Monophony

One melody line

Homophony

A melody accompanied by chords

Polyphony

or

Melody in more than one line

different tones together. Thus we hear meaningful combinations of tones, or harmony. Polyphony may instead involve the combinations of *different* melodies that, when combined, produce harmony. However, although both monophonic and polyphonic music result in harmony, both are primarily melodic, or linear, concepts.

A third music texture, **homophony,** occurs when a melody is accompanied not by another melody line, but by chords. In other words, the voices (instrumental or vocal) accompanying the melody for the purpose of producing harmony are not primarily of melodic interest themselves. Hymns are often accompanied by an organ or piano adding chordal harmony; a band provides harmonic accompaniment while the crowd sings "The Star Spangled Banner" at a football game; folk singers may accompany themselves by strumming chords on a musical instrument. All of these are examples of homophonic, or chordal, texture. (See Figure 6.)

Form

When describing a work of art, we often consider the manner in which it is organized. There are many approaches to formal design, based upon principles of *repetition* and *contrast,* with repetition lending a work unity, symmetry, and balance, and contrast providing the variety necessary to sustain interest. A play, for example, may have one or several acts, a novel a number of

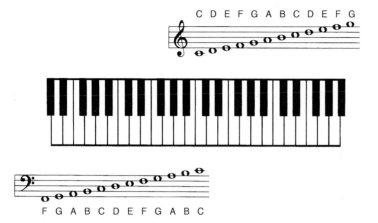

Figure 7
Pitches notated in the treble and bass clefs. Certain tones, including "middle C," may be notated in either the bass or treble clef.

chapters, a poem one or several verses or stanzas. Each act or chapter or verse of a literary work is logically organized within itself, as is each sentence or line of verse. The manner in which the elements of music are organized into a musical composition is called the composition's **form.**

Music Notation

Although one may well enjoy listening to and even performing music without necessarily learning to read music notation, some conception of how music is written may be of interest. For centuries, Western music has been written on a **staff** of five lines and four spaces (see Figure 7). Musical sounds are written as **notes,** and notated silences are called **rests.** The staff forms a kind of "ladder," with each line and each space representing a particular pitch. A sign called a **clef,** placed at the beginning of the staff, indicates that a particular line represents a specific pitch, thus fixing the relative position of all of the other pitches on the staff. For example, the *bass clef* ($\mathbf{9}$:), sometimes called the F clef, on which lower tones are notated, indicates that the fourth line of the staff is (a particular) F. The *treble clef* ($\&$), also called the G clef, on which higher tones are notated, indicates that the second line of the staff represents (a particular) G. In other words, placing a clef on the staff provides a reference point that fixes the pitches of all the lines and spaces.

Understanding just these basic concepts of how music is written allows us, without really "reading" music, to follow the ascending and descending patterns of tones written on a page and have an approximate idea of how the music would sound.

Elements of an American Sound

Because America's early settlers came from many different cultures, it took time for music to acquire a characteristic American sound; but surprisingly soon music, like the English language, changed its accent in the New World.

The manner in which the elements of music are selected and combined, the choice of timbres, various means of musical expression such as changes in dynamic level and in tempo, and the purpose for which music is intended are among the nearly indefinable qualities that determine a particular composition's characteristic sound, or **style.**

In music, as in fashion, style refers to a manner or mode of expression, and again as in fashion, style in music is affected by the time and the culture that produce it. For example, American rhythms often are more flexible than those characteristic of European music; and although the delay or anticipation of accented beats called **syncopation** occurs in music worldwide, its bold and consistent use gives much American classical as well as popular music a distinctive flavor. The long, irregular melodies of pieces such as Samuel Barber's *Adagio for Strings* (Listening Example 69) are sometimes thought to reflect the informality, personal freedom, and lack of physical and cultural boundaries associated with the ideal American life. Jazz musicians, by using traditional instruments in new and unusual ways, caused Americans to alter the timbres of symphonic as well as popular musics, as we hear for example in George Gershwin's *Rhapsody in Blue* (Listening Example 42).

Thus, although much American music is stylistically indistinguishable from music by European composers of the same period, perhaps you will sense in some American pieces a certain audacity, a generous expansiveness, a peculiar irregularity, or some other scarcely definable attribute that simply "sounds American."

How to Improve Your Listening Skills

Attendance at live performances as well as repeated and concentrated study of the text's listening examples are essential to furthering your understanding and enjoyment of music, for no read or spoken words can substitute for the impact music makes on our minds and hearts. It is not difficult to develop skills to enhance your listening comprehension and pleasure—not just for now but for the rest of your life.

First, you must approach each listening experience with expectations of enjoyment. Next, try to memorize music as you hear it so that it will quickly become familiar, and so that you will develop an awareness of a composition's form even as you listen to it for the first time. Remember also to apply the knowledge gleaned from your class discussions and this text to the music you are hearing. By listening actively, even *creatively,* you will participate in the successful collaboration of composer, performer, and listener that makes possible the magnificent experience of enjoying great music.

"I Only Have Eyes for You" (Listening Example 1) offers an opportunity to apply your developing listening skills to an American song popular about the time of World War II and well remembered today.

I Only Have Eyes for You

Title
"I Only Have Eyes for You"

Composer
Harry Warren

Lyricist
Al Dubin

Performer
Ella Fitzgerald

Meter
4 beats per measure

Form
a a' b a"

Tempo
Brisk

Introduction
The band plays an eight-bar introduction to this decidedly upbeat arrangement of the romantic song. You'll probably recognize the 4-beat-to-the-measure metrical pattern, clearly marked by the band instruments, with a strong accent on ONE of each bar.

Chorus 1
Ella Fitzgerald sings the first two lines of the chorus (**a a'**), with eight bars to each line.
The *bridge* (**b**) (beginning, "I don't know if we're in a garden"), a section of different melodic material, consists of eight bars.
The singer sings the last line (**a"**), consisting of eight bars plus four more bars ("*And*—I only have eyes for you"), a kind of "tag."

Chorus 2
The band plays the first two lines of the chorus: 8 + 8 bars, embellishing or creatively altering the melodic lines.
Bridge: Vocal improvisations on the bridge: eight bars.
The voice further embellishes the last two lines of the song, extending the "tag" with four additional bars.

As you listen to this song, try to apply as many of the concepts presented in the Preface as you can recognize. Notice, for example, the band's *dissonant* close, which preserves the good-natured, upbeat feel of the performance. Try to count the *beats,* hear the

I Only Have Eyes for You

variations in the *melody* line, notice that the instruments add
harmony by playing notes different from those the singer sings.
Consider whether the song, and particularly the manner of its
performance, suggest an American sound—and if so, why, or how.
How might the mood and the character of the piece be affected if the
tempo were slower, the accompanying instruments strings rather
than band instruments, and the vocal line "straight" rather than
highly improvised?

Terms to Review

elements of music   The basic materials of which music
is composed.

rhythm   The arrangement of time in music.

tempo   The rate of speed at which music is performed.

meter   The organization of rhythm into patterns of
strong and weak beats.

tone   A sound with a specific pitch.

pitch   The highness or lowness of a sound.

melody   A meaningful succession of pitches.

interval   The distance between two tones.

octave   The interval of an eighth.

scales   A stepwise rising or ascending pattern of pitches
within the range of an octave.

major, minor scales   The tonal scales.

half step   The smallest interval on a keyboard, and the
closest interval in traditional Western music.

whole step   An interval equal to two half steps.

modes   Pretonal seven-note scales whose arrangements
of half and whole steps differ from both the major and
minor scales.

pentatonic scale   A five-note scale within the range of
an octave.

tune   A melody that is easily recognized, memorized,
and sung.

motive   A short melodic phrase subject to development.

harmony   The meaningful combination of two or more
different tones.

tonality, tonal system   The system of harmony that has
governed Western music for about four hundred years.

chord   A meaningful combination of three or more
tones.

consonance (consonant, adj.)   Musical sounds that
seem to be passive or at rest.

dissonance (dissonant, adj.)   Musical sounds that imply
tension, drive, or activity.

tonic   The first and most important note of the major or
minor scale, often indicated by the Roman numeral I.

key   The name of the tonic upon which a tonal piece is
based.

dominant   The fifth tone of the major or minor scale,
often indicated by the Roman numeral V.

subdominant   The fourth tone of the major or minor
scale, often indicated by the Roman numeral IV.

triad   The most basic chord in the tonal system,
consisting of three alternate pitches, or two
superimposed thirds.

timbre   The characteristic quality of the sound of a
voice or instrument.

dynamic level   The level of volume (loudness or
softness) of a musical sound.

piano   Soft.

forte   Loud.

texture   The manner in which melodic lines are used in
music—alone, or combined with other melodic lines
or with harmony.

monophony (monophonic, adj.)   The musical texture
consisting of one melodic line only.

unison   The same pitch, at the same or different octaves.

round   A circular canon, which may be repeated
indefinitely.

polyphony (polyphonic, adj.)   The simultaneous
combination of two or more melodic lines.

homophony (homophonic, adj.)   A melody combined
with chords, producing harmony. Also called **chordal**
texture.

form   The organization or formal design of a musical composition.

staff   Five lines and four spaces on which music is notated.

notes   The symbols with which music is written.

rests   Symbols indicating the cessation of musical sound.

clef   A sign placed on the staff that fixes the pitch of each line and space.

style   A characteristic manner of composition or performance.

syncopation   The occurrence of accents in unexpected places.

Suggestions for Further Listening

Duple meter:

John Philip Sousa, "The Stars and Stripes Forever," Listening Example 21, p. 84

Syncopation:

Scott Joplin, "Maple Leaf Rag," Listening Example 25, p. 117

European music intended to sound American:

Claude Debussy, "Golliwog's Cakewalk" from *Children's Corner*

Darius Milhaud, "La Création du Monde" ("The Creation of the World")

Maurice Ravel, *Violin Sonata*

Igor Stravinsky, "Ragtime"

AMERICA'S MUSICAL LANDSCAPE

Part

1

(Archive Photos.)

Music in Early North America

The Early Years: Historical and Cultural Perspective

Scholars believe that human experience has always included music, although music's sound and its place in society have differed widely from one time and one culture to another. Even today some people differentiate between "music" and "noise"—often disagreeing, however, on which is which—whereas others deny the distinction. Some consider sounds of nature, such as birdcalls or thunder, a kind of music; others do not. For some people, music is art, and for others it is simply an integral part of their everyday experience. Some languages have no word for music at all, although music is fully integrated into their daily experience. But always, it seems, patterns of sound—one possible concept of what we mean by music—have found a meaningful place in human society.

The Beginnings of Music in America

Although today's American music is rooted in the artistic styles and experiences of European and African cultures, long before the first white settlers or black slaves touched the North American shores the people living here were making music of their own. Even though we have no firsthand knowledge of the music of the early North American Indians, Native American music traditions have evolved so slowly over vast periods of time that we may imagine their early music concepts bore a close relationship to those of today.

Native Americans Scholars long believed that the people destined to be called North American Indians or Native Americans began coming to this continent from Asia at the end of the last Ice Age, about 12,000 years ago, crossing the land bridge then existing where the Bering Strait is today, and spreading south from Canada and Alaska into Mexico and Central and South America and eastward to the Atlantic Ocean and the Gulf of Mexico. New archaeological evidence suggests, however, that the New World may have been colonized on numerous different occasions, beginning thousands of years earlier than previously thought and by people arriving from different regions of the Old World. It is possible, for example, that the people who established an ancient campsite 45 miles south of Richmond, Virginia, recently dated at around 18,000 years old, came by sea across the Atlantic rather than by land from Asia. Still, although fascinating research continues as new discoveries occur, it appears likely that *most* of the people who first arrived on the North American continent came from Siberia by crossing the Bering Sea land bridge.

Whatever their distant heritage, all early American Indian cultures shared a close dependence upon and affinity with the natural world. However, over vast periods of time they developed a very broad linguistic and cultural diversity. Thus when Christopher Columbus arrived in the New World, late in the fifteenth century, well over three hundred American Indian cultures with several hundred languages inhabited what is now the United States. Today we generally recognize eight geographic areas, within each of which many tribes share cultural characteristics similar to each other's but distinct from those of Native Americans inhabiting other cultural regions.

Today's descendants of the early Native Americans retain a strong reverence for and a sense of oneness with nature, expressed in their music as in all their arts—although the term "arts" here gives us pause, because traditional American Indian dry (sand) painting, weaving, pottery, basketry, and music all had spiritual and utilitarian significance without which they would have been meaningless. For example, magnificent buckskin shield covers (as shown in Figure 8), designed according to divine

Figure 8

Fight scene painted on a Sioux shield cover. The central mounted warrior shows the manner in which shields were held.
(© National Museum of the American Indian.)

3

instruction, protect the wearer as much by the sacred design etched, incised, or painted on them as by the heavy material of which they are made. The Western separation of sacred and secular concepts has little meaning among Native Americans, for whom religion, art, music, and poetry are the inseparable threads—*the warp and woof*—of life and culture.

Our brief survey can only generalize about important concepts generally shared by members of different Native American cultures, especially up until the early years of the twentieth century, before which time their cultural expression remained quite consistent. During the last century, acculturation brought about significant changes in Indian music, the changes varying from one region to another; yet many basic tenets of Native American culture retain their ancient values today.

European Emigrants

During the sixteenth century, Europeans began to arrive and settle on the North American continent in large numbers, bringing with them their various musical customs. Missionaries, adventurers, explorers, and settlers traversed the land stretching from Florida to the northern California coast. Maps and pictures drawn by these intrepid travelers, vividly depicting American Indians as they appeared to the newcomers, and the great natural beauty of the newly discovered land, encouraged other Europeans to join them in the vast New World. Soon French Catholics and French Protestants (Huguenots) in the southeast, and Spanish Catholics and Sir Francis Drake's Protestant Englishmen in the southwest, were persuading American Indians to join them in singing Christian songs as part of their effort to convert them to Christianity.

The Pilgrims and Puritans arriving in New England early in the seventeenth century were Protestants, whose protests against the Roman Catholic Church included some concerning the performance of religious music. That century also brought English Quakers (members of the Society of Friends) as well as German-speaking Protestants, such as the Mennonites and Moravians.

All of these brave settlers left behind them a rich and varied cultural experience. Roman Catholics had enjoyed generous support for their arts, including music, from royalty and the church. The Protestant New England settlers, sharing simple tastes, generally avoided the extravagant characteristics of the music style (*Baroque*) then prevalent in Europe, but many of them loved art and music and made them a significant part of their life.

Puritan Society

The more we learn about the Puritans, the more we realize how inappropriate is the stereotype of them as plain and wholly serious, for Puritan society included sophisticated men and women of keen wit and high intellect. Some brought with them their personal libraries, but the small ships carrying them to America had scarce room for such luxuries, and before long the colonists began to produce their own new literature, largely consisting of didactic religious tracts but also including memoirs, essays, and poetry.

The New World's first poet, Anne Bradstreet (1612–1672, Figure 9), busy wife of a colonial governor and the mother of eight, composed a significant body of poetry despite her own serious illness and the rigors of colonial life. There is no indication that her

Figure 9
Anne Bradstreet.
(Historical Pictures/Stock Montage.)

peers found her writing of poetry an unwomanly pursuit; on the contrary, she was admired then as now for her learned and well-crafted poems.

Although the practical early New Englanders had little use for art for art's sake and specifically excluded art from their churches, still their daily experience was rich in artistic expression. For example, the graveyards adjacent to their plainly furnished houses of worship often contained elaborately carved and decorated headstones (Figure 10). They furnished their homes with many functional articles of beauty, covering tables and beds with fine needlework to provide protection from cold New England drafts, while beautifully carved furniture, hand-painted dishes, and toys elaborately constructed for the delight of children lessened the severity of New England colonial life.

Although landscape painting held little attraction for early New Englanders more inclined to tame than to admire natural wonders, portraits served the practical purpose of preserving a likeness and so were highly valued. Most portrait painters were amateur artists who earned their living as farmers, shopkeepers, or in some other trade, and who thought of themselves simply as craftspeople producing commodities of practical worth. "Amateur" here, as in Chapter 3, connotes someone who performs more for pleasure than for profit and implies no judgment of quality. Indeed, the rather flat or linear quality of American folk art lends it a pleasing flavor distinct from the professional products of their European contemporaries. Ironically, these early artists often painted their subjects dressed in elaborate finery, suggesting an attraction to worldly goods surprising in the staid Puritan society (Figure 11). But how astonished these modest people would be to know the aesthetic and monetary value their work has acquired today.

The African Experience in Early America

Even before the Pilgrims' 1620 arrival at Plymouth Rock, Africans were being forcibly brought to, and

Figure 10
Gravestone in a colonial churchyard.
(The Bettmann Archive, Inc.)

Figure 11
Elizabeth Davis, *Mrs. Hezekia Beardsley.*
(Yale University Art Gallery, Gift of
Mrs. E. A. Giddings.)

made to work in, the New World. At first African slaves constituted a miniscule portion of society in New York or New England, and even in southern colonies; but after 1700 the importation of slaves increased greatly. By the time of the American Revolution, slaves existed in large numbers in the South, where their forced services made possible the great plantations that produced the coffee, tobacco, sugar, rice, and (much later) cotton on which the southern economy relied.

During the eighteenth century, a surge of humanitarian feeling gave rise to strong movements against the continuing slave trade, which finally was prohibited in the United States, however, only twenty years after the ratification of the Constitution. The strong protests of Quakers and other religious groups notwithstanding, antislavery sentiment had little effect in this country until well into the nineteenth century. In New England, slavery proved unprofitable and disappeared, but in the South the invention of the cotton gin in 1793 made slavery an even more integral part of the plantation system than before.

Forbidden to practice their familiar African religious rituals and to sing songs, dance, and play musical instruments in their accustomed ways, the brutally uprooted Africans and their American-born progeny, starved for religion, attempted to adapt traditional African musical expression to worship of the white people's Christian god. Their early efforts mostly met with ridicule, because their white owners regarded them as "beasts" unfit to receive religious instruction of any kind; but here as in their fatherland, the slaves integrated music and faith into their daily lives.

Revolution, in Classical Style Eighteenth-
century Americans of European descent reflected a strong European influence, enhanced by increased opportunities for travel and communication from one continent to the other. European artists of this time had adopted the *classical* ideals of ancient Greek sculptors and architects, who strove for perfection of form, balanced designs, and relatively restrained emotional expression. Artists on both sides of the Atlantic, in fact, from about 1750 until 1825

applied order, balance, and emotional restraint to their work, rendering the Age of Reason in social and political affairs the Age of Classicism in the arts. To distinguish eighteenth-century visual works of art rendered in this cool, reasoned manner from their ancient classical models, we call them *neoclassical* in style; but too little ancient music remains to cause confusion in terms, and the eighteenth century is known as the Classical period of music.

Paradoxically, the Age of Reason spawned several violent revolutionary movements, and Americans joined a number of European nations in firmly rejecting rule by absolute authority and establishing a republican form of government. Enlightened intellectuals—hardly impassioned fanatics—led the American Revolution, the classical influence evident, for example, in the cool, reasoned language of the Declaration of Independence, which begins "When in the course of human events it becomes necessary for one people to dissolve the political bonds which have connected them with another . . ." America's founders, led by Thomas Jefferson and influenced by outstanding French

Figure 12
Classical influence is reflected in the orderly layout of streets and the prevalence of Greco-Roman architectural style in Washington, D.C.
(National Park Service/Department of the Interior.)

neoclassical architects, designed Washington, D.C., to be an orderly city of wide and regular streets with many grassy parks and shady trees. (See Figure 12.) The simple lines and classical columns of Washington's state buildings, although not constructed until the early years of the nineteenth century, clearly represent the ideals of the Classical period during which they were planned.

Painting in Eighteenth-Century America

Although American artists during this century had more training and sophistication than the folk artists of the settlers' period, their finest works retained an innocence, honesty, and decorative sense distinguishing them from the more elegant European works of the same era. John Singleton Copley (1738–1815), America's greatest colonial artist, was largely self-taught. He developed a highly personal style rooted in the American tradition and governed by classical order and reserve (Figure 13). Becoming increasingly, though reluctantly, involved in events relating to the impending American Revolution, Copley sailed for Europe in 1774, intending to return to America when peace was attained, but in fact he spent the rest of his life abroad.

In Europe, Copley studied with the famous American expatriate Benjamin West (1738–1820), who encouraged him to paint historical and heroic subjects. Although the subsequent paintings were more elegant and polished than Copley's early American portraits, they were correspondingly less distinctive and interesting. One of Copley's later paintings, *Watson and the Shark,* 1778 (Figure 14), is of great interest, however, for in it Copley produced a warm and sympathetic portrayal of an African American man attempting to assist a white man—Watson—desperately floundering in the water. The would-be rescuer has thrown a rope, which Watson has missed, as the shark looms menacingly nearby. (Notice how the African American's outstretched arm, mirroring that of Watson, contributes to the symmetry and the drama of this strong painting.) Such a subtle and sympathetic rendering of relations between African Americans and whites was unusual in that time, and Copley's painting is in every way a masterpiece.

Charles Willson Peale (1741–1827) also studied for a time in Europe with Benjamin West, returning to America to become the leading artist in Philadelphia for many years. Peale revealed the classical thirst for knowledge in his boundless curiosity about a broad range of subjects, implementing his ideas (in the practical, classical way) by establishing the first American museum of natural history, in Philadelphia in 1802.

Peale, who fought in the American Revolution, painted fine, lifelike portraits of the leaders of the young nation. His painting *The Staircase Group* (Figure 15) is so realistic a portrayal of Peale's sons standing on a staircase that George Washington is said to have bowed to the boys as he passed by the painting one day.

Today we recognize the dominant effects of many cultures on the evolution of American music, but the traditions and practices of all the early inhabitants—those native to the land, the early European arrivals, and the people brought by force from their African homeland—have deeply colored the complex landscape of American music. From at least the early seventeenth century, the music heard in the widely separated inhabited regions of the continent reflected highly disparate values and sounds. Nevertheless, Indian, African, and European music shared some things in common: all were more likely to be performed by amateurs than by professionals, in intimate (inside or outside) domestic or worship settings than in a concert hall, and often (although not always) with spiritual connotation. The distinctions we draw now between sacred and secular music and between high and low art—and the difficulties we experience in finding appropriate terminology to distinguish one kind of art from another—had little meaning in the early American experience. ♪

Figure 13
John Singleton Copley, *Mrs. Thomas Boylston*, 1766.
(Courtesy of the Harvard University Portrait Collection, Harvard University, Cambridge,
Massachusetts. Bequest of Ward Nicholas Boylston in 1828.)

Figure 14

John Singleton Copley, *Watson and the Shark*, 1778. Oil
on canvas, 72½ in. × 90¼ in. (184 cm × 229.5 cm).
Although largely self-taught, Copley effectively captured the
seething action and dramatic interplay of emotions between
the desperate characters in his masterful painting.
(Gift of Mrs. George von Lengerke Meyer. Courtesy,
Museum of Fine Arts, Boston.)

Figure 15

Charles Willson Peale,
The Staircase Group.
(Philadelphia Museum of Art,
The George W. Elkens Collection.)

1

North American Indian Music

L ong before European settlers arrived in the New World, North American Indians were practicing their own vital music traditions, essential and integral to their most basic daily experience. Because their music always occurred in association with other activities—dance, religious ritual, prayer, work, recreation—their languages included no word for music itself; yet for American Indians then as today, life without music was unthinkable.

Songs

Never an independent concept but always a part of dance, celebration, games, work, or prayer, Native American music essentially consists of songs imbued with strong powers to accomplish a given end, such as success in fishing, healing, gambling, or winning a bride. American Indians do not think of their songs as *composed,* but as *received,* often in a dream or vision—gifts of power from the spirit world.

Songs, which are highly valued in American Indian cultures, have been preserved through the ages not by notation but by a rich and vital oral tradition stressing the necessity for completely accurate rendition. Navajos, who think of their songs as enriching experiences, sometimes count their wealth in terms of the number of songs they know. And because a basketweaver, for example, sings not only to ease the drudgery of work but more importantly to make a basket pleasing to supernatural spirits, her song must be performed and listened to with propriety.

Native American music certainly does *not* all sound the same to the discriminating ear: The songs of some tribes, for example, are low-pitched, sounding practiced or controlled, whereas songs of others lie very high in the voice, pulsing vibrantly with emotion and energy. Even within a given tribe, songs for gambling, war dances, lullabies, and healing ceremonies vary widely in their sounds.

Although there are as many kinds of Native American songs as there are Native American cultures, some characteristics do apply to all or most. Songs are usually sung by a solo voice or by men and women singing together in **unison** (all singing the same notes at the same time). Although men's voices lie an octave lower than women's, and although **call-and-response**—a solo voice alternating with a group—sometimes leads to an

Figure 16
The pleasing repetition of geometric patterns in this lovely Navajo blanket unifies the design much as melodic repetition unifies a Native American song. (© National Museum of The American Indian.)

overlap between the leader's and the other singers' tones, there is never harmony in the Western sense. In most Native American cultures, melodic phrases generally begin on a relatively high pitch and descend without wide leaps, approximating the inflection typical of a spoken phrase.

A song often consists simply of many repetitions of one or more phrases or partial phrases, much as designs on baskets, blankets, and other Native American art often consist of repeated geometrical patterns. (See Figure 16.) Such aural and visual repetition has a nearly hypnotic effect, enhancing a work's spirituality and artistic coherence while also suggesting the ideal balance of nature for which the Native American constantly strives.

Texts Song texts may be in a native language or, recently, in English. Some texts are simply a series of consonant-vowel clusters or **vocables**—neutral syllables, such as *hey, yeh,* or *neh,* which may in fact convey meaning in themselves. For example, as part of the Navajo Night Way curing ceremony, teams of young men compete in the singing of *Yeibichai (Yeh-be-chy)* songs while masked dancers, personifying the sacred spirits of their grandfathers (*Yei-bi-chai* means "spirits-their-grandfathers"), bring supernatural healing power to help the sick. Every one of the hundreds of Yeibichai songs, consisting entirely of vocables, contains the call of the *Yei: Hi ye, hi ye, ho-ho ho ho!,* immediately identifying the song as belonging to this tradition. You will clearly hear the distinctive call in Listening Example 2.

Sioux Grass Dance

Perhaps easiest to identify of all Native American styles is the singing of the Plains Indians, whose regions stretch from the foothills of the Rocky Mountains east to the Mississippi River and beyond, and from the Gulf of Mexico north into Canada. High in pitch, tense in quality, and harsh in tone, this sound is entirely distinct from that of European-based American music (Listening Example 3).

Usually referred to today as a grass dance, because of the grass braids the dancers wear at their waists, this is the stirring war dance music heard, or imitated, in countless western movies. The strong pulsations, very high pitches

Yeibichai Chant Song

Form
Strophic. A long phrase is repeated many times with minimal variation.

Melody
Repeated high-pitched tones interspersed with even higher cries of indeterminate pitch, producing a rather florid melodic line featuring dramatic upward leaps.

Rhythm
A steady pulse marked by rattle shakes (two to the beat).

Text
Vocables punctuated with the distinctive call of the Yei.

Manner of Performance
On the ninth (last) night of the Night Way ceremony, Yeibichai appears, accompanied by masked dancers shaking their gourd rattles and by the unearthly call of the gods. Although some Yeibichai songs alternate between the extremely high tones produced by singing in the falsetto range (above the normal range of the singing voice) and the normal vocal range, the falsetto tones heard here are particularly characteristic of this and of some other Native American songs as well.

* Listening Example selections are on the three ninety-minute CDs that accompany this text.

sung in falsetto range, and the tense quality of the voices enhance the emotional intensity of this exciting music, as do the elaborate costumes and dramatic steps of the dancers. (See Figure 17.)

Sound Instruments

Although little music is performed by music instruments alone, sound instruments, as they are called, often support or "hold up" a song. Navajo flutes, the primary melody-playing Native American instrument, are usually made of cedar wood and may be elaborately carved and decorated (Figure 18). Traditionally the flute was sometimes used as a courting instrument, played by a young man who trusted the wind to carry his flute-song to the woman he loved, and who hoped the sounds of his flute, by their beauty and perhaps by

Sioux Grass Dance

Form

Strophic. The phrases, some of which are introduced by a leader's "call," are sung in unison by men and women.

Melody

Each phrase begins high in pitch and descends, much as a spoken phrase often ends lower than it began. The melody descends by narrow intervals, the only large leaps occurring from the end of one phrase to the beginning of the next.

Accompaniment

The insistent beat of drums and delicate shaking of rattles accompany the singers, while the dramatic yells of observers as well as participants add to the drama and excitement of the dance.

Manner of Performance

Two teams of costumed dancers enter the area, each dancer carrying a tomahawk or other weapon. Facing each other, the teams dance in place, brandishing their weapons in a threatening manner. Next, forming a circle, they move around clockwise, crouching, leaping, and yelping dramatically. Individually, the dancers simulate the motions of battle, alternately forming and breaking the original formation.

magic as well, would persuade her to become his bride. The Navajo flute, rarely heard during the first three quarters of the twentieth century except among families and occasionally at powwows, is frequently heard today at tribal fairs and powwows and at concerts of traditional music. It has no standard dimensions because its finger holes and air column are based on finger measurements and are therefore never the same. Each flute has its own sound and pitch. Its repertoire now includes newly composed courting songs as well as Western-influenced classical pieces composed especially for this unique instrument.

Far more common and widespread are percussion instruments, especially *container rattles* of several kinds: A rattle element, such as pebbles, sacred corn, or beans, placed into a gourd or pot or into a container made of hide or bark, is shaken in time to the rhythm of a song or swung in a circular motion to produce a continuous sound (Figure 19). For certain sacred ceremonies, the shaking of deer hooves or shells suspended from a stick (*suspension rattles*) produces quite a different sort of rattling effect.

Figure 17

Stirring music performed in the emotional Plains Indian style enhances the drama of the traditional war dance.(© George Catlin/ Art Resource.)

Figure 18

Decorated flute of the Northern Plains Indians. This Kiowa Indian flute with a carved wind cap is decorated with painting, feathers, and braided hair. (© 1980 by J. Richard Haefer. Used by permission.)

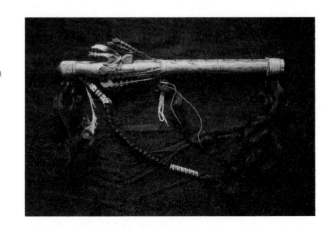

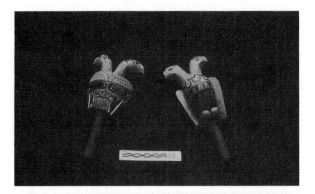

Figure 19
Two Northwest Coast carved wooden rattles from the Tlingit Culture, carved with double birds' heads. These date from the late nineteenth century and come from the area around Sitka, Alaska.
(© 1980 by J. Richard Haefer. Used by permission.)

Rasps, percussion instruments normally made from a long stick of wood into which notches have been carved, are rubbed with another stick or a piece of bone (such as the shoulder blade of a sheep) to make a rasping sound. To amplify the sound, the rasp may be placed on an inverted basket or on a piece of hide over an open hole in the ground.

Drums, carrying great importance in Indian culture, exist in profuse variety. Most are made of wood, with one or two heads of the skin of deer or some other animal. The Zuni, Navajo, and Apache, however, sometimes use less resonant pottery vessels or drum jars. Hollowed-out logs, or *log drums,* tall and thin or short and wide, common to the Plains area, have become the powwow drum of today.

Contemporary Indian Song

The late nineteenth and the twentieth centuries witnessed many changes in North American Indian music, as some cultural traditions nearly succumbed to overwhelming influences from modern American life. Among the earliest changes in traditional Native American music practice was the development of pan-Indian song styles, which evolved as the introduction of the horse and later the automobile increased intertribal contact. Soon Native American peoples from many tribes, speaking various languages, were meeting at large gatherings called **powwows,** to share their dances, songs, and ceremonies with each other and sometimes with a public audience.

The modern powwow is common not only on reservations but also in cities ranging from the states of New York to California, and Montana to southern California. Many Native Americans follow the powwow circuit throughout the year, often traveling 15,000 miles or more to sing, dance, and rodeo. Either English or the use of vocables is particularly convenient for singing powwow songs, which unite the people as Native Americans and also as members of a particular tribe, authenticating their ceremonies and helping keep the people in balance with nature. Powwow songs also allow visitors from other cultures not only to view but sometimes even to participate in the wide variety of music, dance and visual splendor associated with American Indian culture.

A recent surge of interest among Native Americans concerning their own heritage, as well as among other Americans appreciative of the rich Indian culture, has produced a wealth of research and of live and recorded performances both of traditional and new Native American music. Some Native Americans have adopted elements of contemporary popular or vernacular musics, modifying them to suit their needs and desires, and rock bands, country-western groups, and numerous gospel quartets flourish on many reservations today. The **Black Lodge Singers,** for example, one of the most respected drum groups on the powwow trail, perform traditional Blackfeet and contemporary-style songs. The group's northern-style singing, marked by high, falsetto vocals and powerful drumming, evokes strong emotional response in listeners both Indian and non-Indian. Other well-known groups include the instrumental ensemble **Burning Sky** (guitar, Native American flute, and percussion), and **December Wind** (vocals accompanied by acoustic and electric rhythm guitars, drum kit, and native drums). **Sharon Burch,** singing songs inspired by those she heard her mother and grandfather sing, gives contemporary expression to traditional Navajo ways, singing sometimes in the beautiful Navajo language, sometimes in English. Singer-songwriter **Joanne Shenandoah,** whose music was featured on the television program *Northern Exposure,* opened Woodstock '94 and has performed with Willie Nelson and at the White House.

Other Native American musicians have studied music at universities and conservatories, applying their native gifts and experience to composing and performing concert music within the Western music tradition. **Carlos Nakai** (b. 1946, Figure 20), a classically trained cornet and trumpet player, became

Figure 20

R. Carlos Nakai—Native American flutist, composer, and educator.
(Photo © John Running.)

fascinated with the beautiful sounds of the Navajo-style flute and has made exhaustive study of the instrument, which he calls "a sound sculpture—a piece of art that also creates sound." Today Nakai collaborates with musicians in many fields, finding new expression for the Navajo flute in jazz ensembles, piano-guitar combinations, and in the concert hall. He even uses electronic techniques, including synthesizer and digital delay, together with the cedar flute.

Other prestigious Native American musicians include **John Kim Bell** (b. 1953), a symphony conductor and composer; **Edward Wapp** (b. 1943), composer-scholar-professor; and **Louis Ballard** (b. 1931), who has taught for many years at the Institute of American Indian Arts in Santa Fe. Ballard composes for chorus, band, and orchestra, often mixing the sounds of American Indian instruments with the sound of the modern symphony orchestra. His composition *Why the Duck Has a Short Tail* is a musical setting for band and narrator of an American Indian legend.

Paradoxically, to many American listeners Native American music sounds more "foreign" than the music of many distant cultures. However, Americans are becoming more aware of and sensitive to the values of a music born and nurtured in this land we all share. A comment made by Louis Ballard in reference to the uniqueness of each Navajo flute—"Don't ever let 'different' be alien"—applies as well to our approach to Native American music. We may well be grateful that the American Indians share freely the arts by which all humankind receives the most gracious blessings.

Terms to Review

unison The same pitch at the same or at different octaves.

call-and-response A leader's solo voice alternating with a chorus of singers.

vocables Neutral syllables, sometimes called consonant-vowel clusters.

falsetto The singing voice above the normal (full, or chest voice) range.

powwow A contemporary pan-Indian gathering for singing, dancing, rodeo, carnival, and other celebrations.

Key Figures

Carlos Nakai (flutist, composer)
John Kim Bell (conductor, composer)
Edward Wapp (composer, scholar, professor)
Louis Ballard (composer, professor)
Black Lodge Singers (drum group)
Burning Sky (guitar, flute, percussion)
December Wind (vocals accompanied by guitars, drums)
Sharon Burch (singer)
Joanne Shenandoah (singer, songwriter)

Suggestions for Further Listening

Records produced by:
Canyon Records, 4143 North Sixteenth Street, Phoenix, AZ 85016
Indian House, P.O. Box 472, Taos, NM
Smithsonian Folkways, Smithsonian Institution, L'Enfant Plaza, Washington, D.C.

2

Folk Music

Folk music refers to songs and instrumental pieces that appear to have been spontaneously created, or whose origin has been lost or forgotten. Music written (composed) in the informal style of traditional folk music also resides in the folk repertory. Simple, unpretentious, easy to remember and to perform, folk music appeals to inexperienced listeners and sophisticated musicians alike.

The folk music of the United States springs from many ethnic sources: English, Irish, Scottish, Welsh, German, and other European influences abound, and Africa—particularly West Africa—introduced an immeasurable wealth of musical sounds and traditions to folk as well as to other musics in America. From this multiethnic trove, American folk music has reaped the greatest treasure from British and African sources. Much of the recent urban and country folk music we shall consider in Chapter 8 is deeply rooted in the traditional music introduced here.

British Traditions

The early English settlers who arrived in the New World around the turn of the seventeenth century brought few musical instruments with them; but in time, as violins and other, mostly stringed, instruments became available, the settlers and colonists played the fiddle tunes and dances familiar from their British childhood. Many traditional songs acquired new words and altered melodies, reflecting American dialects and New World experience as they were handed down from one generation to the next.

These folk music traditions survive today in rural and mountain areas, where the style of singing and playing instruments is remarkably close to that of seventeenth-century Britain. Simple *lullabies,* such as "The Mockingbird" ("Hush, little baby, don't say a word, Papa's gonna buy you a mockingbird"), delightfully silly and entertaining *nonsense songs,* dramatic sea songs, or *chanteys* ("Blow the Man Down" is a famous example), and *singing games* ("Did You Ever See a Lassie," "Go in and out the Window") all belong to the American folk song repertory.

Folk Ballads
Most common of all folk songs are **ballads,** or stories told in song. Delivered from memory by a solo voice, with or without accompaniment,

ballads offer little background information about the stories they relate, presenting the essential elements and allowing the listener's imagination free reign to flesh out the details. Although the events described often are of a dramatic, even tragic, nature, ballads are presented in a simple, direct, nearly emotionless manner, time and place remaining pleasantly abstract.

A ballad consists of a number of stanzas, or verses, all set to the same tune, repetition of the melody lending unity to the form while the evolving text gives variety. This musical structure, called **strophic form,** is the most common song form of all. Ballads, sung by amateurs for their own or for their families' and friends' pleasure, comprised a major source of entertainment in early America (Figure 21), and many ballads included a very large number of verses, allowing the entertainment to last as long as possible. Because ballads survived through oral tradition, their authors unknown or forgotten, those we continue to enjoy probably evolved as the product of many people over long periods of time, and they still are subject to alteration today. Ballad singers often add, alter, or delete verses as they perform, lending the song local or timely relevance, or simply expressing the irrepressible creativity of the balladeer.

Among the most popular subjects for ballads is that of ill-fated love affairs, such as the one described in the very famous "Barbara Allen" (Listening Example 4), one of the great number of folk ballads to have survived apparently intact since their British origin some time in the Middle Ages. Some of these ancient songs, in fact, seem to have been better preserved in America than in the land that introduced them, and they have long since been adopted into the American folk repertory.

American Ballads

Early emigrants also reflected the influence of another kind of British folk tradition, the **broadside,** written and printed on a very large sheet or as part of a set of sheets called *songsters* (Figure 22). For subjects, the broadsides often took historical or topical events, such as mine disasters, famous murders, or train wrecks, and although performed in the same detached, impersonal manner as the anonymous ballads, many broadsides were related in the first person.

As early as the seventeenth century Americans began not only to alter traditional ballads to fit their New World experiences, but also to write new ballads in the broadside style. Less objective, abstract, and timeless than the ancient songs, however, the broadsides proved less likely to survive beyond the period that introduced them. Thus few of the American folk ballads we remember and enjoy today were written before the second half of the nineteenth century. Preserved through oral or sometimes written tradition, American ballads were performed in the same plain, direct manner as their British counterparts, but their titles, such as "John Henry," "Billy the Kid," "The Erie Canal," "The John B. Sails," or "The Ballad of Casey Jones" (Listening Example 30, p. 133), reflect their uniquely American source and character.

Ballad

Title
"Barbara Allen" (sometimes "Barbery Ellen" or another similar name)

Composer
Anonymous

Form
Strophic. As in most ballads, there are several four-line stanzas.

Text
The story is of the young "Sweet William," who is dying for love of "hard-hearted Barbara Allen." She loves him, too, of course, and soon joins him in death. A red rose and a green briar miraculously grow and join above the ill-fated lovers' adjacent graves. The words are not always the same, because the song has been handed down through centuries by oral tradition.

Melody
The melody, like the words, exists in several versions. It is based upon a pentatonic scale that uses only the tones of the five black notes of a keyboard. Many children's songs and folk melodies are based upon this simple scale.

Texture
This song is often performed with no accompaniment. Sometimes simple chords are strummed on a guitar, banjo, or other instrument. A piano may provide accompaniment if a chordal texture is desired.

Rhythm
There is a steady underlying pulse and a general sense of quadruple meter. The rhythm is refreshingly irregular, and the phrases are sometimes asymmetrical, adapted to suit the informal text.

African Traditions

Unlike the European settlers, who arrived in the New World of their own free will, Africans were forcibly brought to America in European slave ships, beginning early in the seventeenth century—about the time the Pilgrims arrived at Plymouth Rock. By 1700 slavery had become common throughout the thirteen colonies.

Figure 21
Early Americans gather to enjoy informal music and dance.
(Brown Brothers.)

Figure 22
An example of a broadside cover.
(Hutton Getty Picture Archive.)

Most of the slaves forced to work on the plantations in what is now the southeastern United States came from West Africa, where they had commonly integrated music with their daily work. Particular kinds of songs became associated with certain tasks, such as fishing, weaving, hunting, or tilling their farms. In America, the familiar fishing, weaving, and hunting songs lost relevance, but the slaves poured all the anguish of their new, tragic experience into **field hollers** and **shouts**—loud, rhythmically flexible, emotionally expressive chants or cries sung by a solitary voice. The "bent" or slurred notes later applied by jazz and other black musicians to their instruments or voices also colored the hollers and shouts. Some field hollers had words ("Where *are* you . . . ?), but most used neutral syllables that carried over distances, establishing wordless but heartwarming contact with fellow workers who, hearing the poignant cries, could respond with expressive shouts of their own.

Work Songs Another kind of song, the **work song,** accompanied such rhythmic tasks as rowing, hoeing, or chopping trees. Work songs, which set the pace and synchronized the movements of groups of people working in unison, often accompanied the forced labor of American plantation slaves. The songs, strophic in form, were performed in the characteristic West African music practice known as call-and-response, in which the leading lines of each verse, sung by a single voice, alternate with a repeated phrase, or **refrain,** sung by a group.

Traditional work songs expressed joy and pride in hard work for one's family and land and gratitude to the gods for their help. In Africa, drums often accompanied work songs, sometimes providing two or three different underlying rhythmic patterns in a complexity difficult for Western ears even to hear. Using drums for communication as well as for music, West Africans developed an extremely fine sense of changes in tone and timbre, together with truly remarkable rhythmic techniques.

In America, too, slaves made up, or **improvised,** work songs as they labored in pain and sorrow, adapting them, however, to their tragic new condition. Many slaves had brought small drums and simple string instruments with them on the slave ships, where they sometimes were compelled by their captors to perform music to keep them occupied and while away the time; but slaveholders sometimes banned the use of African drums on the southern plantations, fearing the thrilling sounds of the drums might incite revolt. The slaves compensated for the loss of their drums by improvising percussive instruments from empty oil drums, metal washbasins, and whatever else might be available and by clapping, body-slapping, and stamping the rhythms of their songs and dances. Rattles or bits of shell or bone added to simple instruments further enhanced the driving beat. Further, by stretching an animal skin across the open side of a hollowed-out gourd or calabash, slaves created a primitive **banjo** (see Figure 23), derived from the similar African *banjar,* destined in more sophisticated form to be known as the first American musical instrument and to provide limitless entertainment for Americans and others of assorted ethnicity and culture.

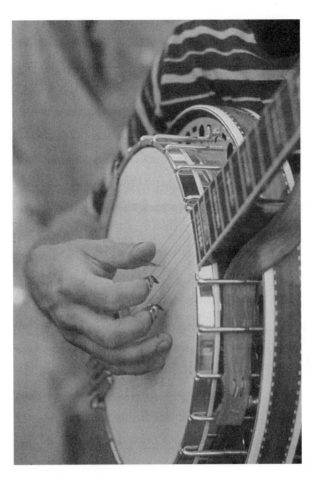

Figure 23
A musician playing a five-string banjo.
(Jerry Howard/Stock Boston.)

In New England, slaves were treated with more leniency than in the south, often enjoying a measure of free time in which to entertain themselves and their masters by singing, dancing, and playing musical instruments. But the admiration excited by the music of the slaves was not always to their advantage: Newspaper lists of slaves for sale and of runaways often referred to their outstanding musical abilities, adding to their desirability as commodities to be owned and abused.

The First African Americans   Many slaveholders harshly discouraged references to African gods and religions in work songs, or in any other traditional expression. Especially British Protestants, who considered African music customs savage and heathen, did everything possible to eradicate their slaves' native religion and culture. Partly to this end, the first babies born to the slaves in this country (unlike those in other areas of the New World, such as Haiti, Cuba, or Brazil) often were separated from their families to be raised on other plantations. There they learned African lore and language from older

Africans, of course, but they also began to accrue experience with America, and with English.

As adults, this first generation of slaves born here began to develop their own music, rooted in African customs and sounds, but genuinely African *American,* expressing their American experience in a new sort of African American language. Whereas the first slaves had sung in the African dialects they knew, the work songs gradually came to be sung more in English, pronounced, however, with African rhythms. For a long time, some African words continued to be used, sometimes for the purpose of obscuring seditious meaning from white people. When even the blacks could no longer understand the African languages, meaningless but rhythmical syllables were used as well.

What of African Music Survives Today?

Today's African American musics are deeply rooted in African traditions that arrived in the New World with the first slaves. Call-and-response, for example, became a basic tenet of African American vocal and instrumental music, as we shall see when we study blues, vocal and instrumental jazz, the religious folk songs called *spirituals,* and many other kinds of contemporary black music. Improvisation is inherent in the concept of jazz and colors much other music as well. Much African American music is still based on the "bent" or flexible tones of the *blues* scale (see p. 153), unheard in this country until the first West Africans arrived. Even more apparent is the emphasis in African American music on rhythm over melody, and the complexity of African rhythms compared with those of Western (European) music.

Terms to Review

folk music   Usually music of unknown origin, orally transmitted.

ballad   A folk story-song, strophic in form.

strophic form   A song form with two or more verses, all set to the same music.

broadside   A topical ballad, printed on a large sheet or on sets of sheets called *songsters.*

field hollers and **shouts**   Loud, rhythmically flexible, emotionally expressive chants or cries sung by a solitary voice, forming a kind of communication between slaves.

work songs   Songs sung by groups of slaves to set the pace and synchronize the movements of rhythmic tasks performed in unison.

refrain   A repeated (textual and musical) phrase, as one interspersed by a group between lines or verses sung by a solo voice.

improvised   Simultaneously invented and performed.

banjo   A string instrument derived in America from the African *banjar.*

Optional Listening Example

"Hammer, Ring" (work song)

Suggestions for Further Listening

Folk songs:

"The Riddle" ("I Gave My Love a Cherry That Has No Stone")

"Arkansas Traveler"

"Down in the Valley"

Useful collections of folk songs:

Anthology of American Folk Music. Folkways 2951/3.

Folk Music in America. Library of Congress.

Folk Music U.S.A. Folkways 4530.

Roots of American Music. Arhoolie 2001/2.

3

The Colonial, Revolutionary, and Federal Periods

B eginning in the sixteenth century, Spanish and French Catholics arriving in the New World brought with them their secular and religious music customs. As part of their effort to convert Native Americans to Roman Catholicism, they taught Indians in Florida and in the Southwest to perform Catholic religious music.

Music at the Spanish Missions

Music was an important part of the religious training of American Indians by zealous Spanish missionaries, who taught their more or less willing converts to sing the songs and prayers of the Christian church, usually set to very simple tunes. Soon American Indians were learning to sing in choirs, play in church orchestras, and even make simple European-style musical instruments. They learned traditional Spanish music, religious praise songs or **hymns,** and even the more difficult *Gregorian chant.* At Christmastime, they participated in musical nativity plays called *Las posadas* (The Lodgings), commemorating the struggles of Mary to find a place in which to deliver the baby Jesus.

The Spanish missions remained active in California, and Catholic church music was regularly performed there by missionaries and by their Native American students, until the Mexican government ordered the missions closed in 1833. A large number of musical instruments, as well as manuscripts of Mass settings and other church music of varying levels of complexity, have been found at some of the mission sites, many of which can still be visited.

Spanish Songs Besides hymns, one of the first kinds of religious song in California, Texas, and New Mexico was the **alabado,** a long praise song (*alabado sea* means "praised be"). The early alabados, some from Spain, some from Mexico, became part of a thriving Spanish folk tradition that remains alive today in some villages of the American Southwest. Long and invariably sad, the alabados project the profound loneliness of the beautiful but remote regions inhabited by those who sing them. Today the alabados are remembered only by a few very elderly people, who sing them with feeling and who describe the significance this music had for their forbears centuries ago.

Spanish secular music had its place in the early American experience as well. Troops guarding forts near the missions sang at their work and danced for recreation with their families and friends. Vendors' songs, work songs, lullabies, and all manner of Spanish folk dances formed an ordinary part of the Spanish settlers' lives in the New World.

New England Psalm Tunes

In 1517, a German Catholic cleric, Martin Luther (1483–1546), instigated the Protestant Reformation by advocating reform of certain questionable practices by the Roman Catholic Church in his day. The movement thus begun stimulated a number of independent-minded people in northern European countries to form their own Protestant sects, each adhering to particular tenets of religious and secular conduct, including the place of music in worship.

Unlike Catholics, whose formal religious music was sung in Latin, Protestants sang their hymns in their vernacular, or common, language. They also preferred simple, folklike tunes that everyday people could sing, to the elaborate Gregorian chant or complex choir pieces sung by trained Catholic monks.

The Pilgrims and Puritans arriving in New England early in the seventeenth century were among the Protestants whose protests against the Roman Catholic church included some concerning religious music. People who followed the strict teachings of the Swiss reformer John Calvin (1509–1564) believed that the *only* texts suitable for singing in a worship service were those of the **psalms,** 150 inspirational verses found in the Old Testament of the Bible. Thus Calvinists forbade the singing in church of hymns, which had freely written texts not necessarily based on passages from the Bible or from church liturgy.

Although poetic in style and expression, however, the psalms as they appear in the Bible are neither metered nor rhymed and therefore do not lend themselves readily to congregational singing. Thus, Calvinists retranslated all the psalms into verses having a regular number of lines, with patterns of weak and accented beats, suitable for setting to music.

The Calvinists did not intend their **psalm tunes** to stir emotions or draw attention to the music itself, because they believed the only purpose for music in a church service was to enhance expression of a religious text. Therefore, because musical instruments cannot express words, harmony increases music's sensuous appeal, and neither instruments nor harmony serve to clarify a text, the Calvinists consistently sang their psalm tunes in church **a cappella,** meaning unaccompanied, and in unison. It is important for us to understand, however, that the separation between sacred and secular experience typical of the modern American experience did not apply in colonial America. Thus it was quite usual for Calvinists to sing the same psalm tunes they performed so austerely in church, in harmony and with elaborate instrumental accompaniment in family and social gatherings at home.

The New Englanders' psalm singing became, in effect, a kind of folk tradition. Psalm tunes were of a folklike nature and generally were learned from oral experience. Strophic in form, most had four-line stanzas, as is common to much folk song, and the ornamentation and variation in the singing of psalm tunes were typical of the manner of singing songs in the folk tradition.

Psalters   The newly metered and rhymed psalm verses were printed in books called **psalters** for use in congregational singing. Some psalters contained notated melodies, whereas others printed no music but only the words of the psalm verses, which could be sung to widely familiar and well-remembered folk, popular, or hymn tunes.

The first collection of psalm tunes was printed in Switzerland in 1539, nearly a century before the Pilgrims and Puritans came to the New World, and the first edition of the famous *Geneva Psalter* appeared in that Swiss city in 1551. (When the Separatists finally settled in the New World, they became known as Pilgrims, and Calvinists coming directly from England were called Puritans.) The texts of these early psalters were in French, the vernacular language of the Geneva congregation. Some of the tunes in the *Geneva Psalter* came from other religious sources; other tunes resemble and may have been derived from secular songs. It was not considered necessary to provide a separate tune for each of the 150 psalms, because all verses with the same metrical pattern could be sung to the same melody. The *Geneva Psalter* contained 125 tunes, and each of the 150 metered and rhymed psalms could be sung to at least one of them.

Among the tunes in the *Geneva Psalter* was a setting of Psalm 100 (Listening Example 5), which has become the most famous psalm tune of all, known today as "Old Hundred" and sung in Protestant churches of many denominations as the Doxology ("Praise God, from Whom all blessings flow"). (Another famous psalm tune, "Windsor," included in the *Instructor's Manual* as an Optional Listening Example, is also widely sung today with a text beginning "Jesus the very heart of Thee.")

An English-language psalter known as *Sternhold and Hopkins* (from the man who had printed the first metrical psalter in English and the man who contributed the most translations to the new version), printed for the use of Calvinists living in England in 1562, became the west's most important religious text next to the Bible for more than a century. It included some tunes from the *Geneva Psalter* as well as several folklike melodies that might have been derived from popular songs of the day, offering seventeen metrical patterns to which the psalm verses could be sung.

As the sixteenth century progressed, some English Calvinists fled persecution in England to seek religious freedom in Holland, where they became known as Separatists. The psalter they printed for their use during this self-imposed exile, called the *Ainsworth Psalter* (Figure 24), included even greater metric variety than *Sternhold and Hopkins*. Both of these famous English-language psalters—*Ainsworth* and *Sternhold and Hopkins*—contain tunes so merry in mood and lively in tempo that skeptics, reminded of the

Psalm Tune

Composer

Louis Bourgeois (c. 1510–28c. 1561)

Title

"Old Hundred." The title refers to the tune's association with Psalm 100.

Form

Strophic

Meter

Each verse consists of four lines, with eight syllables in each line. This is called *long meter.* (Any psalm in long meter could be sung to any long meter tune.)

Accompaniment

In most hymnals and psalters today, the tune appears with chordal accompaniment (for piano or organ). More complex versions, however, were enjoyed even in early Calvinist homes, where the tune might also have been played upon or accompanied by instruments.

Rhythm

Although the melody has remained unchanged for centuries, the rhythm has been altered. Modern Protestants generally sing "Old Hundred" to one of two well-known rhythmic patterns, neither of which has the rhythmic variety, interest, or vigor of the settings enjoyed by early congregations.

syncopated rhythms of popular Renaissance dances, referred to them as "Geneva jigs." In similar vein, in *The Winter's Tale,* Shakespeare described a Puritan who "sings psalms to hornpipes."

Many of the English settlers had enjoyed playing and listening to musical instruments in their homes, but few managed to bring any instruments with them to the New World. Furthermore, because travel between the continents was costly, time-consuming, and dangerous, the settlers soon lost touch with current music events abroad. They had, of course, brought their psalters with them, and for some time the music experience for both Pilgrims and Puritans consisted of singing psalm tunes for worship in church and for entertainment at home.

In a surprisingly short time, the settlers developed an American taste and tongue, making the language of their old psalters seem stilted and old-fashioned. Thus only twenty years after landing at Plymouth Rock, in 1640, an American psalter titled *The Whole Booke of Psalms Faithfully Translated into English Metre* but popularly known as the **Bay Psalm Book,** was printed

Figure 24

Pages from the *Ainsworth Psalter* (Amsterdam, 1612), showing a psalm tune and the manner in which each verse of the psalm has been retranslated into rhymed and metered verse. (Courtesy of the Trustees of Boston Public Library.)

in Cambridge, Massachusetts, the first book printed in the New World (Figure 25).

Early Efforts at Musical Reform

Although each edition of the *Bay Psalm Book* printed after 1698 included several notated tunes, few people knew how to read music, and as the old tunes came to be remembered differently in various towns and villages, New Englanders began to disagree as to how they should be sung. In order to learn the tunes as they thought they should be rendered, some congregations adopted the practice of **lining out,** in which a (more or less musically literate) leader sang one line of the psalm, which the congregation then repeated in unison, performing each successive line in this manner.

But lining out satisfied very few. Some of the leaders, with voices untrained and sometimes unattractive as well, began the songs too high or too low for the congregation, causing people to "squeak above" or "grumble below" their comfortable singing ranges. Leaders and sometimes congregational members also embellished the tunes at will, grossly distorting their original effect. Becoming accustomed to such altered (in a sense, "American") versions of the old tunes, many people were loath to give them up and for a time strongly resisted all efforts to impose the "regular" style of singing the tunes as they were written.

Figure 25

Pages from the *Bay Psalm Book,* the first book printed in the American colonies. (© Historical Pictures/Stock Montage.)

The Singing School Movement As the advantages of being able to read music notation became apparent, certain better-educated ministers printed collections of tunes, prefaced by detailed instructions on how to read music notation, and set out to teach New Englanders to read the tunes printed in their psalters. Although the traditional system of music notation is quite easy to learn (you may want to refer to p. xxix of the Prelude), some amateur teachers attempted to devise even simpler methods, including one based on the four syllables then commonly used to sing pitches (*fa, sol, la,* and *mi*) that placed on the staff the first *letter* of each syllable (*f, s, l,* or *m*) instead of the traditional note heads.

The efforts of the teaching ministers soon were supplemented, and eventually assumed, by talented amateur musicians, who became known as **singing school masters.** Some of these self-taught music amateurs, having previously earned their living as shopkeepers, merchants, farmers, or in other practical trades, became itinerant teachers, traveling from town to town and holding informal singing schools in the local meetinghouse, church, or school for a limited period of perhaps two or three months. People welcomed the singing school masters to their towns, because singing schools became popular social as well as educational events. Interested men, women, and young people attended the singing lessons several times a week and, at the end of their instruction, gave a performance demonstrating their accomplishments to the town's proud public. Then the singing school master traveled on to another place.

The singing school movement, which began in Boston about 1720 and experienced its greatest activity throughout New England from 1760 to 1800, finally spread north into Canada and south through New York, New Jersey, Pennsylvania, Maryland, and into the Carolinas. In fact, singing school masters offered widespread instruction and inspiration, especially in rural and remote areas, well into the nineteenth century. Necessarily hardy and independent individuals, the singing school masters devised their own teaching materials, compiled collections of familiar psalm tunes and other religious songs, and composed tunes of their own. Some wrote extensive introductions to their music primers, including information about the syllables to be sung and the elements of music. The first Americans to write music with a distinctively American (at least, non-European) sound, they are collectively referred to as members of the **First New England School** of composers.

A "school" of artists generally includes people living at about the same time, in the same geographic region, and sharing certain artistic goals and similarities of style. The First New England School composers, who lived in late eighteenth-century New England, shared the goals of teaching people to read music and to sing. Most of the simple folklike songs they composed as teaching tools had religious texts and so were also suitable for congregational singing and for private entertainment at home. The best songs of these "Yankee pioneers" were as rugged, naïve, and honest as the sturdy tunesmiths who made them because, untouched by the influence of their sophisticated European contemporaries, they relied upon old, familiar techniques and their own honest taste. Colonial Americans, after all, had been out of touch with European music since the early seventeenth century, when tonality first became the harmonic system of the Western world, and the singing school masters had only a rudimentary comprehension of the tonal system. More significantly, they did not feel constrained to conform to *anyone's* rules. Sometimes they turned to pretonal techniques, basing some melodies on modes or on simple pentatonic scales.

William Billings (1746–1800)

William Billings, a tanner of hides who became famous as a singing school master and composer, was the first American to produce a book of tunes all of his own composition (see Figure 26). Billings' *The New England Psalm Singer* was printed (by Paul Revere) in 1770. Although Billings had attended singing school himself and continued to study music throughout his career, he considered "nature" the best teacher and confidently judged the quality of a piece according to how much he liked it. Well aware, for example, of the conventional relationships between consonant

(AP/Wide World Photos.)

Virgil Thomson
"The way to write American music is simple. All you have to do is be an American and then write any kind of music you wish."

Figure 26

Circular notation of a
canon by William Billings.
(The Granger Collection.)

and dissonant sounds (see Prelude, p. xxv–xxvi), Billings and other First New
England School composers often remained independent of such rules, making
refreshingly unorthodox musical decisions to please their own ears. (An-
noyed at criticism of his music by certain less adventurous listeners, Billings
flaunted his unconventional ideas by writing a song titled "Jargon," with flagrantly outrageous harmonies sure to offend the sensibilities of delicate
taste.) Considered by his contemporaries to be eccentric but talented above
the ordinary, Billings had many admirers; but he failed to realize much profit
on his tunebooks, because there was no effective copyright law in his day.
Forced to work as a street cleaner late in life, this remarkable early American
composer died a poor man.

A nationalist, in the sense that he wrote to suit his own American tastes
and made no attempt to imitate European sounds, Billings produced a number
of stirring patriotic songs, some of which describe specific events of the
American Revolutionary War. "Chester" (Listening Example 6), a favorite of
the Revolutionary period, is sometimes referred to as the first American popular song, because it was widely sung and played by bands and by solo instruments for general pleasure and entertainment. "Chester" first appeared in
the collection printed in 1770, but Billings added topical verses after the war
broke out.

Unlike most of the music we have studied so far, consisting of one line of
melody without harmonic accompaniment, "Chester" was written and is usually performed in chordal, or homophonic, texture (see Prelude, p. xxviii). In
other words, Billings wrote not only the tune, but also its chordal accompaniment. People had long enjoyed singing harmonized versions of their religious
songs at home if not in church; and by the time of the First New England
School, harmony was no longer excluded from music in the worship service,
where an organ or other musical instrument(s) often accompanied congregational singing.

Revolutionary War Song

Composer

William Billings

Title

"Chester"

Form

Strophic. There are several four-line stanzas.

Meter

Quadruple. "Chester" was the principal marching song of the New England troops during the Revolutionary War.

Melody

The strong tune lies within the range of an octave. It begins with the last four notes of the ascending major scale—the third phrase also uses these four notes only. The second phrase uses the lower notes of the octave, and the fourth phrase uses the complete descending major scale.

Texture

Homophonic. The melody lies in the tenor or next-to-the lowest voice, as was the custom in homophonic vocal music of the eighteenth century. We are accustomed to hearing the melody of a song in the soprano (highest) voice, with the alto or contralto (lower female voice), tenor, and bass (lower male voice) providing harmony. Here we must listen carefully to distinguish the melody line from the other voices, which simply provide harmony and have no melodic interest of their own.

Timbre

"Chester" may be sung a cappella, but it was probably accompanied by instruments in its usual eighteenth-century performance.

Text

Three verses of the words, which were written by Billings, will indicate the stirring spirit and martial mood of his text.

Let tyrants shake their iron rod,
And Slav'ry clank her galling chains.
We fear them not, we trust in God.
New England's God forever reigns.

The Foe comes on with haughty stride,
Our troops advance with martial noise,
Their vet'runs flee before our youth,
and Generals yield to beardless boys.

What grateful off'ring shall we bring,
What shall we render to the Lord?
Loud Hallelujahs let us Sing
And praise his name on ev'ry Chord.

33

Figure 27

A canon. Each voice
enters in turn, singing the
same melody. The resulting
combination of tones
produces attractive
harmonies.

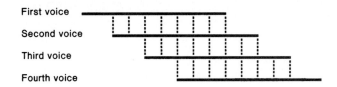

Canons

A **canon** is a melody that forms meaningful harmonies when performed with
"staggered entrances"—that is, when successive voices begin the same
melody at later times (Figure 27). Each voice continues to the end of the
melody, simply dropping out at the end of the tune while any remaining
voices continue until they drop out in turn. (Here "voice" refers to a line of
music, whether sung or played by musical instruments.) Because each of the
lines is melodically conceived—in fact, each line is actually the same
melody—a canon is polyphonic in texture.

"When Jesus Wept" (Listening Example 7), one of Billings' best-known
and best-loved songs, is a circular canon, or **round,** which continues to make
harmonic sense when repeated any number of times.

Fuging Tunes

Late in the eighteenth century, a new kind of song called a **fuging tune** became very popular, and by 1810, about one thousand of these had been written. A fuging tune consists of two sections, which we will call **A** and **B** (Figure 28). The first section (**A**) is chordal, or homophonic, in texture, the
melody lying in one voice (usually the tenor) while the other three (soprano,
alto, and bass) provide chordal harmony.

The second section of a fuging tune (**B**), which begins with staggered entrances, gives each voice melodic interest; thus the texture is polyphonic. But
unlike a canon, in which each voice performs the *same* melody, entering and
dropping out in turn, a fuging tune has four similar but *independent* lines of
music, which finally end together on a chord. The second section is repeated,
rendering the form of a fuging tune **ABB.**

Fuging tunes were fun to sing, offering everyone an interesting and varied
part and challenging housewives, farmers, shopkeepers, tavern owners,
young people, everyone who enjoyed music to put to use their hard-won
singing school skills. "Sherburne" (Listening Example 8) by **Daniel Read**
(1757–1836), another well-known member of the First New England School
of composers, was an immensely popular fuging tune in late-eighteenth-
century America. A comb maker who also owned a general store and taught
singing school, Read probably was the most popular composer of fuging
tunes. "Sherburne" remained widely known until the Civil War period and
still is sung in parts of the country today.

Canon

Composer
William Billings

Title
"When Jesus Wept"

Form
A four-part circular canon or round. There are four phrases, any
two or more of which form harmony when performed together.

Texture
Monophonic when the melody is performed in unison: polyphonic
when performed in canon.

Meter
Triple

Timbre
The canon may be performed by four women's voices, four men's
voices, or by a mixed chorus of soprano, alto, tenor, and bass.

Text
Billings wrote the words, as well as the music, of this famous
canon. The ending is particularly effective; the last voices sing the
moving words in unison, the other voices having dropped out in
turn.

When Jesus wept, the falling tear
In mercy flow'd beyond all bound;
When Jesus groan'd, a trembling fear
Seiz'd all the guilty world around.

Besides Billings and Read, many singing school masters composed psalm
tunes, hymns, canons, and fuging tunes for the edification and enjoyment of
their pupils. Although these practical men conceived of their music as teaching material rather than art, we value it today as strong, beautiful, and genuinely American in character, much as we appreciate the work folk artists of
the period produced, functional in purpose but beautiful in its own right. (See
Figure 29.) Recent American composers have used the tunes of the First New
England School composers and their contemporaries as inspiration and
source material for music of our own period. (Notably, William Schuman, a
Pulitzer Prize–winning composer with strong national interests, wrote a symphonic concert piece titled *New England Triptych* based on three of Billings'
songs, including "When Jesus Wept" and "Chester," see p. 350–351.)

Figure 28

A fuging tune. Section A is homophonic in texture, as represented by the dotted vertical lines. Section B begins with staggered entrances (polyphonic texture) but ends with chords. Section B is repeated.

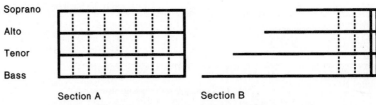

Soprano
Alto
Tenor
Bass

Section A   Section B

Listening Example 8

Fuging Tune

Composer
Daniel Read

Title
"Sherburne"

Texture
The first section, consisting of the first two lines of text, is homophonic in texture. (The fact that the words are sung in the four voices simultaneously implies chordal texture or vertical combinations of sound.) The second section (third and fourth lines) begins with staggered entrances, each melodic line imitative of, but not identical to, the others. (Different words in different voices enhance our ability to hear the music in a linear fashion.) The last few syllables are sounded simultaneously in all the voices, and the section ends on a chord. The second section is repeated.

Text
The words are from a famous hymn written in 1700 by Nahum Tate.

While shepherds watched their flocks by night
All seated on the ground
The angel of the Lord came down,
And glory shone around.

Protestant Hymnody

While John Calvin proscribed all music but the singing of psalm tunes in church, Martin Luther encouraged the joyful singing of simple tunes and light-hearted texts in worship, even composing some hymns of his own. Thus while Calvinists confined their worship music to the unaccompanied singing of psalm tunes, American Lutherans sang hymns, many of which (including Luther's best-known hymn, with a sturdy tune and a strong text beginning "A

Figure 29

The Sargent Family, American School, 1800, canvas, 0.974 cm × 1.280 cm. Folk artists, like the singing school masters, accomplished highly attractive art in their efforts to provide a practical service—here, to preserve the likenesses of this young American family. (Gift of Edgar William and Bernice Chrysler Garbisch, © 1992 National Gallery of Art, Washington.)

Mighty Fortress Is Our God") remain in hymnals currently used by many Protestant sects. The great English writer of hymn texts Isaac Watts (1674–1748) produced a great quantity of stirring hymn verses, including "When I Survey the Wondrous Cross," "Our God, Our Help in Ages Past," "From All That Dwell below the Skies," and "Joy to the World," all of which also are well known and loved today.

In 1735, a strong religious revival movement known as the Great Awakening stirred tremendous waves of religious fervor, further stimulating the rise of hymnody in America.

German-Speaking Protestant Sects Responding to William Penn's policy of religious toleration, a number of German-speaking Protestants fled persecution in their homelands and came to settle first in Pennsylvania, and later in other New World regions as well. Here, free from persecution, they kept much of their Old World culture intact, their language and religious practices largely isolating them from the Protestant Anglo-American mainstream of the thirteen colonies.

The Mennonites (of whom the Amish were a later offshoot) first arrived in 1683, mostly from Germany. From the time of their founding, in the 1520s, their refusal to perform military service and their rejection of a state church led to their severe persecution by their Dutch, Swiss, and German hosts.

Mennonites sang their sturdy, appealing hymn tunes a cappella and in unison, generally in so slow a tempo as to encourage the improvisation of embellishments, thus lending them a highly appealing folklike flavor. Some of their lovely old hymn tunes have, in fact, become part of the folk repertory in Mennonite and Amish communities today. Although the Mennonites remained largely isolated by their language (mostly German or Dutch) and customs from mainstream American society, at least one Mennonite tune is widely remembered today with the addition of a text in English, titled "Flow Gently, Sweet Afton."

Moravians The late seventeenth and early eighteenth century brought further waves of emigrant Protestants, including members of the English Society of Friends, known as Quakers, and Shakers, a later offshoot from the Quaker sect (so-called because of the trembling induced by their religious emotion). Of the new immigrants, however, the German-speaking Moravians had by far the most significant effect upon music in America.

The Moravians arrived in America in 1735 together with the famous Methodist missionaries and hymn writers John and Charles Wesley. Having been severely persecuted for their religious beliefs and practices in their homelands of Moravia and Bohemia, the Moravians wished to settle in America, where many intended to serve as Christian missionaries to African and Native Americans. Settling first in Georgia, the Moravians then moved north to found Bethlehem, Pennsylvania. They also established communities in Salem (Winston-Salem today), North Carolina, and other areas in (what is today) the eastern United States.

Music had been an important part of the Moravians' European experience, and they continued to compose and perform beautiful music in their new land. Integrating hymn singing and other religious music into their daily lives, some Moravians also wrote secular songs and instrumental music, sophisticated and complex beyond that of other early Americans and revealing their strong German and Czech heritage.

The first important American-born Moravian composer, **John Antes** (1740–1811), composed a number of beautiful religious choral pieces called **anthems**—religious songs, longer and more complex than hymns, intended to be sung by a trained soloist or a choir rather than by the members of a church congregation. The text of an anthem is often biblical. The form is usually **through composed,** meaning that unlike a song in strophic form (in which two or more verses are all set to the same music), there is little or no repetition of melodic phrases; rather, the text unfolds to new music throughout the piece. A number of anthems by Antes, including "Surely He Has Borne Our Griefs" (Listening Example 9), are still sung today.

Anthem

Composer
John Antes

Title
"Surely He Has Borne Our Griefs"

Form
Through composed

Meter
Quadruple. Although there is a steady sense of pulse throughout this moving anthem, the tempo is often greatly relaxed at the ends of phrases to heighten the emotional expressiveness of the piece. The term for this expressive "robbing from" and "returning to" the tempo is rubato.

Harmony
The anthem is in the key of C minor, meaning that the tonic note is C and most of the melodic and harmonic material is based upon the C minor scale. Notice how Antes varies the effect, however, by occasionally using a major chord, as at the end of the first phrase on the word "griefs."

Also notice how pungent dissonances, as on "wounded" in the third phrase, enhance the meaning of the text by evoking an emotional response. The sopranos' high pitch on "wounded" and in the last phrase on "stripes" also has an emotional impact upon the listener.

Accompaniment
Whereas most early American composers expected accompanying instruments simply to double the voice lines, Antes wrote full instrumental accompanying parts for his anthems. Here there is a four-part accompaniment for string ensemble, although it may be played on an organ or piano instead. There is no instrumental introduction, but the instruments play an interlude between the two large sections (beginning after "iniquities"). Their ending material, with a descending melodic line, slowing of tempo, and lessening of dynamic level, brings the anthem to a moving close.

Text
Surely He has borne our griefs and carried our sorrows. He was wounded for our transgressions. He was bruised for our iniquities. The chastisement of our peace lay upon Him: And with His stripes we are healed.

Secular Music

Public concerts began to be performed in some of the larger American cities beginning in the late 1720s—about the same time they began to be held in Europe. For most of the eighteenth century, however, Americans showed little interest in formal concert music, most remaining largely unaware of the outstanding composers of their time, the Austrians Wolfgang Amadeus Mozart (1756–1790) and Franz Joseph Haydn (1732–1809). Because even the best-educated American audience had very limited experience with serious music, early concerts consisted of simple and popular pieces—marches, dance tunes, and stirring *programmatic* pieces (instrumental pieces purporting to imitate sounds of nature or to "tell" a story) interspersed with folk songs and popular songs from the contemporary theater. Battle pieces written for keyboard instruments (harpsichord, organ, or piano) as well as for bands numbered among the most popular concert attractions.

Home music, work music, music for entertainment and for dancing dominated American music throughout the Revolutionary and Federal periods. In rural areas, combined work-social affairs such as barn raisings, maple sugaring, and cornhusking often were accompanied by singing, fiddling, or other musical activities and followed by dancing. Music in New Orleans must have been particularly rich and varied, because African, Native American, Caribbean, French, and Spanish cultures all were part of life in that vibrant city.

Music publishing had become an important business by the latter part of the century, producing quantities of sheet music appropriate for the amateur performer that consisted mostly of simple vocal and piano pieces sometimes referred to as "household music." More and more Americans had musical instruments such as violins, guitars, oboes, and flutes in their homes. Popular keyboard instruments included small and often elaborately decorated *virginals* (Figure 30) as well as harpsichords and early pianos, called *fortepianos,* some of which were built in America. The fortepiano was smaller and more delicate than the modern instrument, but as its name implies, it was able to produce varied dynamic levels according to the touch of the performer. Children and young women learned to sing and play simple pieces by taking lessons from immigrant professional musicians.

Servants, both African American and white, sometimes were chosen for their musical abilities and expected to contribute to music making in the home. Talented African Americans sometimes supplied music for social dancing and played at dancing schools, in taverns, and for formal balls. The favored instrument to accompany dancing was the *fiddle:* Smaller and lighter than the modern violin and producing a louder and more vibrant sound than was considered appropriate for genteel listening, the eighteenth-century instrument was heard more often in the barnyard or ballroom than in the parlour.

Figure 30
Double spinet, or virginal, made by Ludovicus Growelus (Lodewijck Grauwels). Early virginals were oblong boxes small enough to be placed on a table, but late in the eighteenth century, the term was applied to various keyboard instruments. (The Metropolitan Museum of Art; The Crosby Brown Collection of Musical Instruments, 1889.)

Prestigious Musical Amateurs

Although Europeans continued to dominate professional music performances, American amateurs became increasingly active in various phases of musical activity. Many joined musical societies founded in a number of larger American cities, which presented instrumental or choral music—mostly written, however, by European composers. Professional foreign musicians often joined the amateur society members for their concerts, which lasted for as long as three or more hours. (See Figure 31.)

The first performances in America of important European symphonic and choral works were given by Moravian musicians, whose compositions and performances were of the highest quality, for they were amateurs only in the sense that they composed and performed music for the love of it (as the root of the word "amateur" implies) rather than for money. As news spread of the Moravians' outstanding concerts, people traveled long distances from other settlements to hear them. George Washington and Benjamin Franklin numbered among the Moravians' most fervent admirers.

Well-to-do patrons and musical amateurs such as the famous statesman **Thomas Jefferson** (1743–1826) supported the efforts of the musical societies by contributing generously of their time, money, and talent. Jefferson, a fine musician himself, participated enthusiastically in music activities, although he insisted that the arts were meaningful only as they bore relevance to everyday life. An accomplished architect who designed buildings to be beautiful as well as efficient, Jefferson apparently considered the musical arts an essential part of the human experience as well. He played the violin, as did Patrick

Figure 31

An eighteenth-century chamber music concert. (The Bettmann Archive, Inc.)

Henry, who sometimes joined Jefferson in duets to entertain themselves, their friends, and (before the Revolution) illustrious representatives of His Majesty's government in Williamsburg, Virginia. Most early Americans agreed with Jefferson that art—especially American art—must be practical to be worthwhile. John Adams considered even "practical" art a luxury inappropriate for the people of a young democracy, although he admired a well-written sermon, political document, or tract.

Benjamin Franklin (1706–1790), who warned that Americans should not cultivate a taste for the arts before they were able to produce them, clearly considered Europeans superior in this regard. Conceding that poetry, painting, and music might be useful under certain circumstances, he complained that America had no musicians of the caliber of outstanding European performers, and that even concerts performed by Europeans in America were inferior to the performances Franklin heard in England and on the continent.

Franklin wrote verses to set to tunes that he enjoyed, learned to play the guitar and the harp very well, and even invented a musical instrument called the **armonica** or **glass harmonica** (Figure 32), which became enormously popular in its day. This instrument consists of a series of hollow, hemispheric glass bowls or bells, each with a short neck. The glasses are mounted on a horizontal spindle, each fitted inside the next largest with a finger width of brim exposed on which to play. The performer keeps the spindle turning through a trough of water by working a pedal, while producing a delicate sound by rubbing the wet rims of the glasses with the fingers.

The mysterious sounds of the glass harmonica were reputed to make women faint, soothe marital disputes, and even to wake the dead! (Mozart frequently played the instrument at the Vienna home of hypnotist Anton Mesmer, who used it to help induce trances in his patients.)

The first secular songs published in America were by Europeans, many from England, and were usually associated with the theater. But about the

Figure 32
Benjamin Franklin playing
his glass harmonica.
(Art & History Archives,
Berlin.)

same time that the singing school masters were writing religious songs to use as teaching tools, other amateur American composers began to write music that had neither a religious nor a practical purpose.

Francis Hopkinson (1737–1791), an extraordinary American who became our first secretary of the navy and one of the signers of the Declaration of Independence, also was much concerned with the artistic dimension of American life. Hopkinson wrote several **art songs**—songs intended for concert or recital performance (amateur or professional) as opposed to folk or popular pieces. The text of an art song is a poem of literary merit, by a known poet. Because the music is intended to enhance the meaning of the poem, it may be expressive or dramatic rather than necessarily pleasing to the ear. Because the essence of an art song lies in the text, and because translations inevitably lose nuances of meaning and sound, art songs are nearly always performed in the language in which they were written.

A zealous patriot in the political sense, Hopkinson nevertheless conceived his songs in conscientious imitation of the English songs of his day. Unlike the sturdily independent singing school masters, Hopkinson held the "cultivated" eighteenth-century American view that the colonists were inferior in the arts and best advised to emulate European styles. Thus his song titled "My Days Have Been So Wondrous Free" (Optional Listening Example) is of far more historical than musical interest today.

Although Hopkinson appears to have been the first American to attempt songs of this nature, soon other Americans also composed songs European in style, with texts, however, often based upon American subjects—several in honor of George Washington. Most early American art songs, unlike their more demanding European models, were suitable for performance by amateurs.

Professional Composers

Many talented and accomplished European musicians who immigrated to the United States greatly enriched the American concert experience before and after the turn of the nineteenth century. For example, **Benjamin Carr** (1768–1831), a composer, singer, conductor, organist, pianist, and music publisher, arrived soon after the Revolution. Aside from his many other activities, Carr also ran a music store in Philadelphia that became the leading center of music activity after the war.

James Hewitt (1770–1827), whose birth and death dates are the same as Beethoven's, became a theater director and music publisher. Hewitt catered to the prevailing American taste by composing a number of programmatic battle pieces, including an orchestral work titled "Overture in Nine Movements, Expressive of a Battle" and an organ piece called "Battle of Trenton."

Alexander Reinagle (1756–1809), who taught music in New York City before settling in Philadelphia as director of a theater company, directed a series of city concerts presenting the music of outstanding European composers. He also composed attractive instrumental pieces, including the Sonata in E for the Piano Forte (Listening Example 10).

The last movement of Reinagle's Sonata in E for the Piano Forte is in the form of a **rondo.** Although a rondo may include any number of sections, the letters **A B A C A** illustrate the general concept of the form. That is, the opening melodic material returns (comes round) a number of times, alternating with other, contrasting, sections. Because the mood of a rondo is often bright and the tempo fast, the form often provides an effective close to a multimovement work.

Early American Theater

Music theater became popular in some areas during the 1730s, as growing numbers of professional musicians from Europe provided performance and educational opportunities previously denied colonial Americans, and many of America's earliest professional musicians were associated with both the theater and the concert hall. Although the songs and instrumental interludes they composed for theatrical works were performed in concerts as well as the theater, it was theatrical performances that made their works popular and afforded them a living. Charleston and Williamsburg, early centers of music activity, had active theaters well before the middle of the eighteenth century. The prevailing religious influence in the South was Anglican, and the English church—unlike the Calvinists—had largely abandoned Oliver Cromwell's seventeenth-century scruples regarding theatrical performances.

Rondo

Composer
Alexander Reinagle

Title
Sonata in E for the Piano Forte, third movement

Form
Rondo (or, since the contrasting sections are extended and rather complex, modified rondo).

Tempo
Allegro

Meter
Duple

(A) The gay opening theme includes two balanced phrases. It is repeated, with only slight variation, to provide classical balance and to enable the listener to memorize it and recognize its return. The left hand plays a simple accompaniment, including some measures of the broken-chord pattern called Alberti bass.

The extended (B) section includes graceful running passages. Notice the strong accents in one passage. (A) returns; there is another contrasting section (C), including contrasts between forte and piano passages. A slow and quiet cadenza, or solo passage for the right hand alone, anticipates the return of (A).

In 1778, under wartime stress, the Continental Congress deemed that "frequenting Play Houses and theatrical entertainments, has a fatal tendency to divert the minds of people from a due attention to the means necessary for the defence of their country and preservation of their liberties." Accordingly, they placed a ban on all theatrical performances; but the lifting of the ban in 1789 and the passing a year later of the first national copyright act, which protected printed materials including music for fourteen years with the possibility of renewal for another fourteen, encouraged a wave of foreign (mostly British) musicians to come to America, where they performed on stage and in the orchestra pits, taught music to aspiring amateurs, and wrote music, including America's first popular songs. After the Revolution music theater developed a growing popularity, interest in music and the theater moving north to New York and then to Philadelphia, which soon dominated the musical scene. The Quakers' disapproval of theatrical performances was overruled by the enthusiasm of such influential patrons as George Washington, who justified his fondness for theater by declaring that it had the practical effect of elevating one's manners.

This hardly appeared the case at performances, however, where informality to the extent of rowdiness prevailed. Those sitting in the cheaper seats, called the gallery, yelled freely at the actors and musicians, demanding to hear their favorite songs and criticizing the performance in the frankest (rudest) terms. Bottles and fruit were tossed into the orchestra pit or onto the stage, and not infrequently, despite the presence of soldiers hired to keep order, pandemonium reigned.

The eighteenth-century American stage offered a potpourri of entertainment, performances lasting four or five hours and usually including a main drama and a shorter, lighter, and often comic piece as well. Music was added even to nonmusical plays, with musical entertainment provided between the dramatic pieces and after the comedy. Sometimes a march played at the end led the audience out of the hall to attend a nearby dance.

Most of the plays performed in eighteenth-century America were English pieces adapted to suit American taste. Shorter and lighter than contemporary European works, they also included more comedy. The most popular type of performance, called a **ballad opera,** was a simple, unsophisticated musical play in which spoken dialogue replaced the *recitative* ("sung speech") of serious opera, and popular songs of the day were interspersed throughout the show. John Gay's *Beggar's Opera,* the first musical play of this kind, became as popular in America as it had been in England since it opened in 1728. (The popular song "Mack the Knife" comes from a twentieth-century version of the *Beggar's Opera* called *Three-Penny Opera* by Kurt Weill.)

A short musical play credited to Francis Hopkinson in 1781 may have been America's earliest original musical theater work, although Hopkinson probably just set new words to music that already existed. In any case, foreign professionals such as Alexander Reinagle dominated the American popular music stage for a considerable period, having significant effect upon the development of music in America.

Terms to Review

hymn   A religious verse set to music suitable for congregational singing.

alabado   A long religious song of praise, from a Spanish folk tradition popular in some villages of the American Southwest.

psalms   One hundred fifty inspirational verses from the Old Testament of the Bible.

psalm tunes   Tuneful settings of the psalms in versions suitable for congregational singing.

a cappella   Unaccompanied (choral singing).

psalter   A printed collection of the psalms translated into metered and rhymed verse, suitable for setting to simple tunes.

Bay Psalm Book   Popular name for *The Whole Booke of Psalms Faithfully Translated into English Metre,* the first book printed in America, which first appeared in 1640.

lining out   A method of group singing in which each line of text is sung by a leader and echoed by the congregation.

singing school masters   Musical amateurs who taught people to read music and to sing.

First New England School   America's first composers, also known as Yankee pioneers and singing school masters, who lived in New England in the eighteenth and early nineteenth centuries, and who wrote music to use as teaching tools.

canon A polyphonic composition in which all of the voices perform the same melody beginning at different times.

round A circular canon, which may be repeated indefinitely.

fuging tune A hymn or psalm tune in two sections, the first homophonic and the second polyphonic in texture.

anthem A through-composed religious song, usually with a biblical text, for performance by a choir rather than a congregation.

through composed A song form containing new music throughout, without the internal repetition characteristic of strophic form.

rubato Flexible rhythm and tempo. *Rubato* means "robbing" and refers to stealing from the tempo and then roughly repaying the lost time.

armonica or **glass harmonica** A musical instrument invented by Benjamin Franklin, consisting of tuned, wet glasses that are rubbed to produce a sound.

art song A secular song, usually with a text of literary merit, intended for concert or recital performance.

rondo A form of composition, usually fast in tempo and merry in mood, in which various episodes alternate with the opening material (**A B A C A**).

Alberti bass An accompaniment pattern consisting of rhythmically regular broken chords.

cadenza An extended passage for solo instrument.

ballad opera An English form of music theater setting comedy and satire to popular tunes.

Key Figures

William Billings
Daniel Read
John Antes
Thomas Jefferson
Benjamin Franklin
Francis Hopkinson
Benjamin Carr
James Hewitt
Alexander Reinagle

Optional Listening Examples

Psalm tune:
"Windsor" (Psalm 15)
Francis Hopkinson, "My Days Have Been So Wondrous Free"

Suggestions for Further Listening

Psalm tunes:
"Old 124th" (Psalm 8)
"Old 112th" (Psalm 34)
Fuging tunes and other songs by First New England School composers, such as the following:
Timothy Swan
Andrew Law
Jeremiah Ingalls
Jacob Kimball
Supply Belcher
Rondo:
Mozart, *Adagio and Rondo,* K. 617, for glass harmonica, flute, oboe, viola, and cello
American instrumental music in Classical style:
Benjamin Carr, *Sonata I,* for piano or harpsichord
Carr, *Federal Overture*
Battle piece:
James Hewitt, "Battle of Trenton," for organ
Music by the following Moravian composers:
Johann Friedrich Peter
Johannes Herbst
John Antes
Jeremiah Denckem
Edward W. Leinbach
Modern compositions based upon the music of the First New England School, including the following:
William Schuman, "New England Triptych"
Schuman, "Chester" Overture, Listening Example 73
Henry Cowell, "Hymns and Fuging Tunes"
Otto Luening, "Fuging Tune for Wind Instruments"
Ross Lee Finney, "Hymn, Fuging and Holiday"

The earliest North American music experience was that of American Indians, whose many musics are associated with ritual, dance, ceremony, or work. Most Native American music was and is song, sometimes supported by sound instruments—primarily percussion instruments, such as drums, rattles, and rasps, or their most common melodic instrument, a flute.

Contemporary Native American music reflects not only the ancient, traditional songs and dances, but also various new styles, some of which are traditional and some borrowed from European neighbors. Even the new songs remain a potent source of power in American Indian culture, confirming Indian-ness, validating ceremonies, and helping keep people "right" and in balance with nature and with the deity who controls all.

Beginning in the sixteenth century, as Europeans came to settle in the New World, Native Americans in Florida and in the missions of the Southwest learned to perform Roman Catholic music and some European secular music as well. Soon German- and English-speaking Protestants established permanent settlements in America, bringing with them their hymns and psalm tunes, as well as folk and other secular music. The first book printed in the New World was the *Bay Psalm Book*. Both African and European Americans enjoyed secular as well as religious music, the settlers singing ballads and playing fiddle tunes, the slaves singing work songs and other songs according to African custom.

Early efforts to improve the quality of singing in New England's churches led to the forming of singing schools, some of whose singing masters wrote their own original tunes, thereby becoming known as members of the First New England School of composers. Their music differed in style and purpose from that of their European contemporaries. William Billings, Daniel Read, and their many Yankee pioneer colleagues produced quantities of psalm tunes, hymns, fuging tunes, and patriotic songs for use at singing school, at church, and in the home.

Americans' musical tastes became more secular and more varied during the eighteenth century, as music supplied entertainment in the home, at concerts, and in the theater. Many people learned to play instruments and sing simple songs, and musical societies were formed for the purpose of performing instrumental and choral music. Talented amateurs participated in informal recitals and composed songs and keyboard pieces. Moravians produced music of a complexity and quality unprecedented by other early American compositions.

Public concerts and music theater had also become a popular form of entertainment by the middle of the century. The important musicians associated with the early American theater were Europeans who adapted popular European plays and ballad operas to suit the less sophisticated American taste.

Part

2

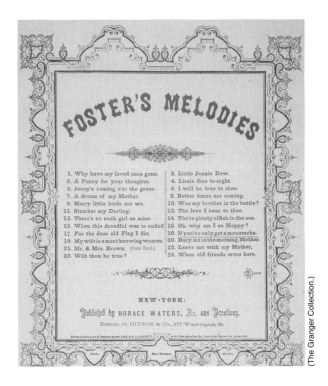

(The Granger Collection.)

The Nineteenth Century

Romanticism in America: Historical and Cultural Perspective

During the nineteenth century, most European writers, painters, and musicians abandoned the coolly reasoned Classical style to reveal in their new art a fierce independence, a fascination with the unknown, and a worshipful love of nature—all characteristics associated with *romanticism* in the arts. From about 1825 to 1900, the emotional, intuitive style called Romanticism (the capital letter distinguishing the nineteenth-century style from romanticism in general) dominated the arts in Europe, and German musicians dominated music in the Western world.

Americans revealed strong romantic tendencies long before the nineteenth century and continue to do so today. Thus the artistic style newly dominant in Europe came quite naturally to this young country, where its spirit seemed always to have been at home. Perhaps the pioneers bred their sense of adventure into later generations of Americans, or perhaps the vast, wild land encouraged the demand for freedom and independence. For whatever reasons, romanticism seemed then, as now, characteristic of the American personality.

The Emergence of Characteristically American Art
Although from about the 1830s one could travel from America to Europe by steamship, such travel was neither safe nor reliable, and most Americans remained effectively isolated from European culture. Little diplomatic exchange took place, and few foreigners immigrated to America during the midcentury period. Although many nineteenth-century American musicians shied away from the fresh, original sounds of the Yankee tunesmiths and attempted to emulate European— specifically German—traditions, the young country's literary and visual artists often expressed their romantic ideals in characteristically American ways.

Independence. Whereas classicists accept the concepts of universal truth and beauty, romantics stress the significance of individual rights and preferences, which of course are basic tenets of the American creed. The brave men and women of the American frontier developed a fierce (if inconsistent) respect for the integrity of the humblest individual, and Puritans, Quakers, and members of other Protestant sects in the cities of the Northeast shared the frontier people's work ethic and concern for the common folk.

In the early 1800s, Americans defended their new and hard-earned political and military independence by resisting the French and British in assorted skirmishes and vigorously fighting the notorious Barbary pirates. American patriots further manifested their fierce independence by vowing, in the Monroe Doctrine of 1823, to resist foreign interference anywhere in the Western Hemisphere. Strong reform movements rising in nineteenth-century America vigorously addressed issues of human and civil rights, as women became active in a number of social causes, including the abolition of slavery, the founding of the American Temperance Society (1826), improvements to the conditions of prisons and asylums, and increased aid to the disabled. In 1828, city and frontier folk alike rejected aristocratic leadership by electing a populist hero president of the United States, and under President Andrew Jackson a new American nationalism evolved as artists and writers, encouraged by their patrons' new interest in American art for art's sake, shed their dependence on Europeans and began to produce works on a wide variety of American subjects.

Claiming a refreshing freedom from European dominance, American literary figures developed their own distinctive ways to express the American experience, and a genuinely American literature evolved. In New York City, the major center of intellectual and artistic activity, and in other large cities as well, the theater thrived, and journalism became an important means of communication and a stimulus for human reform. The prolific literary activity of this period reflected a new American nationalism, as poets and novelists wrote on American subjects placed in American settings. James Fenimore Cooper's *The Last of the Mohicans,* for example, was one of many Romantic works featuring the American Indian.

Mid-nineteenth-century Boston housed an important group of writers and philosophers known as transcendentalists, who in the romantic way trusted intuition, rather than reason, as the guide to truth. Sharing the Protestants' and the frontier people's belief in the integrity and ability of the individual, the transcendentalists also fervently expressed in their literary and philosophical works their love of nature and pride in America's natural beauty.

The year 1852 produced one of the most famous and influential novels of any period, *Uncle Tom's Cabin* by Harriet Beecher Stowe. This book, which gave rise to the expression "Uncle Tom" to denote an African American who accepts a servile position under whites, generated heated reaction from people on both sides of the abolition question. The poets John Greenleaf Whittier and James Russell Lowell joined Emerson and Thoreau in a literary crusade against slavery, while Sidney Lanier (1842–1881) wrote moving verses from a southerner's point of view. From the time Abraham Lincoln was elected president in 1860 until he was assassinated in 1865, sermons, speeches, poems, articles, and proclamations addressed all sides of the slavery issue.

The famous humorist and author Mark Twain (real name Samuel Clemens, 1835–1910) depicted scenes and described relations between blacks and whites as he remembered them from his boyhood along the Mississippi River. An amateur musician who sang and played the piano, Twain frequently referred in his stories to the singing of simple songs and the playing of keyboard instruments. Twain claimed to particularly dislike the piano, an instrument he may have associated with the upper classes, with whom he did not identify. It is also possible that his sensitive ear was offended by the sound of poorly tuned pianos, since few instruments in his day were afforded the regular attention of a professional tuner. In any case, he often wrote approvingly of a simple and increasingly popular keyboard instrument variously called a *reed organ, parlor organ, cabinet organ, cottage organ,* or *melodeon* (Figure 33 and Listening Example 38, *St. Louis Blues*). The player of this instrument, the timbre of which could be varied through the use of levers or buttons called *stops,* pumped one or two treadles to produce the wind that made the sound possible. The reed organ, cheaper and requiring less maintenance than a piano, was very popular in Twain's day.

The Unknown. Unlike classicists, who enjoy the methodical achievement of reasonable, limited goals, romantics are intrigued with the *un*known. Thus romantic curiosity led pioneer men and women to push America's frontier ever farther west, defying great perils in the high spirit of optimism

Figure 33
A melodeon.
(The Bettmann Archive, Inc.)

Figure 34
The Erie Canal.
(The Bettmann Archive, Inc.)

also characteristic of the romantic personality. During the early years of the nineteenth century, surveyors and engineers explored and carefully mapped the wilderness areas of upstate New York, New England, and the West. The Erie Canal (Figure 34) was opened in 1825, and steam railroads soon afforded Americans yet further opportunity to become acquainted with their magnificent land, of which they were justly proud.

Stories and poems concerning abnormal psychology by such writers as Edgar Allen Poe (1809–1849) and Nathaniel Hawthorne (1804–1864) revealed their fascination with the unknown, whereas some Romantic painters, sharing the mutual interest in science and art experienced during the last century by Charles Willson Peale, explored new fields of study and made discoveries of significant scientific and practical worth. James Audubon (1785–1851) gave unprecedented attention to the study of birds, producing an astonishing number of realistic watercolors of American birds in their natural poses and settings.

Samuel Morse (1791–1872), who like Audubon and C. W. Peale had interest and talent in both science and art, helped make the pre-photographic process known as *daguerreotype* popular with Americans, who often had more interest in something new and mechanical than in objects of purely artistic value. Having studied painting in Europe, Morse produced several fine canvases upon his return to America. Ultimately, however, he became discouraged at Americans' preference for landscapes of local scenery over the large European-style "history paintings" he favored, whereupon he turned his attention to another form of communication and invented the telegraph.

Love of Nature. Nature, formerly viewed as a menacing force to be conquered and tamed, now received reverent admiration in American literature, painting, and music idealizing the natural beauty of the American continent. Writers portraying nature as good and beautiful included the poets William Cullen Bryant and Henry Wadsworth Longfellow and the essayists Ralph Waldo Emerson and Henry David Thoreau, each of whom expressed in American ways ideals similar to those of the British Romantic poets.

American painting in the post-Revolutionary, or federal, period also reflected the new American nationalism and the romantic love of nature, as artists captured the clear light, blazing sky, and vast open spaces of the American landscape. Although American viewers lagged behind Europeans in appreciat-

Figure 35

Margaretta Angelica Peale, *Still Life with Watermelon and Peaches*, 1828. Oil on canvas, 13 in. × 19⅛ in. (33 cm × 48.5 cm).
(Smith College Museum of Art, Northampton, MA. Purchased with funds given anonymously by a member of the class of 1952.)

ing art for its own, not necessarily functional, sake, American artists produced paintings and sculptural works of unprecedented numbers and variety. In painting, landscapes predominated, but Charles Willson Peale's cousin Margaretta Angelica Peale (1795–1882), one of very few professional women artists, was widely admired as a painter of still lifes, perhaps considered a more seemly subject than landscape for a woman to interpret (Figure 35). The same democratic spirit that elected Andrew Jackson president stimulated appreciation for scenes in art of everyday life, especially as experienced in the idealized countryside: cornhusking, dancing, and all manner of work and play were charmingly depicted by folk and formal artists.

Painters accompanying explorers and adventurers across the American wilderness depicted the wild beauty of untamed areas, stirring the romantic imagination of city-bound folk. George Catlin (1796–1872), a dedicated artist-explorer, vividly portrayed the vast American wilderness, complete with Indians and wild animals (see *White Cloud, Head Chief of the Iowas*, Figure 36).

Figure 36
George Catlin, *White Cloud, Head Chief of the Iowas.* Canvas, 58 cm × 71 cm (22⅞ in. × 28 in.) (© 1992 National Gallery of Art, Washington, D.C., 1844/1845, Paul Mellon Collection.)

Fusion of the Arts Although comparisons are readily drawn among the various arts of any stylistic period, the relationships between literature, painting, and music of the Romantic period are particularly striking in their strength and significance. Nineteenth-century artists in Europe and America drew inspiration from close association with each other and showed unprecedented interest in each other's work. European artists were, in fact, more dependent upon each other at this time than ever before, because their position in society had undergone significant change: Formerly viewed as servants of the church or aristocracy, which supported artists by requisitioning works to be executed according to the desires (demands) of the patron, artists now considered themselves not only independent, but somehow superior, to such patronage.

In truth, in America as well as in Europe, artists were newly dependent on the approval of a public audience, which lacked both the training and the experience of the earlier limited, even private, audiences of church, court, or salon. Thus during the Romantic period, in this country and abroad, artists relied on each other for moral support, and sometimes for more practical support as well.

The first important group of American painters, known as the Hudson River School, was led for a time by Thomas Cole (1801–1848), whose large landscape paintings capture the spaciousness and grandeur of the Catskill and Adirondack Mountains of New York State. Reflecting the close association between artists so dear to the great Romantics, Cole based his painting *Scenes from The Last of the Mohicans* (Figure 37) on the novel by his friend James Fenimore Cooper.

A mating of the arts also occurred in *Kindred Spirits* (Figure 38) by Asher B. Durand (1796–1886), who succeeded Cole as leader of the Hudson River School. Durand's painting portrays the artist Cole, for whom the painting was a memorial, and the poet William Cullen Bryant sharing admiration for the natural beauty of the Catskill Mountains. This painting embodies the feeling of Romantic artists of various media that their reverence for the natural beauty of their homeland transcended the feelings of more mundane souls.

Music proved a particularly congenial medium for the romantic blending of the arts: An art song, for example, was the setting of a poem to music. Program music often depicted scenes from literature in musical terms. Certain kinds of music theater, especially operas and operettas, constituted even more complex combinations of visual, literary, and musical arts.

The Civil War Era The reform movements begun in the early part of the nineteenth century gathered strength in the 1860s, as tensions heated between blacks and whites and between supporters of slavery and of abolition. Workers, increasingly well organized, forced enactment of tough new labor laws; feminists marched and demonstrated, demanding improved education opportunities for women, liberalized property rights, equitable divorce laws, and the right for women to vote.

Figure 37

Thomas Cole, *Scenes from The Last of the Mohicans.*
(Courtesy of the New York Historical Society, New York City.)

Whereas urban northerners found themselves increasingly repelled by slavery, southerners considered the system essential to the plantation economy upon which they depended, and there seemed no grounds for compromise on this volatile subject.

Finally forced to confront the problems leading inexorably to the Civil War, Americans reflected in their literary, visual, and musical arts every facet of these and other social issues.

From about 1850 to 1875, American painters shared their European colleagues' fascination with the myriad effects of light, which they learned to use as a means of expression in its own right, their best work capturing the clear atmosphere and wide spaciousness characteristic of the American scene.

American artists of the period idealized nature in the romantic way, viewing it as morally uplifting and taking pride in the grandeur of their nation's landscape. Andrew Jackson's optimism and the idealism of the American pioneer were reflected in many moving scenes of mountain splendor and rural calm.

Frederic Edwin Church (1826–1900), Thomas Cole's only pupil, painted New England with a scientific accuracy akin to Peale's and Audubon's fascination with natural history. Church and some of his contemporaries pursued their search for a new frontier all the way to South America, which they rightly considered part of the New World.

But few American patrons shared the artists' appreciation for American art. The best-known American

Figure 38

Asher B. Durand, *Kindred Spirits*. In a scene exemplifying the Romantic image, the painter Thomas Cole and the poet William Cullen Bryant share their admiration for the beauty of the Catskills. Love of nature, nationalism, and the close mating of the arts are among the Romantic characteristics beautifully expressed in this moving painting.
(Collection of the New York Public Library. Astor, Lenox and Tilden Foundations.)

Figure 39
Wooden bucket (c. 1825), whose charming
painted designs must have seemed to lighten
its load.
(Philadelphia Museum of Art.)

Figure 40
Edmonia Lewis, *Bust of Abraham Lincoln*.
(Courtesy City of San Jose Public Library, CA.)

artist of his day, James McNeill Whistler (1834–
1903), spent most of his life in Europe, having become discouraged by the lack of a market for serious art in his own country. Highly eccentric in dress
and manner but widely admired for his great talent,
Whistler became a leading figure in both European
and American art.

American still-life painting matured and flourished, largely independent of European influence,
and folk art became more individual and expressive
than ever (Figure 39). American practicality and
craftsmanship produced fine weathervanes, shop
signs, furniture, and other wares every bit as beautiful as they were indeed useful.

Americans during this time also produced distinctive sculpture, sometimes laden with messages
of social significance. *The Greek Slave* by Hiram
Powers (1805–1873) was seen as an American expression of sympathy for the Greek War of Independence as well as for slaves in the American South.
Another work revealing its creator's social consciousness was *The Indian* (*The Chief Contemplat-*

ing the Progress of Civilization) by Thomas Craw-
ford (1813–1857). Among the few professional
women artists of the time, Edmonia Lewis
(1845–1909), whose mother was Native American
and whose father was black, produced a number of
sculpted pieces of social and political relevance, including a stunning bust of Abraham Lincoln in 1867
(Figure 40).

Music Newly liberated from its former semifunc-
tional position in worship or daily life, and newly
available to an ever-wider public audience, music became an increasingly significant facet of nineteenth-
century American life. Religious and secular music,
for voices and/or for instruments, reflected every
feature of American experience in that turbulent
century. ♪

4

Populist Music of the Nineteenth Century

At the turn of the nineteenth century, a wave of evangelical revival movements gave further impetus to the popularity of the music of the First New England School composers, which continued to be enjoyed by plain and simple folk in New England, New York, New Jersey, Pennsylvania, Maryland, the Carolinas—wherever the singing school masters roamed and set up their short-term but highly effective schools.

While the traditional system of music notation (see Prelude, p. xxix) is quite easy to learn, a new method devised by amateur teachers, known as **shape-note notation,** proved particularly popular and long lived. Shape notes, which evolved from the system of placing the first letters of the four syllables *fa, sol, la,* and *mi* on the staff instead of traditional note heads, were assigned a different *shape* (square, circle, diamond, or triangle) for each of the four syllables and placed in appropriate positions on the staff (see Figure 41).

Although never adopted as the usual way of notating music, the shape-note method proved an effective teaching tool and in fact continues in use today with informal singing groups in certain rural, urban, and suburban areas across the country. Every summer throughout the nineteenth century, singing conventions attracted shape-note singers in large numbers to come together in churches or campgrounds, where they spent several days singing together, picnicking, and socializing much as in the early singing school days.

Figure 41

An arrangement of "Old Hundred" in shape-note notation. The words are placed under the melody line.
(From B. F. White and E. J. King, *The Sacred Harp,* 1844. Copyright © Sacred Heart Publishing Company, Atlanta, GA. Reprinted by permission.)

◁ = fa (used for the 1st and 4th degree of scale)
ο = sol (used for the 2nd and 5th degree of scale)
▢ = la (used for the 3rd and 6th degree of scale)
◇ = mi (used for the 7th degree of scale)

58

Quartets hired by companies publishing shape-note music created a strong interest in the music and a demand for shape-note songbooks; but the purchase of small publishing houses by commercial gospel music companies, more concerned about making money from professional performances than interested in encouraging public singing, was among the modern developments leading to a decline in the number of singing conventions and amateur shape-note singers. As public schools standardized music instruction, and as new roads and automobiles brought new travel and entertainment experiences to young people, musical tastes changed. Yet singing conventions exist today, attended in declining numbers but with no less enthusiasm for the traditional music and for the shape-note method by those who still know and love the music.

Reform Movements

Popular as singing school music and shape-note notation were, however, many educated Americans considered their music inferior to the music of their European contemporaries. These individuals disparaged the unorthodox music of the First New England School composers, fuging tunes in particular. The same nineteenth-century zeal for reform giving rise to labor movements and the Temperance Society also led many American musicians to scrupulously avoid the irregularities characteristic of the music of the self-taught singing school masters.

Thus whereas America's literary figures and visual artists developed indigenous styles of expression, American composers turned to Europe for inspiration and instruction, choosing to emulate the German masters who also dominated European music of that period. In music collections published in America during the first half of the nineteenth century, European pieces and their American imitations largely replaced indigenous American music; and although faithfully retained by steadfast adherents of the singing school, shape notes and other simplified notation systems generally were replaced in favor of the traditional European system of writing music.

Populist Hymns Composers contributing to the important hymn literature of the nineteenth century included the very well-known **Thomas Hastings** (1784–1872) and **William B. Bradbury** (1816–1868). Hastings is said to have written close to one thousand hymns, the most famous of which is "Rock of Ages, Cleft for Me." He also wrote hymn texts, setting them to the music of European composers, frequently selecting secular tunes for this purpose as was customary at that time. Believing that music best served to enhance the sentiment of a religious text without calling undue attention to itself, Hastings composed tunes and harmonies that are simple and unaffected.

William Bradbury's tune titled "Woodworth" is often sung today with a text beginning "Just as I am, without one plea." "Sweet Hour of Prayer" is another of Bradbury's very familiar hymns.

Lowell Mason (1792–1872) A strong proponent of traditional music notation and of music that at least sounded "European," the hymn writer and educator **Lowell Mason** led the movement to reform music in America. The son of a singing school master and schoolteacher, Mason inherited talent both for music and for teaching. Having attended singing school as a child, he continued the study of music as a young man by taking private lessons with a German musician. While making his living by working at a bank, he learned to play several instruments, became a church organist and choirmaster, and began to compose rather conventional but very attractive anthems and hymns.

In 1822, Mason published the first of many editions of the *Boston Handel and Haydn Society Collection of Church Music,* which included some of his own religious songs as well as several that he had arranged from melodies by famous European composers. Amazed at how well the book sold, Mason left his bank job and turned his professional attention to music, a field that previously had not offered Americans significant business opportunities but in which Mason recognized there was money to be made.

Believing that children should not have to depend on the singing school system for their music education, as he had done, Mason declared that instruction in reading and singing music should be provided to all American children by the public schools. It was, in fact, largely due to his efforts that music was first included in the Boston public school curriculum in 1838, and that other school districts soon followed Boston's example. Mason was also a pioneer in providing training for music teachers. He made voice lessons readily available to adults and children in the Boston area, conducted performances of choral music, published collections of choral music and hymns, composed religious vocal music, and generally promoted the improvement of musical taste and performance in America.

Toward this worthy end, Mason wrote hymns and other religious music that he considered of a better (that is, more European) quality than the works of the Yankee pioneers. However, sensitive to the needs of the unsophisticated public he served, he sometimes used—or allowed his publisher to use—shape-note notation, although he clearly preferred that people learn the traditional European system of writing music. Mason also wrote some of his hymns in three-part harmony, more familiar to ordinary people than the modern standard four-part arrangement of soprano, alto, tenor, and bass. He even sometimes placed the melody of a hymn in the middle voice, as the singing school masters had done according to early common practice, instead of in the top voice, as modern listeners were coming to expect (and as we are accustomed to hearing today). Also recognizing the public's fondness for fuging tunes and other early American songs of which he disapproved, Mason wisely included some of them in each volume he published, assuring their commercial success and making him a wealthy man.

Less daring and less original than the efforts of the Yankee pioneers, Mason's attractive hymns appealed to the sentimental taste of his day, and a number of them remain among the most familiar hymns today. "Nearer, My God, to Thee," "My Faith Looks Up to Thee," "Work, for the Night Is

Hymn

Composer
Lowell Mason

Title
"Nearer, My God, to Thee"

Texture
Homophonic (chordal)

Form
Strophic

Meter
Four beats to the bar

The words to this hymn, written by a young American woman, Sarah F. Adams (1805–1848), are based on the Bible story of Jacob, who, while fleeing from his home and his brother Esau, dreamed of seeing angels ascending and descending "steps unto heaven," or to Bethel ("the house of God") (Genesis 28:10–22). Although it makes no reference to Christ, this hymn continues to be found in nearly every published hymnal and is claimed by many people as their favorite. Set to Mason's tune, it is said to have been played by the band aboard the *Titanic* as the ill-fated ship plunged to its icy grave, and it has often brought comfort to grieving people, humble and prominent alike.

Mason's tune, which is called "Bethany," lies comfortably within the range of just over an octave. The high degree of melodic repetition (the four lines of each verse may be described as **a a′ b a′),** and the recurrence of the same last phrase of text at the end of every verse, render the rather conventional but highly attractive tune easy to sing and to memorize and thus well suited to congregational performance.

Notice that unlike Billings's "Chester" and "When Jesus Wept," in which one syllable of text may run through several notes, Mason almost consistently gives each syllable just one tone. Notice, too, that unlike the slightly surprising progressions in Billings's folklike, modal-influenced songs, Mason's simple tonal harmonies follow predictable, academically correct conventions based almost entirely on the I, IV, and V chords.

Coming," and "When I Survey the Wondrous Cross" are still widely known and included in the current hymnals of many denominations (see Listening Example 11).

Hymn

In this performance, the solemn melody is sung by the sopranos, accompanied by harmony in the alto, tenor, and bass voices and by an orchestra.

Nearer, my God, to Thee, Nearer to Thee!
E'en tho it be a cross That raiseth me;
Still all my song shall be, Nearer, my God, to Thee,
Nearer, my God, to Thee, Nearer to Thee!

Tho like the wanderer, The sun gone down,
Darkness be over me, My rest a stone,
Yet in my dreams I'd be Nearer, my God, to Thee,
Nearer, my God, to Thee, Nearer to Thee!

There let the way appear, Steps unto heav'n;
All that Thou sendest me, In mercy giv'n—
Angels to beckon me Nearer, my God, to Thee,
Nearer, my God, to Thee, Nearer to Thee!

Then with my waking thoughts, Bright with Thy praise,
Out of my stony griefs, Bethel I raise;
So by my woes to be Nearer, my God, to Thee,
Nearer, my God, to Thee, Nearer to Thee.

Or if on joyful wing, Cleaving the sky,
Sun, moon, and stars forgot, Upward I fly,
Still all my song shall be, Nearer, my God, to Thee,
Nearer, my God, to Thee, Nearer to Thee!

Revival Movements

The zeal for reform spawned the strong religious revival movement known as the Great Revival or the Second Awakening (see the Great Awakening, Chapter 3, p. 37), which developed rapidly, attracting rural Presbyterians, Baptists, Methodists, and others by the thousands to huge, emotional camp meetings, each lasting for several days (Figure 42). Itinerant preachers called circuit riders led the praying, shouting, singing, and often a kind of frenzied dancing at these social, recreational, and religious events—refreshingly democratic affairs in which men and women, blacks and whites, adults and children participated with equal enthusiasm.

Virtually isolated from European experience throughout the post-Revolutionary periods, frontier Americans evolved a distinctive music suiting

Figure 42
George Bellows, *Billy Sunday.* This lithograph depicts the famous revivalist preaching to a fervent camp meeting crowd.
(Washington, D.C./Art Resource, NY.)

the purposes and pleasing the ears of hardy pioneers. Whereas city dwellers sang the stately, dignified, European-style hymns of Lowell Mason and his colleagues, rural Americans greatly preferred their folk hymns and spiritual songs, a treasured source of comfort and inspiration for those living a difficult life in the South, in the country, and on the frontier.

Spiritual Songs Camp meeting songs included hymns with texts by the famous English clergymen **Isaac Watts** and **Charles Wesley,** as well as popular American folk hymns and spiritual songs, or **spirituals.** Spirituals were a kind of religious folk hymn, strophic settings of religious texts to folk or popular tunes. For those who could read music, songbooks printed in the popular shape-note notation were available, with the melody printed in the middle voice according to old-fashioned custom. One of the most popular such songbooks, *The Sacred Harp,* first published in 1844, is still in use in many rural and some urban and suburban areas today. Its tunes included popular British ballads to which Americans had set their favorite religious verses; hence the songs' folksy, tuneful quality.

We do not know who composed "Amazing Grace" (Listening Example 12), surely the favorite of all white spirituals, or folk hymns. The song appeared in print at least as early as 1831 and remains widely known and loved today.

Because folk hymns or spiritual songs involved a great deal of repetition, even people who could not read words or music learned them quickly and easily. Some songs had many verses in each of which only one or a few words changed—"father" becoming "mother," "sisters," "brothers," or "friends" in succeeding stanzas, for example. "There'll Be Joy, Joy, Joy," Listening Example 13, is typical of the simple but rousing white spirituals sung at nineteenth-century revival camp meetings.

After the Civil War, blacks, free or slave, who had been converted to Christianity participated enthusiastically in the rousing camp meetings, singing psalm tunes and (white) folk hymns with sincerity and fervor and

Folk Hymn or White Spiritual

Title
"Amazing Grace"

Composer
Anonymous

Form
Strophic

Melody
The haunting melody, using only the notes of the pentatonic scale, is often embellished, much as jazz singers embellish the melodies they play or sing. Slides, scoops, and other effects similar to, and sometimes borrowed from, African music are freely improvised.

Meter
Triple (three beats per measure)

Tempo
Slow

Text
The words were written by John Newton, an English evangelist overwhelmed with remorse for his earlier life as a slave trader. They promise God's forgiveness, even for such a "wretch" as he.

Amazing grace, how sweet the sound
That saved a wretch like me.
I once was lost, but now I'm found,
Was blind, but now I see.

developing distinctive spirituals of their own. The African Americans' spirituals, also simple and folklike, ranged from those filled with joy to poignant expressions of sorrow, such as "Nobody Knows de Trouble I've Seen" (Listening Example 14), which black people often referred to as slave hymns or sorrow songs. Joyful spirituals, accompanied by hand clapping, and percussive instruments if available, also incorporated other African effects, such as call-and-response, melodic improvisation, and exciting rhythmic complexities.

Many black spirituals offered hope for eventual release—from slavery, oppression, the harsh realities of the black experience in America, and even life itself. Black spirituals borrowed much imagery from Bible verses describing the anguish of another oppressed people, the Jews; for example, the "promised land" waiting somewhere "over Jordan" was a recurring theme. During the Reconstruction era, black spirituals acquired a new dimension in the form

Listening Example 13

Camp Meeting Spiritual

Title

"There'll Be Joy, Joy, Joy"

Performers

Carter Family (see p. 130)

A. P. Carter sings the melody while Sara and Maybelle Carter add close mountain harmony. Their raw southern twang accentuates the physical and emotional power permeating the stirring camp meeting spirituals.

Form

Strophic. Only the first phrase of each verse, easily introduced by a leader (here A. P. Carter) in call-and-response fashion, has new text; the rest of the verse follows a consistent pattern involving much repetition of familiar words.

Accompaniment

Autoharp and guitar

Text

There'll be joy, joy, joy
Up in my father's house,
Up in my father's house,
Up in my father's house.
There'll be joy, joy, joy,
Up in my father's house,
Where there's peace, sweet peace.

We will all be as one . . .

There'll be no drunkards there . . .

Don't you want to go up there, . . .

There'll be joy, joy, joy . . .

of hymnlike choral harmonies. Beginning in 1871, they were introduced to the world by the Jubilee Singers, a small choral group touring to raise funds for their impoverished Fisk University in Nashville, one of several schools founded for the education of former slaves.

Soon black spirituals entered the solo singer's repertory, a kind of black art song, often performed in moving arrangements written for voice and piano by **Henry Thacker Burleigh** (1866–1949). Thus African American spirituals, many originally improvised and performed in the African style of

Spiritual

Title

"Nobody Knows de Trouble I've Seen"

This folk hymn of tribulation retains its improvisatory flavor, and indeed the words of succeeding verses may vary considerably in performance, as led by a soloist in call-and-response fashion.

There is a simple chorus:

Nobody knows de trouble I've seen,
Nobody knows but Jesus.
Nobody knows de trouble I've seen,
Glory Hallelujah.

This alternates with short verses, the first of which follows:

Sometimes I'm up, sometimes I'm down,
Oh, yes, Lord.
Sometimes I'm almost to de ground.
Oh, yes, Lord.

All participants sing the familiar chorus, and all participate in the refrain, "Oh, yes, Lord," of the verses.

The hauntingly beautiful tune is based upon the pentatonic pattern that can be played on the black notes of a keyboard and that seems particularly comfortable to sing.

call-and-response, became familiar to and well loved by blacks and whites alike, remaining so today.

Secular Music

The great waves of immigration from various European countries enriched America's popular culture, as Germans, Italians, French, Swedish, and other newcomers poured their secular as well as their religious songs into the American stream. Instrumental music, too, had its place in popular culture of the nineteenth century, although then, as now, songs dominated music in the vernacular. Dance tunes of various ethnic heritages entertained informal gatherings in every settled region of the country.

In the Southwest, the Spanish influence remained strong. The religious alabados, rarely heard today, remained important, while a number of Spanish secular traditions took root as well. German music developed a particularly strong presence in nineteenth-century America, as various musical organizations included German vocal and instrumental pieces in their programs. Not only in Pennsylvania, Maryland, and other areas of the East but also in what is today the Midwest and even, by midcentury, on the West Coast, German people and German music—classical and popular—became ever more a part of the American experience.

Of more impact on music in America, however, were ballads from Great Britain. The most popular song in both England and America during much of the nineteenth century was "Home, Sweet Home," written by an English composer, Sir Henry Bishop. The Scottish culture, too, offered a treasure trove of songs, several with verses by the poet Robert Burns (1759–1796) set to lovely folk tunes that became very popular in America before the Civil War. Burns's "Comin' thro' the Rye" and "Auld Lang Syne" soon became and yet remain among the best-known songs in America.

Dominating the British influence, however, were lilting Irish ballads, whose ruggedly beautiful melodies and nostalgic texts appealed strongly to Americans. Even before Ireland's potato famine of the 1840s drove thousands of the starving to abandon their homeland, the Irish had flocked to America's shores in huge numbers seeking economic opportunities. Sentimental songs such as "Believe Me If All Those Endearing Young Charms" and "'Tis the Last Rose of Summer" offered Americans a refreshing change from formal European and American art songs.

Meanwhile, each geographic area of America produced and enjoyed songs and instrumental pieces expressing the typical local experience. As New Englanders became heavily involved in sea trade and traffic, for example, sailors' work songs or **chanteys** appeared, whereas on the frontier people sang songs about freedom, equality, danger, and the beauty of nature in the wild. Songs commemorated the opening of the Erie Canal, the Gold Rush in California, and events of intense local concern. Slaves in the South produced their own characteristic music, expressive of their particular loneliness and suffering, and songs of miners, farmers, railroad workers, even outlaws joined the American repertoire. Lullabies served every segment of the population, and play and party songs were enjoyed by rural adults as well as children.

Among the most numerous folk songs of this, as of any, age were songs of love betrayed, such as the hauntingly beautiful "Shenandoah" (Listening Example 15).

Minstrelsy Most popular of all the songs representative of this fertile period were those included in **minstrel shows,** a form of entertainment popular in England in the late eighteenth century in which white men, their skin darkened by cork or coal, caricatured African American figures. (Spike Lee's 2000 film *Bamboozled* makes reference to a "modern" minstrel show.) Minstrel acts, as they were called, soon were commonly included in American

Folk Song

Title
"Shenandoah"

Performer
Pete Seeger

Meter
Quadruple (four beats per measure). The relaxed tempo and somewhat irregular accents, closely following the natural rhythm of the text, lessen the feeling of beat and almost suggest a rhythm free of metric control.

Tempo
Slow

Accompaniment
Very sparse strumming of a few supportive guitar tones and simple chords.

Text
This lovely, plaintive ballad tells of a white (Canadian or American) trader who courted the daughter of Shenandoah, an American Indian chieftain, and carried her off in his canoe, only to abandon her later on the banks of the Missouri River. A favorite song of sailors—some of whom must have experienced similar conquests and subsequent remorse, and who loved to sing it while away on long, lonely voyages—the song is sometimes thought of as a chantey.

Oh Shenandoah, I love your daughter.
Wa–ay, you rollin' river.
Oh Shenandoah, I love your daughter.
Away, you're bound away
'Cross the wide Missoura.

Oh Shenandoah, I long to see you.
Wa–ay, you rollin' river.
Oh, Shenandoah, I'll not deceive you.
Away, we're bound away
'Cross the wide Missoura.

For seven years I've been a rover.
Wa–ay, you rollin' river.
For seven years I've been a rover.
Away, we're bound away
'Cross the wide Missoura.

circus and showboat performances and even interspersed between the acts of serious plays. The first popular hit in America was a minstrel song called "Jim Crow," written by **Thomas Dartmouth "Daddy" Rice,** known as the father of American minstrelsy. (It was only later that the name of his song became a hostile term synonymous with discrimination against African Americans.)

In 1843, a group known as the **Virginia Minstrels** formed the first completely independent minstrel show. The group was led by **Daniel Decatur Emmett** (1815–1904), who had served in the Union army as a fifer at the age of seventeen and later joined the circus, where he performed in minstrel acts. At their debut, the Virginia Minstrels appeared before a wildly enthusiastic audience in New York City. Wearing white trousers, striped calico shirts, and blue calico coats with tails, they sang, danced, joked, and told stories in a manner imitative of plantation slaves and citified northern African Americans as they understood, or misunderstood, them.

The fiddle and banjo made vital contributions to the minstrel show, which also invariably included a **tambourine** (derived from an African percussion instrument) and a pair of **bones** (commonly replaced in more recent times by a pair of linked castanets, which provides the timbre and rhythmic effects desired for various rural musics). Often there was also a small accordionlike instrument called a **concertina,** with a number of buttons on each side that control the pitch. The concertina is played by alternately pushing the sides inward and pulling them outward, producing the wind that makes the sound.

A minstrel show began with a rousing grand march, during which the players entered the stage and formed a semicircle facing the audience. "Mr. Tambo" and "Mr. Bones" (the players of the tambourine and bones) sat at opposite ends of the semicircle, exchanging hilarious comments that greatly entertained the audience between musical acts (Figure 43).

Notwithstanding its offensive nature by today's standards, minstrelsy was a highly popular form of entertainment in the pre– and even post–Civil War periods, offering a refreshing contrast to the sentimental parlor ballads of the period; and much of the music produced by this unlikely medium remains as enchanting as ever. Although derived from African and European customs, minstrel songs and dances were as indigenous to the American experience as were the folk hymns of New England and the South. The best of the minstrel music—often referred to as America's first popular music—had an unselfconscious and highly infectious charm. After their Emancipation, blacks themselves participated in minstrel shows, forming their own companies and writing songs that remain favorites today.

E. P. Christy, a famous white minstrel composer and skit writer, formed a four-man troupe, the **Christy Minstrels,** which toured the American South and West, bringing theater (of a sort) to people who had never experienced it in any form before. Among the best-known songs they and other minstrel troupes sang are "Carry Me Back to Ole Virginny," "In the Evening by the Moonlight," and "Oh, Dem Golden Slippers," all composed by the first well-known black songwriter, **James A. Bland.**

Figure 43

Scene from a minstrel show, with "Mr. Bones" on the left and "Mr. Tambo" on the right.
(The Bettmann Archive, Inc.)

One of America's favorite songs, "I Wish I Was in Dixie's Land" (Listening Example 16), was written by Daniel Decatur Emmett, who conceived it as a lively plantation song and dance routine called a **walkaround,** performed as the finale of a minstrel show. The troupe stood in a semicircle in front of a plantation background. When the music started, two or more of the members strutted out and alternately sang a stanza while another "walked around" in the inside of the semicircle. Reaching the center, the singers began to dance, accompanied by a musical interlude, after which the entire troupe joined in the frolic.

Stephen Foster (1826–1864)

By far the outstanding American composer of popular songs of the pre–Civil War period was the gifted, self-taught musician **Stephen Foster.** Born into the genteel society of Pittsburgh, Pennsylvania, the young Foster heard his sisters sing and play the piano and other instruments and soon was picking out tunes himself. Because music was not considered a respectable profession for a man in his social position, Foster dutifully went to work as a bookkeeper while still in his teens; but he could not resist jotting down some of the tuneful melodies that filled his mind and—to his own amazement—had his first song ("Open Thy Lattice, Love") published when he was just eighteen. Soon he was writing and publishing professionally.

Minstrel Song and Dance

Composer

Daniel Decatur Emmett

Title

"I Wish I Was in Dixie's Land"

The origin of the word "Dixie" is obscure, although it probably does *not* refer to the Mason-Dixon Line. Some associate it with a French money note called the *dix* (for "ten").

Meter

Two beats per measure.

Form

Strophic

Each verse has two sections, each sung by a soloist and followed by a small group responding in unison, "Look away! Look away! Look away! Dixie Land." The chorus ("I wish I was in Dixie . . .") succeeds each verse.

Emmett wrote "Dixie" as a lively plantation song and dance routine called a walkaround, performed as the finale of a minstrel show with the concluding instrumental music accompanying the spritely dance steps.

Text

I wish I was in de land ob cotton,
Old times dar am not forgotten;
Look away! Look away! Look away! Dixie Land.

In Dixie Land whar I was born in.
Early on one frosty mornin';
Look away! Look away! Look away! Dixie Land.

Chorus: Den I wish I was in Dixie,
   Hooray! Hooray!
In Dixie Land, I'll take my stand,
To lib an' die in Dixie,
Away, away.
Away down south in Dixie.

Old Missus marry "Will-de-weaber,"
Willium was a gay deceaber;

But when he put his arm around 'er.
He smiled as fierce as a forty pounder.

Minstrel Song and Dance

His face was sharp as a butcher's cleaver,
But dat did not seem to greave 'er;

Old Missus acted de foolish part,
And died for a man dat broke her heart.

Now here's a health to the next old Missus,
An' all de gals dat want to kiss us;

But if you want to drive 'way sorrow,
Come and hear dis song tomorrow . . .

Foster's early sentimental love songs suited the self-conscious gentility of his family and their friends, reflecting and reinforcing the mid-nineteenth-century concept of the female identity: domestic, refined, and well-cared-for by father or spouse. The women in Foster's songs, normally described from a male point of view, are passive creatures, entirely idealized, and often asleep ("Beautiful Dreamer"), or perhaps dead, as suggested in "I Dream of Jeanie" (Listening Example 17).

Foster's own personal favorite songs were of two types: the lovely "plantation melodies," reminiscent of the songs he heard African Americans singing as they worked on the Pittsburgh riverfronts, and—especially—the rollicking, comic songs he wrote for minstrel shows. Foster, in fact, experienced a devastating conflict between the music he felt he *ought* to write and the music he wrote and loved best. Although his sentimental songs about home ("Old Folks at Home," for example, and "My Old Kentucky Home"—a nostalgic "remembrance" of the plantation life he never lived inspired by Harriet Beecher Stowe's novel *Uncle Tom's Cabin*), his songs about unfulfilled romantic love (such as "Beautiful Dreamer," "Come Where My Love Lies Dreaming"), and his settings of poems about the Civil War were well-enough received, he felt shamed by his finest pieces, some in black dialect, including such nonsense songs as "Oh! Susanna" and "De Camptown Races."

First performed in public in 1847 in Pittsburgh, "Oh! Susanna" (Listening Example 18) soon traveled across the country and was carried to the western frontier by thousands of adventurers and homesteaders who loved her as their own.

Foster indeed was a man of paradox: His irresistible minstrel and plantation melodies set America and soon much of the world humming his tunes and singing his words about a life he never experienced, for Foster was neither black nor from the South. Analysis of his best songs reveals little that is

Sentimental Parlor Ballad

Composer
Stephen Foster

Title
"I Dream of Jeanie with the Light Brown Hair"

Form
Strophic

Meter
Quadruple

Tempo
Slow

Accompaniment
A guitar accompanies the singer with simple—mostly I, IV, and V—chords, typical of the guitar or piano accompaniment Foster normally provided for his songs. The guitar also plays a brief introduction, interlude between verses, and conclusion, never competing, however, with the voice for primary attention.

Foster seems to have captured in this haunting, mostly pentatonic melody the mystic quality of Jeanie's spirit itself, "borne like a vapor on the summer air." The extreme relaxation of the tempo, called *rubato* ("robbing"), occurring at the end of significant phrases, enhances the romantic character of the piece, which expresses—in the romantic way—a longing destined never to be fulfilled.

Text
I dream of Jeanie with the light brown hair
Borne like a vapor on the summer air.
I see her tripping where the bright streams play
Happy as the daisies that dance on her way.
Many were the wild notes her merry voice would pour,
Many were the blithe birds that warbled them o'er. Oh!
I dream of Jeanie with the light brown hair
Floating like a vapor on the soft summer air.

innovative or even particularly interesting in their form, rhythm, or harmony: The songs are in simple strophic form, with much repetition of the melodic phrases within each verse; there is little rhythmic variety, except for occasional syncopation, as in the **b** phrase of "Oh! Susanna"; and most of the

Minstrel Song

Composer

Stephen Foster

Title

"Oh! Susanna"

Form

Strophic

Meter

Duple

This tune indicates the internal repetition typical of Foster's songs, lending to their immediate accessibility and familiarity. The music of lines 1 and 3 (**a**) is the same, and lines 2 and 4 of the verse and the second line of the chorus (**a′**) only slightly vary the ending of the identical melodic phrase. Only the first line of the chorus (**b**) introduces new material. Thus the song's melodic structure could be outlined as **a a′ a a′ b a′.**

Further, the phrases **a** and **a′** are pentatonic, limited to the pattern of tones represented by the five black notes on a keyboard. Only the first two tones of the **b** phrase (on "Oh! Su-") break the simple pentatonic pattern.

Neither is the rhythm complex or varied, offering only one bit of syncopation, again in the first phrase of the chorus ("Oh! Su-san-**na**!"). Yet the song has the snap and dash of many a banjo or fiddle tune, compelling us to nod or rap along with its beat. The catchy, irresistible tune, pleasing to the ears in many times and cultures, is so strong that repetition satisfies rather than tires the listener, and "Oh! Susanna" seems destined to live forever.

Text

I come from Alabama with my banjo on my knee.
I'm goin' to Louisiana my true love for to see.
It rained all night the day I left, the weather it was dry.
The sun so hot I froze to death; Susanna don't you cry.
Chorus: *Oh, Susanna, oh don't you cry for me.*
I come from Alabama with my banjo on my knee.

I had a dream the other night when everything was still.
I dreamed I saw Susanna a-comin' down the hill.
A red, red rose was in her hair, a tear was in her eye,
I said to her, "Susanna gal, Susanna don't you cry."
(Chorus)

songs were written with simple guitar or piano accompaniments based on the three primary chords of the tonal system.

Foster wrote his songs when the sentimental parlor ballad was in vogue, and some of them may be described as such. But it is particularly difficult to place many of Foster's songs within a particular category or genre. They are hardly art songs, because the texts are not of the quality associated with that form, but they *are* art in the sense that they are long lived and representative of their composer's distinctive style. Foster's melodies, although folklike, are clearly composed. The songs are popular in the sense that they are enjoyed all over the world, but except for the rollicking minstrel songs, they have not been part of our usual concept of popular musc.

It seems a bitter irony that a man so gifted should have been destroyed by his own inability to distinguish between genius and gentility. Unwilling even to acknowledge some of his best songs, he gave them away or allowed them to be pirated. He married in 1850, but his increasing emotional instability and heavy drinking caused his wife to leave him three years later. Stephen Foster died a pauper, alone and unrecognized, at the age of 38.

Patriotic Songs   Some of America's most enduring patriotic songs appeared between the Revolution and the Civil War, and were associated with events during that tumultuous time. Frequently included in theatrical entertainments then, they became, and in some cases remained, widely popular.

The words to "Hail, Columbia," by Francis Hopkinson's son Joseph, were sung to the tune known as "President's March," composed by Philip Phile for the inauguration of George Washington in 1789 and commonly played when that president appeared in public. The stirring patriotic song was among many that sometimes served political as well as artistic aims. For example, the 1798 war between France and England divided American allegiance; some people rallied to the side of the newly democratic French republic, whereas others felt tied to England by affection and tradition. However, the rousing words to the brand new "Hail, Columbia," frequently performed at theatrical entertainments in that year, so exalted the wonders and accomplishments of America that emotional audiences felt united by stirrings of national pride.

The words to "The Star Spangled Banner" were written by a young lawyer, **Francis Scott Key** (1780–1843), under most dramatic circumstances. During the War of 1812, Key boarded a British vessel moored in Chesapeake Bay in order to plea for the release of an important American prisoner. The British agreed to release the prisoner before sailing for England, but they held both him and Key on board through the night while they attacked the city of Baltimore. In two stirring verses, the emotional young lawyer described the agony of suspense he experienced while witnessing the attack and his overwhelming pride and relief at the sight of the American flag waving high the next morning. Key set his romantic text, which he titled "The Defense of Fort McHenry," to the melody of a popular Irish drinking song. In 1813 Thomas Carr (brother of Benjamin Carr, p. 44) musically arranged the tune and rechristened it "The Star Spangled Banner."

Little did either Key or Carr suppose that many years later, during the Spanish American War (1898), the stirring song would be designated the official anthem of the American armed forces. Still less could they imagine that, in 1931, President Herbert Hoover would sign a bill making Key's song the American national anthem. Some have suggested that the melody's wide range and large intervals ("Oh say, can you sing it?") render it more difficult to sing than is appropriate for a national anthem; but defenders stoutly respond that the dramatic nature of the melody (however lowly its origin) and the effort required to sing it properly make it all the more distinctive and ideally suited for this exalted position.

Civil War Songs In 1860, several southern states seceded from the Union, plunging the country into the Civil War. At such times of grief and turmoil, people turn to art and to music—at popular or at more serious levels—to express their anguish and ease their sorrow. Thus it is not surprising that many memorable songs concerned these particularly tragic years.

Indeed, Civil War songs appeared in a rich variety of folklike, religious, comic, and serious styles. "Dixie," as we have seen, began as a minstrel show walkaround. Some songs, lyrical and dramatic in style, suggested their composers' fondness for Italian opera. The haunting bugle call "Taps," commissioned as an elegy for Civil War casualties, evokes the same emotions today as when it was first sounded. Regional favorites, such as "Maryland, My Maryland" (which vied with "Dixie" and "The Bonnie Blue Flag" to become a Confederate national anthem), "Marching through Georgia" (a celebration of General William Tecumseh Sherman's march to the sea), and "The Yellow Rose of Texas" (originally a minstrel tune praising an African American girl as "the yellow rose of Texas" who "beats the belles of Tennessee"), stimulated patriotic fervor and became wildly popular during the troubled period. (The Bonnie Blue Flag, the unofficial first flag of the South, flew from 1860 to 1861.)

What is surprising is how many songs inspired by the Civil War have survived more than a century to please, entertain, and move listeners of other styles and eras. Some tunes acquired new texts in the twentieth century: Thus Elvis Presley sang "Love Me Tender" to the tune of "Aura Lee," and Bob Dylan set "Blowin' in the Wind" to the tune of a slave song, "No More Auction Block for Me." Other songs survive much as they were introduced at the time of America's greatest national trauma.

The stirring "Battle Hymn of the Republic" with its rousing chorus beginning "Glory, glory, hallelujah!" is set to a tune once sung as a tribute to the militant abolitionist John Brown ("John Brown's body lies a-mouldering in his grave"). Dozens of irreverent verses had been set to this simple Methodist camp meeting tune that, according to one writer, "stuck to the ears like burrs to the skirt of a blackberry girl." But upon viewing firsthand the desperate plight of blue-clad Union soldiers, many wounded or ill and all of them lonely and heartsick, published poet and author Julia Ward Howe composed her poignant poem "Battle Hymn of the Republic" to be set to the old tune; and her fervent words sung to the strong melody lifted the morale and stirred the spirits of Union troops and prisoners (see Figure 44).

Figure 44
Julia Ward Howe.
(Corbis-Bettmann.)

After the Civil War, the "Battle Hymn" became one of several patriotic songs (including "The Star Spangled Banner") to serve as an anthem of the reunited nation, its fervent refrain seeming to embody the very soul of American patriotism. Many people were greatly disappointed when it, together with "America the Beautiful," lost the position of national anthem to Francis Scott Key's patriotic creation.

In 1887, Julia Ward Howe wrote, "The wild echoes of the fearful struggle have long since died away, and with them all memories of unkindness between ourselves and our southern brethren. But those who once loved my hymn still sing it." And we still do.

Among the Civil War songs imbued with the robust flavor of Irish jigs was the rollicking "When Johnny Comes Marching Home" (Listening Example 19), which has been revived during all of America's major military involvements since then.

Singing Families Before and after the Civil War, several singing families toured the United States performing songs of many kinds. Like the twentieth-century European Trapp family portrayed in the Broadway musical *The Sound of Music,* these traveling groups performed in churches, meeting-houses, and concert halls.

The most popular American singing family, the **Hutchinsons,** first came to public attention when the thirteen Hutchinson children presented a highly

Listening Example 19

Civil War Song

Title

"When Johnny Comes Marching Home Again"

Tune

The tune is generally attributed to Patrick Gilmore (see p. 81), although some scholars suspect it may have been a folk tune to which he simply set new words expressive of the American Civil War experience. Unlike most popular tunes of the day, this one is based on the minor instead of the major scale. (In the first line, the word "home" occurs on the third tone of the scale, a half step lower than the third tone of the major scale.)

Form

Strophic

Meter

Duple (As explained on page 83, the meter is *compound duple,* meaning that each beat is divided by three (*ONE*-and-a-*two*-and-a).

successful performance of religious and secular music at a New England meetinghouse in the early 1840s. Later, three Hutchinson sons formed a trio; and when, still later, their sister Abby joined them, the popular quartet toured through New England for several years. When Abby married and retired from the group, other members of the family formed various ensembles, and the Singing Hutchinsons remained famous in America and Europe for decades.

The texts of the Hutchinsons' songs, some of which they wrote or adapted themselves, addressed some of the most radical social causes of the day—temperance, women's suffrage, and the abolition of slavery—although their music was refined, genteel, and sentimental. It included secular, humorous songs in strophic form called **glees,** with the melody in the top voice and the other two or three voices providing chordal harmony. Glees, introduced in Europe during the eighteenth century, were originally sung by men only, but by the mid-nineteenth century many glee clubs formed in American cities included women as well as men. These popular ensembles sometimes sang more serious choral literature as well as glees and other lighthearted fare.

Band Music In 1777, General George Washington issued an order requiring "every officer, for the credit of his corps," to provide military music to American troops. The first American military bands, established during the Revolutionary War, consisted only of drums and small flutes called *fifes.* The duties of these **fife and drum corps,** many of whose members were African

Figure 45
A band of drummers.
(© Fridmar Damm/
Leo de Wys, Inc.)

Americans, extended far beyond lifting the spirits and quickening the steps of the amateur soldiers (see Figure 45). They also announced the beginning and end of the day, called the troops to meals and other activities, and transmitted commands on the battlefield that could not otherwise be heard over the noise of musket fire.

Besides fife and drum corps, some military bands in the colonies began to develop, very gradually, along the lines of those in Europe. In 1792, the first laws were passed standardizing the formation of American military bands to resemble European models, which had long included a variety of woodwinds and brasses as well as percussion instruments in their ensembles. Early brass instruments, however, lacking valves that allowed players to change pitches manually, were relatively difficult to play, and only after they were fitted with valves, about 1830, did brass instruments assume the significant melodic responsibilities in military and concert bands they hold today.

Throughout the eighteenth century, New Orleans had its own strong musical heritage, in which military-style bands played a prominent role. Black musicians, both slave and free, provided music for balls and parades in that colorful city, and eventually dominated the traditional military funeral parade's transition to a civic custom. The band attached to the First Battalion of Free Men of Color, which had an active role in defeating the British at the Siege of New Orleans (1815), included people identified as Creole-of-color, meaning they were partly European and active in the French-dominated culture of the city.

Besides their military functions, early military bands also played to entertain the public at parades and informal concerts. Among the popular tunes

Fife and Drum

Title

"Yankee Doodle"

Tune

The origin of the tune and the meaning of its title are unknown. It was composed some time before the Revolutionary War, either in Britain or America, and first appeared in print in 1782. (The words, also anonymous, were often changed for partisan purposes. In fact, the British first sang the song to make fun of the Yankees, who later adopted it as their own!)

Meter

Duple

Form

Strophic

The high-pitched fifes carry the stirring tune, while the drums mark the rhythm with distinctive beats and rolls. The first section of the tune is played and repeated; then the second section, in a version popular during the Revolutionary War, is played and also repeated. As the example tapers off, the corps begins to sound again the first section of the song.

included in such programs, a favorite would have been "Yankee Doodle" (Listening Example 20), which has pleased American ears from the time of its origin to the present day.

Later, during the Civil War, Confederate and Federal bandsmen not only accompanied marching troops and sent them singing into battle; they also waged psychological warfare against each other. Often pitched in close proximity to each other, northern and southern bands tormented their counterparts, pitting loud and enthusiastic renditions of "Dixie" and "The Bonnie Blue Flag" against equally vigorous performances of "Yankee Doodle" and "Hail, Columbia." One Confederate musician confessed that at such musical battles he "grew desperate, and was filled with unchristian desire to slay the musicians, and so end their performances."

Concert Bands By the time of the Civil War, **concert bands** (Figure 46) were playing an entertaining variety of novelty pieces. The early nineteenth-century addition of valves having facilitated playing intricate melodies on trumpets, horns, and cornets, these instruments now assumed a prominent role in marching and concert bands.

Figure 46
A concert band, circa 1875.
(Culver Pictures, Inc.)

Bands provided an important stimulus for music publishing in America, although much of the music printed for American bands throughout the nineteenth century was written by European composers. Besides marches and dance tunes, **programmatic** pieces, describing in musical terms a sequence of scenes or events, were particularly popular at band concerts, with "battle" pieces featuring the sounds of gunshots, cries of the wounded, trumpet calls, and other warlike effects especially well received.

Soon after the Civil War, two outstanding band directors established the balanced ensemble of woodwinds, brass, and percussion we are accustomed to hearing today.

Patrick Gilmore (1829–1892) was among the thousands who fled Ireland's potato blights and famine to make a new life in America. A virtuoso cornet player, he was appointed bandmaster of the Union army and soon became the most famous bandleader of the 1860s. Gilmore wrote several attractive pieces, probably including (although the tune sounds very much like an Irish folk melody) the popular Civil War song "When Johnny Comes Marching Home Again" (Listening Example 19).

When military bands broke up after the war, Gilmore formed America's first band conceived entirely as a concert ensemble. A master entertainer who, like Louis Moreau Gottschalk and Louis Antoine Jullien (see Chapter 5), organized huge concerts in which thousands of performers participated, he also brought outstanding European bands to perform in America. Soon, through their influence and his own good taste, Gilmore achieved an effective balance between brass and woodwind instruments in his Grand Boston Band, which toured America, Canada, and several European countries to very popular acclaim.

Figure 47
John Philip Sousa on a
sheet music cover.
(EKM-Nepenthe.)

John Philip Sousa (1854–1932) The year Gilmore died, a young American violinist named **John Philip Sousa** (Figure 47) formed a band destined to surpass in size of ensemble, variety of repertoire, and quality of performance any previous concert band, including Gilmore's. Sousa's Marine career began when his father learned that his thirteen-year-old son was planning to run away from home and join a circus band. The elder Sousa promptly enlisted John Philip in the Marine Corps, where, as an apprentice in the Marine Band, he soon learned to play all of the band instruments. Since its founding through an Act of Congress signed by President John Adams in 1798, the Marine Band's primary mission has been to provide music for the President of the United States and the Commandant of the Marine Corps. In

1801, the prestigious ensemble played for the inauguration of President Thomas Jefferson, and it has performed for every presidential inauguration since that time.

Sousa left the band at age twenty to pursue a career as violinist and conductor of theater orchestras; but five years later he became the director of the Marine Band, and in that capacity he faithfully served five presidents (Hayes, Garfield, Arthur, Cleveland, and Harrison). He brought the band to a peak of perfection, regularly astonishing audiences with incredibly soft dynamic levels and other expressive effects previously thought possible only for the symphony orchestra. Later, Sousa formed his own Sousa Band, which traveled widely and earned a worldwide reputation.

Although Sousa wrote songs, comic operas, operettas, and programmatic orchestral music, he is best remembered as the march king; for although Sousa's marches conform in most respects to many marches by European composers, their wealth of melodic invention and their stirring spirit render them distinctively American and irresistibly attractive works.

Marches
Although differing widely in mood and tempo, marches—be they military, funeral, patriotic, or concert pieces—normally share duple meter, with a strongly marked beat to correspond with the marching pattern LEFT-right-LEFT-right. Meter, which refers to the number of beats in a measure, may be *simple* or *compound* according to the manner in which each beat is divided.

Simple meter means that each of the beats in a measure is divided by *two.* For pieces in *simple duple meter* (for example, "Yankee Doodle" or Sousa's "The Stars and Stripes Forever"), we count the two beats in each measure as *ONE*-and-*two*-and, and so forth.

In *compound meter,* each beat is divided by *three.* For pieces in *compound duple meter* (such as "My Bonnie Lies over the Ocean," "When Johnny Comes Marching Home," or Sousa's "Washington Post March"), we also count two beats per measure but divide them as *ONE*-and-a-*two*-and-a, or *ONE*-two-three-*four*-five-six.

A march, which may begin with a short (four- or eight-measure) introduction, consists of a series of melodic sections called **strains,** each usually sixteen or thirty-two measures long, and each repeated at least once. One of the strains, scored for fewer instruments and therefore softer in dynamic level, and also typically sweeter or more lyrical than the others, is called the **trio.** Some marches include a section called the **break**—dramatic, highly rhythmic, and often percussive in style and timbre, thus providing effective contrast to the melodic strains.

Whereas tonal pieces normally end in the tonic key, a march often ends with a repeat of the trio, which is usually in the subdominant key. This is the case in Sousa's very famous "Stars and Stripes Forever" (Listening Example 21).

March

Composer
John Philip Sousa

Title
"The Stars and Stripes Forever"

Meter
Duple

Key
E-flat major

Outline of the Form   A A B B C D C D C

       A = *first strain*
       B = *second strain*
       C = *trio (third strain)*
       D = *break*

After the four-measure *introduction* (counting the four measures of the short introduction will help you define the length of each strain), the *first strain* (16 measures) begins with several repeated notes. The first strain is repeated.

The *second strain* (16 measures), which has a wide range of pitches and several large leaps between tones, is played and repeated.

The *third strain,* softer and more melodic than the others and twice as long (32 measures), is the *trio.* You may sense that it is in a different key (the subdominant, A-flat major), or perhaps you will simply be aware that its character is distinct from the first two strains.

There is a bold, dramatic *break.*

The *trio* returns with a perky *countermelody,* a simultaneous independent melody played by the piccolo, providing intense polyphonic or *contrapuntal* interest.

There is another *break.*

The march ends with the *trio,* still in the subdominant key, accompanied by a new countermelody in the trombones.

Terms to Review

shape-note notation   A method of music notation assigning a shape to the pitches *fa, sol, la,* and *mi,* placing them in their normal positions on the staff.

spiritual   A folklike religious song with a simple tune.

The Sacred Harp   A popular nineteenth-century collection of hymns and spiritual songs.

chantey   A folk song about sailors and/or the sea.

minstrel show   An entertainment, popular in the nineteenth century, in which white men perform music and comedy in imitation of stereotypical African Americans.

tambourine   A small drum with metal disks that jingle when the instrument is struck or shaken.

bones   A folk percussion instrument consisting of a pair of castanets tied together and held in one hand.

concertina   A kind of accordion or portable reed instrument. Melody and chords are achieved by depressing buttons or keys, and the wind is supplied by a folding bellows.

walkaround   A lively plantation song and dance routine often forming the finale of a minstrel show.

glee   A part-song with three or more lines of music, in chordal, or homophonic, texture, usually with the melody in the top voice.

fife and drum corps   An early band, consisting of fifes and drums, which performed for military and later for entertainment purposes.

concert band   An instrumental ensemble including brass, woodwind, and percussion instruments.

programmatic music   Instrumental music describing a story, scene, idea, or event.

strain   Term used for a melodic section in a rag, march, or other vernacular form of music.

trio   A strain that is lighter in texture, softer in dynamic level, and more melodic than the other strains in the piece.

break   A dramatic, unstable, strongly rhythmic section, as in a march.

Key Figures

Thomas Hastings
William B. Bradbury
Lowell Mason
Isaac Watts
Charles Wesley
Henry Thacker Burleigh
Thomas Dartmouth "Daddy" Rice
Virginia Minstrels
Daniel Decatur Emmett
E. P. Christy
Christy Minstrels
James A. Bland
Stephen Foster
Francis Scott Key
The Hutchinson Family
Patrick Gilmore
John Philip Sousa

Suggestions for Further Listening

Hymns by Lowell Mason:
"My Faith Looks Up to Thee" (tune known as "Olivet")
"Work, for the Night Is Coming" ("Diligence")
"When I Survey the Wondrous Cross" ("Hamburg")
"Watchman, Tell Us of the Night" ("Watchman")
Hymns with texts by Isaac Watts:
"From All That Dwell Below the Skies"
"O God, Our Help in Ages Past"
"Joy to the World!"
"When I Survey the Wondrous Cross"
Hymns with texts by Charles Wesley:
"Come, Thou Long-Expected Jesus"
"Hark, the Herald Angels Sing"
"Jesus Christ Is Risen Today"
"Love Divine, All Loves Excelling"
Spirituals:
"Go Down, Moses"
"Deep River"
"Swing Low, Sweet Chariot"
Chantey:
"Shenandoah"(Listening Example 15)
March:
John Philip Sousa, "Washington Post March"

5

Early Concert Music

Although still far less distinct than the highly subjective lines drawn today between vernacular music ("for the people") and art or concert music (for an audience viewed as somewhat select), differences between the popular and the classical worlds of music assumed more significance in the American experience as the nineteenth century progressed. While household music and religious songs retained their vital position in American life, the decades before and after the Civil War witnessed growing interest among composers, performers, and listeners in music for the concert hall.

Romantic Virtuosos

Nineteenth-century Europeans, who enjoyed expressive extremes, responded with equal enthusiasm to the sounds of a large symphony orchestra and an intimate solo recital. Americans, however, with more access to the latter than the former, attended concerts in much the same frame of mind with which they viewed a circus or minstrel show and particularly enjoyed dazzling displays of technique by solo **virtuosos.** Certainly virtuosity is among the qualities of *musicianship*—the broad combination of talents possessed by the consummate performer—which also includes sensitivity to the *style* of the music, differing from one period and one culture to another; *originality* of interpretation; and of course *accuracy.* But the spectacular performance of difficult passages of music, thrilling to see and hear, held sway in the romantic minds and hearts of the mid-nineteenth-century American audience, where romantic glorification of the individual made virtuoso performers objects of intense hero worship.

Also, Americans then (as often now) preferred to hear familiar pieces rather than anything new or unusual. Thus a serious gap developed and slowly widened between composers, who of course sought to create something original, and listeners, who preferred something comfortably familiar. This gap affected musicians on both sides of the Atlantic, but American composers were further frustrated by the conspicuous lack of interest in American music on either continent.

The Swedish Nightingale
The great nineteenth-century virtuosos, on the other hand, benefited from the passion Americans felt for their brilliant

Figure 48
Jenny Lind.
(The Bettmann Archive,
Inc.)

performances at the very time that Europeans had begun to tire of them. Performers flocked gratefully to America, where an adoring public eagerly applauded their showy performance techniques. Among the best known and best remembered of the outstanding concert artists who toured America are a Swedish singer, a Norwegian violinist, and a pianist from Louisiana.

P. T. Barnum arranged the United States tour for Jenny Lind (1820–1887) (Figure 48) much as he promoted his famous circus acts. Although Lind's talent was prodigious, she wisely confined her programs in this country to the kind of repertoire she—or Barnum—knew would entertain an American audience: familiar well-loved arias from European operas and oratorios, with "Home, Sweet Home" and songs by Stephen Foster as encores.

Jenny Lind stayed in America for about two years, traveling by steamer from New Orleans to Memphis, Nashville, and St. Louis and visiting many other cities as well. The most successful virtuoso singer of her period, she thrilled Americans with her lovely voice, amazing vocal technique, and charming personality. "Jenny Lind fever" spread quickly, and many who previously had never heard or been interested in concert music became adoring admirers of "the Swedish nightingale." Concert halls were built specifically to accommodate her performances, and thus the way was prepared for other European performers to follow.

Ole Bull The Norwegian composer Ole Bull (1810–1880), best remembered as the outstanding violinist of his day, made five long visits to the United States, on one of them marrying an American woman. A dedicated nationalist who believed art should represent the culture that produced it, Ole Bull encouraged Americans to develop a characteristic music of their own. To this end, while managing a fledgling opera company in New York City, he offered one thousand dollars to any American composer who would write an opera on an American subject; no one, however, accepted the challenge, and the company soon collapsed.

Like Jenny Lind, Ole Bull accepted the limitations of his inexperienced American audiences and performed little serious music, entertaining them instead with his virtuosic tricks—playing on all four strings of the violin at once or producing incredibly soft *pianissimos* that romantic ears must have perceived as coming from another world. In one of his own compositions, Bull portrayed the American Revolution by alternating phrases of "Yankee Doodle" with "God Save the King," to the delight of his admiring audience. Original, flamboyant, hugely talented, and entertaining, Ole Bull added a valued dimension to nineteenth-century America's music experience.

Louis Moreau Gottschalk (1829–1869)
Among the outstanding pianists of the period was an American who amazed and entertained audiences on both sides of the Atlantic with his virtuosic performances of his own compositions. **Louis Moreau Gottschalk** (Figure 49), whose English/Jewish father had been educated in Germany and whose mother was descended from a wellborn French family that had emigrated from the West Indies a generation

Figure 49

Louis Moreau Gottschalk at the piano.
(The Bettmann Archive, Inc.)

before, was born into the brilliant cultural milieu of New Orleans. (Gottschalk's mother was called a *Creole,* meaning someone born in this country of a foreign family. Later the word Creole referred to people of mixed racial heritage, causing some to believe erroneously that Gottschalk had African American ancestors.) Gottschalk's first and strongest language was French, although he also spoke Spanish and English fluently.

New Orleans teemed with a rich variety of cultural experiences, as French, Spanish, Creoles, and African Americans mixed freely in a sophisticated atmosphere unlike that of any other city in Europe or America. From this fertile environment, Gottschalk absorbed the musical sounds of each culture, frequently finding inspiration for his compositions in exotic Creole tunes based on French folk and popular melodies.

Gottschalk's sophisticated family had no genteel compunctions regarding professional musicians and, recognizing their son's precocious talent and the lack of opportunities at home, they sent him to France at the age of thirteen to study music. He stayed abroad for eleven years, becoming a great favorite of aristocratic European society, who admired his youthful compositions for piano and his astonishing virtuosity. Frederic Chopin (1810–1849), the famous Polish "poet of the piano," predicted that Gottschalk would one day be the "king of pianists."

The Piano

By 1800, the piano had almost displaced the harpsichord as the keyboard instrument likely to be found in homes or heard in concert. The piano constituted, in fact, the ideal Romantic instrument, providing access to every facet of emotional expression. The *damper* or "loud" pedal (to the player's right) held the tones, connecting one to another for a **legato** or smooth and lyrical melody line, or allowing the sounds to accumulate to thunderous effect. The "soft" pedal (on the left), by shifting the keyboard, considerably damped the volume. And on some large pianos, a center pedal, called the *sostenuto,* allowed the player to sustain some tones while others sounded cleanly above them.

Piano music enjoyed immense popularity in the United States, where the varied concert programs of the day often included a virtuosic piano performance by a resident or visiting concert artist and much "household" piano music was available at a level of difficulty appropriate for the average young lady to master. Lowell Mason's son Henry cofounded the famous Mason and Hamlin piano company in 1854, and Jonas Chickering, William Knabe, and Henry Steinway all lived in America, producing pianos unsurpassed anywhere in the world.

Although Gottschalk composed songs, orchestral works, and even operas, it is for his delightful piano music that he is remembered, especially works based on popular dances and his moving **character pieces** (mood pieces), such as "Berceuse" ("Lullaby") and "The Banjo."

Gottschalk's Piano Music

The rhythms and forms of popular dances had long invigorated many kinds of concert music, and Gottschalk continued this tradition by writing several *waltzes* and *mazurkas* for the piano. The

waltz, a dance in triple meter, was very popular in nineteenth-century ballrooms on both sides of the Atlantic; the **mazurka,** a Polish folk dance also in triple meter, has a more robust character than the graceful waltz. Concert pieces based on these and other traditional dances were not intended to be *danced* but rather to capture in concert music the mood, style, tempo, form, and meter of a popular step. Gottschalk's stirring "La Bamboula" (an Optional Listening Example), which he subtitled "Danse des negres," is based on a dance popular with whites and blacks alike in the vibrant city where Gottschalk grew up.

Theme and Variations. Another formal design serving well to organize piano and other instrumental musics is known as **theme and variations.** Here a melody or *theme* recurring throughout the piece provides unity through repetition, although each presentation of the theme is *varied* for purposes of variety or contrast. (An apt comparison may be made with the musical theme of a movie, which recurs throughout the film arousing any number of conflicting emotions according to the way it is performed.) Listening Example 22 is a well-known theme and variations by Louis Moreau Gottschalk.

Having amazed and delighted concert audiences in Spain, France, and England, Gottschalk returned in 1853 to America, where audiences, perceiving his long stay abroad to have made him respectably foreign, responded with unbridled enthusiasm to his performances of his own melodically simple but technically demanding piano pieces. Next Gottschalk spent several years in the West Indies, whose tropical sounds and flavors he captured in some of his later compositions, returning to America in 1862 to find the country desperately at war.

Although a southerner by birth, Gottschalk sided firmly with the North and began an exhausting concert tour across America, reaching people who had never heard concert music before and contributing most of what he earned to the Union cause. Criticized by an elite few for playing his own tuneful pieces instead of the great classical music of Beethoven, Chopin, and others, Gottschalk replied that he played what the audience wanted to hear; but he also commented late in his short life on the marked improvement he perceived in the level of American taste.

Gottschalk never married but was adored by women, who screamed and swooned and fought to grab pieces of his clothing whenever he appeared. Finally forced by a scandal (in which he probably was quite innocent) to leave the country in 1865, he traveled to South America, where he organized huge concerts, much like the musical extravaganzas popular in Europe at the time involving hundreds of performers. The exact cause of his death in South America at the age of forty, usually attributed to yellow fever, yet remains a mystery—as is fitting, perhaps, for this quintessential Romantic man.

Rise of Nationalism in Music

At about the same time that American paintings began to reflect America's natural splendors, a few composers set out to capture the American spirit in

Theme and Variations

Composer
Louis Moreau Gottschalk

Title
"Le Bananier" ("The Banana Tree")

Form
Theme and variations

The theme, a Creole melody, begins with an ascending broken minor triad. Strong accents and irregular phrase lengths enhance the exotic effect of the tuneful melody.

The first section of the theme (**a**) is played by the right hand while the left hand plays an "obstinately" repeated rhythmic pattern called an **ostinato,** which marks the duple meter. Section **a** is repeated.

The second half of the theme (**b**), higher than **a** in range, begins with three repeated and accented notes. Section **b** is repeated.

a is heard in the higher range, accompanied by a new ostinato. Repeat.

b is delicately embellished by the right hand, accompanied by chords in the left.

A variation of **a** is played in a major key.

There is a section of new material that sounds improvisatory.

The major version of **a** is played by the left hand while the right hand performs dazzling runs.

b recurs briefly.

The delightful piece concludes with fragments of **a** in the left hand and rapid, virtuosic figures in the right.

music and to promote performances of American music. These early seeds of **nationalism** fell on dry ground, however, largely ignored by audiences on both sides of the Atlantic, who considered Americans to have great mechanical and industrial capabilities but to be novices in matters of art. Musicians struggling to establish a characteristic American style faced formidable odds.

These early nationalists were resisting German Romanticism, which dominated the arts and especially the music of the nineteenth-century Western world. The great German composers wrote lengthy pieces with long, expansive melodies accompanied by rich and full harmonies. Extreme contrasts of dynamic level also characterize their music, much of which was based on programmatic ideas suggesting the most intense emotional expression.

Despite efforts of the nationalists, the German sound increasingly dominated music in America, where audiences preferred to hear music by the earlier Handel, Haydn, Mozart, and Beethoven and the more modern Robert Schumann, Felix Mendelssohn, and Richard Wagner than music by composers of any other nationality, including their own. Americans also chose to study music with German teachers when possible, the great wave of German immigration to this country in the middle of the nineteenth century making this possible for amateur and professional musicians alike. Those who could afford it traveled to Germany to further their music education.

The second half of the nineteenth century witnessed strong European nationalistic efforts as well, as certain nations not bordering directly on Germany began to assert their artistic independence and to establish characteristic styles of their own during the second half of that period. Artists in Russia, Bohemia, Norway, and Finland soon established strong national styles, as writers, painters, and musicians drew inspiration from and based their works on the colorful folk tales, legends, and religious music of their own experience. Suddenly the local peasant became more interesting than the generic noble. By the later part of the century, after the ruling aristocracies of several nations had been overthrown and popular states established, nationalism became a significant political and cultural movement throughout western Europe.

Although most Americans remained unready to defy the established wisdom that Germans knew best how to write music, a talented and highly eccentric Bohemian American composer boldly set out to establish a genuine "American" concert music.

Anthony Philip Heinrich (1781–1861)

Forced by financial reverses to leave his home and family in 1810, **Anthony Philip Heinrich** arrived in the United States, where he soon became music director of a popular theater in Philadelphia. Unable to make a good living, however, he moved to Kentucky in 1817 and settled among the Indians of that area.

In Kentucky, Heinrich lived alone in a log cabin, practicing his violin and composing programmatic pieces based on his own ideas and experiences. He also conducted what was apparently the first performance of a Beethoven symphony in this country. Profoundly struck by the beauty of the American wilderness and charmed with the music of his Native American friends, Heinrich wrote several works that expressed his appreciation and praise for America in such extravagantly titled orchestral pieces as *The War of the Elements and the Thundering of Niagara, The Columbiad, or Migration of American Wild Passenger Pigeons,* and *Pushmataha: A Venerable Chief of a Western Tribe of Indians!* Well known and admired in this country and abroad, Heinrich was acquainted with many of the outstanding figures of his age and reflected their influence in some of his compositions: *The Ornitho-*

logical Combat of Kings: or, The Condor of the Andes, for example, reveals an interest he shared with his friend John James Audubon.

Although Heinrich's music often quoted more-or-less legitimate Native American themes, he harmonized them according to Western tradition, idealizing and romanticizing the Indian experience much as James Fenimore Cooper's novels and George Catlin's paintings presented it in an attractive but unrealistic light. Nevertheless, although not a great composer, Heinrich furthered the American music experience by expressing American ideas, quoting Native American themes, and enthusiastically promoting the performance of music by himself and other American composers (as he resolutely considered himself to be). His music is rarely performed today, but "Father Heinrich" is remembered and revered for his important contributions to our musical heritage.

Orchestral Music

Whereas the great virtuosos continued to attract an ever wider and more appreciative public audience, the large orchestral ensemble held little interest for the young republic. Few American orchestras existed throughout the nineteenth century, although dedicated professional and amateur musicians endeavored to make the orchestral sound appealing to an American audience. In 1820, the Moravians founded a Philharmonic Society for the performance of orchestral music in Bethlehem, Pennsylvania; and in Philadelphia, American and immigrant musicians organized a Musical Fund Society, which performed symphonic music and also choral music accompanied by an orchestra. The New York Philharmonic Society, the nation's oldest orchestra still in existence today, was founded in 1842, but it remained a loosely organized and rather haphazard association for many years.

A Growing Awareness

Musical activity increased significantly across America as the nineteenth century waned. For example, some of our finest professional music schools, or **conservatories,** were established and several concert halls and opera houses were built. The Metropolitan Opera House, built in 1882 (Figure 50), and Carnegie Hall (1891) attracted enthusiastic audiences to New York City; and Americans across the country had access to more concert music of a greater variety and finer quality than ever before. Choral and chamber societies presented programs not only on the East Coast but also in cities farther west such as Cincinnati and Chicago, and both serious and light operas became more and more popular.

The European orchestras that played in America generally performed European works, of course. The first organization to give serious attention to orchestral music by American composers, however, was a visiting orchestra directed by the celebrated French conductor Louis Antoine Jullien (1812–1860).

Figure 50
Metropolitan Opera House, circa 1900. (The Bettmann Archive, Inc.)

A showman in the tradition of P.T. Barnum, Louis Gottschalk, or more recently Liberace, Jullien wore white gloves when he conducted and used a jeweled baton. But however flashy he might have appeared, he led his ensemble in fine performances of great orchestral music. Jullien added American musicians to his orchestra during the year he spent in New York (1853) and, strongly prompted by the local press, included some American works in his programs.

William Henry Fry (1813–1864) Among those who benefited from this opportunity was one of the most outspoken American nationalists of the period, **William Henry Fry.** Fry first became known as a composer of operas. His *Leonora* (1845) was the first American opera to be produced in this country—but he had to pay for the production himself, for although Italian operas presented by European companies were popular in New Orleans and New York, even those enlightened cities had little interest in an opera by an American composer. In fact, although *Leonora* was written in the familiar

Italian style with lyrical melodies, attractive harmonies, and the lavish staging expected of Romantic operas, it was not very well received here. Later, while working for an American newspaper as a music correspondent in Paris, Fry had no success in arranging for a performance of his opera there.

Fry next ventured to offer a series of public music appreciation lectures. Complaining bitterly that the New York Philharmonic Society never commissioned and seldom performed any music by an American composer, he exhorted American musical societies to perform American works, audiences to listen to them, and critics to review them objectively. At one lecture, Fry asserted that "the American composer should not allow the name of Beethoven or Handel or Mozart to prove an eternal bugbear to him," further declaring, "It is time we had a Declaration of Independence in Art and laid the foundation of an American School of Painting, Sculpture and Music."

William Henry Fry's four symphonies and other orchestral works are rarely heard today, his music having been surpassed in quality by many other American and European compositions. Nevertheless, Fry is respectfully and rightfully remembered for his efforts in support of American music.

George Bristow (1825–1898)

George Bristow (1825–1898) The other well-known American composer of orchestral music from this period was **George Bristow,** a violinist who once resigned as a player for the New York Philharmonic Society in sympathy with Fry's complaint at the Society's lack of support for American music. Bristow rejoined the orchestra later but continued to promote acceptance of American music.

Better trained than Fry, Bristow became a successful conductor, teacher, and church organist as well as a composer and violinist. (It is significant that Heinrich, Fry, and Bristow all supported themselves by means other than their meager earnings from the composition of music.) As the conductor for eleven years of an orchestra known as the Harmonic Society, Bristow tried to introduce American works and have them favorably reviewed. Yet his own orchestral and choral works *sound* more German than American, and although he used an American Indian melody in his Symphony no. 4, his Western harmonies, rhythms, and orchestral timbres belied the achievement of a genuine Native American sound.

The second American opera, written by Bristow ten years after Fry's *Leonora,* had a modestly successful run in New York. Bristow based his opera on an American subject—Washington Irving's *Rip Van Winkle*—but like Fry, he set his story to Italian-sounding music.

The individual who finally raised the level of orchestral performance and appreciation in America was a musician of German background, Theodore Thomas.

Theodore Thomas (1835–1905)

Theodore Thomas (1835–1905) Soon after the ten-year-old **Theodore Thomas** (Figure 51) arrived in America from Germany, already an accomplished violinist, he became a member of the New York Philharmonic Society, playing as well for various theater and opera orchestras. But he

Figure 51

Cartoon depicting Theodore Thomas conducting in Central Park. (Reproduced from *Theodore Thomas: A Musical Autobiography*, ed. George P. Upton, 1905, rpf. New York: Da Capo Press, 1964. Used by permission.)

A REMINISCENCE OF CENTRAL PARK GARDEN

intended to become an orchestral conductor and in that capacity to raise the level of Americans' appreciation for orchestral music. And so he did.

Scornful of the casual rehearsal and concert procedures of the New York Philharmonic Society, Thomas formed his own ensemble, the New York Symphony Orchestra, hiring only the best musicians, rehearsing them rigorously, and presenting public programs guaranteed to please an audience. His method was to subtly but systematically alter the balance in his concerts between light, familiar pieces and more serious, challenging works as his listeners became more experienced with orchestral fare.

Recognizing Americans' familiarity with varied and entertaining programs, Thomas invited solo virtuosos—including Gottschalk on at least one program—to dazzle the listeners, who then dutifully received perhaps one movement of a more serious piece. Thomas also was careful not to plan programs that were too long. He traveled widely with his orchestra, bringing symphonic music to people who had never heard it before and extending the season's employment for his musicians; in the summer he offered outdoor "garden concerts," where refreshments were served. The quality of his performances was always superb, and America gradually developed an enthusiastic appreciation for the thrilling orchestral sound. Inevitably, German composers formed the core of Thomas's programs, although he also gave generous attention to outstanding American composers of the day.

With the support of some Chicago businessmen, in 1891 Thomas established the Theodore Thomas Orchestra, later known as the Chicago Symphony Orchestra, conducting it until his death in 1905. By that time several other American cities had formed their own orchestras, and smaller towns enjoyed short orchestral seasons as well. During the next several decades, Americans continued to form numerous school, civic, and professional orchestras and to absorb the great symphonic literature of the world. By the mid-twentieth century public school, civic, and professional symphonies across the country rendered America a veritable nation of symphony orchestras.

Terms to Review

virtuoso   A performer who possesses dazzling technical brilliance.

legato   Smooth, without perceptible interruption between notes.

character piece   A relatively short piano piece with a characteristic style or mood.

waltz   A ballroom dance in triple meter; also a concert piece with the character of a waltz.

mazurka   A Polish folk dance of varying character, in triple meter; also a concert piece.

theme and variations   An instrumental form in which a theme or melody recurs to provide unity, but in altered guises for variety.

ostinato   A repeated melodic and/or rhythmic pattern.

nationalism   The expression in art of particular cultural characteristics. The nineteenth century witnessed strong nationalistic movements in several countries.

conservatory   A professional music school.

Key Figures

Louis Moreau Gottschalk
Anthony Philip Heinrich
William Henry Fry
George Bristow
Theodore Thomas

Optional Listening Examples

Louis Moreau Gottschalk: "La Bamboula"
George Bristow: Fourth Symphony (*Arcadian*), op. 49, third movement ("Indian War Dance")

Suggestions for Further Listening

Louis Moreau Gottschalk: "The Banjo"
William Henry Fry: excerpts from *Leonora*
George Bristow: Third Symphony in F# Minor, op. 26
Bristow: Overture to *Rip Van Winkle*

6

American Concert Music Comes of Age

Although most French and Italian composers had their New World partisans, nineteenth-century Americans who enjoyed hearing orchestral music preferred the German Romantic style to any other. Romantics (German and otherwise) approached the elements of music differently from their Classical forbears. Their melodies were long and lyrical rather than short and motivic, their phrases asymmetrical rather than balanced in the classical way. Also, Romantic composers were more likely to repeat their long, songlike melodies with variation or embellishment, than to develop brief intellectual melodic ideas. Chordal harmony became fuller and steadily more dissonant, as ears adapted to richer and ever-more-pungent combinations of sound. As Romantic composers added new tones to familiar chords, they expanded the concept of tonal harmony and achieved newly varied and colorful effects.

Romantics also treated rhythm more freely than had the Classicists, avoiding regularly recurring patterns of a certain number of beats per measure. Their love of freedom and their stress on individuality encouraged Romantics to use *irregular meters* (five or seven beats to the bar instead of two, three, or four), *changing meters* (a different number of beats in succeeding measures within a piece), or *polymeters* (two or more meters at the same time), lending an exciting new rhythmic variety to their concert music.

About the same time that painters began to use color for expressive rather than realistic purposes, composers began to explore the timbres, sometimes called the colors, of sounds. Thus nineteenth-century music includes increasingly rich and imaginative instrumental effects. Technological changes increasing the capabilities of woodwind and brass instruments encouraged their wider use in the symphony orchestra, whereas the percussion section of the orchestra also was greatly expanded, making it necessary to add more strings in order to balance the sound. Accordingly, the Romantic orchestra was not only larger than that of the Baroque and Classical periods but also included a richer variety of timbres. When you attend orchestral performances today, you will probably notice that pieces written in the eighteenth century are played by a small or **chamber orchestra,** whereas Romantic pieces require a much larger ensemble.

Despite the continuing tendency among America's best-known composers to make their music sound as German as possible, a strong nationalistic urge developed among a few dedicated American musicians and listeners as the nineteenth century drew toward its close. In 1892, Mrs. Jeanette M. Thurber, one of the few Americans genuinely interested in establishing a nationalistic style of composition, invited an outstanding Bohemian nationalist composer to direct the National Conservatory of Music in New York City. While in America, the prestigious Antonín Dvořák (1841–1904) listened to the music of African Americans and Native Americans with the same fascination with which he had absorbed the folk music of his own beloved homeland, expressing amazed regret that Americans seemed relatively uninterested in their "native" sounds. Dvořák did not always distinguish between genuine spirituals developed by African Americans and the derivative minstrel songs; nor did he specifically recommend that American composers quote or imitate black or Indian effects. He strongly suggested, however, that these particular musics offered unique and important sources of inspiration.

To illustrate his ideas of how American music should sound and to express appreciation for the scenic beauty of the land he was visiting, Dvořák wrote his Symphony no. 9 (*From the New World*) and two chamber pieces. Each of these works includes melodies that seem to be based on the scales of black or Indian music as Dvořák understood them—although he harmonized the melodies and orchestrated the music according to Western custom.

After fewer than three years, when Dvořák's homesickness compelled his return home, he had raised very little interest in American-sounding music. At least a few Americans reflected his influence, however, by using black or Indian references in their music. Among them was the distinguished African American composer, Henry Thacker Burleigh (see p. 65), who inspired Dvořák's interest in spirituals.

The Second New England School

Although New York City remained the center of music performance activity, the intellectual atmosphere of the Boston area nurtured significant developments in music as well as in philosophy and literature, and New England produced most of the important American composers of the late nineteenth century. The Boston Symphony Orchestra, founded in 1881, loyally supported the efforts of local composers by bringing their music to public attention, often with repeated performances of a well-received work.

Members of the **Second New England School** of composers, much of whose music was comparable in quality as well as in style to that of many of their European contemporaries, shared a dedication to the principles of German music theory and a concern for careful craftsmanship leading some to dub them the "Boston classicists." They contributed to every genre of concert music. Many were church musicians and organists who included organ **transcriptions** of opera arias and symphonic music in their recitals, bringing this literature to Americans who had little access to opera or orchestral concerts. These intrepid pioneer composers also contributed strong compositions for organ and a significant body of choral music to the American music repertoire.

John Knowles Paine (1839–1906)

As a young man, **John Knowles Paine,** the oldest member and the leader of the Second New England School, made the decision—unusual for an American of his day—to become a professional musician. Having progressed in his music studies as far as possible with a German teacher in America, he traveled to Germany to polish his skills, giving organ concerts while he not only studied music theory and composition but also composed.

While in Europe, Paine wrote his Mass in D for chorus, soloists, and orchestra based on a well-known Mass by Beethoven, taking his text, although he was a Protestant, from the Roman Catholic liturgy according to choral music custom. In this first large composition by an American to be performed in Europe (where it was better received than at a later American performance), Paine neither intended nor achieved a distinctively American sound.

Returning to America in 1861 to find the country at war, Paine became the university organist at Harvard University, where, eager to share his newly acquired expertise, he offered free noncredit lectures in music (not considered a proper course of study at American universities) to Harvard students. To the surprise of the university administration, Paine's lectures were very well received. Thanks to his efforts, in 1875 America's oldest college became the first to include music in its formal curriculum, and Paine became the first American professor of music.

Paine's orchestral music is far more significant than that of Heinrich, Fry, or Bristow, who are mainly remembered today for their valiant efforts to promote American music. His much-admired Symphony no. 1, first performed by Theodore Thomas's orchestra in 1876, was the first American symphony to be published—but in Germany rather than America, and only after Paine's death. He wrote many other kinds of music as well, including songs, hymns, an opera, and several fine keyboard compositions for organ or piano, including his cheerful Fuga Giocosa (Listening Example 23).

Fugue

Although originally conceived as a form of keyboard music, the highly structured *fugue* serves as well for every performing medium, including the singing voice. A **fugue** is a polyphonic composition with three to five melodic lines or "voices" entering one at a time in imitation of each other. (To "fugue" is to chase—think of "fugitive.")

The principal theme or **subject** of a fugue enters alone. After it has been heard all the way through, it is imitated by each of the other voices in turn until each has made its entrance. The first entrance—the subject—is on the *tonic,* and the second voice, or **answer,** begins on the *dominant.* The remaining voices (usually there are a total of three or four) alternate entrances between tonic and dominant until each voice has been introduced (Figure 52). Whereas the imitation in a round or canon is literal, the melody in a sense chasing itself, the answer in a fugue begins on a different tone from the

Fugue

Composer
John Knowles Paine

Title
Fuga Giocosa, op. 41, no. 3

Form
Fugue

Key
G major

The subject, which is based on an old baseball song, "Over the Fence Is Out, Boys," includes a distinctive upward leap of an octave. It enters on the tonic note (G) and is soon answered at the level of the dominant (D). The third voice enters (tonic), and then the subject is tossed—like a baseball, perhaps—from one voice to another.

Paine explores several major and minor keys throughout the rest of the fugue. He sometimes treats the first four notes of the subject as a motive, repeating the figure sequentially. Occasional large chords provide effective contrast to the polyphonic texture, and the piece becomes increasingly virtuosic and dramatic. It is never pretentious, however, and the end, like the beginning, is light and humorous.

Figure 52

Diagram of the exposition of a four-voice fugue.

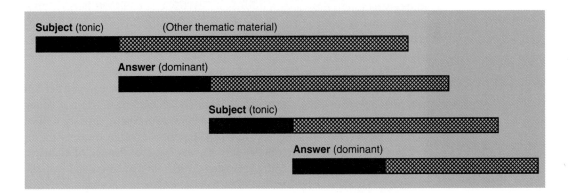

subject (dominant instead of tonic) and is only similar, rather than identical, to the subject.

This rigid structure applies only to the beginning section, or **exposition,** of a fugue, in which all of the voices are introduced ("exposed"). Thereafter, each voice proceeds with independent material, referring to the subject and answer more or less frequently throughout the piece. There may be a second theme, or *countersubject,* introduced in the same manner as the subject and also recurring throughout the fugue. Thus, although intellectually conceived and tightly structured, the form is quite flexible after the exposition is completed.

Other Members of the School A large number of capable and prolific composers, many of them trained in Europe, were soon active in the New England area. Most, however, found it necessary to acquire academic positions in order to make a living, because American audiences offered little support to American composers.

The music of **George Chadwick** (1854–1931) has energy, humor, and a kind of audacity lending a refreshing American flavor to some of his works. For many years the director of the prestigious New England Conservatory of Music, Chadwick, like Paine, taught a number of younger musicians who became important members of the Boston group.

Horatio Parker (1863–1919), like Paine and Chadwick, was an organist who composed for "the king of instruments," as the pipe organ is called, and also for virtually every other vocal and instrumental medium. Becoming head of the new music department at Yale in 1894, he also formed the New Haven Symphony Orchestra, served as guest conductor for other ensembles, played for and directed a church service each week, and composed prolifically. Parker's music, which clearly reflects his German training, was widely admired both here and in Europe, and his sacred choral cantata *Hora Novissima* is still widely known.

Amy Cheney Beach (1867–1944) Mrs. H. H. A. Beach (Figure 53), as **Amy Cheney Beach** preferred to be called, was well-known as a pianist and a composer. While not the first American woman to write music, she was the first to rank with such highly educated and sophisticated musicians as Chadwick and Parker; and she was, in fact, the first American woman to write a successful Mass and a symphony. Women of her day and before simply were not afforded the education, the financial support, the social support, or the patronage required to succeed as professional composers of music.

Both Beach's parents and her husband recognized and encouraged her talent, although to a limited extent. Although she studied piano from a young age, her formal training as a composer was minimal. She rigorously trained herself, however, translating into English important foreign treatises on instrumentation and orchestration. Before her marriage, at the age of eighteen, she performed as a pianist with the Boston Symphony Orchestra and with the Theodore Thomas Orchestra; but after their marriage her husband preferred

Figure 53
Amy Cheney Beach.
(Corbis.)

that she concentrate on her compositions, because a married lady's professional appearance on stage was not well accepted in her day. After her husband's death, Beach resumed her concert career, performing to great acclaim both here and in Europe.

Although her compositions were widely performed and well received on both continents, Beach could not escape references to her sex in reviews of her work, reviewers sometimes criticizing her for trying to sound masculine, or praising her graceful melodies and more gentle symphonic passages as properly feminine in style. Thus, although she handled the symphonic medium very capably, it is little wonder that Amy Cheney Beach composed more art songs, including her charming "The Year's at the Spring" (Listening Example 24), than any other form, because her contemporaries readily accepted songs as fitting examples of feminine creativity.

Only recently, as enterprising contemporary musicians have performed and recorded some of their well-crafted, attractive works, have we begun to fully appreciate the music of the Second New England School composers. Reviewers of numerous recent recordings of symphonic works from this period have expressed both admiration for the quality of the music and regret that it has been virtually ignored for so long.

Edward MacDowell (1860–1908) Although the Second New England School composers wrote effectively in all of the symphonic, choral, and solo genres, as we have seen their music predominantly conformed to the sounds of their European contemporaries. **Edward MacDowell,** who was too romantic to be called a classicist of any sort and too individual to be included

Art Song

Composer
Amy Cheney Beach

Title
"The Year's at the Spring"

The song is the setting of two verses by Robert Browning, from his poem *Pippa Passes*.

Meter
Triple

Accompaniment
The piano marks the triple division of the beats with rich chords that add interesting harmony and enhance the dramatic expression of the song.

Form
Modified strophic. The music of the second verse is similar, but not identical, to that of the first verse.

The first melodic phrase is repeated sequentially at higher levels of pitch at the beginning of each verse. Notice how this, together with an expressive crescendo, increases the dramatic intensity of the song. Key phrases ("God's in his Heaven," "all's right") are repeated for emphasis. The highest note is reserved for the word "right" toward the end of the song.

Text
The year's at the spring,
And day's at the morn;
Morning's at seven,
The hillside's dew pearled;
The lark's on the wing;
The snail's on the thorn;
God's in his heaven,
All's right with the world.

in a school of composers, became the first American to write concert music in a style distinctly his own.

In his teens appearing equally talented in music and art, MacDowell was sent to Paris to study in both fields (Figure 54). But finally deciding to become a professional musician, he traveled to Germany, where he followed the prevailing custom of studying theory and composition. An accomplished pi-

Figure 54
Edward MacDowell—
composer, painter, poet,
and lover of nature.
(Bettmann Newsphoto,
Inc.)

anist, he concertized widely during his long stay abroad, and some of his songs and piano pieces, written in the accepted German style, were published in Germany before he returned to America in 1888.

After several years of performing, composing, and teaching in the Boston area, MacDowell accepted the position of head of the newly established music department at Columbia University in New York City, in 1896, which afforded him the opportunity to implement his ideal of teaching music as related to the other arts. We have already noted that Romantics often were talented in more than one of the arts and found particular significance in relationships between music and literature. Thus MacDowell, who not only composed music and painted but also wrote poetry, believed that the arts could not be understood in isolation from each other and established at Columbia a curriculum similar to a modern humanities program.

MacDowell professed not to espouse the nationalists' claim that quoting African American or Indian themes would establish a characteristically American music, suggesting instead that American music should seek to capture the youthful, optimistic spirit of the country. Nevertheless, he was unable to resist references to American Indian music in several of his compositions. For example, each section of his orchestral *Indian Suite* is based on Native

American lore or experience, and each uses American Indian or Indianlike melodies, though the harmonies and orchestral effects are entirely European. (A **suite** is an orchestral work consisting of several sections or semi-independent pieces.) Similarly, his famous set of character pieces titled *Woodland Sketches* includes one called "From an Indian Lodge," which imitates American Indian sounds within a Western framework.

MacDowell's piano pieces, including the *Woodland Sketches,* reflect his romantic love of nature, painting in musical terms idyllic scenes of woodland lakes and hills. These delicate, intimate, and modest piano miniatures capture the very essence of the sounds and moods of nature as MacDowell loved it.

His vision of music as one of the integrated arts has profoundly benefited American arts to this day, for after his death, MacDowell's widow established a summer colony on their estate at Peterboro, New Hampshire, where artists, musicians, and literary figures are invited to spend uninterrupted summers working within their chosen fields at the **MacDowell Colony.**

Arthur Farwell and the Wa-Wan Press

Arthur Farwell (1872–1952), who like so many Americans studied music in Germany, decided upon his return home that American composers should be writing something other than imitation German music. Farwell intended to exalt in his music "the common inspirations of American life"—by which he meant, somewhat surprisingly, the experiences of the American Indian. To this end he imaginatively arranged some Native American tunes and composed several original pieces based on Indian melodies. Understanding that Native American music signified more than art or entertainment, Farwell attempted in his *American Indian Melodies* (1900) to reflect the essence of the myths or legends upon which the songs were based. Nevertheless, the worthy intentions of Farwell and other composers interested in Native American music were overwhelmed by their thorough indoctrination into tonal concepts.

Farwell's music was coolly received by audiences and routinely rejected by publishers, who gave an unfriendly reception to music by other American composers as well. So in 1901, Farwell established the famous **Wa-Wan Press** (the name is from a ceremony of the Omaha tribe), dedicated to producing American music. Although it existed for only a decade, the Wa-Wan Press published several hundred compositions, effectively boosting the reputations and careers of several struggling American composers.

Yet the market for their music remained minimal. And few composers *or* listeners of the late nineteenth century showed much interest in music that *sounded* American. Although by the latter part of the nineteenth century American composers were producing impressive works in all of the large instrumental and vocal forms—symphonies, concertos, sonatas, operas, and choral works—and finally were being afforded a respectful, if limited, hearing, most of them not only studied in Germany but also wrote most of their music in the firmly established German Romantic style.

Terms to Review

chamber orchestra   A small orchestra, with only a few instruments per line of music.

Second New England School   The first American composers to write significant works in all of the large concert forms. Sometimes referred to as the Boston classicists.

transcription   An arrangement of a piece originally composed for a particular instrument or ensemble so that it can be played by a different instrument or combination of instruments.

fugue   A polyphonic composition in which imitative entrances of two or more voices alternate between tonic and dominant. Originally conceived for keyboard instruments, fugues now are written for other instruments and for voices as well.

subject   The principal melodic theme of a fugue.

answer   The second presentation of the subject, on the dominant.

exposition   The first section of a fugue.

suite   An instrumental work consisting of several dances or other semi-independent pieces.

MacDowell Colony   A colony for artists in every medium established on the estate of Edward MacDowell by his widow, in Peterboro, New Hampshire.

Wa-Wan Press   A publishing company established in 1901 by Arthur Farwell, dedicated to the publication of American music.

Key Figures

John Knowles Paine
George Chadwick
Horatio Parker
Amy Cheney Beach
Edward MacDowell
Arthur Farwell

Optional Listening Example

Horatio Parker: Fugue in C Minor

Suggestions for Further Listening

Amy Cheney Beach: Symphony in E♭ (Gaelic), op. 32
Beach: Mass in E♭, op. 5
George Chadwick: "Tam O'Shanter"
Edward MacDowell: "Will o' the Wisp" and "To a Wild Rose" from *Woodland Sketches*
John Knowles Paine: Second Symphony ("In the Spring")
Paine: Fantasie über "Ein' feste Burg"
Paine: Mass in D

PART 2 SUMMARY

By the turn of the nineteenth century, Americans had become more romantic than classical in their style of expression. The romantic zeal to improve the conditions of life initiated religious and social reform movements as well as efforts to reform American music by making it sound more European. Lowell Mason, who led the movement to reform musical taste in America, wrote attractive—although quite conventional—hymns, brought music education into the public school system, and systematically attempted to raise the level of musical awareness and appreciation.

Lowell Mason's efforts notwithstanding, country folk continued to practice and enjoy their accustomed ways of reading and singing music; the singing schools remained popular in rural areas, using shape-note songbooks such as *The Sacred Harp* as teaching materials. During the Great Revival, people of all ages, both black and white, attended religious camp meetings, where they enjoyed singing rousing hymns and spirituals. Secular songs became popular, too, often reflecting the experience of everyday life. In the cities, theaters offered popular entertainment that was primarily musical. Religious songs, sentimental ballads, songs of social protest, and glees were sung in parlors and concert halls and were included in the performances of well-known singing families such as the Hutchinsons.

In the most popular entertainment of the period leading to the Civil War, the minstrel show, white men blackened their skin and imitated the songs, dances, and dialect of stereotypical African Americans. Stephen Foster was the finest composer of minstrel songs, although the genteel society preferred his love songs, Civil War songs, and sentimental ballads about home. Concert bands directed by Patrick Gilmore and John Philip Sousa became balanced ensembles capable of performing transcriptions of orchestral and operatic literature as well as more popular pieces, and—under the superb direction of Sousa, the march king—achieved the highest levels of professionalism.

Mid-nineteenth-century Americans particularly enjoyed concert music performed by virtuoso soloists, and Jenny Lind and Ole Bull were among several outstanding European performers who toured throughout the United States, thrilling audiences with their dazzling virtuosic displays. America's own piano virtuoso, Louis Moreau Gottschalk, gained popularity on both sides of the Atlantic. Gottschalk introduced American audiences of the Civil War period to piano music, generally performing his own light but stirring compositions. After the Civil War, conservatories, concert halls, and opera houses were built in several American cities, as concert music grew in significance. Theodore Thomas presented orchestral programs that pleased audiences and gradually raised their level of appreciation, but primarily for European orchestral music.

The seeds of American nationalism, sown during the nineteenth century, bore fruit slowly, although several ardent nationalists, including Anthony Philip Heinrich, William Henry Fry, and George Bristow, sought to awaken American appreciation for American-sounding music. Dvořák encouraged Americans to develop a characteristic sound of their own; but the Second New England School composers produced the first significant American concert music writing primarily in the German Romantic style.

Edward MacDowell developed a characteristic, although not distinctively American, idiom of his own. The MacDowell Colony in Peterboro, New Hampshire, continues to invite artists in every discipline to spend summers working there.

Part 3

(Hulton Getty Picture Archive.)

The Growth of Vernacular Traditions

Music in the Vernacular:
Historical and Cultural Perspective

The common, or vernacular, language of a country is the language spoken by most of its people—the language they hear and use throughout their lives. A culture's vernacular music also is commonly heard and understood, without conscious effort on the part of listeners, and with less training and experience required for its performance than for the performance of so-called classical, concert, or art music. Often the term *popular* is applied to much of the music we shall cover in this section of the text, but popular music does not adequately embrace such disparate fields as jazz, folk, rap, country-western, and rock. In fact, *pop* has become a genre in its own right, distinguished from other vernacular sounds.

(© Janet Somer/Archive Photos.)

Walt Whitman
"I hear America singing, the varied carols I hear."

Vernacular Art and Literature Besides music, the other arts of the post–Civil War period also captured new American flavors. The picturesque stories of Bret Harte (1836–1902), for example, brought Western local color to appreciative readers in the great cities of the East, while Mark Twain (1835–1910) made everyday scenes of his youth in the Mississippi River region internationally, and hilariously, famous. The poet Walt Whitman (1819–1892) frequently used colloquial language to express the American experience of his day in an eloquent, distinctively American, idiom. Whitman's simple, anguished words in his famous poem "O Captain! My Captain!" reached the hearts of a nation in mourning for the death of Abraham Lincoln.

After the turn of the twentieth century, other poets variously expressed themselves in colloquial terms. The years between the late 1930s and the early 1950s were a thriving time for popular culture, when pulp novels, adventure comic books, swing music, and B movies enlivened the humdrum lives of working Americans. Some of the work of the midcentury Beat poets, who borrowed vocabulary from jazz musicians and sprinkled their verse with obscenities in an effort to bring poetry "back to the streets," was undeniably powerful and moving.

The visual arts, too, showed a new interest in the mundane facts of everyday American life and, by the turn of the twentieth century, the robust vigor of city life replaced the idyllic rural American landscape as the subject of choice for many American artists. Ben Shahn (1898–1969), among many socially conscious painters of the period, emulated newspaper cartoons in the effort to attract large numbers of people to his paintings. By the 1950s, Jasper Johns (1930–) and Robert Rauschenberg (1925–) were introducing everyday objects (flags, numbers, street signs) into their paintings, and in the 1960s a new art, known as "Pop," presented soup cans, Coke bottles, light bulbs, comic strip characters, and movie stars in hugely glorified detail. George Segal (1924–2000) cast life-sized plaster figures from live models, outfitted them in familiar commercial products, and placed them in lifelike settings, to amuse and sometimes fool the viewer's eye.

Among the best-known of the Pop artists, Andy Warhol (1928–1987) puzzled and intrigued his

111

contemporaries as he continues to compel our attention today. Working with silk-screen prints made from images taken from newspaper and magazine photos, Warhol ran colors through the screen directly onto his canvas, achieving surprising—some said audacious—new color harmonies. His finest pictures are "serial" paintings, multiple repetitions of the same image on a single canvas. For subjects he chose ubiquitous objects of popular American culture: movie stars, advertising logos, political figures, and popular musicians, many of whom he counted among his personal friends. It has been said that art and music are separate mirrors that reflect some of the same things, and certainly Warhol identified closely with some vernacular musicians of his day. In 1965, the punk rock group The Velvet Underground accompanied the showing of one of Warhol's artworks, and the next year he painted a banana for the cover of their first album (*The Velvet Underground and Nico*, released in 1967) (Figure 55).

One of America's most distinguished black artists, Romare Bearden (1912–1988), worked in *collage,* a cut-and-paste technique combining objects of varying content and material to form a work of art. Attempting, as he said, to "establish a world through art in which the validity of my Negro experience could live and make its own logic," Bearden defied conventional rules of art, sharply cutting the human features in his stunning collages with sudden breaks and surprising repetitions that functioned for him, it has been suggested, as a visual equivalent to the jazz he loved. *Empress of the Blues* is one of his most famous works (Figure 56).

Vernacular Music As we have seen, art or classical music gained favor in the New World only very slowly, over a long period of time, and much of the music already considered in this text belongs in the realm of the vernacular. Native American music never was conceived as an elite form of art; nor were Anglo-American or African American dances or songs. The hymns and psalm tunes written by self-taught amateurs formed a part of their educational and recreational as well as their worship

Figure 55
Andy Warhol's cover for the album *The Velvet Underground and Nico.*
(© 2001 Andy Warhol Foundation for the Visual Arts/Artists Rights Society [ARS], NewYork.)

Figure 56
Empress of the Blues by Romare Bearden.
(Smithsonian American Art Museum, Washington, D.C./Art Resource.)

experience. The composer Stephen Foster had no formal music training and did not intend his music for concert performance. Spirituals and *alabados* were really religious folk songs.

However, although vernacular music has always formed a significant facet of American culture, it was during the period between the Jacksonian era and the Civil War (1829–1861) that popular music as we know it emerged. Americans wrestling with rapid industrialization, economic uncertainty, slavery, westward expansion, and other overwhelming issues of social, religious, political, and economical import, found popular songs a helpful means through which they could cope with reality, sentimental songs on such sensitive topics as slavery, women's suffrage, or alcoholism, for example, allowing emotional release without requiring direct confrontation of the issues on a personal level.

At least until recently, vernacular music like popular art has evolved in an unself-conscious manner, spontaneously reflecting cultural characteristics indigenous to the region where it occurs. Thus long before art music achieved anything recognizable—however controversially—as an American sound, the young nation's vernacular music revealed strongly characteristic American traits. About the time of the Civil War, when popular culture included minstrel shows, band and circus music, the songs of Stephen Foster, and stirring performances by popular singing families, many songs, dances, and instrumental pieces acquired a new, distinctively American flavor. The rhythms, timbres, melodies, and harmonies of many songs, dances, and instrumental pieces, unfettered by conventional (European) rules, introduced new sounds suited to the pace and moods of American life and articulated in regional American accents. Some music, written down or passed along by aural tradition, was conceived to provide popular entertainment at home, in the theater, or in some other structured setting.

Some tunes evolved on an open range, in a cotton field, on a chain gang, or on the field of battle, where they offered self-expression and relief to the lonely and oppressed.

Again until recently, there has been little studied attempt to preserve vernacular traditions, favorite pieces surviving from one generation to the next simply through unchanging, or slowly changing, performance practice, as we observed with the early ballad "Barbara Allen" (Listening Example 4). New sounds also gain recognition as styles or genres or kinds of vernacular music in their own right, to be short lived or long lived according to the vagaries of popular acceptance and of the music business. Some very old tunes remain familiar today, whereas some highly popular songs have been largely forgotten by the fickle public who loved them a few months ago.

Recent Decades In the twentieth century, popular or vernacular music became a significant cultural concept in its own right as well as an important business, as it remains today. Recent decades have produced an unprecedented variety of popular, or vernacular, music: grunge, hip-hop, alternative rock, women-in-rock, new country, teenybop, Latin pop, and rave, all of which have not replaced but have joined rhythm-and-blues, classic rock, light pop, and all the other musics that belong to and express our popular culture. The nineties proved to be one of pop's most experimental periods, aided by technological advances that brought down the costs of recording, and computerized inventories that allowed stores to carry more stock. The downloading of music has changed the nature of the pop marketplace, challenging major labels to find new ways to make money in what may soon be the post-CD era.

And so we are in the midst of a prodigiously productive period, richer than any earlier time, and than any other contemporary culture, in the variety, quantity, and quality of our vernacular music. ♪

7

The Rise of Popular Culture

The gap between classical and popular music grew ever wider during the last half of the nineteenth century. Before that time, songs by the Austrian composer Franz Schubert and excerpts from operas by the Italians Giacomo Bellini and Donizetti were commonly hummed by Americans who perhaps never attended a concert or an opera, but who heard such tuneful melodies on someone's parlor piano, or in a theater performance, and loved and imitated them. The harmonies of such music were relatively simple, too, posing no challenge to untutored but receptive ears, and songwriters often modeled their own songs on those of the classical composers. But as the century progressed, composers such as Chopin, Wagner, Debussy, Richard Strauss, Gustave Mahler, and Arnold Schoenberg steadily increased the complexity and dissonance of their music, and writers of popular songs correspondingly simplified their melodies and harmonies to make them more accessible, more acceptable, to a wide audience.

The last decade of the nineteenth century, known (somewhat deceptively) as the Gay Nineties, witnessed two phenomenal movements in American music, each of which proved long lived and influential far beyond initial intentions or expectations. These two American musics—one (ragtime) instrumental, led by black musicians, the other (the songs of Tin Pan Alley) vocal, led by American Jews, aroused the enthusiasm and the lasting admiration of listeners here and abroad.

Ragtime

During the rather hectic and at least superficially carefree last decade of the nineteenth century, talented black pianists began to play a new, highly syncopated and very danceable music in more or (especially) less reputable places of entertainment. By 1897, the hot new music was being called "ragtime," and to "rag" a melody meant to syncopate it in the new way.

Although certain recent scholars suggest that the term had more general meaning in the music's early days, normally we consider **ragtime** specifically a written piano music—that is, music composed rather than improvised, and intended to be played on the piano. Uprooted from their homeland and transplanted in a harsh new world, blacks were restructuring their old modes of musical expression to fit their new cultural experiences; thus, in effect,

114

ragtime was a new and essentially American music that black musicians created, based on both white European and black African traditions.

From Europe, ragtime derived its march form and tonal harmony. Like a march, a rag generally begins with a brief introduction. Next we hear several strains in the order **A A B B C C D D,** each different letter representing a new strain. Usually one of the strains is a trio, often in the subdominant, and many rags, like some marches, end in this key. The pattern is not rigid, however, and certainly does not dictate the content; the first strain may return later in the piece, and many other variants of this basic march form also are possible.

Although some of the early ragtime players were self-taught, others with solid music training brought their knowledge of European harmony to the popular piano style. Thus, even though early rags were clearly tonal, some of them included rather complex harmonies using numerous **chromatic** tones—tones other than those of the major or minor scale on which the piece was based.

The rhythms and the "flavor" of ragtime, however—the characteristics that made it wildly popular in Europe as well as in America—derived from Africa and were practiced by singers, brass bands, and other instrumental ensembles long before ragtime was established as a piano form. Although syncopation had enlivened Western music from its beginning, the spicy nature and consistent application of syncopated rhythms were distinctive characteristics of the vigorous new vernacular music, ragtime.

Late minstrel shows constituted a strong source of inspiration for the hot new piano style: After the Civil War, minstrelsy provided a lucrative source of income for black as well as white performers, and blacks formed their own lively shows in which they syncopated, or ragged, banjo tunes. The high-stepping plantation dance called a **cakewalk,** based on the syncopated figure *short-LONG-short,* became a regular feature of the **finale,** or last scene, of a minstrel show. This distinctive cakewalk rhythm also appears occasionally in the music of many composers—Gottschalk's "La Bamboula" and "The Banjo," Stephen Foster's "Oh! Susanna," and Daniel Emmett's "Dixie" to name a few. (Because *duration* implies *accent,* we hear the long note of the cakewalk rhythmic pattern as stronger than the short notes that surround it.) This pattern consistently served the ragtime pianist, whose left hand marked the regular duple meter while the right hand played a highly syncopated melody.

Outstanding ragtime pianists included **Eubie Blake** (see Chapter 19), who died at the age of one hundred in 1983, **James Scott** (1886–1938), and Ferdinand DeMenthe, known as **Jelly Roll Morton** (1890–1941), among many others, each with his own style of writing and playing rags. Ragtime pianists recorded their performances on **piano rolls** by playing on a special piano that marked dots on a paper, which then could be punched and duplicated, making it possible for eager listeners throughout America and abroad to hear the music "live" on the new **player pianos.** A "pianist" played this novel instrument by pumping two pedals controlling a set of vacuum bellows that forced air through the holes in the paper as it wound over a tracker bar, causing the piano hammers to strike the appropriate piano strings. Player pianos brought recorded performances of the great ragtime players into people's homes before phonographs—and long before radios—became widely available.

Scott Joplin (1868–1917)

The childhood experience of **Scott Joplin** (Figure 57), the acknowledged king of ragtime, was rich with music, for his father, a former slave, played the violin, and there were other instruments in the Joplin home as well. The young Joplin studied piano with a German immigrant musician, who also provided him basic studies in music theory.

While still a teenager, Joplin left his home in Texarkana, Texas, and traveled east to Missouri, earning some money along the way by playing ragtime piano. In Sedalia and later in St. Louis—the early center of ragtime creativity—Joplin addressed both white and black music markets, playing in black bars and saloons while writing sentimental songs and arrangements in the white popular style. A shy and gentle man, he liked composing and teaching far better than playing in the rough environments where ragtime was first popular; and finally, the huge commercial success of his "Maple Leaf Rag" (Listening Example 25), published in 1899, allowed him to concentrate on the activities he preferred.

Although very easy to enjoy, good rags may be quite difficult to play, Joplin's own rags revealing a change from the (relative) simplicity of such early rags as "Maple Leaf Rag" and "The Entertainer"—both irresistibly tuneful and entirely unpretentious—to some of his later rags such as "Euphonic Sounds," which sound more like music for the concert than the dance hall. Although he insisted that rags should be played as written, Joplin regularly improvised complex embellishments in his own playing—which, however, was never very fast, for Joplin knew that a dashing tempo trivialized the strength and dignity of a great rag.

Figure 57
Scott Joplin (1868–1917) was honored with a commemorative stamp by the U.S. Postal Service in 1953 as part of its Black Heritage series. (Copyright 1983 U.S. Postal Service.)

[handwritten margin notes:] St. Louis – early center of Ragtime creativity

[handwritten:] Influence
• Dance

Influence of Ragtime

Ragtime had a phenomenal effect on many kinds of music both in the popular and classical realms. Social dancing was strongly affected as Americans, who even before the Civil War had largely abandoned popular eighteenth-century country dances for couple dances such as the waltz and the energetic polka, after the rise of ragtime avidly adopted the **two-step,** or **fox-trot.** The frequent syncopations of the popular new dance delighted young people and soon replaced all other dances in popularity.

James Reese Europe (1881–1919), an African American composer and bandleader, composed some of the most popular fox-trots of his day. And by the early twentieth century, many forms of American popular music reflected a strong black influence, although most of the rags, blues, and jazz recordings were made by white performers. African American vocalists especially were excluded from recording, though instrumental groups, such as those led by Europe and by **W. C. Handy** (1873–1958), were allowed to record because listeners were less likely than in vocal performances to discern the performers' race.

Soon white composers also were writing songs using ragtime rhythms, such as "Hello, My Baby!" by Joseph E. Howard, "Waiting for the Robert E. Lee" by Lewis F. Muir, and "Yessir, That's My Baby" by Gus Kahn and

Ragtime

Composer
Scott Joplin

Title
"Maple Leaf Rag"

Meter
Duple

Key
A-flat major

Outline of the Form   A A B B A C C D D

The *first strain* (A) (16 measures) features the short-LONG-short cakewalk figure, which first occurs in the second half of the first measure and recurs frequently throughout the piece. The first two measures are repeated. Notice the accented chromatic notes in the next two measures and the dramatic ascending figure that follows.

The *first strain* is repeated.

The *second strain* (**B**) (16 measures), rhythmically similar to the first, is higher in pitch. It begins with a chromatically descending melodic line and is marked **staccato,** meaning that it should be played in a crisp, detached manner.

The *second strain* is repeated.

The *first strain* is played again.

Notice the rich chordal texture of the *trio* (**C**), also 16 measures, which is played and repeated. The key is the subdominant, or D-flat major.

The *fourth strain* (**D**), 16 measures, returns to the tonic and is more similar in texture to strains 1 and 2.

Walter Donaldson. By 1914, when thousands of rags had been published, several European composers also reflected the influence of ragtime by writing syncopated concert pieces with "rag" or "ragtime" in their titles.

By the end of World War I, however, ragtime had declined in popularity. Some composers were producing rags that were too complex for popular appeal, and the commercial effort to reach a broad audience often diluted the very characteristics that made early rags exciting.

In the second decade of the twentieth century, many songs with little or no syncopated rhythm and no reference to ragtime in their titles were perceived as "ragtime songs" because of the style in which they were sung and played on stage and on recordings. In fact, performers capitalized on the popularity of ragtime by "ragging"—that is, by syncopating—almost any popular song of the day.

✳ Tin Pan Alley

The popular music publishing business expanded rapidly after the Civil War, with busy publishing houses active in many cities, including Boston, Chicago, Philadelphia, Baltimore, and Cincinnati. Well before the turn of the century, popular music had become an important business, and songs were being written for the purpose of making money. Songs with piano accompaniment printed in sheet music form sold in amazing quantities, made popular by variety shows, music theater performances, and piano rolls (Figure 58).

In 1881, the brothers Alex and Tom Harms established a publishing firm in New York City, achieving such commercial success with their business that many other companies followed their lead and also based song-publishing firms in New York. This music publishing activity first centered on East 14th Street, in what was then the heart of New York's theater district; but by the 1890s, nearly every major music publishing house was situated on or near 28th Street, soon dubbed **Tin Pan Alley,** in reference to the sounds of many

[handwritten margin note: Publishers New York Base]

Figure 58

Couple enjoying Tin Pan Alley songs on piano rolls. (Jane Kramer/EKM Nepenthe.)

pianos playing at once, as house composers worked out new compositions and **song pluggers** demonstrated them by playing and perhaps singing them for customers. Theater performers also stopped by when in town to try out and select new songs for their shows, the primary means by which most listeners became familiar with popular music. (In the 1920s, the new recording industry began to assume some of the responsibility for popularizing songs; but although radio stations were playing popular recordings in the thirties, it was yet another decade before radios became widely enough available to make that medium influential in determining the popularity of a song.)

The Songs Tin Pan Alley publishers produced only popular songs, and these were nearly uniform in style, beginning with a brief piano introduction, which might include references to the melody of the song or might simply set the key and the tempo, and proceeding with the **verse-chorus form** that had become standard well before the time of Tin Pan Alley. Nevertheless, the dozen or so superb songwriters of the period developed their own styles and sounds to produce hundreds of great songs that continue to please listeners today.

The verses of a Tin Pan Alley song narrated a story or described a situation or a portrait, whereas the chorus, which was repeated after each verse, echoed or commented on the story. Even the songs of the so-called Gay Nineties often told tales of tragedy and loss, although their chorus might not reveal the sad nature of the song text: only those who sang or heard the last verse of a song, for example, might be aware that the loved one extolled in the chorus has passed away.

Most songs had at least two, and often several, verses, but in time the verses became less and less important, listeners clearly preferring the memorable chorus melodies and often scarcely recognizing a song's less-tuneful verse(s). For this reason, by the 1920s, Tin Pan Alley composers were writing shorter verses and fewer of them. Further, since early recordings could only contain three or four minutes of music on a record side, the verse of a song might well be omitted in recorded performances—another reason for composers not to spend precious time and effort writing them. Even when time allowed for a verse, performers often chose to repeat the familiar chorus instead, inviting an audience, if present, to sing along; and finally many Tin Pan Alley composers simply wrote songs without any verses at all.

Although largely writing songs to order, early Tin Pan Alley composers nevertheless produced many wonderful tunes still well remembered today. A large number, including "After the Ball" (1892), "The Sidewalks of New York" (1894), "Casey Would Waltz with the Strawberry Blonde" (1895), "Meet Me in St. Louis, Louis" (1904), and "Take Me Out to the Ball Game" (1908), were waltzes, reflecting the popularity of European operettas (see p. 252) and other European music.

Ragtime, although an instrumental music, had strong influence on a number of early Tin Pan Alley songs, although most so-called "ragtime songs" only approximate the mood and style of ragtime without following ragtime's systematic opposition of a syncopated melody and a nonsyncopated bass.

(AP/Wide World Photos.)

Sammy Cahn
"The popular song is America's greatest ambassador."

Shorter verses
↓
sometimes no verses
↓
more emphasis on the memorable chorus (the catch)

Ragtime influence

"Hello! Ma Baby" (1899) by Joseph E. Howard, "Bill Bailey, Won't You Please Come Home" (1902), and "Waiting for the Robert E. Lee" by Lewis F. Muir (1912) are among the lilting ragtime-flavored songs of early Tin Pan Alley.

Jewish American songwriters dominated Tin Pan Alley's years—those lying between the two World Wars, or from about 1920 to about 1945. Although forming a small percentage of the population in the early years of the United States, Jews had been actively involved as performing musicians and music teachers in various urban areas of the country, and had contributed significantly to the popular song industry from its beginning. As their population in this country increased dramatically, Jewish Americans made phenomenally successful careers in various areas of show business, including popular song.

uneducated

Figure 59
Irving Berlin.
(The Bettmann Archive, Inc.)

used the black keys on piano
—had a trick keyboard built

Irving Berlin (1888–1989)   The long-lived **Irving Berlin** (Figure 59) was born Israel Baline in western Siberia, but his only memory of his native country was of himself lying huddled in a blanket, watching from the outskirts of town as Cossacks set fire to his Jewish neighborhood. Fleeing Russia with his family, who settled in 1893 in a poor tenement in New York City, the small boy began selling newspapers on the streets and soon became fascinated with the popular songs he heard pouring through the doors of busy taverns and cafés. Singing for pennies on street corners and in saloons, and as soon as he was old enough (eighteen) as a singing waiter, he soaked up the sounds that later emerged in his own hugely varied body of work: barroom ballads, ethnic songs, folksongs, novelty songs, ragtime, the blues, and jazz.

While working on Tin Pan Alley as a song plugger, Berlin began to write songs for vaudeville and other forms of musical entertainment. "Alexander's Ragtime Band," written for a vaudeville show in 1911, became his first hit song. Totally immersed in the American popular music and music theater scene, Berlin went on to become one of the best-known and most popular of all American songwriters.

A self-taught musician, Berlin was only comfortable playing on the black keys of the piano, which limited him to playing in one key—strangely, a key (G-flat or F-sharp) many pianists consider particularly difficult. This posed a problem, since a composer must be able to write in different tonalities to match the range of a singer's voice or add variety to a piece of some length by **modulating** (changing systematically) from one key to another. Different keys also seem to have varied effects, some warm and rich, for example, others cool and light, making one key more suitable than another for a particular song. So Berlin had a trick piano built on which he could slide a board to change mechanically the key in which he was playing while still using primarily the black keys on the keyboard.

In 1919, Irving Berlin formed his own publishing company, while continuing to write prodigious numbers of songs, many of them for the Broadway stage. In the 1930s, he moved to Hollywood to write for movie musicals. He wrote about 1,500 songs, and close to 1,000 of his songs are still in print. There seemed no limit to the range of his talent and his musical imagination.

Listening Example 26

Tin Pan Alley Song

Composer
Irving Berlin

Title
"Blue Skies"

Written for a 1926 musical *Betsy* (long since forgotten), this appealing song was later used in several movies, including *Blue Skies* (1946) with Fred Astaire and Bing Crosby.

Form
Strophic, verse-chorus. Each four-line verse is succeeded by the more tuneful eight-line chorus.

Meter
Duple. The lively piano accompaniment and interludes give the song a distinct ragtime flavor.

The rollicking tunes and jolly rhythms of many Berlin songs reveal his attraction to syncopated popular dance music; others have a warm, romantic character. "White Christmas," "Easter Parade," "Always," and "Blue Skies" (Listening Example 26) name only a few of Irving Berlin's many songs that have become classics of American music, as much a part of American culture as any folk song. "A good song embodies the feelings of the mob," he once said. "And a songwriter is not much more than a mirror which reflects those feelings."

Berlin's patriotic song "God Bless America" has a curious history, having sparked controversy from the time singer Kate Smith introduced it in 1938. The public received the song with wild enthusiasm, and Berlin, thrilled, donated all royalties from that song in perpetuity to the Boy Scouts and Girls Scouts of America: but liberal commentators attacked it as jingoistic, flag-waving, and sentimental, whereas on the right, according to a 1940 *Time* magazine story, the song "brought on a wave of snide anti-Semitism directed at composer Berlin." Leftists attacked the song's lack of respect for separation of church and state, and right-wingers resented a non-Christian born in another country telling God that He should bless America. Yet not a few Americans enthusiastically proposed replacing "The Star Spangled Banner" with "God Bless America" as the country's national anthem.

A painter as well as a musician, Berlin passed his last years in quiet retirement, universally acknowledged—long before the world celebrated his hundredth birthday in 1988—as the elder statesman of American popular song.

Jerome Kern (1885–1945) Born to a prosperous New York family, **Jerome Kern,** unlike his near contemporary Irving Berlin, had a sound music

[handwritten marginal notes: attraction to syncopated pop. dance music & romantic character]

[handwritten marginal notes: controversy in Berlin's "God Bless America"]

[handwritten marginal notes: educated studied in London → influence of European sound.]

education. He studied in London for a time, composing songs for the British musical stage, and absorbing something of a European sound that would affect his music always. He intended, in fact, to become a composer of classical music but found himself irresistibly drawn to the popular music theater and began writing songs for Broadway.

Kern's first songs were simply interpolated into British shows imported to Broadway, according to the custom of that day, when songs usually were unrelated to the plot of a show and therefore could be added or substituted at will. Many composers took advantage of the opportunity to write one or more songs for a show without having to be responsible for the entire score.

Like Berlin, Kern worked as a Tin Pan Alley song plugger and a rehearsal pianist for Broadway theaters before he began writing for his own shows (see Chapter 15, p. 259). His songs often resemble those of Irving Berlin, although they often include more complex harmonies and sophisticated chord changes than had been used by Berlin and other early Tin Pan Alley songwriters. Also like Berlin, Kern wrote for Hollywood sound movies, finding them a congenial medium to introduce many of his finest late songs, including "The Last Time I Saw Paris" (from *Lady Be Good,* 1941) and "Long Ago and Far Away" (from *Cover Girl,* 1944). We shall consider music for theater and films in Chapters 15 and 16; but many of Tin Pan Alley's greatest hits, written for plays or movies that have been largely forgotten, still live prominent lives quite independent of the theatrical vehicles that launched them long ago.

Cole Porter (1892–1964)

The early life of **Cole Porter** (Figure 60), another major contributor to the Golden Age (1920s–1950s) of American

Figure 60
Cole Porter (1892–1964). (The Cole Porter Musical and Literary Property Trusts.)

popular song, could hardly have differed more from Irving Berlin's. Wealthy, privileged, and very highly trained (in Paris under classical musicians), Porter took his career as composer/lyricist seriously, working every bit as hard as anyone dependent upon his job for a living. His witty, sexy, sophisticated lyrics expressed basic human emotions in clever, fresh, and subtle ways—often so risqué as to earn him the nickname "the genteel pornographer."

Unlike Berlin's tuneful melodies, many of Porter's sophisticated tunes are quite difficult to sing. Often extremely chromatic, they wind their stepwise way sequentially up and down the scale, arriving just where and when they should but posing hazards to the vocalist along the way. "I've Got You Under My Skin," "In the Still of the Night," "You Do Something to Me, "All of You," "Begin the Beguine," and "Just One of Those Things" all illustrate the narrow steps and chromatic intervals typical of a Porter melody, and "Night and Day" (Listening Example 27) makes clear why many musicians prefer to listen to Cole Porter than to perform his music. (Porter is said to have referred

[handwritten margin notes: career composer/lyricist took that seriously ↑ (risque) difficulty in singing fluctuation of vocals from high to low]

Cole Porter Song

Title
  "Night and Day"

Form
  Verse-chorus

The melody, designed by Porter to fit the narrow range of Fred Astaire's singing voice, seems uniquely suited to enhance the text. The singer describes the voice within him which, like "the beat, beat, beat of the tom-tom," keeps repeating, "you, you, you." Thus the melody of the verse repeats one note thirty-three times and another note, a half-step higher, twenty-nine consecutive times. (Porter once suggested that he had been inspired to write the song after hearing religious chanting from a mosque in Morocco.)

Astaire introduced the song in Porter's 1932 musical *Gay Divorcée,* and despite the severely compressed vocal range and the tortuously chromatic chorus melody, it was a sensation from the start. Irving Berlin shared the public's enthusiasm for the song, declaring to Porter, "I think it is your high spot."

After the accompanying ensemble plays the chorus through once, Astaire sings the verse and chorus, and the instrumental ensemble plays a brief but effective closing passage.

to creating a new melody as "delicious torture," a sentiment hardly likely to have been expressed by the practical, down-to-earth Irving Berlin.)

George Gershwin (1898–1937)

Born and bred in Brooklyn, New York, **George Gershwin** (Figure 61) worked as a song plugger on Tin Pan Alley while still a teenager, banging out tunes for singers and dancers. Soon his own tunes began attracting the attention of Broadway publishers, and before he was twenty he became a house songwriter for the T. B. Harms publishing firm, one of the most important on the street. An excellent pianist, Gershwin was also in demand as an accompanist for professional singers.

An early Gershwin song, "Swanee," written for a Broadway *revue* (a variety show—see p. 250) when he was twenty-one, garnered little attention until the popular singer **Al Jolson** (1888–1950) adopted it as a regular part of his performances. Jolson's dramatic, full-voiced singing style and impassioned delivery made the song an instant hit—the biggest hit song of his career—and brought Gershwin into great demand to write songs for the musical theater. During his short lifetime he wrote the scores for some 30 musicals and composed over 600 songs, many of which, including "Someone to Watch Over Me," "'S Wonderful," and "I Got Rhythm," were defined not only by Gershwin's beautiful melodies and complex harmonies, but also by clever lyrics written by George's brother Ira. (**Ira Gershwin** [1896–1983] wrote the words to one of George Gershwin's most beautiful songs, "Our Love Is Here to Stay," in moving tribute to his brother's tragic death from a brain tumor, at age thirty-nine.) The youngest Gershwin brother, Arthur, was also a songwriter, although he never became very well known.

Handwritten margin note: Al Jolson – "Swanee" (singer) → Put Gershwin in the music light

Figure 61
George Gershwin (1898–1937). (The Bettmann Archive, Inc.)

Gershwin, like Berlin, Kern, and Porter, also wrote for Hollywood movies, bringing to them the same sophisticated skills he had honed on Broadway. But unlike the other great Tin Pan Alley songwriters, Gershwin had strong, even compelling interest in classical music and jazz. Although not a jazz musician himself, his musical language has the sounds and the flavor of jazz, and his songs lend themselves particularly well to jazz interpretations. His richly dissonant harmonies include sometimes humorous, sometimes plaintive turns and embellishments, making his music absolutely recognizable as his own; and his hauntingly beautiful melodies render his songs as meaningful and as well loved today as ever.

[handwritten margin note: had strong interest in classical music & jazz]

Decline of Tin Pan Alley

Several factors contributed to the gradual lessening of the influence of Tin Pan Alley on American popular music. Inevitably, popular taste began to change after half a century of domination by one powerful system. Sentimental songs that retained significance through the years of World War II became less relevant after the war was won, the troops were home, the economy boomed, and youthful tastes came to the fore. Humorous, nonsensical "novelty" songs accommodated the lightened mood; Latin rhythms attracted wide audiences; songs from the country and from the West joined and in some cases replaced the urban song style that had dominated American popular music for so long.

Coincidentally, in 1940 the American Society of Composers, Authors, and Publishers (ASCAP), founded in 1914 to assure its members just compensation for the public use of music, enforced a strike against the major radio networks, which would not meet ASCAP's demands for fees significantly higher than were currently paid. For over a year, pending settlement of the strike, radio stations could play no new recordings of Tin Pan Alley music. Desperate for new music to program, the stations readily accepted music offered them by a newly formed organization, Broadcast Music Incorporated (BMI), whose members were generally younger than and largely unaffected by the professionals of Tin Pan Alley, and whose music reflected varied regional tastes.

The tide was about to turn, bringing a wave—many waves—of new sounds in popular music.

[handwritten margin note: Decline: • tastes in music changed • strike made by Pan Alley associates]

(Archive Photos.)

George Gershwin
"True music must repeat the thought and inspirations of the people and the time. My people are Americans and my time is today."

Terms to Review

ragtime   A written piano music, duple in meter, moderate in tempo. The left hand marks the beat while the right hand plays a syncopated melody.

chromaticism (chromatic, adj.)   Use of tones not belonging in a particular major or minor scale.

cakewalk   A plantation dance with syncopated melodies, including the *short-LONG-short* figure that became characteristic of ragtime.

finale   In music theater, the final scene of an act or of the show.

piano roll   A perforated paper roll on which pianists of the late nineteenth and early twentieth centuries recorded their performances.

player piano   An instrument for playing piano rolls by pumping pedals to force air through the holes in a piano roll as it wound over a tracker bar.

staccato   Short, detached.

two-step or **fox-trot**   A popular American dance derived from ragtime. The meter is duple, the rhythm syncopated, the tempo moderate.

Tin Pan Alley   The name for the popular-music publishing industry from the late nineteenth through the first half of the twentieth centuries. Also, the street(s) in New York City where the publishing houses were located.

song plugger   A music store employee who demonstrated popular songs for customers by playing them on the piano and sometimes by singing them as well.

verse-chorus form   A common song form in which verses relating the song's story alternate with a tuneful chorus, or refrain.

modulate   To change systematically from one key to another, usually by using one or more tones common to each key as a pivot.

Key Figures

Eubie Blake
James Scott
Jelly Roll Morton
Scott Joplin
James Reese Europe
W. C. Handy
Irving Berlin
Jerome Kern
Cole Porter
George Gershwin
Al Jolson
Ira Gershwin

Suggestion for Further Listening

Recordings of Tin Pan Alley songs performed by Joan Morris and William Bolcom

8

Country-Western and Urban Folk Music

As various vernacular musics evolved in America's urban and rural environments throughout the nineteenth century, people living in certain remote areas of the eastern hills continued to sing and play their traditional music much as it had been performed in the countries and in the times of their ancestors. Relatively isolated from mainstream popular music and largely unaffected by modern trends, they passed the old tunes and performing customs from one generation to the next by oral tradition, thus faithfully preserving many early folk ballads—especially those brought to America from the British Isles.

After the Civil War, however, new influences invaded even isolated mountain areas, inevitably affecting the music as well as every other aspect of life. Migrant workers seeking jobs laying railroad lines, mining coal, or working for the textile mills being established in remote hill areas where tough union rules could safely be ignored brought new kinds of music and new musical instruments with them into the hills. Of particular significance was the five-string banjo, on which one string played a constant or repeated pitch called a **drone,** ideal for accompanying hill or country music.

Conversely, mountain people began to take temporary jobs in the cities, from which they brought home new subjects for songs and new musical sounds. Soon new "folk" songs evolved, similar to the traditional ballads but characteristically American in subject and style. Sometimes people lost track of the origin of a song so that one included in the "folk" repertoire might actually have been composed rather than improvised, memorized, and passed down in the traditional way.

From Country to City

In the early 1920s, commercial recording companies began to send talent scouts into the hill country both to search for folk singers and instrumentalists with a distinctive sound and to entice country musicians to come to the cities, where the market for recordings of "old time" music was increasing. In 1925, four musicians from Virginia recording under the name Hill Billies gave rise to the term **hillbilly music,** somewhat scornfully applied to the music of country fiddlers, harmonica players, and singers of traditional country ballads.

127

The hill musicians traveling with tent shows, medicine shows, and vaudeville shows, appearing at county fairs, and participating in fiddlers' contests sang songs concerning the elemental subjects of human experience—love, work, entertainment, family life, death—expressing the deepest emotions in a semidetached, impersonal way that made their music all the more moving. As city listeners perceived the wealth of beauty and entertainment in this unfamiliar style, country music's audience continued to expand.

The trend toward popularity and commercialization, however, signaled the end of the old way of preserving original folk songs and performance practices. Professional country musicians soon adapted to the requirements of the commercial market, expanding their limited repertoire by writing new songs and learning to perform them in a manner acceptable to a city audience. Story-songs, or ballads, were particularly popular, many of them written on dramatic topics of the day: a coal mine disaster, a hanging, the sinking of a ship. By the mid-1920s, when recordings of country music became widely available and brought the country sound to an ever-larger audience, even the country people themselves began to lose track of which folksongs were traditional and which modern creations.

In 1927, two different strains of hillbilly music were introduced to the public—one by a soloist from the Deep South and the other by a singing family from the mountains of Virginia.

Jimmie Rodgers (1897–1933)

Jimmie Rodgers (Figure 62) came from Mississippi but wandered through several states in the course of his tragically brief career. He had little formal training but many creative ideas, and he was willing to try anything suggested by the record producers who promoted him. Although accompanied on his recordings by various and unusual combinations of instruments, Rodgers probably was most effective when he accompanied himself on the guitar, providing appropriately simple support for his clear, pleasant tenor voice that he sometimes used in the falsetto range. He also had a natural **yodel**—a rapid alternation between the full voice and falsetto—later imitated by many country singers. The thirteen songs called "blue yodels," for which Rodgers was particularly famous, had the form and harmonies of the twelve-bar blues (see pages 152–153), with his distinctive yodel added at the end of each verse.

Known as the "singing brakeman," Rodgers drew on his experiences as a former railroad man for some of his songs. Others concerned love gone wrong, cowboys, the southern home he missed, and country folk whom his listeners either recognized or idealized. Although country songs more commonly paid homage to mother than to dad, Rodgers, whose mother died when he was only six, paid sentimental tribute to the father who raised him in "Daddy and Home" (Listening Example 28).

Although Rodgers performed professionally only for about six years, dying of tuberculosis at the age of thirty-six, he became extremely popular

Figure 62
Jimmie Rodgers and The Carter Family, pictured during a recording trip to Victor Studios in New Jersey.

Listening Example 28

Jimmie Rodgers

— Yodel

Title
"Daddy and Home"

Composers
Jimmie Rodgers and his sister-in-law Elsie McWilliams

Meter
Triple; in fact, a relaxed waltz

Form
Strophic (verse-chorus). Notice the irregular number of beats in certain phrases, reminding us that although this is commercial music, the country flavor is strong and effective.

Rodgers plays a brief introduction on the guitar. There are two verses, each followed by the chorus or refrain and Rodgers's beautiful yodeling.

during his short career, during which he established the solo song as an important part of hillbilly music. He had the honor of becoming the first person elected to the Country Music Hall of Fame, established in Nashville, Tennessee, in 1961.

first to be elected in Country Music Hall of fame (1961) Nashville, Ten.

[handwritten margin notes:]
represented close, conservative family.
vs.
Rodgers = soloist

Virginia origin

The Carter Family **The Carter Family** (Figure 62) represented a tradition quite different from that of Jimmie Rodgers: Whereas he typified the hard-living solo wanderer, they represented the close, conservative family. Rodgers's relaxed, bluesy voice made the solo country song popular, whereas the Carters performed as a group, their harmony close and their voices high-pitched and tense.

Alvin Pleasant Carter (1891–1960), his wife Sara, and his sister-in-law Maybelle came from the mountains of Virginia and sang traditional songs, ballads, and hymns in the high-pitched, rather pinched or nasal voices characteristic of mountain people. The innumerable songs the Carters recorded included many joyful camp meeting spirituals, such as we heard in Listening Example 13 (p. 65).

The Carters accompanied themselves with guitar, on which Maybelle Carter developed considerable virtuosity, and with autoharp, a simple folk instrument whose strings are strummed or plucked with one hand while the other hand depresses buttons to form chords. Many of their recordings include fine instrumental breaks between the verses of a song, but "Chinese Breakdown" (Listening Example 29) is a rare example of a purely instrumental piece recorded by Maybelle and Sara Carter. Here Maybelle Carter demonstrates the now widely used country guitar technique of picking a melody on the bass strings, known as the "Carter scratch."

During the 1920s and 1930s, members of the Carter family collected, arranged, and recorded hundreds of American traditional, spiritual, and folk songs, thereby laying the foundation for modern country music, and several generations of Carters have continued to perform country music professionally. **June Carter** is widely known in her own right as a singer who delivers

[handwritten margin note:]
Instrumental —

Listening Example 29

The Carter Family

Title
"Chinese Breakdown"

Composers
The Carter Family

Meter
Duple

Style
Mountain music

This is the music bluegrass was based on: good-natured, virtuosic string playing, steady in tempo, happy in mood. Notice the marked **backbeat** (accents on *two* and *four*) in Sara Carter's autoharp, which accompanies Maybelle Carter's melody cleanly picked on the bass strings of the deeper, more mellow guitar.

great country songs, earthy or spiritual, with the plaintive wail of a mountain girl. Appearing regularly on Nashville's Grand Ole Opry in 1950, she befriended Elvis Presley and Hank Williams (she is godmother to Hank Williams, Jr., as well as Roy Orbison's sons) and met Johnny Cash, who would become, in 1968, her third husband. In 1997 she appeared in the film *The Apostle,* and two years later, at the age of 70, she released a new album titled *Press On.* June Carter and Johnny Cash's daughter Roseanne Cash has been a major country music performer since the 1980s. Roseanne's stepsister Carlene, who kept the Carter name, carried her country roots to England, where she recorded with assorted rockers, combining the sounds of rock with country in her own distinctive way.

Styles of Country Music

By the late 1920s, most Americans had radios, which brought hillbilly or "old-time" music and religious country music, called **gospel,** into homes across the country. The typical country radio program, of which *The Grand Ole Opry* in Nashville was the best known, included sentimental parlor songs, gospel hymns, old English and American ballads, and work songs performed by country singers, usually accompanied by a fiddle or banjo and sometimes by a guitar. String bands, consisting of several fiddles, one or more banjos and guitars, and sometimes a string bass, played rollicking dance tunes. The popular radio shows also included "dance songs," in which string bands alternated verses with a solo voice.

Country and folk musicians seem gifted with the ability to absorb and reflect in their music various eclectic influences and life experiences, thereby developing characteristic sounds, country in flavor but distinctive in style. Many kinds of rural music have evolved across America, reflecting local experience and preference in a rich variety of ways, producing a great body of modern country and folk musics of seemingly endless variety and charm.

Some rural music reflects country folks' perception of and reaction to urban developments that inevitably bring change to the country way of life. The opening of mines in the hill country, highways sprawling through pristine country fields, economic depressions, wars, the commercialization and urbanization of modern life all spurred folk expression.

American Folk Ballads Topical songs—personal stories relating current political or social events—have always had a place in American folk music, but their topical nature discouraged their survival beyond memories of the events they described, and few we remember today are much more than a hundred years old. About the turn of the twentieth century, however, the growth in the trade union movement and passionate interest in numerous social causes produced a large number of topical songs, most of them aimed at a city rather than a rural audience, and most with a decidedly leftist bent. Throughout the early years of that century, railroads, representing progress and the future, had a sheen of glamour and proved a popular subject for ballads,

[handwritten margin notes:]
radio expanded the listening of country music

life's events sparked folk expression.

railroad subject matter

including the very familiar "Wabash Cannon Ball," written and recorded by Roy Acuff in 1936. Although composed, written down, and commercially disseminated, such ballads had much of the flavor and appeal of the traditional folk ballads discussed in Chapter 2 and are reminiscent of the broadside ballads whose topics were relevant to an earlier age.

One of the most popular and enduring American ballads, "The Ballad of Casey Jones" (Listening Example 30) describes a train wreck that actually occurred in 1900—although not exactly as the song relates the tale. The famous ballad has an uncertain history: A laborer named Wallace Saunders (or Wallis Sanders), who had known and liked the engineer Casey Jones, seems to have set the story of the wreck to an old railroad song called "Jimmie Jones," altering the events, however, to be more dramatic than they actually were and thereby making Casey Jones a folk hero.

Saunders, who was black, never received a penny for the song, which white entertainers made into a grassroots hit and which in time acquired a catchy chorus, repeated after each verse. Today, a century after the famous crash occurred, this early American song lets us relive the heroic last moments of a flawed but courageous man, whose legend survives today.

Bluegrass   In the 1930s and 1940s, **Bill Monroe** (William Smith Monroe, 1911–1996) blended old-time string band music with the holler of the blues and the improvisation of jazz to create a music called (since the 1950s) **bluegrass,** a virtuosic instrumental style rooted in mountain music such as The Carter Family performed. This revival of a traditional music took its name from Monroe's string band called the Blue Grass Boys (Figure 63), named for his home state of Kentucky, whose music on the radio and on recordings soon became widely popular and commercially important.

Bluegrass is unique among country musics, which consist mostly of song, in being primarily an instrumental concept. The bluegrass ensemble includes a fiddle, a guitar, a string bass, a five-string banjo, and often a mandolin—a popular Italian instrument that produces a delicate yet vibrant sound when its strings are plucked. The **acoustic,** or natural, instruments of a bluegrass band make the characteristic timbres light, but the fast tempos and virtuosic playing provide plenty of excitement.

Besides being a virtuoso performer on the mandolin, Monroe also set a new vocal standard with his haunting calls and high-pitched harmonies (the high lonesome sound) based on hymn-singing techniques learned in his youth, as heard in "It's Mighty Dark to Travel" (Listening Example 31). Even with bluegrass ballads, however, sung in the high tones and with the close mountain harmony introduced to urban music by the Carters, the emphasis is on important instrumental interludes or breaks. No less than other country musics, bluegrass has absorbed varied influences and adapted its sound to suit evolving tastes. The verse-chorus form of bluegrass ballads reflects the style of Tin Pan Alley; the virtuosic instrumental playing owes homage to jazz; the manner in which Monroe and his musicians sometimes

American Folk Ballad

—tells a story

Title
"The Ballad of Casey Jones"

Words
Wallace Saunders

Tune
Anonymous

Performer
Johnny Cash

Form
Verse-chorus

Meter
Four beats to the bar

Tempo
Fast

The engineer John Luther Jones, nicknamed Casey for his hometown of Cayce, Kentucky, had safely delivered the fast passenger express known as the Cannonball to Memphis, Tennessee. Tired from his long run from Canton, Mississippi, Jones intended to rest for the night; but learning that the engineer scheduled to run the Cannonball south was ill, Jones agreed to take over the run which finally began an hour and a half late. Proud of his record for meeting schedules, Jones determined to make up the lost time and nearly succeeded in doing so by running his train at more than 100 miles an hour at a time when speeds of 70 or 80 miles an hour were considered highly daring for passenger trains. But his reckless speed caused him to miss signals warning that several cars of a derailed freight train lay sprawled across the tracks straight ahead of him. Had he slowed as he properly should have, approaching the end of his run, a collision could have been averted; but Jones saw the danger too late, commanded his fireman to save himself by jumping off the train, and stayed in the cab himself to meet certain death. Desperately squeezing the throttle and brakes to slow the train to less than 50 miles an hour before it finally slammed into the train ahead, he spared his passengers injury, and all escaped unharmed.

Verse
Singer/guitarist Johnny Cash begins the tale, singing slowly, almost tentatively, lightly accompanied by the guitar in a manner reminiscent of *recitative.*

American Folk Ballad

Verse
Cash launches into the story, revving up the tempo and establishing a driving beat, to which the audience responds by clapping along.

Chorus
(begins, "Casey Jones mounted to the cabin")

(Brief "brassy" instrumental interlude)

Verse

Chorus
(Interlude)

Verse

Chorus
Having maintained the steady tempo and upbeat flavor of the song in the impassive country manner, Cash slightly slows the tempo to bring the song to a close.

Figure 63
Bill Monroe playing the mandolin with his Blue Grass Boys at the Nightstage in Boston, MA. (© Cheryl Higgins 1989/ Decisive Moment, Inc.)

took turns playing lead and making virtuoso displays suggests the inspiration of western swing (see p. 141).

The virtuosic performances in Listening Example 32 ("Earl's Break-down") indicate why bluegrass remains among the most appreciated styles of country music today. The musicians **Lester Flatt** (guitar) and **Earl Scruggs** (banjo), who left Bill Monroe's Blue Grass Boys in 1948 to form their own group (the Foggy Mountain Boys) and develop a distinctive style of blue-grass, greatly popularized this stimulating country music: The smoother vocal

Bluegrass

Composer
Bill Monroe

Title
"It's Mighty Dark to Travel"

Performers
Bill Monroe and his Blue Grass Boys

Form
Verse-chorus

Meter
Four beats to the bar

Tempo
Fast

This classic bluegrass piece has all the characteristics that made bluegrass popular. A hard-driving song full of lonesome imagery, it features virtuosic interplay among the acoustic instruments, and the high-pitched, close harmony associated with country singing.

Instruments
Besides the smooth, blue-tinged fiddling and the solid string bass line, we hear Earl Scruggs's three-finger-style banjo playing, the dramatic guitar runs of Lester Flatt, and Monroe's outstanding mandolin playing.

Vocals
Monroe sings several of the verses, accompanied by the instruments. Flatt joins him in the choruses, his high voice piping above the main melody, country style.

Chorus
The instruments play the chorus as an introduction to the song.

Chorus
Vocal duet.

Chorus
Instrumental.

Verse
Monroe, with instrumental accompaniment.

Chorus
Vocal duet.

Further verses and choruses alternate, with Monroe singing the verses, and the choruses performed either as vocal duet (accompanied) or as instrumental sections. Throughout, the rhythmic intensity, instrumental virtuosity, and tight vocal performance exemplify all that bluegrass lovers enjoy about this brand of country music.

— fast vocals fast tempo

fast tempo —
(Banjo)
(Fiddle)

almost has an improvpou effect to it between the banjo r fiddle

Bluegrass

Title
"Earl's Breakdown"

Composer
Earl Scruggs

Instruments
Guitar (Lester Flatt), banjo (Earl Scruggs), mandolin, fiddle, bass

Form
Variations on a tune

1. The banjo presents the tune, which has two parts, acompanied by the other instruments. In the second part, Scruggs uses a tuner to bend the pitches expressively.
2. The fiddle offers virtuosic variations on both parts of the tune.
3. Scruggs takes the tune back, with chromatic variations, again bending the strings in his distinctive style.
4. The fiddle ranges ever more widely in pitch, treating only the first half of the tune.
5. The banjo introduces a new picking style as the excerpt tapers off.

Throughout the example, as the soloists trade turns, please listen attentively to *all* the instruments, including those playing stimulating accompaniment to the exciting solo performances.

Flatt and Scruggs's band breaking of from Monroe –

harmony of Flatt and Scruggs's band, as well as Scruggs's dazzling banjo technique and Flatt's guitar trick called the Lester Flatt G-run, in which the guitar concludes another instrument's solo break with a strong bass figure, all attracted a wider audience to classic bluegrass. Monroe strongly resented the success of Flatt and Scruggs, but during the folk revival of the early 1960s (see p. 146), he accepted the title they and other young bluegrass musicians bestowed on him as the Father of Bluegrass. Monroe continued to perform at the Grand Ole Opry until shortly before he died.

During the 1960s, the vibrant sound of the acoustic string instruments and the brilliant playing of the instrumentalists made bluegrass particularly popular on college campuses, in coffeehouses, and at folk festivals around the country. Bluegrass has flavored television shows—*Beverly Hillbillies* (theme song by Flatt and Scruggs), *Petticoat Junction, Green Acres*—and films—*Bonnie and Clyde,* and the famous "Dueling Banjos" of *Deliverance,* for example. In 1954, Elvis Presley recorded a revved-up rockabilly version of

Monroe's song "Blue Moon of Kentucky." Other references to bluegrass include Steve Wariner's 1990 "Domino Theory," sung in the high-pitched tones of mountain music and accompanied by mandolin, steel guitar, and fiddles. The title cut of Vince Gill's 1996 album *High Lonesome Sound* beautifully updated the traditional bluegrass sound.

Today's performers in bluegrass style include Alison Krauss and Rhonda Vincent among many others. In 1995, songwriter-singer-instrumentalist Steve Earle accompanied "Train a Comin'" with unamplified instruments only, and his 1999 CD *The Mountain,* on which he played his songs accompanied by the Del McCoury Band (mandolins, banjos, guitars, fiddles, and upright basses) became a standard-bearer of contemporary bluegrass. Recently several bands, including one from New England called Northern Lights, have gained national attention playing tight instrumentals and close-knit harmonies in so-called *newgrass* style. And the passionate bluegrass fans who gather every summer at bluegrass festivals around the country burn with a zeal approaching that of old-fashioned religious camp meetings.

Cajun Music Evicted by the British from their homeland in Acadia (Nova Scotia) in the mid-eighteenth century, the French Acadians (later called Cajuns) sought asylum in the bayous of southwest Louisiana, finally settling in a remote area south of New Orleans. There, relatively isolated from most of American society, they shared space with African Americans, many descended from French-speaking "free men of color." Continuing to speak French, they slowly evolved a *patois,* or mixed language, of their own.

Although the sensitive listener may detect a hint of tragedy in **Cajun music,** the sound is prevailingly light-hearted, with dance rhythms and catchy melodies dominated by the wonderfully raucous sound of the accordion. The Cajun accordion, with ten melody buttons (instead of piano keys) on one side and two bass accompaniment buttons on the other, produces a loud, vibrant sound requiring singers to produce a high, strained tenor voice that will carry over the roaring accordion and droning fiddles. Often one hears shouts ("Oh, ya, yaie!") reminiscent of bluegrass sounds.

Cajuns particularly enjoy waltzes and other dances, such as the two-step in Listening Example 33, which they perform with rhythms and timbres as spicy as their highly seasoned food.

Zydeco A more recent black Cajun style called **zydeco** (zy-deh-CO) is distinguished by spicy hot rhythms and unusual sounds (Listening Example 34). The word is a corruption of the first two words of the French phrase *les haricots sont pas sales,* meaning "the snap beans aren't salted," a traditional indicator of hard times. But there is no misery to the rich zydeco sounds of accordion and harmonica, accompanied by a tambourine and sometimes by a *frottoir,* or a rub board (a washboardlike instrument that the musicians may strap to their chests for ready access—Figure 64) marking the hotly syncopated rhythms. Heard mainly along the Gulf Coast, where a blend of African American French Creole traditions has created a rich gumbo of

Dance effect to it (handwritten margin note)

Cajun Music

Title
Cajun Two-Step (excerpt)

Tune
Traditional

Form
The two-step is a dance organized much like a rag or march in a series of four-measure strains. The taped excerpt includes AABBAAC . . . , and we sense, probably accurately, that the dance could continue almost indefinitely were it not for constraints of concert and/or recording time.

Meter
Duple, as the title implies

Tempo
Fast. The insistently rapid tempo contributes to the exuberant nature of the piece.

Instruments
Accordion, or concertina, and triangle. The instrumentalists punctuate their peformance with occasional joyous shouts.

Gulf Coast – heard (handwritten margin note)

musical flavors, contemporary zydeco bands combine the energy and amplification of the hottest rock groups with the exotic melodies and dialect of the Cajuns to produce their own intoxicating music.

Mainstream artists, too, show the influence of the compelling Cajun and zydeco musics. Paul Simon's tribute to zydeco and its late "king," Clifton Chenier—"That Was Your Mother"—formed one of the highlights of Simon's multimillion-selling *Graceland* album, for example. When asked what drew her to Cajun, country singer Mary Chapin Carpenter (who won a Grammy in 1992 for her Cajun-spiced "Down at the Twist and Shout") replied, "In no particular order: percussion, fiddle, spices, waltzes, Acadian accordion, the tempo, lyrics of love and spirit, gumbo, wails, Highway 10, darkness, dance halls."

Nashville Sound
When rock and roll exploded on the popular music scene in the early 1950s, the country-western music industry faced imminent disaster. **Rockabilly** responded to the new music by combining country themes with the rhythms and instrumentation of rock and roll as the audience for traditional country music fell away, record sales decreased, and radio

Zydeco

Title
"Tu le ton son ton" ("Every Now and Then")

Form
Twelve-bar blues

Meter
Quadruple

Tempo
Moderately fast

The famous zydeco vocalist and accordion player Clifton Chenier (1925–1988) performs here, accompanied by electric bass, drums, and washboard (sometimes called the rub board). The song, probably improvised by Chenier, begins with an instrumental three-line, twelve-bar verse. Some of the succeeding verses are sung, others are performed by the instruments accompanied by encouraging shouts from Chenier.

Notice the steady walking bass and the rasping rhythms of the washboard. Generally the performance suggests the influence of rock, or rhythm and blues, more than the country effect of white Cajun music.

[handwritten note: Black vocalist (Blues sound)]

listeners vanished. Nashville, Tennessee, thereupon met rock and roll on its own ground.

Roy Acuff (1903–1992)—a mountain boy from east Tennessee who symbolized the link between old-time early-morning radio, medicine shows, and hotel room recording sessions with modern commercial country music—founded the first modern music-publishing company in Nashville in 1942. Acuff sang in a high, dry, tense, sometimes spine-chilling voice, loud enough to draw crowds to medicine shows before amplification systems were available. Equally at home with gospel, sentimental ballads, and southwestern honky-tonk (pp. 142–143), he retained his immense popularity until his death at eighty-nine—long before which time Nashville had become established as the preeminent center of the country-western music business.

[handwritten note: Found 1st modern music-publishing company in Nashville in 1942.]

Nashville met the threat of rock and roll by combining country themes with pop instrumentation in what came to be known as the **Nashville sound.** Nashville soloists singing of traditional country topics jived up their rhythms and used a "hot" guitar; their accompanying instruments included electric guitars, drums, electric bass, a "tinkly" piano (as played by Floyd Cramer),

[handwritten note: combination of rock and roll ⇅ country music ↓ in order to stay popular]

Figure 64

Left to right: Robert Clemon—accordion; Clifton Edmond—rub board; and Albert Chevalier—accordion. (Photo © by Chris Strach Witz, courtesy of Arhoolie Records, 10341 San Pablo Ave, El Cerrito, CA 94530. From the booklet of Arhoolie CD 307: "Zydeco—The Early Years.")

and sometimes a string section; and often there was a background chorus of voices singing not in the close mountain harmony of the Carters, but in a trained, professional style, much like the doo-wop singers of Motown rock and roll (pp. 221–223). As the strong rhythm and lively instrumentation of recordings by Johnny Cash attracted members of the rock and roll audience, and Tennessee Ernie Ford's recording of "Sixteen Tons" (written by the brilliant country guitarist Merle Travis) soared rapidly to the top of the best-selling charts, other country artists felt compelled to modify their styles by adopting techniques of rock and roll in order to survive as commercial entertainers.

Country Goes Western

Even before bluegrass and the Nashville sound established popularity in the eastern United States, country music moved west, where it developed further dinstinctive styles. People displaced from their jobs by the economic turmoil of the Great Depression, or forced to abandon farms located in drought-stricken areas, left their accustomed environments and roamed west, carrying

Great Depression = movement of people ↓ movement of music

Figure 65
Bob Wills.
(Frank Driggs Collection/
Archive Photos.)

with them their traditional music customs, if little else. This kind of forced migration continued during World War II, as people leaving familiar rural areas to find jobs in the cities brought along their country music tastes. Young people in the armed services had an unprecedented opportunity to associate with others from diverse backgrounds, and many who were from the city discovered that they liked the country music sound.

As the western states welcomed and absorbed country music, they added distinctive flavors of their own. Texans reflected the mariachi sounds of Mexico, the Cajun music of Louisiana, the Hawaiian steel guitar, and the songs of lonesome cowboys in their own versions of country music, which may properly be called **country-western.**

Western Swing Whereas country music in the eastern United States generally reflected the conservative mood and morality of the Christian home, the western country flavor was closer to that of the dance hall. Thus Texans responded to the big band dance craze of the thirties and forties with a dance band style of their own, called **western swing:** To the piano, sax, brasses, and jazz rhythm section of the eastern big band, Texans added fiddles and the steel guitar, and their singers added Jimmie Rodgers–style yodeling. Fast tempos, hot rhythms, and wonderfully virtuosic instrumental solos also indicated a strong jazz influence on western swing.

Bob Wills (1905–1973), the major figure in the development of western swing, knew firsthand and in fact performed country fiddle tunes, Hispanic folk music, African American folk blues, and jazz (Figure 65). His recording of "New San Antonio Rose" (Listening Example 35) became a huge national success in the late 1930s.

Horns —
Dance —

Western Swing

Title
"New San Antonio Rose"

Composer
Bob Wills

Meter
Four beats per measure

Form
A series of strains (**A, B,** and **C**) in the order **ABABCA′CA′**

After a four-measure introduction by the horns, typical of swing danceband music, the horns play **A** in a relaxed fox-trot style (16 measures).

The horns play **B**; then **A** returns, sung this time, with saxophone accompaniment. The vocal, with sax accompaniment, continues with **B** ("It was there I found beside the Alamo . . .")

A new strain, **C** ("Moon in all your splendor"), is sung, accompanied by trumpets, adding a *mariachi* (Mexican) flavor to the sound.

The vocal continues with **A′** ("Broken song, empty words I know . . ." only slightly altered from the original presentation), accompanied by saxes.

The piece ends with *mariachi* trumpets playing **C, A′,** and a concluding measure.

Texas origin

Honky-Tonk While Texas dance halls rang with the sounds of western swing bands, another country-western style developed in the intimate Texas bars and clubs called honky-tonks. The patrons in these small crowded rooms were more interested in listening than dancing to the **honky-tonk** songs, which frankly expressed harsh subjects relevant to the experience of returning servicemen and uprooted or separated families: infidelity, divorce, alcohol, home sickness, separation, loneliness, prison. Singers delivered the rough and realistic lyrics in an earthy, matter-of-fact manner typical of the country style.

loud piano
involvement

Accompanying bands, if any, had a distinctive instrumentation borrowed from the blues, jazz, or Hawaiian ensembles, but electrified in order to be heard in the noisy honky-tonks. An amplified piano, loud enough to carry above the noise of rough drinking crowds, often provided the sole accompaniment.

Although Kitty Wells's 1952 recording "It Wasn't God Who Made Honky-Tonk Angels" was a great hit on the country-western charts—and even though Charley Pride, the only black country music performer to have a long and distinguished career, has found honky-tonk a congenial medium—historically the stars of honky-tonk were white males from the Southwest, including Ernest Tubb, Lefty Frizzell, Hank Thompson, Ray Price, Buck Owens, Merle Haggard, George Jones, and George Strait. For a time, honky-tonk shied away from the wrenching honesty that, like the blues (pp. 151–158), historically helped its listeners confront hard times and death; but recent honky-tonk responds to the new public frankness on subjects such as sex, drugs, and violence with strong new lyrics—often delivered by independent young women teeming with talent and fired with the spirit of female independence.

Cowboy Songs From the time of the earliest talking pictures, Americans flocked to western films, and by the mid-1930s the craze for westerns was full-blown. Films portrayed the West as Hollywood envisioned it: full of wide-open spaces, dramatic scenery, beautiful and virtuous women, and despicable villains, inevitably vanquished by brave and handsome cowboys—many of whom sang romantic cowboy songs.

Hollywoods depictions of cowboys

Some of the Hollywood singing cowboys actually were from the West. **Gene Autry,** born near Tioga, Texas, in 1907, was working as a telegraph operator when, one night in 1927, the great humorist Will Rogers overheard him singing and strumming his guitar and encouraged him to try his luck in New York. Unsuccessful in New York, Autry got a job with a radio station in Tulsa, where he was known as Oklahoma's Yodelin' Cowboy, a tribute to the "Singing (and yodeling) Brakeman" Jimmie Rodgers. A good businessman as well as a highly talented musician, Autry started his own publishing company and film-production company and became the first movie star to get into television. Today the Autry Western Heritage Museum in Los Angeles, California, presents a multiethnic history of the American West and its impact on pop culture.

Autry → Oaklahoma's "Yodel" Cowboy

Tex Ritter, another famous singing cowboy, also came from Texas; but many of the songs he, Autry, and other "cowboys" sang were written by Tin Pan Alley professionals. Among the most famous of these were "Tumbling Tumbleweeds" (featured as a tremulous harmonica solo in the 1991 film *City Slickers*) and "Cool Water," both written by Bob Nolan, a founding member of the famous singing trio called the Sons of the Pioneers. Most of the songs sung by Roy Rogers, who, like Autry, starred in about one hundred western films, were also written by Nolan. Of course there were real cowboy songs as well, many of them with lilting Irish tunes to which nineteenth-century immigrant Irish cowboys set new words describing life on the American range. These, together with the songs composed for western films, became part of the country-western repertoire.

Tin Pan Alley Professionals wrote the cowboy songs most often

By the late 1940s, cowboy songs had largely faded in popularity. Gene Autry, who earlier had recorded songs from the African American blues tradition ("Black Bottom Blues," "Wild Cat Mama," and "Traveling Blues," for example), went on to sing songs in the popular rather than in the western vein. (His best-known songs today are "Here Comes Santa Claus" and "Rudolph, the Red-Nosed Reindeer.") Tex Ritter's biggest hit, "High Noon," was high on the pop rather than on the country-western charts.

The western sound that Autry helped popularize has recently experienced something of a revival, however, partly spurred by movies such as the 1993 hit *Sleepless in Seattle,* which included Gene Autry's "Back in the Saddle" on its multiplatinum soundtrack, and *The Horse Whisperer* (1998). The simple melodies and straightforward lyrics of country-western songs often appeal to listeners less comfortable with the electronics and indecipherable words of some popular musics.

Country Pop

Patti Page's 1950 recording of "Tennessee Waltz" (written by western-swing bandleader Pee Wee King and his vocalist Redd Stewart) proved how popular a country-style song could be if presented in pop format to a general audience, and soon **cover recordings** of country hits were being made by Tony Bennett, Frankie Laine, and other popular singers. The smooth voices and polished styles of Eddy Arnold and Jim Reeves, often accompanied by a string orchestra, also represented country pop, whereas Chet Atkins sang country songs and played his guitar in a style close to that of Tin Pan Alley.

The songs of **Hank Williams** (1923–1953), firmly rooted in the genuine rural tradition of country music, combined elements of blues, gospel, mountain music, and honky-tonk; but his performance style was widely accepted by the country pop audience. At the time of his early death, Williams was the best-known and most financially successful country singer.

Urban Folk Music While bluegrass musicians sought to perpetuate traditional country music values, urban folk musicians performed folklike music in a polished, suave manner designed to appeal to popular music fans. Some songs were settings of new words to traditional tunes, others were newly composed in the folk or country style.

Of great inspiration to the urban folk enthusiasts was a singing hobo, Woody Guthrie, one of many songwriters stirred by the Great Depression to write movingly of injustice and inequality in American society.

Woody Guthrie (1914–1967) The singer-songwriter Woodrow Wilson **"Woody" Guthrie** (Figure 66) evolved from a simple hillbilly singer into a sophisticated composer and performer of protest songs while surviving as a hobo riding the rails, or thumbing rides on the highways, of America. Having seen his own family decimated by forces beyond their control (devastating dust storms, fire, bank failures), Guthrie was convinced that only by

Figure 66
Woody Guthrie.
(Frank Driggs Collection/
Archive Photos.)

banding together—in unions or otherwise—could the common people survive, and these were the beliefs he expressed in his songs, many set to traditional folk and religious tunes.

In the winter of 1940, barely recovering from the trauma of his Great Depression years, Guthrie came to despise Irving Berlin's stirring patriotic ballad "God Bless America." Directly protesting what he heard as cloying sentiment and overblown sophistication, Guthrie composed "This Land Is Your Land (to the tune of a Baptist hymn, "Oh My Lovin' Brother"), which he originally titled "God Blessed America." To Berlin's romantic pastoral imagery ("From the mountains / To the prairies / To the oceans, white with foam"), Guthrie responded, "When the sun come shining, then I was strolling / In the wheat fields waving, and the dust clouds rolling / The voice was chanting as the fog was lifting: / God blessed America for me."

Protest was not a traditional characteristic of country music, but social commentary was, and Guthrie's stirring poems and songs on a variety of social topics formed a major inspiration for the folk revivalists of the late 1950s and the succeeding socially turbulent decade. Indeed, many consider him America's greatest folk poet.

unity = survival theme in his songs

← protest to Berlin's "God Bless America" (Great Depression)

the Weavers (group)
↓
*protest song
tradition is kept
alive.*

Among those inspired by Woody Guthrie, **Pete Seeger,** the son of a famous musicologist specializing in American folk music (Charles Seeger), left college to collect folk songs, learn to play the banjo, and travel with Guthrie in the years before World War II. The younger Seeger formed the Weavers (so-named to reflect "the qualities of rhythm and work"), a folk group dedicated to preserving the political-activist protest song tradition. The Weavers' first great hit, "Goodnight Irene," was written by **Huddie Ledbetter ("Leadbelly"),** a gifted black blues singer and songwriter discovered, while serving a term in jail, by musicologists John Lomax and his son, Alan. The Lomaxes arranged for Leadbelly's release, and the great country blues singer's subsequent performances and recordings were of tremendous influence on hillbilly performers and fans.

The popularity of the Weavers would seem to have rendered them impervious to attacks from the suspicious political right; but the Cold War and the McCarthy era's Red Scare hysteria forced them, temporarily, to restrict their appearances to union halls, civil rights and peace benefits, and college concerts. By the end of the 1950s, however, their popularity was again on the rise. Pete Seeger, too, faced Congressional censure. Hauled before a subcommittee investigating supposed subversive influence in entertainment in 1955, Seeger refused to cooperate and was blacklisted from television for his leftist leanings. His fortunes soared, however, at the end of the decade, when he left the Weavers and forged a highly successful solo career. Ironically, perhaps, in the late 1990s he was inducted into the Rock and Roll Hall of Fame. (Queried recently about his reaction to appearing on that particular roll of honor, Seeger replied, "Rock is what future centuries will probably say is twentieth-century folk music.")

As popular attention diverted to the Kingston Trio's 1958 recording of "Tom Dooley," a murder ballad innocent of political overtones, the **urban folk revival** came into full bloom, forming an important tie between country music and mainstream pop. The Kingston Trio and other suburban, collegiate, clean-cut groups, including the Limelighters, the New Christy Minstrels, and (especially) Peter, Paul and Mary, joined such city-bred singers of "acceptable" protest songs as Joan Baez, Bob Dylan, and of course Pete Seeger to produce commercial music for a sophisticated urban audience. Performing in coffeehouses, in big-city nightclubs, and on college campuses, they also effectively revived interest in early folk music—at least among themselves. The Kingston Trio's four-million-selling "Tom Dooley" had first been recorded in the 1920s by a blind fiddler descended from the sheriff who had arrested the eponymous murderer, Tom Dula. Bob Dylan's haunting "Blowin' in the Wind" (recorded by the Weavers in 1963) is an adaptation of an old slave song, "No More Auction Block for Me." And Joan Baez made serious studies of folk and country music, learning traditional songs and performance customs and bringing them to a receptive modern audience. Baez's recordings of Carter Family songs introduced them to a new audience and also to musicians who composed original "folk" songs modeled on such country classics.

Figure 67
Bob Dylan.
(AP/Wide World Photos.)

Having formed a link between country music and mainstream pop, the urban folk revival can be seen at the other end of a hypothetical chain to connect with rock as well, in the surprising move of Bob Dylan from leader of urban folk to electric rock.

Bob Dylan (1941–) **Bob Dylan** (Figure 67), born Robert Zimmerman in Duluth, Minnesota, followed Woody Guthrie to New York, where Dylan began performing in clubs and recording his original folklike protest songs while learning as much as possible from his ailing idol, Guthrie. His singing voice was harsh, his guitar self-accompaniments unsophisticated; but the passion in his voice and the stirring messages of his texts—written by himself, some on intensely personal issues—made him the favorite figure of the folk revival. This initiated a significant change in the popular music industry: the folk revivalists, like performers in the Tin Pan Alley tradition, had mostly sung songs composed, or handed down, by others; but Dylan's original songs inspired others in the folk revival movement also to write their own material. Rather than new arrangements of traditional tunes, the folk revival movement now produced original "folk" songs, written by the performer(s)— as would become standard in the early days of rock. (We shall meet Dylan again, in Chapter 13, at the 1965 Newport Folk Festival.)

Women in Country

The road life, honky-tonk settings, and all-male bands typical of the country music experience did not encourage participation by women at least during the first half of the twentieth century, when women's seemly, or proper, place in American society was quite rigidly defined. Most of the women who made early successful careers in country music were heavily influenced by pop stars and may be seen as crossover artists bridging country and pop: Thus **Patsy Cline** (1932–1963), who came from a country background and had a strident, powerful country sound, gained high positions on both pop and country charts. **Kitty Wells**'s status as "Queen of Country Music," which she held through the 1950s, faced strong competition from a number of great female singers in the 1960s. **Loretta Lynn,** who also favored honky-tonk instrumentation, and who appealed to beleaguered housewives with such songs as "The Pill," perhaps had the strongest claim to inherit the title.

In the 1990s, women established a commanding, even a dominant, presence in country music, both as writers and singers of "new country." Mary Chapin Carpenter and Reba McIntyre, among others, broke new ground by singing country-style songs about contemporary city people. Mixing old-fashioned values and country instrumentation with frank sexuality and samplings of other vernacular sounds, women, including Shania Twain, LeAnn Rimes, Deana Carter, and Mindy McCready, have reigned securely at the top of the country charts. For much of the summer of 2000, Lee Ann Womack's single "I Hope You Dance" (on the album of the same name) was the top country single.

Harmony singing, too, shows a new strong female influence. Close, tight country music harmonies between a man and a woman, as in the duets of George Jones and the late Tammy Wynette, or Porter Wagoner and Dolly Parton, constituted a kind of musical dialogue, the combination of enormously different but compatible voices implying sexual tension, resolved or not. But even more characteristic of country harmonizing are same-sex combinations, in which the blending of voices is tantalizingly close. The recent somewhat unlikely collaboration of Dolly Parton, Emmylou Harris, and Linda Ronstadt pits three enormously talented but strikingly different country singers together in an amazingly successful sound. Growing up, **Dolly Parton** sang traditional ballads and gospel songs with her eleven brothers and sisters. Besides her pure, clean soprano voice, she also has a genuine talent for songwriting. **Emmylou Harris**'s background is more diversified, but she now sings country songs with a rare combination of strength and fragility. **Linda Ronstadt,** from the Southwest, has a background in Mexican and Spanish music and began her career singing rock-and-roll. A true crossover artist, she has sung operetta and classical songs, but since the 1970s seems to have settled on country. All three women have a wide range of emotional expression, and their combined vocal talents are impressive indeed. Their first album *Trio,* released in 1987 (including "To Know Him Is to Love Him" by Phil Spector), is an outstanding example of traditional harmony singing. As a point of interest, one song on their new album, "After the Gold Rush," is accompanied by synthesizer, strings, and a glass harmonica (see p. 42).

Recent Country

More sophisticated in performance and broader in scope than ever, country music continues to hold a wide audience, as in the early years of a new millennium "new country" vies with "traditional country" on the radio stations and in the hearts of country music lovers. Successful releases by Dwight Yoakam, George Strait, and other popular country singers now come out of California, which competes with Nashville for influence in the country market, as country music faces a veritable identity crisis, challenged by traditionalists (mostly in Nashville) on one hand and modernists (many in California) on the other. At the 2000 (West Coast–based) Academy of Country Music Awards, George Strait and Alan Jackson performed "Murder on Music Row" (Music Row refers to Nashville, where the Country Music Association presents its own annual awards), a stinging indictment of all that West Coast people find wrong with country radio today: "The steel guitars no longer cry and the fiddles barely play, but drums and rock-and-roll guitar are mixed up in your face." Songs such as the Kentucky Headhunters' hit "Rock 'n' Roll Angel" illustrate a new confidence that allowed country musicians in the 1990s to refer good-humoredly to their formerly dreaded competition. Yoakam and others regularly give the hillbilly twang a happy rock-and-roll spin.

A new traditionalism leads other country stars to replace synthesizers, string sections, and pop drumbeats with acoustic guitars and fiddles, whereas some seek to recapture the friction and grit of original honky-tonk. Fiddling and banjo contests regularly draw huge crowds to folk festivals and state fairs. The catch in the throat, the plink of a mandolin, the woozy swoop of a steel guitar, even a modest mountain twang have returned to current country, and the Hawaiian sound, western swing, and—especially—bluegrass have a strong presence in country music today.

Terms to Review

drone   A single tone, sounded continuously or repeated many times.

hillbilly music   A term applied to early country music.

yodel   A singing technique that involves changing rapidly back and forth between the normal and falsetto voices.

backbeat   A heavy accent on the normally weak second and fourth beats of a measure in quadruple meter.

gospel   A folklike religious music. White gospel includes camp meeting spirituals; black gospel has had far more influence on popular music.

bluegrass   A commercial instrumental style, for acoustic instruments, derived from mountain music.

acoustic   A natural, as opposed to electric, instrument.

Cajun music   A country music of the Cajuns (Acadians), vibrant, light hearted, often with a strong dance beat.

zydeco   A rock-flavored Cajun style of country music.

rockabilly   A close amalgamation of country music and rock-and-roll.

Nashville sound   Country music's commercial response to rock-and-roll, with country themes, pop instrumentation, and a heavy beat.

country-western   Western music with a country flavor.

western swing   The Texas swing band style, influenced by Mexican and Hawaiian sounds and by jazz.

honky-tonk   A Texas vocal style, featuring harsh, honest lyrics.

cover recording (cover)   A rerecording of a popular record, sometimes intended to appeal to a broader audience than the original recording addressed.

urban folk revival   A movement popular in the sixties, relating country music and mainstream pop.

Key Figures

Jimmie Rodgers
The Carter Family
June Carter
Bill Monroe
Lester Flatt
Earl Scruggs
Roy Acuff
Bob Wills
Gene Autry
Hank Williams
Woody Guthrie
Pete Seeger
Huddie Ledbetter (Leadbelly)
Bob Dylan
Patsy Cline
Kitty Wells
Loretta Lynn
Dolly Parton
Emmylou Harris
Linda Ronstadt

Suggestions for Further Listening

The Carter Family: "Keep on the Sunny Side" (their theme song)
The Carter Family: "Can the Circle Be Unbroken"
Cajun music: "Fais Pas Ça" ("Don't Do That")
Zydeco albums by Clifton Chenier or by Queen Ida and the Bon Ton Zydeco Band
The *Smithsonian Collection of Classic Country Music*

9

The Jazz Age

As Americans danced into the twentieth century, turn-of-the-century saloons and dance halls rang with the sounds of ragtime, the two-step, and various Latin dances (see p. 202) soon to become even more popular. Fast tempos, syncopated rhythms, and dance band timbres replaced the sedate ballroom dances played by the string orchestras of an earlier time. As dance rhythms became more complex, solo instrumental lines more independent, and instrumental timbres more varied, Americans discovered that listening to the new music was just as exciting as dancing to it. By 1917, they were calling it **jazz.**

The popular writer F. Scott Fitzgerald dubbed the 1920s—the decade of dance marathons, speakeasies, a stock market boom, Babe Ruth, Greta Garbo, and Valentino—"the jazz age," and so that period is often called today (see Figure 68). Of course the roots of jazz lie far earlier, and jazz was not the *only* music popular in the Roaring Twenties, but that was when the new music came to wide public attention through the performances and recordings of a large number of tremendously talented musicians who would dominate the field for decades to come.

The roots of jazz, rich and varied, include white European marches, hymns, and various popular dances; Creole and Caribbean influences; and of course and most significantly the stirring, hot rhythms, dramatic percussive effects, and distinctive vocal and instrumental performance techniques derived from black Africa. It is not surprising, then, that jazz styles vary widely—in mood, instrumentation, tempo, and even artistic intent, although generally jazz is regular in meter, involves so-called *blue notes,* and is improvised to a greater or lesser extent, depending on the performers' inclinations and abilities. Although rooted in folk and popular styles, jazz rarely entered the popular music mainstream. It reached an enthusiastic segment of the popular music audience, of course, but it belongs to America's art music tradition as well.

Blues

The foundations of jazz, primarily an instrumental music, lie in the **blues,** a vocal form whose origins, although stubbornly obscure, derive from African American traditions and date from some time in the nineteenth century (Figure 69). Just when the blues emerged is the subject of dispute, but certainly

Figure 68

Blues, Archibald Motley. The syncopated rhythms of Motley's swaying musicians and dancing couples superbly evoke and reflect the influence of the music of the Jazz Age. (© Archibald Motley/ Chicago Historical Society.)

new emancipated Blacks laid the foundation of blues (theme) - distress

after the Civil War intimations of what we call the blues were heard from slaves and from newly emancipated blacks, who often found their lives *more* rather than less difficult than before they received their freedom. Away from their familiar plantation environment, lonely and in desperate need of money, some became migrants, some went to prison, others held backbreaking, un-rewarding jobs such as digging ditches or laying railroad lines. In their new distress, they sometimes expanded field hollers into simple solo songs, laden with emotional content and highly expressive of their loneliness and pain. In effect, they were singing the blues.

This new kind of solo song, introduced by blacks, was folklike in sound but highly distinctive in character and form. The texts of the early, rural blues addressed every aspect of life, but most concerned work or, especially, love—unrequited, betrayed, or gone wrong. Blues singers expressed their troubles in an unaffected, straightforward manner, without sentimentality and often with a wry or whimsical humor that lessened the sadness while increasing the poignancy of their tale of woe.

They could hardly have guessed the inestimable influence their simple music would have upon the development of every genre of American music.

Form The earliest blues stanzas probably consisted of one line of text sung three times to a familiar or improvised melody. But in time it became

Figure 69
The origin of the blues.
(North Wind Picture Archives.)

customary to sing the first line twice and add a conclusion or response, in the form **AAB** (statement, repeat, response). Because each stanza had *three* lines, and each line had *four* measures or bars, the form is called the **twelve-bar blues**—the only purely American contribution to *musical form*.

> *Hard times here, worse times down the road.*
> *Hard times here, worse times down the road.*
> *Wish my man was here to share the load.*

Melodic Characteristics Blues singers and later instrumentalists adopted the African custom of treating the *third, seventh,* sometimes *fifth,* and less often *sixth* degrees of the scale as neutral or ambiguous tones, the wonderfully flexible **blue notes** the jazz musician lowers or slightly raises to produce gracefully fluid, emotionally expressive melodic lines. Besides these "bent," "tired," or "worried" notes, vocal and instrumental scoops and slides, or **glissandos,** also derived from black African singing, further colored the performance of early blues melodies.

Blues Harmony In time, a simple harmonic pattern emerged in which the tonic, subdominant, and dominant chords occurred in unorthodox order, providing a strong, simple, and distinctive harmonic framework for the blues musicians to improvise around.

> *Line 1: stays tonic*
> *Line 2: IV goes to I*
> *Line 3: V goes to IV goes to I*

It is in the third line that the distinctive harmonic irregularity occurs, as V—which implies a movement toward tonic—surprisingly "regresses" to IV.

Improvisation This asymmetrical, strictly tonal, textually simple form beautifully served the improvising musician in several ways. Vocal and instrumental timbres were limited only by a performer's imagination and the availability of musical instruments, whereas possibilities abounded for subtle rhythmic adjustments over the solidly steady beat. Each of the characteristics of text, form, melody, and harmony described previously further supported the musician's improvisational efforts:

1. Each line of text took about two-and-a-half bars to complete, leaving a measure-and-a-half of thinking time to be filled with half-spoken, half-sung nonsense syllables, later called **scatting** or **scat singing,** or by improvisation on accompanying instruments.
2. Repetition of the first line of text gave the singer additional thinking time to plan the response.
3. Melodies could be embellished and colored by scoops, slides, blue notes, and other creative and expressive effects.
4. The basic harmonic pattern allowed ample harmonic variety, the simple chords supporting without getting in the way of creative ideas.

Soon the rural blues evolved from intensely personal introspection to a form of entertainment, sung around campfires or in the poorest living quarters in the evening when the labor of the day was done. Any available instrument might accompany the voice, perhaps adding its own melodic interest in competition with the vocal (Listening Example 36).

Classic Blues Blues conceived *primarily* as entertainment, performed in theaters and clubs and on commercially distributed recordings, is called **classic blues.** Whereas the country singers accompanied themselves usually on guitar or banjo, classic blues performers often had a band backing them up. More professional, more stylized, more universal than the earlier, primitive or rural blues, classic blues found a wide audience among white as well as black Americans.

The outstanding singers of rural blues were men, famously including Huddie Ledbetter (see p. 146) and Blind Lemon Jefferson among many others, but the early classic blues singers were mostly women, and nearly all of the great blues lyrics are written from a woman's point of view. Again in contrast to folk or country blues, which embraced a wide range of topics, most classic blues concern love—especially "love gone wrong." By the 1920s, theatrical performance was becoming recognized as an acceptable profession for women (white or black), and the field offered many unprecedented social and economic opportunities.

Gertrude "Ma" Rainey (born Gertrude Pridgett, 1886–1939), one of the most imitated and influential classic blues singers and composers, established something of a link between early rural blues and sophisticated blues performances recorded for commercial distribution. Ma Rainey, sometimes called Madame Rainey, and the Mother of the Blues, taught **Bessie Smith** (1894–1937), who became perhaps the most famous of all classic blues singers (Figure 70). Bessie Smith is remembered today for the intense personal feeling with which she imbued her performances, embellishing melodies and bending tones—as in Listening Example 37—to communicate the deepest emotions to her rapt and sympathetic audiences.

Country Blues

Title

"Hellhound on My Trail"

Performer

Robert Johnson (1911–1938), one of the great country blues singers, accompanying himself on his guitar

Form

Twelve-bar blues

The bluesy mood fits the impassioned nature of the text, whereas the varying length of the lines indicates the informality and improvisatory nature of country blues. Notice, too, the manner in which Johnson fills out each line with repetitions of fragments of the text and with eloquent commentary on his guitar. The frequent blue notes and intricate melodic embellishments add to the individuality and the passion of Johnson's performance.

I got to keep movin'. Blues fallin' down like hail.
I got to keep movin'. Blues fallin' down like hail.
I can't keep no money with a hellhound on my trail.

If today was Christmas Eve, and tomorrow Christmas Day,
If today was Christmas Eve, and tomorrow Christmas Day,
I would need my little sweet rider [lover] *just to pass the time*
    away.

You sprinkled hot-foot powder [a voodoo spell?] *all around my*
    door.
You sprinkled hot-foot powder all around my door.
It keeps me with a ramblin' mind, Rider, every old place I go.

I can tell the wind is risin', the leaves tremblin' on the tree.
I can tell the wind is risin', the leaves tremblin' on the tree.
All I need is my little sweet woman to keep me company.

Ma Rainey, Bessie Smith (Empress of the Blues), and a number of other great classic blues singers brought a professionalism and theatrical polish to blues it had never had before, and the blues became a highly profitable medium of entertainment. Of the great classic blues recordings, Bessie Smith's earned the most money for her recording company, but although Columbia Records paid her well, she never received any royalty monies for her efforts, and she died, as the result of an automobile accident, nearly penniless.

Figure 70

American blues singer and
songwriter Bessie Smith.
(Frank Driggs Collection/
Archive Photos.)

"Strange fruit"

Billie Holiday (1915–1959)

Billie Holiday (born Eleanora Fagan) trod softly between the worlds of jazz and pop, although her interpretations of many great blues songs were undeniably those of a great jazz singer. Jazz scholar Nat Hentoff said that Lady Day, as she was respectfully known, could simply say hello, and the sound and rhythm of that one word became the very definition of jazz. Among her most striking innovations was her way of "microphonizing" her voice—using the microphone, at that time a new enhancement, not only to amplify but to alter her voice and add expressive effects.

A tragic figure in her own right, who died possessed of just seventy cents despite having earned a lot of money during her career as singing and recording artist, she once recorded an unforgettable ballad, "Strange Fruit," concerning the appalling tragedy of lynching. The words of the ballad—devastating to hear or even just to read—have a strange history of their own, written not by a black but by a first-generation Jewish American whose parents came to the United States from Russia. Abel Meeropol (1903–1987), whose pen name was Lewis Allen (and who later adopted the two children of Ethel and Julius Rosenberg, whom he had never met, after their parents' execution in 1953), was inspired by a picture of a lynching to write the poem and to set it to music.

Classic Blues

Title
"Lost Your Head Blues"

Performers
Bessie Smith (singer, who probably also created the song by improvisation);
Louis Armstrong (trumpet)

Form
Twelve-bar blues

Harmony
The harmony is entirely based on the I, IV, and
V chords, which occur in the order described on page 153.

Tempo
Moderately slow

The trumpet and piano play a four-bar introduction.

There are five three-line verses. To each line of each verse sung by Bessie Smith, the trumpet responds, answering, mocking, encouraging the singer in turn.

Lightly dissonant piano chords lope along throughout the performance, supporting both voice and trumpet.

The melody remains fairly constant for each verse, although always subject to Smith's supple vocal manipulations. Especially in verses 3 and 5, she ranges slightly afield, but never far, from the original melodic line.

Notice the slight slowing in tempo, or *ritardando,* at the end of the last line, signaling the conclusion of the song.

The performance seems tightly organized and professionally delivered, yet both voice and trumpet suggest literally endless possibilities for interpretation of this famous blues piece. The straightforward delivery of complaint, unburdened by sentimentality, and relieved by slight, wry humor, is characteristic of the blues. Listen for expressive slides and blue notes throughout the piece in both trumpet and voice.

Billie Holiday happened to be performing at that time (the late 1930s) at the Café Society, a club owned by a friend of Meeropol, who persuaded her to sing the new ballad; and her powerful interpretation (she almost never sang a song as it was written) was, and is, breathtaking. So sensitive, so threatening was this first civil rights protest song that for years it was rarely heard, and Holiday's normal label, Columbia, refused to record it, forcing her to go to the far more obscure Commodore. But recent recordings and performances have brought "Strange Fruit" to new audiences, who hear it as hushed and awed as the audience that sat in eerie silence following Holiday's first performance.

Urban Blues It was only a matter of time before the professional publishing and recording industries recognized the commercial potential of the blues, and blues pieces began to be published in sheet music form. White composers started to write blues, and the word "blues" appeared in the titles of many pieces, including some that were not blues at all. Published blues first appeared about 1912, and by the 1920s so-called blues **race records** (the unfortunate industry term for recordings intended for an African American audience) were being mass produced.

As the blues entered the popular music stream, blues composers adapted the twelve-bar form in a manner they supposed would better appeal to a mainstream (white) audience. Intended for performance by professional musicians, the so-called **urban blues** could be more complex in form and more sophisticated in harmony than their rural predecessor; and although some or even most of the stanzas of an urban blues retained the three-line form, one or more verses had the conventional four- or eight-line (sixteen- or thirty-two-bar) form. Soon urban blues, recorded by professional blues singers, were being disseminated to a wide and increasingly appreciative public. As the great blues singers made some of their finest recordings with the outstanding jazz musicians of their day, close connections were established between instrumental jazz and urban blues, both of which shared a folk or popular heritage, a regular beat, subtle rhythmic variations, versatile blue notes, and fluent improvisation.

Although W. C. Handy (see Chapters 7, 19), the African American bandleader and composer who called himself "father of the blues," hardly invented the form, he certainly led it into the world of commercial popular music. As a young man, Handy (Figure 71) learned to play a cornet and (to his Methodist father's dismay) joined a minstrel troupe. He then formed his own dance band, which played in Memphis for a while before moving to Chicago and finally to New York. There Handy began writing and publishing urban blues, including the best-known example, the beautiful *St. Louis Blues* (Listening Example 38). Notice how complex the formal arrangement of this blues piece has become in contrast to the improvised, twelve-bar country blues: Here we have an extremely sophisticated vocal and instrumental performance of a published composition in which the verses vary in melodic content and even in the number of lines per verse.

New Orleans Jazz

As music instruments left over from Civil War military bands became readily and cheaply available, black musicians began playing them in their own manner, improvising freely on favorite familiar tunes. In New Orleans, small brass bands played for parades, concerts, and even for funerals, developing a

Figure 71
W. C. Handy (at left) with Duke Ellington. (Frank Driggs Collection.)

famous tradition that survives today: Having performed solemn music to accompany the funeral party both to the cemetery and—for a dignified interval—on the way back to town, the band breaks into joyous music whose familiar tunes and hot rhythms virtually compel the mourners' healthy return to the normalcy of everyday life.

In time, the bands' instrumental techniques became more individual, the tempos faster, and the mood more high-powered and intense. Although some of the musicians read music, most did not and simply improvised freely on familiar tunes. In a word, they were playing jazz. Soon small bands or **combos** (Figure 72) of black musicians were providing indoor entertainment, their hot new dance music combining the steady beat and stirring tempo of European march and dance tunes with the subtle and complex syncopations of black African and Caribbean effects.

As already noted (see p. 89), New Orleans, which had alternately been under French and Spanish rule and to which many Afro-Latin people had fled from Caribbean settlements such as Haiti and Cuba, offered a rich cultural climate, whose music included popular French, Spanish, Creole, and black tunes; serious and comic opera; and airs from marching, dance, and concert bands. The city generously nourished the exciting new vernacular sound, with the notorious Storyville red-light district of gambling saloons, bordellos, and dance halls offering ample job opportunities for jazz musicians. Thus it is not surprising that New Orleans produced a large number of astonishingly talented jazz musicians who soon attracted others to their city, making it the first important center of jazz.

Urban Blues

Composer
W. C. Handy

Title
St. Louis Blues

Form
Modified twelve-bar blues

Verses 1 and 2 follow the twelve-bar form.
Verse 3 has four lines; the first two rhyme, as do the last two.
The song ends with a fourth stanza, in twelve-bar form, but with
a melody different from verses 1 and 2.

Performers
Bessie Smith, accompanied by Fred Longshaw on reed organ and
by Louis Armstrong (see pp. 160–162) on trumpet. Although the
reed pump organ suggests the rustic flavor of country blues, the
young Louis Armstrong already reveals his mastery as a jazz
musician, competing with Bessie Smith for virtuosity and
emotional expression.

Notice the rhythmic freedom with which Bessie Smith delivers
the words in her big, robust voice and the manner in which she
bends pitches, as on "sun" in the first phrase of the song, with
Armstrong echoing her effects on his trumpet.

Most **New Orleans jazz** combos contained three to eight people playing
clarinet, cornet or trumpet, and trombone, with a rhythm section including
banjo, tuba, and drums. Later, combos playing inside rather than on the
streets added a piano and sometimes replaced the tuba with a string bass.
Having selected a hymn, rag, march, popular song, or blues and agreed upon
the harmonic patterns to be repeated throughout, the musicians began improvising around the tune: The cornet handled the melody; the clarinet wove
countermelodies around it; the trombone provided supporting harmonies; and
the rhythm section marked the beat, a straight four-to-the-bar, with an accent
on *ONE* and a secondary accent on *three*. Early New Orleans performances
were basically collective improvisations played in this manner, the soloists
taking turns improvising complex variations on given (known) melodies
while the other musicians provided rhythmic and harmonic support.

Louis Armstrong (1900–1971) **Louis Armstrong** (Figure 73) survived a violent childhood in New Orleans to become a gentle, kindly,

Figure 72
Members of a jazz
combo.
(© *Washington Post.*
Reprinted by permission of
the D.C. Public Library.)

good-natured man and an incredibly talented musician. He played the cornet
in King Oliver's band as a boy, and in the early 1920s followed Oliver to
Chicago, where Armstrong formed his own band (The Hot Five, later The
Hot Seven) and began making important jazz recordings, including the performance of his wife's composition "Hotter Than That" heard in Listening
Example 39. Switching to the trumpet, Armstrong developed previously inconceivable virtuosic techniques for that instrument, producing pure, clarion
tones that had never been heard before.

Even more significant than his virtuosity, however, were Armstrong's
original and highly creative solo improvisations, as beautifully expressive as
they were technically brilliant. The extraordinarily wide emotional range of
his playing greatly expanded musicians' and listeners' concepts of what jazz
was all about, leading the great bebop trumpet player Dizzy Gillespie (see
pp. 180–181) to express the feeling of many musicians when he said of Armstrong, "No him, no me."

Figure 73
Louis Armstrong.
(© UPI/Bettmann
Newsphotos.)

New Orleans Jazz

Composer

Lillian Hardin Armstrong

Lil Hardin, an outstanding jazz pianist who became Louis Armstrong's wife, performed regularly with The Hot Five, the group that recorded this and many other early Armstrong hits.

Title

"Hotter Than That" (excerpt)

Instruments

Cornet, trombone, clarinet, piano, banjo, guitar

The cornet, trombone, and clarinet take turns improvising while the other instruments provide a rhythmic accompaniment. Armstrong's cornet solos dominate of course. And in his scat singing he "plays" his voice like another instrument revealing a seemingly limitless range of creative and expressive techniques.

Armstrong also sang (in a manner of speaking), scatting in an amazingly creative, often humorous, always expressive way. Finding sadness or humor or elation in a song, he let it issue forth as a purely natural, purely human statement. In this and in every way, he personalized his performances as no one had before, taking the music and making it his own.

Chicago Jazz

Out of New Orleans to Chicago

In the 1920s, after the law shut down New Orleans' lucrative Storyville district, many outstanding jazz artists moved to Chicago, which then became the new performing and recording center for jazz. Chicago's large population, thriving speakeasies, and fledgling recording opportunities—as well as a plentiful supply of jobs in the railroads, stockyards, and mills—soon attracted jazz musicians from all over the country.

In Chicago, many young white musicians became enamored of the sounds of the New Orleans combos and, in the sincerest form of flattery, set out to imitate them. **Dixieland,** the term for this white imitation of New Orleans jazz, in time came to be applied to all early jazz, although musicians distinguished between New Orleans Dixieland and Chicago Dixieland music: The Chicago combos usually added a saxophone to the New Orleans instrumentation and replaced the banjo with a guitar; further, a big-city tension and drive characterized Chicago jazz, which often began and ended with more complex

Figure 74
The Original Dixieland
Jazz Band.
(Frank Driggs Collection.)

improvisations than New Orleans musicians used, and which emphasized the role of soloists to a greater degree. A marked backbeat often enhanced the excitement of the newer style. It has been suggested—but one can never know—that the white musicians actually strove to outdo their models (see Figure 74).

Before the end of the Roaring Twenties, the heart of jazz shifted again, this time to New York City, where numerous combos and many jazz pianists continued to evolve distinctive sounds.

Jazz Piano

Jazz pianists, whose instrument sounded its own harmonies and who could practice independently of other musicians, enjoyed greater opportunity than other jazz instrumentalists to maximize their individuality; and indeed a number of jazz pianists developed distinctive styles extremely influential in the transition from ragtime to jazz. Jelly Roll Morton (see Chapter 7) combined ragtime and *boogie-woogie* techniques to produce his own inimitable jazz piano style, with rhythms looser and melodies less embellished than those of ragtime. Earl Hines (1903–1983) played with a swinging, flexible style usually associated with band instruments rather than with the piano. And Art Tatum (1910–1956), one of the most admired pianists in jazz history, combined his gifts for complex and ingenious harmonic changes and incredibly powerful technique with elements of the piano style called *stride*.

Boogie-Woogie
As accompanying instruments assumed ever more significant roles in performing the blues, the next logical step was adapting the blues to instrumental forms. Thus before 1920, certain ragtime pianists carried the twelve-bar structure, and often the characteristic harmonic progressions of the blues as well, to the piano.

*dancing
+
listening*

*"The Charleston"
(Great Gatsby)*

Unlike the written ragtime pieces, the **piano blues** or **boogie-woogie** was freely improvised, the new jazz pianists accompanying a syncopated melody in the right hand with a characteristic highly rhythmic left-hand ostinato. This **eight-to-the-bar** accompanying pattern (subdividing the four beats of a measure into eight pulses, usually in the pattern *LONG-short-LONG-short-LONG-short-LONG-short*) resulted in complex cross rhythms, which—combined with a brisk tempo and a new driving intensity—quickly made boogie a music popular to dance and listen to (Listening Example 40).

Stride

Stride piano retained the regular left-hand metrical pattern of ragtime, alternating low bass notes on *one* and *three* with midrange chords on *two* and *four* under an improvised melody in the right hand. **James P. Johnson** (1894–1955), "the father of stride piano," certainly furthered the transition from ragtime to jazz, with playing that was more dissonant, more loosely structured, more strictly improvisational, and more highly syncopated than other jazz piano music of the 1920s. Although Johnson composed other kinds of music as well, including "The Charleston," which flappers joyously danced through the Roaring Twenties, he is best remembered for his great stride compositions such as "Carolina Shout" (Listening Example 41).

Fats Waller (1904–1943), who studied with James P. Johnson, developed his own legendary jazz piano style, more driving, intense, and virtuosic than his mentor's. Although Waller went on to become one of the great jazz entertainers and a composer of hundreds of tunes, he never surpassed the beauty of Johnson's technically demanding stride pieces. And although Waller's stride piano playing was a direct descendant of ragtime, Waller rarely wrote out his pieces in full, generally writing only a simple melody line and the most fragmentary additional notations. (All that was required to copyright an original tune was a melody and a title.) Some of his compositions were published as sheet music during his lifetime, and he did record some piano rolls, but neither are considered representative of the performances Waller would have realized from the same pieces.

Sweet Jazz *(Paul Whiteman Orchestra)*

Throughout the twenties, as the center of jazz innovation and performance shifted from New Orleans to other cities, especially Chicago and New York, a tame but attractive music that came to be known as **sweet jazz** reached a wide audience through the sophisticated, classically tinged performances of the **Paul Whiteman** Orchestra, the most popular dance band of its day. Whiteman, a (white) classically trained violinist who adored jazz, but lacked the gift to emulate the uninhibited improvisations of the jazz musicians he admired, formed his band in the early twenties to play jazzy arrangements of popular and even classical melodies. Although Whiteman was known for a time as the King of Jazz, his music bore only a marginal relationship to real jazz. Most of the notes were written out for his musicians, who did not indulge

(Everett Collection.)

Paul Whiteman

"Jazz came to America three hundred years ago in chains."

Boogie Improvisation

Title

"Shout for Joy"

Form

Twelve-bar blues. After a four-bar introduction reminiscent of the familiar "Westminster Chimes," we hear eight three-line verses. (The easiest way to count phrases is to tap your foot on each beat: Eight beats constitutes one line or phrase; each verse contains three lines.)

Accompaniment

The jumping "eight-to-the-bar" left-hand ostinato nearly compels a rhythmic response from the listener—as well as a probable happy smile.

Melody

Over the pounding beat, the pianist's right hand plays joyous melodic improvisations.

Verse 1: After two bars introduce the ostinato, a light-hearted melody enters in the right hand, occasionally embellished with a kind of "shake" between tones.

Verse 2: Dissonant chords mischievously accent the space between beats.

Verse 3: A three-note pattern (da-DA-dum) recurs throughout this verse.

Verse 4: This verse begins with a slightly higher-pitched four-note pattern.

Verse 5: A rising pattern, lower in pitch, with longer note values, is enhanced by the characteristic boogie "shake" for a shimmering effect.

Verse 6: Happy new melodic ideas play over the relentless, compelling ostinato.

Verse 7: This verse is colored by the "shake" and by distinctive chromatic harmonies.

Verse 8: Highest in pitch of all the variations, this one involves intricate finger work in the right hand. The final phrase tapers down to a quiet, unassuming end.

in creative flights of improvisational fancy; but their jazzy timbres and syncopated rhythms suggested to listeners the flavor of jazz.

Not only did the new arrangements relieve musicians from the necessity for extensive improvisation; they also made it possible for jazzy music to be played by larger ensembles than the New Orleans or Dixieland combos,

improvisation wasn't present in Whiteman's music.

↓

less pressure on musician form larger ensembles

Stride Piano

Composer
James P. Johnson

Title
"Carolina Shout"

A shout was a form of religious dance popular on plantations through the nineteenth century in which slaves expressed according to African custom their new Christian fervor. While singers standing around the cabin or praise-house room clapped and sang a spiritual or other religious song, the shouters (dancers) walked and shuffled in a ring, careful not to cross their feet—or sometimes even to raise them from the floor—as for ordinary dancing, for the shout was specifically a form of religious devotion. As the movements quickened and the religious frenzy approached a state of ecstasy, shouters often fell to the ground in complete exhaustion.

Meter
Duple

After a four-measure introduction, the first phrase of the first strain begins its deceptively lazy descent, accompanied by a left hand that ingeniously shifts the accents back and forth from *one* to *two,* or to the "and" between beats.

The first strain is repeated.

The second strain, lower in pitch, further varies the rhythms, rocking the beat from hand to hand.

The harmonic complexity increases with the third strain, implying a quickened pace—though the tempo actually holds steady—as chords in the left hand *respond* to the high-pitched *calls* of the right hand.

Shorter, more fragmented phrases further intensify the last two strains, as the vigorously striding left hand offers ever new variations on the beat.

A cascading four-bar **coda,** or ending section, brings the stunning piece to a fitting close.

providing a more sensuous sound relatively easy on white middle-class ears. It was even possible for two or more instruments to play melodies in unison, making the tunes easy to identify and follow. In this manner, Whiteman often arranged melodies from the familiar light classics, which added to the "respectability" of the sound. And although hardly constituting jazz in any legitimate sense, his arrangements often were quite beautiful in their own right.

As a number of other bandleaders joined the sweet jazz bandwagon, gifted arrangers and orchestrators learned to create arrangements that *sounded* improvised, the best providing leeway for musicians to be as creative as their talent and inclination allowed. Thus sweet jazz marked an important step in bringing jazz to public favor. It also introduced the art of the arranger, which was to become even more significant in the era of the big band.

Symphonic Jazz

In a further effort to exalt jazz in the public mind, Whiteman decided, in 1924, to present a performance of jazz, not in the usual dancehall setting, but in a concert hall, to prove that this music merited the respect of a more serious venue. Anxious to include a new work by George Gershwin in "An Experiment in Modern Music," as he proposed to call this concert (which also included pieces by Victor Herbert and Irving Berlin), he told Gershwin of his plans and requested him to write a piece combining the qualities of symphonic music and jazz only a few weeks before the scheduled concert date. To that point, Gershwin had composed in neither medium; but he understood orchestral music, and his Tin Pan Alley songs captured a jazzy flavor and seemed made for jazz interpretation. Thus he was perhaps uniquely qualified to write the first example of **symphonic jazz.**

Gershwin's *Rhapsody in Blue* (Listening Example 42), originally conceived for jazz band and piano but more often heard today as a piece for piano and orchestra, in all but technicality might be considered a piano **concerto**—normally defined as a three-movement duet between orchestra and solo instrument. As its title implies, however, *Rhapsody* is a loosely organized work, a glorious venture from one beautiful theme to another unhampered by preconceived structural concerns.

Rhapsody vividly demonstrates Gershwin's gift for pianistic writing, exploiting the keyboard instrument's magnificent capacity for wide-ranging timbres, moods, and techniques. Only a virtuoso pianist need attempt to play this piece! Gershwin also used symphonic techniques with skill and originality, weaving motives throughout the fabric of the orchestra and transforming his beautiful themes with seemingly endless creativity. The blues theme that begins the piece, for example, sounds every bit as appropriate in its fast and jazzy reincarnation as in the plaintive, haunting version heard before.

Rhapsody in Blue confused American critics, who were not sure on which grounds to attack it: They found the piece too jazzy for concert music but unacceptable as jazz because it involved no improvisation. But the public

Symphonic Jazz

Composer

George Gershwin

Title

Rhapsody in Blue

Instrumentation

Gershwin originally conceived this piece for jazz band and piano. However, Ferde Grofé (composer/arranger/pianist, 1892–1972) arranged *Rhapsody,* including many orchestral instruments in his score, and the complete version was published for piano solo and orchestra, as it is generally performed today.

Form

The word "rhapsody" implies a loosely organized work, and indeed the one-movement piece consists of a series of melodic sections related in key and style, but following no prescribed formal design. References throughout to the blues theme heard at the beginning help unify the work.

Rhapsody begins with a clarinet run that evolves into the famous wailing slide, or *glissando.* Then the clarinet introduces the memorable blues theme—syncopated, moderately slow in tempo, and emotionally expressive. A muted trumpet takes an irreverent turn with the theme before the piano enters to play an extended, dissonant, and extremely virtuosic *cadenza,* or solo passage. Next the romantic blues theme returns, passionately performed by the full orchestra.

Piano solos alternate with sections for orchestra, or for orchestra and piano. Although some of the piano cadenzas sound improvisatory, all the notes are, in fact, written: Gershwin did not intend performers of the piece to improvise at all.

Several new themes are introduced, including a warm, romantic melody played first by the strings. Gershwin's gift for conceiving sweeping, memorable melodies had much to do with *Rhapsody*'s great success.

Notice as you listen to the piece the manner in which orchestral instruments sometimes are played using jazz techniques. The score (the written music) sometimes calls for the musicians to use

Listening Example 42—Continued

Symphonic Jazz

"fly swatter or brush." The banjo and bass are occasionally directed to "Let string snap."

Wonderful melodies, rich orchestration, intriguing rhythms and timbres, and virtuosic piano playing all contribute to the charms of this popular and enduring work.

greeted *Rhapsody* with enthusiasm, and it remains probably the best-known and best-loved symphonic composition in the world.

Gershwin continued to be interested in concert as well as popular music, although his later concert music never achieved the acclaim of his first *Rhapsody.* He wrote a *Second Rhapsody,* a tone poem (one-movement programmatic orchestral piece) titled *An American in Paris,* Three Preludes for piano, a *Cuban Overture,* and the Concerto in F for piano (Optional Listening Example), each of which reflects the jazz implications that were an inherent part of Gershwin's music vocabulary. (He also wrote the most popular of all American operas, *Porgy and Bess*—pages 291–293—and many of the most affecting love songs ever heard.)

A number of European composers, taking symphonic jazz and especially *Rhapsody in Blue* to their hearts, also created several works in the symphonic jazz idiom. Sweet and symphonic jazz remained in fashion through the late twenties, soothing the troubled audiences of the Great Depression years, while *real* jazz—hot, mostly black—went underground.

But during the 1930s, jazz finally found a popular audience as big band music came into its own. Now Americans were ready to swing!

Terms to Review

jazz   A means of performing music. There are many moods and styles, but improvisation is an inherent characteristic of jazz.

blues   A black vocal music.

twelve-bar blues   The standard form of the blues, consisting of three-line stanzas with four bars, or measures, in each line.

blue notes   Flexible tones, usually (not always) slightly under the normal pitch.

glissando   An expressive slide between tones.

scatting, scat singing   Improvisation on neutral syllables.

classic blues   Blues conceived primarily as entertainment, performed in theaters and clubs and on commercial recordings.

race records   The term used before 1949 by the popular music industry for recordings intended for an African American audience. (Later called rhythm and blues.)

urban blues   Blues pieces written for publication and professional performance, often slightly altered from the standard twelve-bar blues form.

combo   A small jazz ensemble.

New Orleans jazz   Virtuosic improvisation by members of a jazz combo on a given (already known) melody.

Dixieland   A white imitation of New Orleans jazz, faster and more intense than the original style, introduced in Chicago.

piano blues or **boogie-woogie**   A popular piano style with the form and harmony of the twelve-bar blues, but faster in tempo and with a dance beat.

eight-to-the-bar   The ostinato accompanying a boogie, dividing each of the four counts in a measure into a long and a short beat.

stride   A jazz piano style in which the left hand alternates low bass notes on *one* and *three* with midrange chords on *two* and *four*.

coda   A closing section.

sweet jazz   Music with the sound and flavor of jazz, but so arranged as to require little improvisation.

symphonic jazz   Concert music with some of the sounds of jazz but with no improvisation.

concerto   A multimovement (usually three-movement) work for orchestra plus solo instrument.

Key Figures

Gertrude "Ma" Rainey
Bessie Smith
Billie Holiday
Louis Armstrong
James P. Johnson
Fats Waller
Paul Whiteman

Optional Listening Example

George Gershwin: Concerto in F

Suggestions for Further Listening

Abel Meeropol, "Strange Fruit," sung by Billie Holiday
Examples of blues, boogie, and Dixieland included in *The Smithsonian Collection of Classic Jazz*
George Gershwin: *An American in Paris*

10

Jazz 1930–1960

J azz reached a peak of popularity in the mid-1930s, a relatively optimistic period when the Great Depression was finally receding and America's involvement in World War II lay ahead. Recordings and radio programs having made the sounds of sweet jazz widely familiar by then, multitudes of people craved more adventurous listening, and with Prohibition ended, real jazz came to be performed in an atmosphere more congenial to the general public than the small, illegal speakeasies of the twenties. Crowds flocked to hear the *big bands* play, and by 1935 big band music resounded from radios, recordings, juke boxes, and dance halls all over the country.

[handwritten note: 1935 - Big Band Popularity]

Big Band Swing

While sweet and symphonic "jazz" soothed more timid listeners, black jazz musicians were adding instruments to their small combos and developing the vibrant sound that came to be known as **big band** jazz, or **swing.** The new sound was of such huge appeal to whites and blacks of virtually every stratum in society that jazz and popular music came together for a time and swing constituted *the* popular music of the thirties.

[handwritten note: Bigger Sound in comparison]

Both "big band" and "swing" need clarification. The earliest big bands actually had only five or six members, but the standard soon became twelve to eighteen players, in three sections of instruments:

1. Brass (trumpets, trombones).
2. Woodwinds, called **reeds,** in which the player causes small flexible pieces of cane to vibrate (saxophones, sometimes also a clarinet).
3. Rhythm (a guitar and/or double bass, piano, drums).

"Swing," like many terms in art, has several meanings, some rather technical: For example, *swing eighths* are strings of eighth notes performed in uneven rhythm, alternating long and short notes of subjective rather than of measured length. This contributes to the flexible give-and-take, or expressive *rubato,* within the steady jazz beat. But "swing" also refers to a mood, a lilt, a magical effect that great jazz achieves and that sympathetic listeners recognize and respond to. When every element of a jazz performance comes together and works, the music swings.

[handwritten note: Swing - give + take sound mood]

Bring together of Black + white

Eventually the big, or swing, bands experienced the stimulating interaction between black and white musicians characteristic of many developments of jazz, for although the makers of recordings and the managers of commercial radio stations still severely segregated popular music intended for blacks or whites, African American music inevitably became more familiar to and popular with a greatly widening audience. White people often traveled to Harlem, a black neighborhood in uptown New York City, where they could hear the finest jazz musicians in the world collectively improvise, or **jam.** And even people who hardly understood the complex new music found themselves intoxicated with its nearly indefinable trait called *swing*.

arranged music was necessary with the bigger band.

Art of Arranging Whereas early jazz combos functioned well with free improvisation, these larger groups of players needed to follow some kind of structured plan, relying upon arrangements that were either written down or thoroughly worked out in rehearsals. Because many such arrangements were based on New Orleans originals, listeners perceived much the same music as New Orleans and Dixieland jazz; but the larger combos, more sensuous orchestration, and more structured atmosphere made the new sound more intelligible to a wide audience. Because most of the big band musicians had more formal music training than most of the jazz pioneers, big band harmonies were more adventurous and their pieces more highly structured than those of early jazz. Solo improvisations were still hot, but they were brief, the band playing together much of the time.

Solos were still found to be improvised

Jelly Roll Morton (1920's)
First to provide arranged music

The great ragtime and jazz pianist Jelly Roll Morton was one of the first bandleaders to provide arrangements for his band, beginning in the mid-1920s. Even more influential on later jazz bands, however, were the arrangements of **Fletcher Henderson** (1897–1952), who made large groups *sound* as if they were improvising and in fact left room for improvisation, within limits. A fine pianist with a degree in chemistry, Henderson in effect transformed the large "sweet" dance band into a jazz band, skillfully alternating the independent use of each section (trumpets, trombones, saxophones, rhythm) with outstanding solos. So successful were his innovations that they were copied by nearly every dance band of the Big Band era and in fact remain standard for many high school and college jazz bands today.

Music dominated Kansas city Jazz

Count (Bill) Basie (1904–1984), who defined jazz as "music you can pat your foot to," became one of the most popular of all big band arrangers and leaders. A quiet, unobtrusive pianist and leader whose music dominated the Kansas City jazz scene with its refined "less is more" style of playing, Basie proved that *space,* or *silence,* is as important to music as *sound*. He chose his notes—whether as pianist or arranger—meticulously, giving each utmost significance. Basie's band was particularly admired for its rhythm section, in which guitar, bass, and drums were so closely integrated as to produce a perfectly balanced sound. And Basie's unique style of piano playing gave further grounds for some to consider his ensemble the best swing band of all.

The brilliant tenor saxophonist **Lester Young** (1909–1959) seemed uniquely comfortable with Basie's style. In "Taxi War Dance" (Listening

Big Band Swing

Title
  "Taxi War Dance" (excerpt)

Composers/Arrangers
  Count Basie, Lester Young

Instruments
  Four trumpets, three trombones, three saxophones, piano (Basie),
  guitar, double bass, drums

  Basie introduces a rolling figure in the lower piano range, which
  continues as trumpets make brief, emphatic comments,
  accompanied by trombones and drums.

  Lester Young begins his relaxed, swinging saxophone
  improvisation, which he extends and develops.

  The trumpet figure returns, and then we hear a trombone solo
  accompanied by the rhythm section.

  The trombones play a four-note motive (a distinctive rise, then a
  fall, in pitch), answered by the trumpets. This figure recurs
  several times, interspersed between solo passages for the other
  instruments, as the piece continues.

Example 43), we hear Young answering Basie's spare, rolling piano figures
with his own light and elegant melodic saxophone phrases.

Benny Goodman (1909–1986) The white clarinetist and bandleader (*White man*)
Benny Goodman (Figure 75) brought big band music to national attention
through his many recordings and radio programs. Although Goodman's unprecedented inclusion of outstanding African American soloists in his band
was warmly appreciated, his exploitation of the contributions of black musicians sometimes caused resentment. Many of the Goodman band's best
arrangements, for example, were by Fletcher Henderson, but although the
band made Henderson's arrangements extremely popular, Henderson never
earned the money that Benny Goodman and his band accrued. Both Goodman and Henderson had received classical music training; both insisted on
disciplined musicianship from their band members; and the fact that Goodman's band became more popular than Henderson's was a source of some
bitterness by the end of the decade.

  Goodman later divided his playing and recording between big bands and
various smaller ensembles, for while big bands remained highly popular well
into the forties, the range of jazz styles expanded greatly during that decade,
offering musicians and listeners alike a wealth of exciting new musics.

Figure 75
Legendary jazz clarinetist
Benny Goodman in
performance.
(Culver Pictures, Inc.)

Mood Indigo

Edward Kennedy "Duke" Ellington (1899–1974)

In 1922, **Duke Ellington** (Figure 76) moved from his hometown, Washington, D.C., to New York City, where he formed his own small dance band. By 1927 he had transformed the ensemble into the ten-member Duke Ellington Orchestra, playing hot New Orleans jazz at the popular Cotton Club in Harlem. The talking brass instruments, wailing clarinets, ritualistic drumbeats, beautiful melodies, and precise orchestration of the Ellington sound astonished black and white listeners alike. Ellington hired the best musicians available and deftly exploited the unique sounds of each in his gifted orchestrations, writing for specific musicians to capitalize on special talents they sometimes didn't know they had. Already famous as a great jazz pianist, Ellington is said to have used the jazz band as his real "instrument," exploring its entire range of sounds with unprecedented imagination and creativity. By juxtaposing instruments in nontraditional combinations and using them in the extreme limits of their range, he transformed their sound, sometimes effectively obscuring their identification.

Listening Example 44 presents *Mood Indigo,* a haunting tune Ellington composed in 1930 and arranged innumerable times for many combinations of instruments. The chromatic melodies, *bitonal* harmonies (juxtaposing one key over another), and dreamy mood made *Mood Indigo* music to listen to, as well as to dance to; and lyrics added later rendered the piece a popular song of lasting appeal.

Figure 76
Duke Ellington.
(Courtesy of Ray Avery.)

During the early days of rock and roll, Ellington's jazz was heard less often, but at the 1956 Newport Jazz Festival his orchestra made a tremendous hit, leading to a best-selling album, "Ellington at Newport," and to prestigious new concert dates. From then Duke Ellington's fame soared to unprecedented heights. We will meet him again (pp. 183, 184) in the discussion on concert jazz.

Women in Jazz

Besides the internationally known big bands of Duke Ellington, Count Basie, Benny Goodman, Fletcher Henderson, and three or four other outstanding

Concert Jazz

Composer
Duke Ellington

Title
Mood Indigo

Tempo
Rather slow and bluesy. Although the performance is of a quality and style suitable for intense listening, it is also eminently danceable.

Instruments
This big band arrangement includes five trumpets, three trombones, five saxophones (two tenor, two alto, one baritone), two clarinets, bass, drums, and Duke Ellington at the piano.

After a relaxed introduction played by muted sax accompanied by walking bass, the lovely theme is introduced by trumpets playing in a style appropriately warm and mellow, rather than brilliant or virtuosic as in standard dance pieces. The bass continues to provide steady support as the piano delicately embellishes the highly chromatic melody.

Even in this brief rendition, the colors of the sounds change continuously, rendering the timbres endlessly interesting in their own right. Listening to other versions of *Mood Indigo* provides further insight into Ellington's incredibly versatile and imaginative approach to orchestration.

War brought women jazz bands to the spotlight

men, from 1937 to 1948 there was also an all-female band that can only be described as a blazingly hot jazz force. Women wishing to play jazz in those days faced nearly insurmountable odds: it was widely assumed that they didn't have the strength, or the temperament, or the talent to measure up to the men.

Nevertheless, during World War II, all-woman bands (all-girl bands, they were called then) flourished as men went off to war, and people grew accustomed to seeing women in various nontraditional roles. Well-known all-white female bands included one led by Phil Spitalny (note the male leader) and another led by Ina Ray Hutton. Most impressive of all, however, were the **International Sweethearts of Rhythm.** Predominantly black, with Chinese, Indian, Hawaiian, and white representation as well, they were also all female and thus were largely ignored by white audiences, films, and print media, who would not take a bunch of women seriously as jazz musicians. Yet at

Figure 77

Jazz musician and composer Mary Lou Williams. (Metronome/Archive Photos.)

Harlem's Apollo Theater and Savoy Ballroom—drawing probably the most demanding jazz audiences in the land—they made a tremendous, and a lasting, hit.

Mary Lou Williams (1910–1981) One of Ellington's employees, **Mary Lou Williams** (born Mary Elfrieda Scruggs), was a rare exception, a woman soloist highly successful in the field of instrumental jazz (Figure 77). Having played the piano in public since the age of six, she married a carnival band member, and when her husband left the band to join another she hired a replacement for him and ran the group herself. Later she worked as freelance arranger for several bands, including Benny Goodman's, and became a staff arranger for Duke Ellington, producing highly original and distinctive arrangements while also performing as pianist both here and in Europe. Having contributed to all of the evolving styles of popular piano music, from ragtime to bebop and beyond, in 1977 she was recognized as the best-known player of free-jazz piano. After arranging and composing for Duke Ellington for many years, she became his close friend in later life and played at his funeral. In 1996, she was honored with the first of an annual series of Mary Lou Williams Women in Jazz festivals at the Kennedy Center in Washington.

Reactions against Big Band Music

A new generation of young Americans unfamiliar with early jazz danced to the happy sounds of big band music through the 1940s. Many older people enjoyed the music as well, finding the repertory familiar because the big bands, like the earlier combos, based their music upon marches, hymns, and the made-to-order songs of Tin Pan Alley, whose formula had altered only slightly from the 1890s.

Complication in the
arrangement of the
jazz songs leads to
an inability to receive
it as dance music
~~Repression dance~~

a music to be listened
to rather than to
dance to.

music put to be
observed.

Reactions against big band music began to set in, however, even while crowds continued dancing to its swinging beat, as increasingly complex band arrangements, emphasizing rhythm and swing rather than melody, sometimes rendered the source tune unidentifiable. Repeated rhythmic patterns, or **riffs,** held the arrangements together while effectively heightening the intensity of the mood; but the swing crowd began to resist the challenging instrumental arrangements in favor of simple songs.

Although primarily an instrumental concept, early jazz had important reciprocal relationships with popular song: Early combos improvised on the melodies or harmonies of popular songs, and many songs of the twenties and thirties were jazz flavored. The big bands played arrangements of old and new songs from Tin Pan Alley. Thus it is not surprising that at some point in the thirties, big bands began to work closely with vocalists. Slowly the style of big band music changed as the bands assumed the role of accompaniment and as great instrumental soloists vied for popularity with outstanding vocalists, regularly alternating instrumental and vocal choruses. Ella Fitzgerald (1918–1996) became famous for her scat singing, and crooners such as Rudy Vallee and Bing Crosby became increasingly popular as the technology of microphones and recording engineers allowed their more intimate personal styles to project to a listening audience. In time, crowds came not so much to dance as to hear Crosby, Frank Sinatra, and other popular singers, for whom the bands provided support. A lush string sound returned to favor, replacing the brassier sound of big band jazz; and by the mid-forties singers accompanied by orchestral ensembles supplanted the big swing bands in the white public's affections.

Meanwhile, largely unnoticed at first, a sophisticated new style called *bebop* emerged, destined to exert great influence on the future of jazz.

Bebop 1940's

Retaliation to the
arranged,
commercial Jazz
that was being played

going back to the
Roots of jazz

performed by small
ensemble

Disliking the polished performances of written, rehearsed "jazz" and resentful of the broad popularity of a music that had once belonged to an exclusive few, a few black jazz musicians introduced in the early 1940s a tight, difficult, virtuosic instrumental music called **bebop.** Although its inventors conceived it as a return to the ideals of early jazz—improvisation, virtuosity, and close interaction between soloist and combo—bebop or bop is generally considered the first truly modern jazz.

Like much of the concert music of the forties and later, bebop was performed by a small ensemble of virtuoso performers. Each instrumental line was stark, clear, and technically demanding, the angular melodies moving by large unpredictable leaps instead of narrow steps. Rather than following prearranged or familiar harmonic progressions, bop musicians challenged each other to chart new harmonic paths and make them work. Their chords, large and richly dissonant, startled ears accustomed to tame and forever-pleasant sounds. Conversely, they sometimes improvised on the *harmony* of a famous tune rather than on the *melody,* which remained obscure to puzzled listeners.

The best bebop musicians in fact achieved a revolutionary sound that effectively changed the course of jazz.

The typical bebop combo consisted of trumpet and saxophone, double bass, piano, and percussion. The melody instruments (trumpet and sax) sometimes began a composition by playing a pop, blues, or original melody in unison, then alternating with increasingly complex improvisations while supported by the other players. The double bass, which marked the beat, sometimes took melodic responsibility as well in a pattern inherited from the swing era called the **walking bass,** while the piano and percussion supplied unexpected, irregular accents.

A saxophonist who died tragically young and a trumpet player who remained active until shortly before his death at seventy-six were among the innovators and outstanding exponents of bebop.

Charlie "Bird" Parker (1920–1955)

As a youngster in Kansas City, Missouri, **Charlie Parker** (Figure 78) absorbed the sounds of Lester Young, Count Basie, and other outstanding jazz musicians active in his musical hometown. Later Parker moved to New York City, where he jammed in Harlem clubs with pianist **Thelonious Monk** (1920–1982) and trumpeter Dizzy Gillespie (see pp. 180–181), inspiring and inspired by them to develop the complex new music.

Not only was Charlie "Bird" Parker an amazing saxophone virtuoso, his sax tone dry and biting and his melodies highly jagged in contour, but he also introduced new rhythmic, melodic, and improvisational techniques that lifted jazz to a different plane. A knowledgeable musician, he sometimes quoted

Figure 78
Charlie Parker.
(The Bettmann Archive,
Inc.)

fragments of popular and classical compositions, moving rapidly from such familiar phrases to soaring flights of melodic virtuosity. Parker often performed with a fiercely rapid tempo and an unrelenting emotional intensity that left the weak behind but offered adventurous listeners glorious new insights to jazz.

Addicted to drugs and alcohol and ill for much of his short life, Parker—whom some consider the most influential of all jazz musicians—died when he was only thirty-four. In 1988, the movie *Bird* brought the story of Charlie Parker to popular attention; but among serious jazz afficionados, his memory and influence have never faded.

John Birks "Dizzy" Gillespie (1917–1993)

Dizzy Gillespie (Figure 79) improvised rhythms of a complexity unprecedented in Western culture, reached notes no one knew the trumpet could play, and devised harmonic changes defying the accepted rules of harmony. But even more important, his music touched the human spirit with passion and beauty.

Gillespie enjoyed African Cuban rhythms and sounds, which he included in such pieces as his big band number "Manteca," among the earliest pieces to bring Latin American sounds to modern jazz. Less zealous than Parker and apparently comfortable with a variety of jazz styles and techniques, Gillespie remained an active performer until shortly before his death, his

Figure 79
Dizzy Gillespie.
(© Ray Avery.)

famous balloon cheeks highly visible on television programs and in concerts around the world.

Parker and Gillespie's performance of "KoKo" (Listening Example 45) demonstrates the incredible virtuosity, musicianship, and compatibility of these outstanding musicians.

Although popularity was never a primary goal of the bebop musicians, their style might have attracted a wider audience had the public been able to experience its evolution. At the very time Parker and Gillespie were leading the bebop revolution, however, a recording artists' strike caused a ban on commercial recordings of popular music that lasted for about two years (see p. 125). Thus even the devoted jazz audience was largely nonplussed by the sophistication and complexity of the first bebop recordings produced when the strike finally ended. One tends not to like what one does not understand, and there were many who did not understand bebop.

But bebop is an important music, which not only challenged and stimulated talented musicians and conscientious listeners but also ushered in the age of modern jazz. Meant for listening more than dancing, bebop had significant implications for musicians interested in establishing relationships between concert music and jazz.

Jazz as Concert Music   1950's

A number of Americans writing music in the vernacular tradition have applied their knowledge of classical techniques to popular pieces; and many composers have simply refused to distinguish between classical and popular musics in terms of either quality or preference. Among those we have studied, John Philip Sousa, the march king, composed operettas and symphonic works; Scott Joplin, the king of ragtime, wrote operas; and George Gershwin wrote one opera and several symphonic pieces as well as the many Broadway show tunes we still listen to and romance to today.

Thus during the forties, as jazz steadily grew more serious, dissonant, intellectual, and complex, some jazz musicians absorbed influences from contemporary classical music, reversing the process by which classical musicians had borrowed jazz techniques for their purposes. No longer music for dancing and entertainment alone but for serious *listening* as well, jazz had become, in fact, a kind of classical or concert music in its own right. By the early 1950s, jazz was performed frequently in concert, especially on college campuses or at huge jazz festivals. Both black and white jazz musicians and their listeners as well took a more intellectual approach to jazz than had earlier been customary, and jazz criticism became a recognized field. Today, as we shall see in Chapter 11, certain jazz composers collaborate with poets, choreographers, and classical musicians to produce serious concert works.

Jazz Composition Because the essence of jazz is improvisation, musicians wishing to combine classical and jazz techniques faced a new challenge: They had to create a balance between what was written, what was

Bebop Improvisation

Title
  "KoKo"

Performers
  Charlie Parker (alto saxophone), Dizzie Gillespie (trumpet, piano), Max
  Roach (drums), Curley Russell (bass)

Tempo
  Extremely rapid

At a session intended to record a swing standard titled "Cherokee," by Ray
Noble, Parker and Gillespie improvised halfheartedly on the tune until
Parker, tired of the familiar melody, decided to improvise instead on the
chords rather than the tune of the popular piece. Therefore, instead of
beginning as usual with the "head," or reference to the standard tune, Parker
used bits of his own melodic material, skillfully weaving them over and
through the rather unusual chord changes of "Cherokee." The resulting
historic recording—one of Parker's greatest solos—is based on no prewritten
melody at all (incidentally requiring Parker's recording company to make no
royalty payment for "Cherokee," because chords, unlike melodies, did not
bear copyright). Neither is Parker's "KoKo" related to Duke Ellington's
earlier composition of the same name.

Introduction: The alto sax and muted trumpet begin the elaborate, rather eerie,
  introduction, playing in unison, accompanied by lightly brushed drums.
We hear a brief muted trumpet solo, an alto sax solo, and the sax and muted
  trumpet playing in parallel harmony, all accompanied by a complexity of
  accents on the drums.
Parker plays the first chorus, accompanied by drums, a fast-walking bass, and
  (soon) sparse piano chords, played by Gillespie, who has put down his
  trumpet and moved to the keyboard. Technically, the chorus is in **AABA**
  form, the bridge (**B**) beginning about fifty seconds into the piece.
Parker maintains his extremely brisk tempo and astonishing virtuosity
  throughout the second chorus (beginning at 1:15).
An intricate drum solo varies the texture and sonority—and allows Gillespie to
  return to his trumpet.
The alto sax and muted trumpet play in unison, accompanied by brushes on the
  cymbals.
We hear a muted trumpet solo, then an alto sax solo, both backed up by
  cymbals.
The parallel harmony of alto sax and muted trumpet heard in the introduction
  return to round out and conclude the remarkable piece.

improvised by the soloists, and what an ensemble achieved collectively. Certainly there were precedents for requiring performers in the classical tradition to improvise:

1. During the Baroque period, composers wrote the melody and bass lines of a composition, leaving the harmonies to be filled in by a lute or keyboard player.
2. In the early Classical period, soloists improvised one or more cadenzas in performing a solo concerto.
3. Church organists often are expected to improvise music that connects one part of a service, or one verse of a hymn, to another.

In all of these cases, however, musicians improvised within established guidelines appropriate for a given style of music. Jazz as classical music was a *new* concept, and musicians involved in its evolution faced new situations. The symphonic jazz of the twenties was simply concert music with some of the flavors of jazz, and the big band arrangements approached the concept of composed music but were hardly original compositions. By the 1940s, however, jazz composers were doing more than arranging familiar tunes—they were writing original jazz compositions. At that point, jazz entered the world of art music. Some will question whether concert jazz is jazz at all; but the question remains blessedly moot if we value each style and each piece of music according to its merits, no matter the label it wears.

Duke Ellington, whom we have already met as an outstanding big band leader and as the composer of *Mood Indigo* (pp. 174–175), also wrote serious concert, or classical, music. His scope, in fact, was enormous: In addition to his beautiful ballads and inspired band arrangements, he composed tone poems, ballet suites, concerto-like miniatures for star sidemen, sacred music, topical revues, film scores, and extended jazz works, and at the time of his death he was writing a comic opera, *Queenie Pie,* intended for public television. Finally staged in Philadelphia and Boston in 1986, *Queenie Pie* has enjoyed occasional performances in other cities since.

Ellington has, in fact, been referred to as America's most prolific composer of the twentieth century, in both number of pieces (almost 2,000) and variety of forms. In title and content, his serious compositions often reflected the black experience in America with extraordinary depth, wit, tenderness, and strength. Among his best-known symphonic works, for example, is *Black, Brown, and Beige,* subtitled "A Tone Parallel to the History of the Negro in America," premiered by Duke Ellington and his orchestra at Carnegie Hall in 1943 and played by the New York Philharmonic Orchestra in 1949 and by many other major orchestras since. Ellington returned to Carnegie Hall on a near-annual basis until 1948; and when the nation mourned the death of President Franklin D. Roosevelt in 1945, Ellington's orchestra was the only dance band selected to pay tribute to the fallen president in a memorial radio broadcast.

Ellington wrote *Concerto for Cootie* (Listening Example 46), one of his most beautiful compositions, to feature the trumpeter Charles "Cootie" Williams.

Concert Jazz

Composer
Duke Ellington

Title
Concerto for Cootie

Form
ABA. Although titled *Concerto,* normally indicating a multimovement work, *Concerto for Cootie* is a one-movement piece.

Meter
Four beats to the bar

Instruments
Saxophones, clarinet, trumpets, trombones, bass, drum

Although not written in the classical concerto form, which includes three movements, this piece retains the masterful interplay between soloist and orchestra characteristic of the classical form.

The trumpet (Cootie Williams) begins the piece on the downbeat with a phrase later adapted to begin an Ellington popular standard, "Do Nothin' Till You Hear from Me."

Williams presents the beautiful **A** theme in several ways, skillfully altering the timbre of his instrument by using various mutes and playing techniques. The accompaniment also changes each time the theme recurs, producing rich and varied sonorities.

The dramatic **B** theme differs from **A** in key and timbre. Williams plays it with the open horn, creatively extending and elaborating upon the melody.

A returns, and the piece ends with a brief *coda,* or ending section.

Progressive Jazz

PRESENCE OF
Latin American
drums

In 1949, pianist-arranger **Stan Kenton** (1912–1979) led a twenty-piece orchestra in a jazz concert at Carnegie Hall, where his tightly organized and beautifully balanced ensemble played with elegance and precision. Kenton's name for this music, **progressive jazz,** became the name of a new jazz movement.

Kenton also made other important contributions to modern jazz, including serious exploration of Latin American drums and rhythms in his big band jazz. A typical Latin rhythmic feature called *double-timing,* which subdivides the beat (into eighths instead of quarters, for example), *implies* a faster tempo without actually increasing the rate of speed, because the musicians play twice the number of notes per beat; and Kenton's band greatly increased the intensity and excitement of some of their music by employing this technique.

While Kenton and Woody Herman promoted progressive jazz in the East, **Dave Brubeck** (b. 1910) was in the forefront of progressive jazz on the West Coast, where performances such as that in "Take Five" (Listening Example 47) brought his quartet increasing fame and prestige. Brubeck, a pianist and composer who played with Dixieland and swing bands as a youngster, majored in music in college and then studied composition with the French composer Darius Milhaud (*Me-oh'*) (1892–1974), one of several important European composers who sought to escape the horrors of World War II by living and teaching in America, profoundly affecting the course of our music history. Milhaud, who was particularly interested in jazz and had written several symphonic pieces with jazzy rhythms and timbres, encouraged Brubeck to apply jazz techniques to his concert compositions.

But Brubeck also absorbed ideas from European art music. For example, intrigued by the responsibility of Baroque keyboard players to improvise chords over a given bass line, he produced polyphony reminiscent of the Baroque style. His harmonies, however, are those of his own century, including **atonal** (without a tonic) and **polytonal** (with two or more tonics) effects, and his rhythms are the complex rhythms and sometimes polyrhythms of modern jazz. He frequently uses **irregular meters**—five or seven beats per measure instead of the usual two, three, or four.

Dave Brubeck's Quartet (Brubeck as pianist, Paul Desmond on alto saxophone, Joe Morello as drummer, and David Wright on bass) achieved unprecedented popularity and sales for a jazz recording with Desmond's engaging piece "Take Five."

Cool Jazz

At the same time that Desmond, Brubeck, and Charles Mingus (see pp. 188–189) were evolving their "progressive" ideas, other jazz musicians were developing a style they called **cool,** closely related to and sometimes indistinguishable from progressive jazz. In reaction to the complexity and exclusive nature of bebop, they organized larger bands that included the sensuous sounds of symphonic instruments such as the French horn and oboe. More elegant and less hot than bebop, cool jazz clearly reflected the influence of European concert music—especially the Impressionistic harmonies of Claude Debussy and the sharp dissonances of Russian composer Igor Stravinsky.

The important musicians involved in cool jazz included **Miles Davis** (1926–1991), Figure 80, who in 1949–1950 led the nine-piece orchestra that recorded the album later titled *Birth of the Cool.* But cool jazz was only one of the myriad interests of Miles Davis, who made important contributions to several jazz styles over many years. He became particularly interested in expanding the melodic possibilities of jazz by basing melodies on modes rather than on the major, minor, or blues scales. The music on Davis's album *Kind of Blue,* largely modal, had important influence on many jazz musicians of

Progressive Jazz

Composer
Paul Desmond (saxophonist)

Title
"Take Five"

Performers
Dave Brubeck Quartet (piano, sax, bass, drums)

Meter
Quintuple, or five beats per measure. The beats are divided in the pattern *one*-two-three-*four*-five.

The piano marks the beginning of each measure with a low accented pitch, while the sax and drum solos weave intricate patterns over the steady five-beat accompanying figure.

Figure 80
Miles Davis.
(© Shooting Star.)

varied tastes. A virtuoso trumpet player, Davis was also an outstanding band-leader, composer, and innovator who continued throughout his life to experiment with creative ideas in jazz.

Hard Bop (Funk, Soul)

In the late fifties, certain black musicians reacting against the detached, intellectual, "white" sounds of West Coast cool jazz combined driving rock-related rhythms with the "amen chords" of gospel to produce a sound variously called **hard bop, funk,** or **soul.** Funk—earthy, emotionally exuberant, intensely physical in concept—derives from the blues and embodies strong rhythms and bluesy phrasing. Melodies are straightforward, harmonies simplified, the rigid beat punctuated with strong backbeats. Whereas bebop musicians generally improvised around the structure—although not the melody—of a popular or familiar tune, the less cerebral, aggressive hard bop often worked around new, unknown melodies.

The drummer **Art Blakey** (1919–1990), who worked with many of the biggest names in jazz, formed his own group, the Jazz Messengers, in the late forties and retained the name for other groups active in fifties-style music. His 1955 recording "The Preacher," a funky blues piece with elements of gospel, clearly reflected the increasing influence of rhythm and blues and gospel on jazz.

Ever more varied, increasingly sophisticated, jazz acknowledged at the end of the fifties—as it does today—continuing awareness and appreciation of its roots.

Terms to Review

big bands   Popular dance ensembles of the thirties and forties, consisting of from twelve to eighteen players.

swing   A term with many meanings, including (*a*) a mood of lilting spontaneity; (*b*) a danceable music played by the big bands in the thirties and forties.

reeds   Wind instruments in which the player causes small, flexible pieces of material called reeds to vibrate. Clarinets and saxophones are single-reed instruments; oboes and bassoons have double reeds.

jam   To improvise together with other members of an ensemble.

riff   A repeated rhythmic pattern that provides unity in a jazz composition.

bebop   A complex, highly improvised jazz style, largely developed by Charlie Parker and Dizzy Gillespie.

walking bass   A steadily moving pattern in the plucked string bass, having melodic as well as rhythmic implications.

progressive jazz   A symphonic approach to jazz, introduced by Stan Kenton.

atonal   With no tonic note and no tonal relationships.

polytonal   In two or more keys at the same time.

irregular meters   Meters other than duple, triple, or quadruple. (Usually five or seven to the bar.)

cool   A jazz style introduced about 1950 for large bands including some symphonic instruments.

hard bop, funk, soul   A style combining rock-related rhythms with gospel.

Key Figures

Fletcher Henderson
Count Basie
Lester Young
Benny Goodman
Duke Ellington
International Sweethearts of Rhythm
Mary Lou Williams
Charlie Parker
Thelonious Monk
Dizzy Gillespie
Stan Kenton
Dave Brubeck
Miles Davis
Art Blakey

Optional Listening Example

Dizzy Gillespie: "Shaw 'Nuff"

Suggestions for Further Listening

Thelonious Monk: "'Round Midnight"
Miles Davis: *Birth of the Cool*
Art Blakey: "The Preacher"

11

Jazz since 1960

As emerging new styles joined without replacing established trends in jazz, the jazz experience increased in complexity and sophistication, although hardly in popularity. From the time bebop entered the fray—well before rock and roll swept the popular music industry off its feet—jazz has belonged as much to the classical as to the popular music world. Jazz pianist, composer, and scholar Billy Taylor refers to jazz, in fact, as America's classical music.

Throughout the sixties, jazz musicians explored relationships between classical and popular music, placing less emphasis on outstanding solo performances accompanied by players who obligingly yielded the spotlight until it became their turn to take it, and favoring instead collective improvisation by several, or even by all, the ensemble members at the same time.

exploring relationship between classical and popular music. ——>

collective improvisation vs. solo improvisation

Charles Mingus (1922–1979)

Charles Mingus (Figure 81), a double bass player intimately involved with progressive jazz in the fifties, made important contributions to jazz history both as a <u>bass player</u> and <u>as a composer</u> with unprecedented ideas of jazz

Figure 81
American jazz musician Charles Mingus. (Bob Parent/Archive Photos.)

188

composition. Mingus made the bass line significantly more interesting and important than it had been in early or traditional jazz styles, his magnificent bass solos sometimes imitating saxophone or piano lines.

During the 1960s, his ideas concerning jazz composition made Mingus an extremely controversial, although ultimately influential, figure. Perhaps more than any other jazz musician, Mingus explored the complex relationships between jazz composition and improvisation, for which purpose he established the Charles Mingus Jazz Workshop in New York in 1955. Although he prescribed a formal framework for each composition, Mingus encouraged individual freedom and creativity within that framework, disapproving, for that reason, of a written score.

Mingus's "unwritten compositions," in the tradition of progressive jazz, are rhythmically very complex. Instead of the requisite steady beat of earlier jazz styles, his rhythmic pulse is flexible, and he changed meters frequently. Further, he defied the traditional steady tempo of jazz, sometimes prescribing a gradual *accelerando* (increase in tempo) throughout a piece or through part of a piece. His bass line is sometimes modal, precluding the use of traditional chord changes and requiring musicians to improvise new kinds of melody lines instead of those based on given tunes. In short, Mingus revolutionized the conception of jazz as well as of jazz composition.

Mingus = "unwritten compositions"

Free Jazz

The innovations of Charles Mingus and others during the fifties encouraged a number of jazz musicians to seek new approaches to improvisation, which remained at the core of the concept of jazz. Some shared with Mingus the conviction that jazz was not necessarily—or primarily—about individual solos, but about rhythm and interplay best expressed by the **collective improvisation** of several or all members of the ensemble. In 1960, **Ornette Coleman** (b. 1930) introduced free collective improvisation in an album titled *Free Jazz,* which defied the perception of jazz as generally accessible to the ordinary listener, for **free jazz** was a difficult music, challenging to performers and listeners alike, with no familiar chord changes, no references to popular songs or blues, and no steady beat. In free jazz, each musician improvised independently, aware of and responsive to the other players but bound by no preset obligations. Even the initial phrases of a composition, played by the ensemble's soloists together, were not necessarily in unison.

Free Jazz = without limitations or standards.

Free jazz further released musicians from the strictures of tonality, of recurring rhythmic patterns and/or a fixed pulse, and of predetermined themes. (It has been suggested that free jazz expressed in musical terms the same sorts of freedom African Americans were demanding and finally achieving in many areas of life during that turbulent decade. And the new assertive independence free jazz offered rhythm instruments might be compared to the respected positions African Americans were now assuming in life.) The new music also bore a relationship to chance music (discussed in Chapter 20), and Coleman stated that he thought his playing had some rapport with abstract

free Jazz offered a freedom for the musician

piano was substituded for other instruments that had more ~~flexibility~~ in tone. flexibility

expressionist art. The cover of Coleman's recording *Free Jazz* features, in fact, a reproduction of a Jackson Pollock painting (Figure 82).

Free jazz also reflects the interest in some non-Western music that intrigued many twentieth-century composers of classical music. Having no chord changes to play relieved free jazz ensembles from including a piano, with its restrictive keyboard limited to the tones of the black and white keys. This freed musicians to explore non-Western scales and encouraged them to include instruments from other cultures in their ensembles and to play Western instruments in nontraditional ways. The use of *microtones* (lying between the tones of a piano keyboard) and certain rhythmic techniques derived from the music of India heighten the emotional effect and intellectual challenge of Coleman's performances.

Spiritual leader of Jazz →

Jazz saxophonist **John Coltrane** (1926–1967) (Figure 83) became in a sense the spiritual leader of free jazz during the last years of his short life. Widely known and admired for the beautiful tone and the variety of effects he achieved on his tenor and soprano saxophones, he countered Ornette Coleman's concept of collective improvisation by playing individual solos of unprecedented length, most famously in "Chasin' the Trane" (1961). Coltrane, who had worked with Miles Davis on the influential album *Kind of Blue*, continued to use modal effects in some of his own compositions. Generally dissonant and complex, and charged with emotional, often spiritual, intensity, Coltrane's music features frequent harmonic changes and some polytonal passages.

Figure 83
John Coltrane.
(Historical Pictures/Stock
Montage.)

Third Stream — *combination of jazz & classical music*

Third stream *combines* jazz and classical music in a manner that—unlike the *blending* of classical and jazz effects in symphonic, cool, and progressive jazz—allows each style to retain its characteristic qualities. The composer who first attracted attention to this new idea, which had not yet been named, was **John Lewis** (1920–2001), a classically trained African American pianist who was interested in the forms of European art music, especially of the Renaissance and Baroque periods. Lewis founded the Modern Jazz Quartet (MJQ) (Figure 84) in 1952 and wrote many compositions for that ensemble, often using forms—such as *canon, fugue,* or *variations*—of the earlier periods he admired. Some of Lewis's compositions were to be performed by the MJQ with a symphony orchestra or with another classical music organization, the members of the jazz quartet improvising some of their music while the classical ensemble played what was written. Thus each group remained true to its traditions, and their collaboration formed a new style of music combining classical forms with jazz improvisation and the feel of swing.

The term for the new style was introduced in 1957 by Gunther Schuller, who, for a time at least, believed that jazz and classical music should be treated as separate but congenial entities.

Gunther Schuller (1925–) A classically trained musician who divides his interests about equally between jazz and classical composition, **Gunther Schuller** has played the French horn with major symphony orchestras and is currently a conductor, arranger, orchestrator, music critic, and composer of many kinds of music. Recognizing no qualitative distinction between categories of music, Schuller admires a good rag as much as a good symphony. His transcriptions of several Joplin rags were used in the 1972 movie

Figure 84
The Modern Jazz Quartet (MJQ). Drums: Connie Kay; piano and director: John Lewis; bass: Percy Heath; vibraphone: Milt Jackson.
(Courtesy of Atlantic Records.)

first stream = classical music
second stream = jazz music
together = third stream

The Sting, and the resulting revival of interest in ragtime led him in 1975 to orchestrate Joplin's opera *Treemonisha* and direct the Houston Opera Company in its successful premier performance.

Although Schuller found the interaction of jazz and classical music effective, he distinguished between their blending as practiced by symphonic, cool, or progressive jazz musicians and the new style introduced by John Lewis. In 1957 he referred famously to classical music as the "first stream" of music and jazz as the "second stream," calling their combination in a manner allowing each to retain its characteristic qualities *third stream* music.

Perhaps a painting analogy might help distinguish between the concepts of symphonic jazz, such as Gershwin's *Rhapsody in Blue,* and third stream: Think of an artist who places some red paint on a palette next to some yellow pigment, mixes the two colors together, and applies the resulting orange to the canvas; and compare this to a painter who applies pure red next to pure yellow on the canvas, causing the viewer to *perceive* a particularly vibrant "orange." The first visual example suggests symphonic jazz, whose composer has blended concert and jazz effects to achieve a finished product, while the second may be compared to third stream, in which the jazz and concert music each retain their integrity as distinct means of making music. In other words, the third stream composer requires the *listener* to mix distinct sounds, much as an Impressionist painter expects the *viewer* to perceive orange when yellow and red are juxtaposed.

Third stream music as Schuller conceived it was in vogue for only a short time; but the collision—or cooperation—it represents between classically trained musicians, who depend on fixed ideas of standard Western notation, and jazz musicians, whose art is predicated on pliability and invention, persists. Ornette Coleman, who remains interested to this day in the concept that used to be called third stream, has been writing classical music since the 1950s, when he produced several string quartets, and in the sixties he combined jazz and classical concepts much as John Lewis and Gunther Schuller were doing. His **concerto grosso** for symphony orchestra and solo jazz improvisers titled "Skies of America," written in the mid-sixties, gives the conductor something of an improvisatory role as well by choosing between an array of notated inserts to be cued to the orchestra by means of hand signals. Of course the piece poses quandaries for classically trained orchestral musicians accustomed to relying on a straightforward interpretation of the notes printed in a score: thus when Coleman suggested at a 1997 rehearsal of the piece by the New York Philharmonic that the musicians might choose to play notes *other* than those he had written, a violinist complained that this concept was very hard to understand, to which Coleman replied, smiling, "Just because it's hard to understand doesn't mean it's not true."

The Seventies

Before 1970, it is possible to define a dominant, though hardly exclusive, style characteristic of each decade: we may see the twenties as the Jazz Age, the thirties as the era of swing, the forties reacting to bebop, the fifties staying cool, the sixties exploring relationships between jazz and classical music. Although no one style reigned exclusively at any time, and all existed concurrently with other important kinds of jazz, each of those decades is associated with a particular approach to jazz distinguishing it from other such periods. It is even possible to discern the alternation between *classically* cool and *romantically* emotional music decade by decade: the emotional intensity of the Roaring Twenties, followed by the soothing sounds of big band music, succeeded by the challenge of bebop, countered by *The Birth of the Cool,* to which the sixties offered the intellectually rigorous free jazz.

The seventies, too, were mainly "cool," but further than that we do not recognize a defining style for that—or for the succeeding—decades. From 1970 to 1980 several important movements not only coexisted but seem to have had relatively comparable influences on the jazz of succeeding periods. Tenor saxophonist **Coleman Hawkins** led a *swing* comeback, which remains strong today. European *chamber music–style combos* held appeal for many musicians and listeners alike. And *bebop* made a powerful and lasting comeback. Besides these, two distinctive movements vied for prominent attention during that era: *fusion* and *world music.*

Fusion (Jazz-Rock)
Jazz and rock, which came from the same roots (blues, gospel, work songs) both faced crises as the 1970s began. Jazz seemed to have lost its identity, foundering somewhere between classical and foreign ethnic musics; and rockers, mourning the deaths of some of their greatest stars, struggled to find the means to address the tragic social and political events of the day (see p. 233).

Miles Davis's ensemble incorporated rock rhythms in some of their music beginning in the mid-sixties, and early in the new decade numerous other jazz musicians, who after all had grown up to the sounds of rock and roll, also began to invigorate their music with the rhythms of what had become the most compellingly popular music in history. Introduced in Great Britain in 1963, the movement sprang to life here with Miles Davis's 1969 recording of "Bitches Brew."

Jazz-rock, or **fusion,** or **jazz-rock-fusion,** as it is variously called, melds rock rhythms and the use of electronic instruments with collective improvisation, extreme ranges of volume (from very loud to whisper soft), and rapid shifts in meter, tempo, and mood that are uncharacteristic of rock. Further, fusion is an instrumental music, without the vocals generally inherent to rock. But the use of bass guitar or electric bass instead of jazzers' traditional stand-up bass allowed fusion groups to play faster and to alter their sounds with electronic effects; and the manner in which snare and bass drums replaced the rhythmic effects previous jazz ensembles had assigned to piano and cymbals raised the rhythmic section to a position of dominance unprecedented in the history of jazz.

By the mid-seventies, some jazz ensembles included electronic organs and other keyboards, on which many jazz pianists enjoyed working, as well as a variety of synthesizers. Electroacoustic instruments—those on which sound is mechanically generated and then electronically amplified and altered—were often included as well. (Electric instruments belonging to the second category include piano, clarinets, guitars, saxophones, trumpets, and drums.) These ideas were not new: Benny Goodman's sextet featured an electric guitar in 1939, the electric organ first gained popularity in black rhythm and blues, and the multi-talented singer pianist Ray Charles (see p. 226) played an electric piano for "What'd I Say" in 1959. But electric instruments affected jazz to a new degree in the 1970s. Recording technology also acquired unprecedented importance for jazz musicians, rendering the sound engineer an artist as well as a technician, responsible for manipulating the musicians' sounds to best advantage.

Pianist **Chick Corea** (Figure 85) who, like so many innovators of the seventies and later had worked with Miles Davis, in 1970 founded a popular and influential fusion group, Return to Forever. An accomplished acoustic piano player, Corea turned more and more to a wide variety of electronic keyboard instruments during this decade and the next. He also reflected the influence of Latin American rhythms, as did—and as still do—a large number of important jazz groups and individuals. (See pp. 208, 210 for reference to Corea and the *bossa nova.*)

Thus fusion, which implies a bringing together, also brought about serious schisms within the world of jazz, as musicians chose between acoustic and electronic instruments, between the flexible rhythms of free jazz and a soul- or gospel-influenced steady beat, and among African, Latin (including a huge variety of sounds from Spanish, Portuguese, and even French cultures), and European concepts.

Figure 85
Pianist Chick Corea on
stage at the San Sebastian
Jazz Festival, Spain,
July 25, 1998.
(Reuters/STR/Archive
Photos.)

Another influential musician who found inspiration (and huge success) with electronic instruments, **Herbie Hancock** (1940–), produced an album, *Headhunters* (1973), which became the best-selling jazz album in history. The electric bass and keyboards and synthesizers on this album gave jazz a radical new sound and attracted a sizeable international following for its creator.

Integration of Foreign Sounds In the late sixties, John Coltrane sparked interest in bringing characteristics of many foreign ethnic musics into jazz, and after his death this became a compelling concept for a number of outstanding jazz musicians, who integrated music from India, Brazil, Arabia, Bali, Japan, China, various African cultures, and many others into their own distinctive performances. European concert music also attracted many jazz musicians, some of whom moved to Europe, where they lived for several years. One such was **Don Cherry** (1936–1995), who worked with Ornette Coleman and John Coltrane and performed and recorded in Europe and in New York during the 1960s. Having traveled extensively in Asia and Africa as well, Cherry settled in Sweden in the early seventies and became active there in music education and performance. Referring to himself as a "world musician," Cherry played many ethnic instruments from Tibet, China, India, Bali, and other countries besides the trumpet for which he first became known. In 1978 he and two colleagues, a Brazilian percussionist and an American who played sitar, tabla, and percussion, formed a trio, Codona, that performed a seemingly boundless array of ethnic musics for schoolchildren, enthusiastic adult audiences, and recordings.

[handwritten margin note: music that had no true identity – a "melting pot" period (?)]

The Eighties

For jazz musicians, the eighties proved a fragmented period of enormous diversity, exploration, and discovery. So much information, so much technology, so many musics were available, jazz greatly extended the range of its identity. World music remained important. Electronic techniques retained their roles. The crossover of jazz and classical attained a new significance. And a strong revival of interest in traditional jazz led to extensive quotation and emulation of early styles. In many cases, a single musician or group participated in a number of kinds of jazz, establishing no definitive identity with any one.

Crossover Music John Lewis's Modern Jazz Quartet, seen as both a black response to the intellectualism of the Dave Brubeck Quartet and New York's answer to West Coast cool jazz, was both popular and controversial, but by the seventies negative feelings outweighed positive feelings concerning the group, and they played their "Last Concert," as they titled the performance and its subsequent album, in New York in 1974. Sensing a change of sensibilities in 1981, however, the Modern Jazz Quartet regrouped for a tour of Japan, which was so well received they resumed touring and in 1984 returned to the recording studio to resume their recording career as well.

Traditionalism The eighties' reflection of earlier styles, updated to modern tastes, is sometimes referred to as *neoclassicism,* although with no particular consistency or agreement among musicians or critics alike. In any case, a return to the steady beat associated with swing and other traditional jazz was likely to be tempered by freely flowing rhythms within the regular metrical pattern. Hardly a new idea—flexible rhythm and meter are indigenous to much music in Africa—this seemed a new application of such ideas to the music we call jazz.

　　Rock-related sounds proliferated in the jazz world of the eighties, as danceable funk and rock rhythms protested against the white, European concert sounds of much crossover music.

The Nineties and Beyond

Relationships to rock loomed ever more important as the twentieth century drew toward a close. Soul and funk, world music, and crossover remained strong, while a new style, called *no wave* or *noise* evolved alongside all of them. According to the multitalented reed player–composer–jazz scholar **John Zorn,** no wave seeks the emancipation of noise: pieces in this style are extremely brief, in very fast tempos, and loud. Some have described this music as a collage of very short, isolated sound events.

　　Zorn is among an impressive number of contemporary jazz musicians who are following Duke Ellington's lead in integrating composition and improvisation. Although none has yet attained the renown or adulation accorded

[handwritten margin note: no wave • brief • fast tempos • loud]

[handwritten margin note: Zorn — Integrate composition and Improvisation]

Ellington during his lifetime, or accomplished Ellington's seemingly effortless negotiation between popular culture and the fine arts, several visionary composers are attracting the attention and admiration of critics and fans of jazz. Many of them are masterful improvisers, several are scholars, all seem interested in putting to their own various uses many or all of the various ethnic, technological, traditional, and experimental resources offered in these early years of the twenty-first century.

Henry Threadgill (1944–)

Henry Threadgill, who plays saxophone and flute, has traveled with gospel musicians and blues bands. In the early sixties, he became associated with the highly influential collective called the Association for the Advancement of Creative Music (AACM), formed to help Chicago musicians present their new, commercially unacceptable, music. In the seventies he formed the group Air, a trio that explored African music, ragtime, and assorted other traditional musics; and since 1980 he has formed a number of groups using unusual instrumentation, such as the Very Very Circus, which uses trombone, two tubas, two guitars, and drums.

Anthony Braxton (1945–)

Anthony Braxton, also a former member of AACM, created a milestone in jazz history by recording a double album of solo alto saxophone music *For Alto,* released in 1971, and soon other alto sax players followed his lead by making their own solo recordings. In the eighties Braxton toured in Europe, but recently his attention has been as much, or more, on composing than on improvising, although he is a master improviser (see Listening Example 48).

Braxton, endlessly exploring and restlessly seeking creative new means of expression, has written for everything from the solo saxophone to huge orchestral ensembles and opera. A highly intellectual composer, he has devised systems for composing music, some based on mathematical relationships, diagrams, or formulas as a means of generating improvisation within the framework of an orchestral composition. In some of his pieces, parts can be played by different instruments, depending on what is available or desired for a particular performance. Some of his compositions can be played together, in a concept related to the ideas of John Cage and chance music (see pp. 341–343).

Anthony Davis (1951–)

Anthony Davis, sometimes referred to as a crossover musician, frequently blends jazz and classical styles in his compositions. A fine pianist and improviser, he prefers to write out most of his own music, having said he considers improvisation just one compositional tool within the framework of a piece. His compositions draw on classical and Eastern musics, and his avant-garde jazz ensemble Episteme has been involved in some third stream–style performances with traditional, or classical, performers. Davis's first opera, *The Life and Times of Malcolm X,* was first performed at the Metropolitan Opera House in 1986, and in 1988 he wrote a science fiction opera called *Under the Double Moon.*

Jazz Composition

Composer
Anthony Braxton

Title
92 + (30, 32, 139) + (108c, 108d) for Creative Orchestra

Anthony Braxton has said that for him, "titling" is similar to composing: in each case, he thinks long and hard about the image or concept he intends to convey. This title reveals his compelling interest in math, but also the spiritual dimension to his work and his love of mystery and the unknown. He says that his titles have moved away from the ingredients of the music; that he prefers not to provide definitive titles but "to leave a little room for something unknown to come into the music."

Soloists
Alto saxophone, trombone, piano, three trumpets

Although this is a written composition, the effect is one of collective improvisation. The soloists demonstrate virtuosic mastery of their instruments, creatively exploiting their extreme possibilities. Unorthodox playing techniques, as well as unusual combinations of instruments, produce highly intriguing timbres.

Rhythm
Changing

The bass often marks a steady rhythmic pulse, anchoring the unstable music above with its solid underpinning. Notice how rhythmic changes add variety and interest to the piece and how, despite the complexity of the piece, it really swings! There is even a light-hearted reference (about ten minutes in) to the sound of an old-time swing band.

Harmony
Dissonant

This is a piece to hear in *linear* fashion, concentrating on each line and on the relationships between the lines, which do not produce chordal harmony. *Tone clusters* in the piano and the combinations of instrumental lines contribute to the clean, sharp dissonance of the piece.

Texture
Dense

Jazz Composition

Because the combinations of these musical lines do not have harmonic significance in the traditional sense of Western harmony, we can define texture here in terms of the density of the sound, which varies from thick and complex, with all of the instruments playing together, to thin and transparent, as one or two instruments dot the aural screen with slight, pointillistic gestures.

Melody

Disjunct

Angular melodic lines dominate, with occasional references to tuneful melodies (as in the trumpet about nine minutes into the piece) sounding more like parodies of an earlier style than significant melodies in their own right.

With each listening to this piece, try to focus on one aspect of the composition—the colors of the sounds, the independence of the solo lines, the complexity of the rhythm, for example. Then hear and enjoy the piece as a whole, considering Braxton's assertion that "I'm looking for a music that expresses everything in one moment."

Davis has a classical appreciation of formal structure, believing that "the ultimate freedom is to command form." His orchestral music, organized according to clear formal designs, often includes improvisatory passages, and his recent Violin Concerto and orchestral piece *Notes from the Underground* have effective jazz undertones.

Wynton Marsalis (1961–) **Wynton Marsalis** (Figure 86) is a classicist, who believes that bebop is the foundation of modern jazz, and who continually defends, updates, and modernizes early jazz styles in his own compositions, A Julliard-trained trumpet virtuoso who achieves on his instrument an extremely beautiful quality of sound, Marsalis is also known as an educator and composer and, since 1992, as the artistic director of jazz at Lincoln Center in New York. Having toured for a time with Art Blakey's Jazz Messengers, Marsalis took time off to steep himself in the roots of the tradition he so admired, and his deep study of blues, gospel, work songs, and the work of Louis Armstrong and Duke Ellington brought to his playing and to his composing new passion, depth, and technical brilliance.

Having voiced his concern to restore "respect and seriousness" to jazz, Marsalis also believes the future of jazz holds more emphasis on composition than on soloing, and like many other jazz composers today, he writes music intended to last. Indeed jazz recordings in general are turning toward more

Figure 86
Jazz musician Wynton
Marsalis.
(New York Times
Co./Stephanie Berger/
Archive Photos.)

closely arranged projects than in earlier times, when outstanding soloists reigned supreme.

In 1998, Marsalis received the Pulitzer Prize for Music for his extended composition "Blood on the Fields," and in 1994, his book *Sweet Swing Blues on the Road* also received high praise. However, he remains a controversial figure among jazz fans, some of whom consider him too intellectual and too narrow minded as to what constitutes "real jazz." Nevertheless, his inspired trumpet playing, tireless proselytizing for jazz, and impressive compositions suggest that his will continue to be an important name in jazz.

Jazz Today and Tomorrow

Thus the important American music we call jazz continues to evolve, offering performers and listeners alike a full range of creative experience. Composed or improvised, entertaining or a challenge to the intellect, jazz remains a vital feature of the American musical landscape.

Terms to Review

collective improvisation   Simultaneous improvisation by some or all members of a combo.

free jazz   A style of free improvisation introduced by Ornette Coleman in 1960.

third stream   A term coined by Gunther Schuller referring to the combination, but not the blending, of jazz and classical music. Today the term is loosely used in reference to avant-garde jazz styles.

concerto grosso   A composition for orchestra and a small group of solo instruments.

jazz-rock, fusion, jazz-rock-fusion   A jazz style melding rock rhythms and the use of electronic instruments with collective improvisation, extreme ranges of volume, and rapid shifts in meter, tempo, and mood.

Key Figures

Charles Mingus
Ornette Coleman
John Coltrane
John Lewis
Gunther Schuller
Coleman Hawkins
Chick Corea
Herbie Hancock

Don Cherry
John Zorn
Henry Threadgill
Anthony Braxton
Anthony Davis
Wynton Marsalis

Suggestions for Further Listening

Gunther Schuller: *Transformation* (for an eleven-piece ensemble)

Schuller: *Conversation* (for the MJQ and the Beaux Arts String Quartet)
Schuller: *Seven Studies on Themes of Paul Klee* (orchestral)
Charles Mingus: *Better Git It in Your Soul*
Coleman Hawkins: *Body and Soul*
Ornette Coleman: *The Shape of Jazz to Come*
John Coltrane: *Giant Steps*
Chick Corea: *Now He Sings, Now He Sobs*

12

Latin Popular Musics

Music from Latin America, having enriched the popular and concert music of the United States for at least a century and a half, is of more significance to North American popular music today than ever before. In the Southwest, where venerable Spanish traditions remain strong, traditional dance music is played much as it has been for many generations. In other parts of the country, Latin American dance music has strongly affected North American pop and jazz. And today "Latin Pop" is a category in its own right—a strong one—on the *Billboard* trade magazine popular music charts.

Early in the twentieth century, Latin popular dances took the United States by storm, first as exotic curiosities, next as fads, finally entering the mainstream of American popular music. The first of the Latin rhythms to affect American pop was the Argentinian **tango,** a graceful dance, sedate in tempo but highly sensuous in performance. Introduced to Broadway audiences in 1911 and made widely popular as danced by Irene and Vernon Castle in a 1913 musical (see p. 261), the tango represents a sophisticated fusion of European and African ingredients.

Lyrical tango *melodies* often suggest the influence of Argentina's large Italian population, whereas the basic tango *rhythm* is that of an older Cuban dance, the **habanera** (named for Havana, Cuba), which subdivides eight eighth-notes (four beats) into 3 + 3 + 2. The habanera beat has been of enormous significance to popular music in the United States; for example, in the mid-nineteenth century, Louis Moreau Gottschalk used the rhythm in several of his popular piano pieces (see pp. 89–90); Jelly Roll Morton claimed that New Orleans ragtime players often applied the "Spanish tinge," as he called this beat, to their left-hand accompaniments; and in 1914, W. C. Handy used the rhythm in the four-line verse—the "tango section"—interspersed between the blues stanzas of *St. Louis Blues* (Listening Example 38). Since those early days, the habanera beat has been heard as the basic rhythm of numerous pop styles.

In the thirties several Latin dances entered American pop through big band music, especially that of the popular bandleader **Xavier Cugat** (Figure 87), who was born in Spain but raised in Cuba. Several renowned Latin performers, including Desi Arnaz and Carmen Miranda (Figure 87), began their careers about that time, appearing in popular stage shows in the thirties and later in film musicals.

Three Latin areas—the Caribbean, Brazil, and Mexico—have particularly influenced the popular, classical, and religious music of North America.

Figure 87
Xavier Cugat and Carmen Miranda, stars of Latin music in concerts and film musicals of the 1930s and 1940s.
(The Kobal Collection.)

The Caribbean

The slave trade bringing blacks to North America carried many slaves to the Caribbean islands (and even more to Brazil). Slaves in these Latin American areas managed better than their northern counterparts to preserve their cultural traditions, partly because the traditional drumming largely forbidden in the north was tolerated south of the border, and also because the African tribal religions blended far better with the Christian Catholicism prevalent in Latin America than with the Protestantism characteristic of the north.

Since 1898, when Puerto Rico became a protectorate of the United States, a steady influx of Puerto Ricans has arrived to settle primarily in New York City. Cubans, too, have come to New York in some numbers, although far more have settled closer to home and to where they land by boat, in Florida. Chicago and Los Angeles also have sizeable populations of Caribbean peoples, including those from Haiti, Trinidad, and other areas of the West Indies. Both Cubans and Puerto Ricans brought numbers of African-derived musical and dance forms to the United States; but because Spanish colonizers transported far more African slaves to Cuba than to Puerto Rico, the black Cuban population is sizeable and the African influence on their culture particularly strong.

A Popular Religion: Santeria The traditional rhythms of the Cuban *bata* drums accompany the most sacred and complex rituals of *Santeria,* a religion rooted in African practices. (Bata are double-headed, hourglass-shaped drums, generally thought to be in the shape of the thunder axe of the god they represent. Both heads of the drums are sounded with the hands.) Brought by immigrant Caribbeans to North America, Santeria has attracted not only members of the Cuban and Puerto Rican communities but many African Americans and a growing number of Anglo-Americans as well. Today Santeria enjoys a large following, especially in New York and southern Florida, where it is practiced in a manner closely related to West African traditions.

Santeria songs, each associated with a particular deity, normally are sung without harmony in call-and-response fashion between leader and group, the leader often improvising phrases in an open, relaxed vocal style characteristic of some African practice. The rhythms of the accompanying bata drums also have specific ritual significance, each rhythm constituting a musical prayer that honors and represents a specific god. Because bata drumming is an oral tradition, living in the minds of performers rather than on a printed page, bata ensembles continue to evolve their own individual performance style and technique, always rooted, however, in ancient African tradition.

Bomba

Among the first Latin dances to become popular north of the border was the **bomba,** a distinctive African-derived Puerto Rican couple dance allowing the man great flexibility and freedom to display his dancing skills while his female partner performs relatively fixed steps. They dance to a song, whose text—performed in call-and-response fashion—usually concerns everyday or topical events, accompanied by drums plus optional maracas, *guiro* (a notched gourd, open at one end, scraped with a stick or with metal wires), and/or cowbell. A pair of sticks strikes a fixed rhythmic pattern on the side of a drum or other hard resonant surface, as the male dancer and lead drummer respond to and compete with each other in rhythms of increasing complexity.

Rumba

Rumba is actually a generic term for a group of Afro-Cuban musical and dance forms derived from the *son,* which somewhat like *swing* describes a particular type of instrumentation and feeling rather than a specific formal structure. Couples dancing a rumba hold each other slightly apart, shoulders level, while moving their hips provocatively from side to side. The basic rhythm of two or four beats to the measure is divided according to the *clave* rhythm, tapped out by cylindrical sticks called *claves,* which underlies all Cuban dance music: The first of two measures is in habanera rhythm, and the second measure sounds on beats two and three (see Figure 88). The tempo varies but is never very rapid.

Traditional Cuban instruments add to the exotic flavor of the rumba: *Bongos* are pairs of drums of different size, held between the knees and usually played with the fingers and hand, sometimes with a stick. *Conga* drums, largest of the Latin instruments, also often are played in pairs, the sound produced by their muleskin head varying according to whether it is struck by the heel, palm, or fingers of the hand. Pairs of metal drums called *timbales* are

Figure 88

The subtle syncopated clave rhythm.

CLAVE RHYTHM

mounted on a stand and struck with a stick. *Maracas* are pairs of gourds filled with pebbles or seeds and shaken or rotated by handles attached to one end.

While Cuban and Puerto Rican musicians performed rumbas during the thirties in New York's *uptown* Latin district known as El Barrio, Xavier Cugat and other bandleaders entertained *downtown* ballroom crowds with a rhythmically simplified hybrid Latin/American version of the dance. Soon the rumba's extreme popularity led Tin Pan Alley songwriters to join the Latin bandwagon, producing such wonderful songs as Irving Berlin's "Heat Wave" and Cole Porter's "Begin the Beguine." (The *beguine* is a native dance of the West Indies.)

Cu-bop
By the forties, Cuban instruments and instrumentalists were strongly affecting jazz, among the most popular influences that of yet another dance, the **conga,** danced in a line or chain essentially as a march but with a heavy accent every fourth beat emphasized by a side kick by the dancers. Having added a conga drummer to his Afro-Cuban jazz orchestra, Dizzie Gillespie in a 1947 bebop concert at Carnegie Hall introduced **cu-bop,** merging Latin rhythms with his bebop style. From then on, Gillespie, Duke Ellington, Stan Kenton and other United States musicians flavored much of their music with Brazilian, Cuban, and other Latin influences.

Mambo
Tito Puente (1923–2000), born in New York City to Puerto Rican parents, became known as the mambo king for his sophisticated "downtown" versions of yet another Latin dance craze, the **mambo.** Puente, who had studied at Juilliard and other professional music conservatories, tempered his Latin rhythms with cooler European harmonies, timbres, and tempos. But hot or cool, the mambo, developed in this country by Latin and Latin-influenced musicians, merged Afro-Cuban sounds with those of big band jazz. Couples danced the mambo moving forward and back, either holding each other in rumba fashion, touching one hand only, or not touching at all. The slower, simpler **chachacha,** popular in the fifties, is closely related to or even a form of the mambo, adding a double step between the fourth (last) and first beats. The mambo's influence proved more far-reaching than its originators or even the mambo king might have envisioned: Having merged with big band jazz and having inspired many Tin Pan Alley songs recorded by such popular singers as Perry Como and Nat "King" Cole, the mambo also strongly affected rhythm and blues in the fifties and introduced Latin rhythms into early rock. Bo Diddley, Ray Charles, and James Brown number among the many musicians who absorbed the Latin percussion sounds and rhythms into their own unique musics.

Salsa
By the late seventies, a Cuban music that had been considered a sub-style of popular music for decades emerged as a major ingredient in virtually every vernacular field, receiving with its new status a new name as well—**salsa.** The word, meaning sauce, had long been applied to peppy Cuban sounds, but the young people who coined it as a name seemed to think of the

remained closer to
Cuban music than
any other Latin
style.

Danceband music

music it defined as something new. In fact, as its popularity spread, salsa drew from a wider range of Latin sounds than before while yet remaining closer to Cuban music than any other Latin style. Today the term is sometimes used generically to denote all African-Latin popular musics.

Salsa indeed was danceband music, but with instrumentation, rhythms, and a general flavor quite unlike the swing band sound. Its timbres were primarily those of voices and trumpets or, alternatively, flutes and violins, while its complex rhythms continually absorbed varied Puerto Rican and South American elements, which sophisticated jazz musicians enthusiastically incorporated in their highly virtuosic performances (see Listening Example 49).

Listening Example 49

Salsa

Title
"Ojos" (1978)

Performers
Ruben Blades (vocal), Willie Colón (trombone)

Rhythm
Clave rhythm

Instrumentation
Brass (with trombone playing the lead lines instead of salsa's traditional trumpets or flutes); percussion, including conga drum, timbales, bongos, maracas, and claves. A piano plays repetitive syncopated patterns.

Form
Two-part: *canto* (narrative) and *montuno* (rhythmic, more instrumental than vocal in concept)

This performance of "Ojos" exemplifies the manner in which salsa musicians absorb varied influences and apply them to this basically Cuban style. Trombonist, composer, and bandleader Willie Colón, born in New York City but of Puerto Rican heritage, replaces the traditional trumpets or flutes of salsa with trombone, and blends jazz harmonies and jazz-style soloing into his salsa performances. Thus the brass instruments in this performance sound much like those of big band jazz. Panamanian Ruben Blades (whose mother was Cuban, and who often is referred to as the Latin Bruce Springsteen) adds a showman's flare to his vocals. (Blades has acted in and written songs for a

Salsa

number of movies and recently performed on Broadway in Paul Simon's musical *The Capeman.*)

Canto After a brass introduction, the first section, much like the verse of a Tin Pan Alley song, presents the narrative content of the song, accompanied by the band.

Montuno The second section alternates instrumental and vocal performances. During the vocal solo, a chorus of male voices intersperses calls of "Ojos." Later the vocalist encourages the instrumentalists with improvised phrases. Notice that the intensity and rhythmic complexity of the piece increase as the performance proceeds. Listen for intricately woven and highly syncopated rhythmic patterns governed by the clave rhythm— which has, however, been too thoroughly internalized by these sophisticated musicians to be readily identified by the casual listener. Try to follow one or more independent instrumental lines at a time, noticing the manner in which their accents fall on, or between, different beats. Hear the strong ostinatos played by the piano. Notice, too, the manner in which the vocal line becomes rhythmically and melodically freer and more complex toward the end of the piece.

Reggae **Reggae** fused elements of North American rock and African Jamaican music to form a kind of "acculturated rock" popular in England in the 1960s and in the United States a decade later. **Bob Marley** (1945–1981), a leading Jamaican reggae performer, became very well known and highly revered in North America.

Reggae comes in several styles, all roughly related to rhythm and blues, although reggae's African polyrhythms are more complex, the bass lines stronger, and the tempos more relaxed than those of r&b. Reggae combos consist of electric guitars, electric organ, electric bass guitar, and drums, with electronic studio techniques sometimes making significant contributions as well. A technique developed by Jamaican disc jockeys of rapid patter talking over the sound of spinning records, called **toasting** or **dubbing,** was destined to have far-reaching effects on the development of rap music in the seventies and eighties (pp. 239–240).

Reggae—a vernacular music (rock) borrowed and transformed by a culture (Jamaican) other than the one that introduced it (African American) to form yet a new style—reveals the possible complexities and enrichments afforded by such wide acculturation. Reggae also exemplifies a *popular* music with strong *religious* connotations, for it is closely associated with a black religious movement called Rastafarianism. In addition, many reggae songs have urgent *political* content, promoting the "back to Africa" movement that emerged in the sixties.

Brazil

It seems logical to relate the relaxed, easy pace of Brazilian music to the sounds and inflections of the Portuguese language spoken in the country that spawned it. In any case, Brazilian dances—more gentle, slower, and less intense than the exciting Cuban and Puerto Rican musics—achieved their own popularity in the United States, although never to the degree of the hot Caribbean sounds.

Samba and Bossa Nova
The African-derived **samba,** sometimes called the national dance of Brazil, arrived in New York around 1949 and quickly became popular as sung and danced by the glamorous Carmen Miranda. In the sixties, a variation of the samba, with modern harmonies and more syncopation than the earlier dance, became known as the **bossa nova,** sometimes called jazz samba, because it fused elements of cool and progressive jazz with its Latin beat.

Less vibrant and more melancholy than Cuban-flavored music, the bossa nova adapted beautifully to the world of jazz, where its flexible rhythms and colorful instrumentation continue to stimulate sophisticated musicians. But much like bebop in the United States, the subtle bossa nova met initial resistance from traditionalists who did not understand its elusive flavors and new sounds. Also like bebop, it is a music primarily for listening. In fact, unlike the rumba, samba, and other Latin musics popular north of the border, the bossa nova is a rhythm—rather, a number of subtle, flexible rhythms—not a dance. Although *nova* means "new" in Portuguese, *bossa* has no literal meaning but seems to be a slang term implying approval (perhaps related to "boss" in recent lingo?).

Eventually the bossa nova won a wide audience through many popular recordings by Sergio Mendes; and in 1962, Stan Getz (Figure 89), a tenor saxophonist who enjoyed mixing jazz with Latin rhythms, won a Grammy for his solo performance of "Desafinado," featuring a bossa nova rhythm (Listening Example 50). Most familiar of all to a general audience was another bossa nova by the composer of "Desafinado" (A. C. Jobim), the lovely and very popular "Girl from Ipanema" (with vocalist João Gilberto).

In the early seventies, several important groups and individuals adopted the quietly sensuous rhythms and melodies of the bossa nova sound to flavor their own distinctive music. Weather Report famously added Brazilian percussionists to their ensemble. Brazilian singer Flora Purim, who appeared equally comfortable performing both jazz and Brazilian music, sang first with Stan Getz, next with Gil Evans, and finally with avant-garde pianist Chick Corea and his Return to Forever group. Purim's husband, percussionist Airto Moreira, also joined Corea's group, enhancing their sounds with the Latin

---

Handwritten margin notes:

Brazilian
gentle
slower
less intense
compared to
Cuban
Puerto Rican
music

1949 - samba
arrived in NY

60's – Bossa Nova
↓
adapted to the
world of Jazz

Like Bebop
- initially not understood
- music for listening

70's & 80's
musicians
adapted music

Bossa Nova

Composer
Antonio Carlos Jobim

Title
"Desafinado"

Performers
João Gilberto (vocalist, guitarist) and Stan Getz (jazz tenor saxophonist)

Meter
Four beats to the bar

Tempo
Slow, relaxed

Form
Strophic

Gilberto's calm voice seems uniquely suited to present the long, sinuous melodic line, accompanied by subtle but insistent rhythms in the drums, bass, piano, and guitar. Everything about the performance seems gentle; the softly dissonant harmonies, lightly syncopated rhythms, even the Portuguese language, all fall easily on the ear.

After Gilberto sings four four-line stanzas, with a fifth line added to his last verse, Stan Getz gives an instrumental version of the piece, similarly accompanied by drums, bass, piano, guitar, and—at the very end—by Gilberto's soft syllables in the background. The muted tenor sax, like Gilberto's singing voice, has all the warmth and subtlety of a sultry tropical night.

Figure 89
Stan Getz playing tenor sax.
(Bob Parent/Archive Photos.)

209

bells, rattles, and shakers he had used earlier when performing with Miles Davis. And through the eighties, the subtlety and flexibility of bossa nova had strong appeal for Pat Metheny's jazz-rock groups, free jazz musicians, and bop.

Mexico

The southwestern states of Texas, New Mexico, Arizona, and California absorbed many sounds from nearby Mexico, where the folk and popular music strongly reflect the songs and dances of African slaves. The country music of the Southwest naturally shows the Mexican influence. Woody Guthrie, who began playing music in Texas in the late 1920s (see pp. 144–145) sometimes adapted Mexican topical ballads, or *corridos,* to his own inimitable style; and the Mexican *ranchera* (ranch song) "El Rancho Grande" became a standard of western swing bands. It has even been suggested that the "blue yodel" of Jimmie Rodgers and others may have been stimulated by Mexican singing styles.

Any number of dances also traveled back and forth between Spain and Mexico, acquiring changes in name, instrumentation, and performance style as they continued to develop. *El cutilio* (Listening Example 51) is a traditional Spanish social dance, or *baile,* that was popular in the pre– and post–Civil War Southwest and that remains so in that region today. Unlike the religious *alabados,* rarely heard today, *bailes* continue to delight people

---

Listening Example 51

Spanish Dance

Title

El cutilio (The Cotillion)

The lively *cutilio,* the last of a set of square dances popularly danced in New Mexico through the nineteenth century, posed a challenge to the dancers to keep up with its fast tempo and complex steps. This is only one of many tunes to which they danced *El cutilio.*

Notice the irregularity of the phrases, unusual in a popular dance. The first phrase, which has an ascending melodic pattern, contains five measures of four beats each. (You can count the accompanying "stamps"—one-two-three-four—five times.) This phrase is repeated.

The second phrase, descending and covering only three-and-a-half measures, also is repeated. The accompanying stamps mark a steady beat through the repetition of the phrases, which occur again, and through the one-beat pause between phrases.

of every age and social situation. Performed now as then to celebrate engagements, weddings, birthdays, and other joyful events, these rollicking dance tunes lighten the hearts of those who hear them—although few remember how to dance the intricate steps popular over a hundred years ago.

Conjuntos

During the late nineteenth century, as Mexican Americans, or Chicanos, spread not only throughout the southwestern United States but well to the north and east as well, they carried with them their traditional **norteño** (Texas Mexican American) style of music. An accordion, usually together with a guitar and sometimes a double bass and drums, dominated the sound of the accompanying ensemble or **conjunto** for this popular regional folk music.

folk music that came from late 19th century Mexican Americans

Traditional norteño conjuntos played polkas, waltzes, and other European dances popular in Mexico and along both sides of the border, and by the forties they also accompanied the singing of rancheras, corridos, and other traditional Mexican songs. During the middle decades of this century, norteño conjuntos (Figure 90) entertained in cantinas throughout the southwest, sometimes adding a saxophone to further color their distinctive sound.

Mariachis

By the late seventies, folk, country, and rock rhythms and instrumentation increasingly reflected vibrant Mexican traditions, including the sounds of strolling **mariachis** (Figure 91), an important Mexican folk music frequently heard in the southwestern United States. Originally a string ensemble, mariachis now add one to three trumpets to the violins, guitar, and perhaps *guitarron* or bass guitar (the instrumentation is quite flexible) making up the traditional ensemble. It is thought that because their joyous music so often entertained at weddings, they may have derived their name from a corruption of *mariage,* French for marriage.

folk music

Latin Music Today

Once an exotic flavoring added to light classical or early popular American music, Latin music has become a vital force of great complexity, variety, and

Figure 90
The 1950s were a peak period for southwestern Chicano music, and among the leading norteño groups was Los Alegres de Teran.
(Photo © by Susan Titelman, courtesy Brazos Films, 10341 San Pablo Ave, El Cerrito, CA 94530. From the film: *Chulas Fronteras.*)

Figure 91
Strolling Mariachis
entertain passersby.
(Corbis/Bettmann.)

Influenced American music rhythmically.

significance in the American music experience. Of strong interest in its own right both here and abroad, Latin music has influenced rhythmically progressive American music as well. Not only the rhythms, but also the varied timbres of Latin instruments, have greatly expanded the American musical palette.

Terms to Review

tango   A graceful, sensuous Argentinian dance, the first of the Latin rhythms to become popular in the United States.

habanera   A Cuban dance, whose rhythm is the basis of the tango.

bomba   A Puerto Rican couple dance derived from Africa.

rumba   A group of Afro-Cuban musical and dance forms, with many variants.

conga   A Cuban carnival dance-march: the dancers, having formed a chain, mark every fourth beat with a heavy kick.

cu-bop   Dizzy Gillespie's fusion of Latin rhythms with bebop.

mambo   An Afro-Cuban form of big band dance music.

chachacha   A slower version of the mambo, with a double beat added between the last and first beats of each measure.

salsa   Popular Cuban dance band music with rhythms derived from African-American dances.

reggae   A blend of rock and African-Jamaican styles.

toasting or **dubbing**   A technique developed by Jamaican disc jockeys of rapid patter talking over the sound of spinning records.

samba   The most famous Brazilian song/dance; duple meter.

bossa nova   Brazilian rhythm, slower, more subtle than Cuban dances, reflecting the influence of cool and progressive jazz.

norteño   A Texas Mexican American style of music.

conjunto   An ensemble accompanying dance and song in norteño music, north and south of the Mexico-Texas border.

mariachis   Mexican groups of strolling musicians playing string instruments and often led by one or more trumpets.

Key Figures

Xavier Cugat
Tito Puente
Bob Marley

Suggestions for Further Listening

Bossa nova: *Getz-Gilberto* (Stan Getz and Brazilian composer-singer-guitarist João Gilberto)
Reggae: *This Is Reggae Music* (various artists)
Salsa: *Machacha* (features Clare Fisher and Salsa Picante)

13

Rock and Roll

The baby boom of World War II produced a fifties teen boom of unprecedented numbers, wealth, and influence. Little interested in the sentimental popular music of the depression and war years, these numerous young people craved excitement and a music expressive of *their* frustrations and needs, a music to which they could dance. And for the first time in American history, the teenage population had money enough to command the attention of the popular music industry.

The Generation Gap

Several postwar conditions fostered an unprecedented sense of independence and even rebellion among American youth. Many failed to understand in such prosperous times the frugal ways of their parents, who had survived but not forgotten the Great Depression and years of wartime austerity. Military families experienced frequent relocation, particularly unsettling to children and teens, whereas youths in more stable conditions often had mothers working outside the home, filling jobs vacated by men still in the military, or continuing jobs to which they had become accustomed during the war or upon whose income they felt dependent. These and numerous other social and economic conditions caused a serious, unprecedented gap in communication and understanding between adolescents and their parents.

The spirit of rebellion also waxed strong among young African Americans returning from war to find the equality they had experienced on the battlefield bluntly denied them in the domestic workforce. Spurred by the injustice of social discrimination, the civil rights movement steadily gained momentum, and black power became a force to be reckoned with.

Meanwhile, popular music after World War II became increasingly diversified, generally moving away from instrumental music back to song. This young generation perceived swing bands as too polished, the performers' dress too formal, and the shows too structured to please them. Mainstream pop's sentimental ballads, suitable for the slow dances popular among young adults, could not satisfy the restless teenage audience, and the complexity of modern jazz—primarily instrumental, often dissonant, intended more for listening than for dancing—simply antagonized them. More and more young white people preferred the vital, stirring sounds of black *gospel* music and *rhythm and blues* to the music their parents had enjoyed.

Gospel (Religious Blues)

Gospel music, also called the religious blues, descends from the religious spirituals developed by the slave culture, later celebrated in camp meetings, and later yet in concert environments. *Gospel* actually refers to a family of religious musics, white and black, including the white spirituals discussed in Chapter 4 (p. 63); however, only black gospel music has profoundly affected popular music, becoming in effect a branch of rhythm and blues and contributing vitally to both jazz and rock.

Originated from religious spirituals

The line between sacred and secular is often thin, and gospel generally refuses to draw that line, simply combining religious expression with techniques generally associated with secular music. All of the elements of black gospel music—including a steady beat underlying strong rhythmic complexities, hand clapping, percussive accompaniment, call-and-response, melodic improvisation, and enthusiastic, unrestrained body movements and dancing—found their way into the music called **rhythm and blues (r&b).**

Gospel music's aspects found their way into rhythm & Blues

Rhythm and Blues

For many years, the popular music recording industry, as mentioned previously, applied the term "race records" to popular musics, ranging from country and urban blues to jazz, white-style ballads, and gospel, performed by and marketed primarily for blacks. Much black popular music was based on the form and harmonic pattern of the blues; most of it was in quadruple meter, with strong backbeats on the normally weak second and fourth beats of the measure; and most of it was danceable. Religious or secular, it generally involved syncopated rhythmic improvisation, call-and-response between a leader and group/congregation, and vocalizations utilizing African techniques—extremely high and low ranges, the use of falsetto, numerous blue notes, and expressive vocal catches strengthening the emotional character of the music.

Although performed in an idiom deemed unacceptable for mainstream markets, black popular music steadily developed an enthusiastic audience among young white listeners. Finally, in 1949, the industry trade journal *Billboard* abandoned the offensive term "race records," grouping all the popular music intended for a black audience under the term rhythm and blues, and for several years that was the phrase generally applied to black popular music.

1949 - Termed Black popular music under the title of Rhythm & Blues

Rhythm and blues ensembles, whether swing-style bands or small combos, were *loud,* usually featuring an electric guitar and sometimes other electrified instruments as well. The music had a strong vocal orientation, with at least one singer and often an all-male vocal group involved, the need for singers to shout or scream to be heard above the instrumentalists contributing to the

LOUD music & vocals

emotional intensity of the music. The lyrics of most r&b songs—though frankly, unself-consciously, and even blatantly sexual—remained primarily good-natured.

Although white listeners readily accepted the soothing music of certain black male ensembles, they did not yet accept black music per se: The performances of such **doo-wop** ensembles as the Mills Brothers and the Ink Spots, featuring high falsetto voices, smooth harmonies, and subtle rhythmic backgrounds sung to nonsense syllables, were relatively white in style. The Platters' doo-wop recordings "Only You" and "My Prayer" are other well-known examples of early doo-wop music. The black soloists Lena Horne, Nat "King" Cole, and Ella Fitzgerald also had hits on the pop charts in the late forties and early fifties, but most of their repertoire was from Tin Pan Alley, and their performances, too, generally conformed to white practice. Black listeners tended to prefer rhythm and blues, and by 1950, increasing numbers of young whites did, too.

Finally, the unexpected but quite congenial blending of rhythm and blues and country-western—each lying *outside* the mainstream—invigorated and in fact revolutionized American popular music.

Country Music Meets R&B

Black rhythm and blues and white country-western shared a number of important characteristics: Both lay outside the popular mainstream; both were rooted in the South; both were danceable; both consistently involved the guitar—acoustic, electric, or amplified; both featured frank lyrics and earthy delivery styles; and both were sung in dialects different from that of the standard white urban population.

Thus it is not surprising, given the restless climate of young listeners hungry for something hot and new, that in the early fifties the two dissident styles met and fused to produce the most widely, the most wildly hailed popular music the world has known: rock and roll.

Birth of Rock and Roll

Convinced that white listeners would reject the raucous sound, producers and directors generally refused to program rhythm-and-blues hits on mainstream radio. But a disc jockey in Cleveland, Ohio, named **Alan Freed** soon realized that many white teens preferred r&b hits to mainstream popular music, and beginning in 1951 he played increasing numbers of rhythm-and-blues records on his radio programs, which reached a broad general audience. Freed also promoted live stage performances of music in r&b style, with both blacks and whites present on the stage and in the audience.

Then two young white country singers with black delivery styles entered and forever altered the popular music picture. The terms "rock" and "roll" had long been familiar, and sexually suggestive, in black popular music; but Alan Freed is credited with coining the term **rock and roll** for the new style with which Bill Haley and Elvis Presley revolutionized the popular music world.

Bill Haley (1925–1981)

When **Bill Haley and His Comets,** initially a country-western group, began to combine white western swing with elements of black rhythm and blues, they seemed temporarily displaced musicians—at home in neither popular music camp. They didn't know it then, but they were playing a brand *new* music—rock and roll, soon to replace all others in popularity. In 1954, their cover recording of Joe Turner's r&b hit "Shake, Rattle and Roll"—widely played by radio stations that would not have touched the r&b version—quickly soared to the top of the popular music charts. And the next year, the Comets' recording of "Rock around the Clock," used as the theme for the movie *Blackboard Jungle,* became the first international rock-and-roll hit.

[handwritten margin note: Combine white western swing with black rhythm & Blues]

[handwritten margin note: "Rock around the Clock"]

Elvis Presley (1935–1977)

Elvis Presley (Figure 92) another country boy, followed much the same course from country to rock and roll, but the astonishing degree of popularity he achieved was unprecedented then and, for a solo singer, remains unsurpassed. Through a combination of talent, persistence, and luck, Presley achieved a recording contract and soared to the top of his profession with dizzying speed.

Presley's early rockabilly or country rock records actually found more favor with blacks than whites, but his appeal soon became interracial and international. His 1956 cover recording of "Hound Dog," recorded earlier by Willie Mae "Big Mama" Thornton, reached the top of first the black and then the white pop charts. Another early recording, "Heartbreak Hotel," suggested the range of his expressive gifts from wild and raucous to wrenchingly warm and tender.

Elvis, almost entirely self-taught, played little more than simple chords on his guitar; but he had a beautiful and amazingly versatile voice to which he added warmth and intensity by the use of the slight wavering between pitches

Figure 92
Elvis Presley.
(Wide World Photos.)

called **vibrato,** with which singers and instrumentalists color their sounds. The vocal slides and catches typical of black singing styles came to him naturally, and he used them with great effect. He could shout or croon, sing gospel (his personal favorite), folk, or rock and roll, and virtually electrify an audience with his voice and his dynamic stage presence. Known as Elvis the Pelvis for his sexy gyrations on stage, he epitomized all that youth loved and middle-class adults feared about rock and roll.

Chicago

Early Characteristics

African Americans migrating north to Chicago after World War II found a wealth of music happening there as jazz musicians, country and urban blues musicians, boogie-woogie pianists, and others played for self-entertainment, for commercial clubs, and for the recording studios. Some of the new arrivals began to develop their own distinctive kinds of rock and roll, more closely related to rhythm and blues than was Presley's, which was rooted in country-western music. Their accompanying instruments included one or more amplified guitars, a saxophone, and sometimes a trumpet, over which a singer screamed or shouted. The meter was quadruple, with strong backbeats, and the tempo danceable. Bo Diddley (whose real name is Ellas McDaniel and whose nickname is assigned various and conflicting origins) played his electric guitar with terrific rhythmic vitality, achieving an extreme range of sounds in an age before technology made such effects commonplace. Little Richard (Richard Penniman) thumped his piano and screamed his lyrics, sacred or profane, with equal fervor.

Chuck Berry (b. 1926) (Figure 93), among the most talented early black stars of rock and roll, fused with rhythm and blues more country-western elements than had other outstanding black musicians of the mid-fifties. A great guitarist and a talented songwriter who wrote most of the material he performed, Berry was also an effective singer, shouting protest and rebellion in a high, clear tenor voice over his highly amplified guitar. Berry became as

Figure 93
Chuck Berry.
(© UPI/Bettmann
Newsphotos.)

famous for his "duckwalk" across the stage—knees bent, head thrusting forward and back as he played his guitar—as Elvis was for his pelvic gyrations; but more significantly, Berry's music strongly influenced both the Beatles and the Rolling Stones, who later sang his songs and imitated his distinctive style. Berry's many hit recordings included "School Day" (1957, Listening Example 52).

End of the First Era The end of the fifties proved a dark time generally for the promising new music, rock and roll: Elvis had been drafted into the army; Little Richard walked away from rock and roll (temporarily, for religious reasons, returning after several years to resume his highly successful career); Buddy Holly lost his life in a plane crash. Scandal plagued several stars, notably Jerry Lee Lewis, who had married his very young third cousin, and Chuck Berry, who had been arrested for taking a minor across state lines.

White performers, seeing their profits slip away to the r&b market, began to make tame, toned-down cover versions of r&b songs, with sexual references less blatant and rhythms less hot; and radio stations that had never

---

Listening Example 52

Rock and Roll

Composer/Performer
Chuck Berry

Title
"School Day"

Meter
Four beats to the bar

Form
Twelve-bar blues

Tempo
Brisk

Here the form is the blues, but the mood is light and the energy level high! Berry does not follow the text repetition within each three-line verse typical of the classic blues.

Of the seven verses, all but the fifth—which is a guitar solo—involve call-and-response between the singer and the guitar, which often imitates the vocal line it follows. The subtle roll of the piano, playing a triplet pattern at half the speed of the guitar and drums, is best heard during the fifth (instrumental) verse.

Throughout the song, the uneven subdivisions of the strongly accented beats that lend the rhythm a "shuffle" effect nearly compel a physical or, at least, an emotional response from the listener.

programmed "black music" willingly played the "whitened" cover record-ings, which they considered more suitable for listening by the general audi-ence. Television's popular *American Bandstand* program, hosted by Dick Clark, featured white teen idols such as Paul Anka, Bobby Darin, Fabian, and Frankie Avalon singing respectable, urban versions of rhythm-and-blues hits.

The **payola** investigations of 1959 to 1960, which revealed that disc jock-eys were routinely accepting money and gifts for playing (plugging) certain records, tarnished even the popular Dick Clark and virtually destroyed Alan Freed: Convicted of "commercial bribery," Freed received a fine and a sus-pended sentence, was blackballed by the music industry, and died, penniless, of results of alcoholism, at the age of forty-three.

As rock and roll lost its hard edge and energy, pop became more bland than ever, sending the sixties off to a slow, unpromising start.

Surfing Music

Social unrest and violence reached unprecedented heights during the early 1960s, as the civil rights movement made dramatic breakthroughs, often at tragic cost, and President Kennedy spoke movingly of a new frontier, chal-lenging young people to make heroic sacrifices in order to realize high ideals. But to warm, relaxed, materialistic youths living in sunny southern Califor-nia, Kennedy's challenge sounded remote and unreal. *Their* ideal existence consisted of sun, fun, and—essentially—the beach. And **surfing songs** de-scribing the relaxed California life also provided vicarious pleasure to young whites living in less idyllic parts of the troubled country.

The Beach Boys, formed in the early sixties by Brian Wilson, included two of his brothers, a cousin, and a friend. Wilson, who led the group and wrote some of the songs, had a pleasant falsetto voice, and the Beach Boys sang their simple songs with smooth and soothing harmony.

But the Beach Boys evolved into sophisticated concert and studio musi-cians, effectively articulating such teen concerns as school spirit and fast cars besides the (supposed) comfortable California surfing life. Temporarily side-lined by a nervous breakdown, Brian Wilson poured his talent into song-writing to produce, in 1966, *Pet Sounds,* which became an influential theme album in a market whose albums primarily had consisted of single, unrelated songs. Later the same year, the Beach Boys released their best-selling single, "Good Vibrations," accompanied by such nontraditional rock music sounds as sleighbells and the electronic *theremin* (see p. 281).

After 1966, the Beach Boys changed both their leader and their image, growing long hair and beards and adding sophisticated electronic effects to their music, now darkened by protest songs. In the eighties, the Beach Boys enjoyed something of a comeback, but in 1983 Dennis Wilson drowned, and the later Beach Boys' albums made limited impact on the volatile rock mar-ket. Their lasting fame and influence seems fated to reside in their songs of sun, sand, and surf.

[handwritten margin note: Kids related to this type of music of "fun in the sun" an escape from all the social unrest and violence.

— for white audience]

Motown

Surfing music meant little to young African Americans facing challenges of a more serious kind. Angered to see white performers reaping huge profits from covers of black hits and from bland surfing songs, some black musicians set out to earn a higher share of the wealth. Most notably, in 1959, a young black songwriter named **Berry Gordy, Jr.,** formed a company called **Motown** for the purpose of marketing black rock and roll as aggressively and lucratively as the products of white musicians.

Motown was established in the "motor town," Detroit, which became to rock and roll what Nashville was to country. Under Gordy's guidance, the new company turned out hit records as efficiently as assembly lines turned out cars, each one technically perfect, efficiently marketed, and of broad crossover appeal. Gordy custom-designed his singers, carefully supervising their repertoire and requiring them to take classes in diction, grooming, stage presence, and choreography. Thus the Motown sound was lighter, smoother, and less sexy than other, blacker, rock and roll. There was usually a lead singer and a background vocal doo-wop group, who enriched the sonority by singing nonsense syllables in pleasant harmony. Whereas early Motown records used very simple instrumentation, strings and other orchestral instruments accompanied later performances.

The outstanding Motown group was the female trio The Supremes (Figure 94), with their famous lead singer Diana Ross (Listening Example 53). Well-known male vocal groups sponsored by Motown included the Four Tops and the Temptations. Michael Jackson was only five years old when Motown discovered him and his brothers, a family group—The Jacksons—

Detroit = Motown

adding some sophistication to black music

Figure 94
The Supremes.
(The Bettmann Archive, Inc.)

Motown

Title
"Stop! In the Name of Love"

Performers
The Supremes

Form
Modified verse-chorus

Meter
Four beats to the bar

Tempo
Moderate

Here the chorus, or refrain, serves as the "hook," a catchy four-measure phrase that begins the song and that recurs after each sixteen-measure (four-line) verse.

Refrain: Sung by the Supremes (four measures)
Instrumental phrase: Four measures.
Verse: Sung by Diana Ross (sixteen measures). We hear the Supremes in the background, and toward the end of the verse, the Supremes sing a brief phrase ("Think it o-o-ver") that serves as a further unifying factor— besides the refrain—throughout the song.
Refrain: The Supremes sing it twice, adding the "Think it o-o-ver" motto, also twice.
Verse: Diana Ross, with the Supremes in the background. As Ross sings the fourth line of the verse, the Supremes join her, repeating "Think it-o-o-ver."
Refrain: As before.
Verse: Diana Ross sings just two lines of the verse, and all bring the song to an end with repetitions of the refrain and the unifying motto.

Notice the constant steady pulse, with accents applied about equally between downbeat and backbeat throughout the song.

[handwritten margin note: Music of uniformity and left little room for individual development]

perfectly illustrating both the virtues and liabilities of Motown: That is, the conformity and uniformity Gordy demanded left little room for individual development. Stevie Wonder, who also recorded for Motown, became the first member of the group to achieve artistic independence and gain control over his own recordings.

Although Motown made a lot of money for black singers, the music they produced was actually more popular with white than with black listeners, and by the mid-sixties, black musicians were effectively asserting themselves with their own new music, *soul.* First, however, an invasion from abroad revitalized the fading American rock and roll.

The British Invasion

The baby boom following the war years produced a generation of underemployed, undereducated, and often underfed English teenagers, some of whom vented their frustrations in assorted antisocial ways. Many joined one of two rival gangs, the Rockers or the Mods, which provided a sense of identity and belonging while fostering rough, delinquent behavior.

Many young gang members were avid fans of rhythm and blues and rock and roll, for by the late 1950s popular American recordings were well known in England, where several successful concert tours had taken place. But young English fans were profoundly disturbed at the commercialization they perceived diluting their favorite music—in fact threatening to render rock and roll obsolete. Ultimately, the unlikely combination of four English Rockers effectively revitalized the fading American style.

The Beatles The remarkable group that came to be known as the **Beatles** (in punning reference to Buddy Holly's Crickets, whom they greatly admired, and "beat" music) began as a Liverpool gang more interested in finding trouble than in changing the course of rock and roll. John Lennon formed the group, which included Paul McCartney and soon George Harrison. Music was among the more innocent activities of these three talented, although largely untrained, musicians, who performed their early songs, most of them pleasantly simple and naive, in a rather primitive performance style. Whereas Lennon was more inclined to shout than to sing, McCartney had a beautiful voice, and Harrison played the guitar extremely well.

In 1962, having replaced their early drummer Pete Best with the already popular Ringo Starr (Figure 95), the Beatles shared a London performance with Little Richard, recently returned to rock and roll, and became an overnight sensation. They attracted a producer, quickly became famous in England, and very soon were rocking the musical world with their own brand of rock and roll.

Impressed with the growing fame of the young rock and rollers, whose records by 1963 were hugely popular in America, television host Ed Sullivan invited the Beatles to perform on his popular television show in 1964—little anticipating the riot of enthusiasm their arrival in America would cause. Their clothes, hair styles, and foreign accents made a terrific impression on American teens, who screamed and swooned with adulation. The Beatles's lighthearted, good-natured songs with their catchy melodies and quite innocent lyrics ("I Want to Hold Your Hand") lifted the spirits of American youth, inaugurating Beatlemania.

Figure 95

The Beatles in 1963.
Pictured left to right: bass
guitarist Paul McCartney,
guitarist George Harrison,
guitarist John Lennon, and
drummer Ringo Starr
(AP/Wide World Photos.)

Also during 1964, the Beatles made their first film, *A Hard Day's Night,* which included several hit songs compiled into a loosely structured album. Later Beatles albums, however (especially *Sgt. Pepper's Lonely Hearts Club Band* and *Abbey Road*), constituted sophisticated productions, tightly integrated around a unifying theme. Hugely successful and well-to-do by 1966, the Beatles stopped touring, preferring to record in studios using the new technological facilities to supreme effect. They also made several more films.

Lennon, McCartney, and Harrison all composed for the group. Lennon's poetry was especially effective, his later verses, symbolic and complex, addressing subjects of universal interest and often laden with idealistic messages. The band's instrumental music had more significance in later days as well, for their playing had improved by then, and their albums began to include more, and more interesting, instrumental passages. Eclectic in their interests, they proved to be incredibly versatile musicians, reflecting in their compositions and performances toward the end of the sixties the influences of Harrison's travels in India, for example.

But at the end of just a decade, the Beatles separated, each wishing—needing—to satisfy his own creative needs. John Lennon remained largely secluded from that time, working with his wife Yoko Ono on various artistic projects until his tragic death in 1980. Today the three surviving Beatles continue to generate innovative musical ideas, occasionally collaborating on new projects. Paul McCartney formed a successful group of his own, Wings, which has periodically disbanded and re-formed. He now lives quietly at his home in England, where he has recently completed a new record album in his private studio. The other two Beatles have remained less active musically, although George Harrison has made several record albums and worked on films with members of the British comedy team Monty Python, and Ringo

Starr continues to perform as a singer, actor, and drummer. Starr toured the United States during the summer of 1992, having just released *Time Takes Time,* his first studio recording since 1983.

Post-Beatles English Rock The music of Elton John (born Reginald Kenneth Dwight), who became a popular rock pianist and singer in both England and America in the early 1960s, is distinctive among English rockers in that it clearly reflects country-western styles. Although Elton John attracted as much attention with his appearance as with his songs, wearing outlandish clothes and spectacular spectacles, these could not detract from his talent, which was prodigious. (In 1988, no longer needing such gimmicks, he sold some of his adornments very profitably at auction.) His songs written for the 1994 film *The Lion King* revealed his enduring ability to charm the young and young-at-heart with his music.

The Who evolved later in the sixties, an unlikely combination of talented but disparate individuals. Although each member of the group performed in a style unlike the others, somehow their brand of chaos worked, and they became quite popular in the United States. Their rock opera *Tommy,* written in 1969, was made into a successful film in 1975, and a revival of the show toured the United States to highly favorable reviews in the mid-nineties.

The Rolling Stones, another hugely influential English group, also began to perform in the early sixties; but because their style and influence belong to the next decade, we will discuss them in Chapter 14.

Back to Black Rock

Relationships between black and white rock and roll have been and remain curious and complex: With roots in both cultures, rock was primarily a black concept; yet white country singers who *sounded* black made the style popular, and the Beatles gave it the shot of energy that rescued it from early death. American blacks, however, soon sought to regain the initiative they had temporarily lost to English groups and soloists.

By the mid-sixties, "black power" and "black is beautiful" were potent slogans in the United States, where blacks generally had less interest in integrating with whites than in establishing their own cultural identity. Many, resentful of the basically white flavor of the Motown sound, began to perform a kind of updated rhythm and blues, which they named *soul,* a post-fifties term for black pride and the term with which *Billboard,* in 1964, replaced rhythm and blues.

Soul At first, **soul** evolved as a new blues, sung by small vocal groups with harsh voices and a rough delivery style, accompanied by small combos, usually including a saxophone. The added intensity of conviction, passion, and sincerity characteristic of the new black music, blending secular lyrics and gospel energy, remained inherent even in the broader stream of music to which the term soul came to be applied.

Figure 96

American blues, gospel, soul, pop, and jazz singer Aretha Franklin. (Hulton Getty Picture Archive.)

Aretha Franklin (Figure 96), known as "Lady Soul," began her music experience singing in church and, like many soul singers, transferred the emotional gospel style to popular and rhythm-and-blues songs. The African roots of soul are apparent in the harsh, intensely emotional singing of another great soul singer, James Brown ("Mr. Dynamite") (heard in Listening Example 54).

Blind from glaucoma from the age of seven, the acknowledged genius or "father" of soul Ray Charles (b. Ray Charles Robinson in 1930) received excellent music training in his teens, becoming a fine pianist and singer and also learning to play the saxophone. Among the first blacks to become technically expert with studio recording technology, Charles thereby enhanced the quality of recordings by himself and other blacks. He also has a great gift for involving an audience in his performances, singing secular songs with gospel music abandon and using call-and-response to capture listeners' attention and participation. A knowledgeable and complex musician who continues to work year-round, Charles blends the improvisation of jazz, the beat of rhythm and blues, and the emotional fervor of gospel in his own infectious but inimitable style.

From Rock and Roll to Rock

Ominous, often tragic, social events of the mid- to late sixties, including riots in the ghettos of Harlem and Watts in 1965, further race riots in 1967, and the murder of Martin Luther King, Jr., in 1968, again changed the mood and the music of youth. As students held sit-ins at colleges across the land protesting

Soul

Composer/Performer
James Brown

Title
"Papa's Got a Brand New Bag"

Meter
Four beats to the bar

Form
Twelve-bar blues

After a brief instrumental introduction—announcement, really—Brown sings six verses, praising "Papa's brand new bag" and the way she dances. Brown generally conforms to the twelve-bar blues form and harmony changes; however, the second line of text in each verse is original, rather than a repeat of the first line as in the classic blues. Notice, too, that the fourth verse consists of only two lines, instead of three.

The accompanying instruments (bass, horns, drums, guitar) play overlapping, independent rhythmic patterns (*polyrhythms*), punctuating the vocal line and adding rhythmic as well as timbre interest. We do not hear the competition or interaction between voice and instruments typical of classic blues performances.

discrimination, authoritarianism, and eventually the war in Vietnam, popular music closely reflected the new mood. The vivid new music replacing the carefree early rock and roll was collectively called **rock,** of which many and diverse branches or brands evolved.

Folk Rock

The mood of protest having strengthened, rock crowds demanded more than entertainment, and by 1965 urban folk singers who included protest songs in their college and night club performances were addressing rock audiences as well, reflecting the serious new mood by blending light rock effects with tuneful melodies and protest lyrics in what became known as **folk rock.** Mellow groups such as Peter, Paul and Mary, unable or unwilling to update their lyrics and their style, quickly became less relevant and less popular.

On the other hand, urban folk singer Joan Baez (Figure 97) was among those who intensified the emotional content of their songs and addressed topics of current controversy and concern. Drawing upon her examples and those of Woody Guthrie and Pete Seeger, other folk musicians also began adding elements of rock to their performances, thereby reaching a wider audience.

Figure 97
Joan Baez performing
at Big Sur.
(Bettmann Newsphotos.)

To the confusion of some fans, Bob Dylan switched from urban folk to folk rock in 1965, replacing the acoustic instruments of his early days with an electric guitar and a rock rhythm section. And when Dylan began to sing of personal rather than of social or universal problems, he antagonized many previously loyal listeners. Some think today, however, that the powerful messages of protest and reform in Dylan's moving poetry are destined to survive his music.

Several groups joined the folk rock movement: The Mamas and the Papas added a light rock flavor to their familiar style of folk music; Crosby, Stills, Nash, and Young also updated their sound by adding light rock effects; Simon and Garfunkel and The Fifth Dimension performed in folk rock style as well. But The Byrds, even more strongly affected by Bob Dylan's new approach, became the group most closely allied to the folk rock style, using the amplification and distortion of instrument sounds for expressive effect. Their recorded versions of Dylan's "Mr. Tambourine Man" and Pete Seeger's "Turn! Turn! Turn!" made a very strong and lasting impact on a wide audience (Listening Example 55).

Acid Rock "Psychedelic" or **acid rock** began, in San Francisco, about 1965 as an attempt to reproduce the sensations experienced by someone under the influence of LSD ("acid" in street slang). Because the music was to be *felt* as well as heard, the sound was amplified to unprecedented levels, the extremely—even excruciatingly—loud volume and heavy distortion of sounds causing emotional, psychological, indeed psychedelic effects in the listener. Improved amplification systems and other technical advances made stadiums and large arenas the perfect venue for huge concerts, perfectly suited to the acid rock experience. During performances, which often were extremely long (time being meaningless to someone in a psychedelic trance),

[handwritten margin notes:] Began in San Francisco in 1965

music was to be felt as well as heard

music used to reproduce the feelings of taking LSD

Loud - Distortion sound.

Folk Rock

Composer
Bob Dylan

Title
"Mr. Tambourine Man"

Performers
The Byrds

Meter
Four beats to the bar

Tempo
Slow, relaxed

Form
Verse and refrain

During the four-bar instrumental introduction, the drums and tambourine punctuate the sounds of the twelve-string electric guitar, electric bass, and other instruments with a strong backbeat.

The Byrds sing the song's familiar two-line (eight bars in each line) refrain in their close, country-style harmony, the main melody sometimes lying below a higher melodic line, or *countermelody,* as often occurs in country music. Their simple chords occur in slightly surprising order compared with the harmony of earlier popular music

The soloist (singer/guitarist Roger [Jim] McGuinn) sings two verses of irregular length: fourteen lines in the first, ten in the second. (Such irregularity of phrase length and stanza lines is reminiscent of the traditional manner of performing folk songs such as "Barbara Allen," Listening Example 4.) Perhaps the several other verses Dylan wrote for the song, expressing loneliness and the desire to find relief in the sound of the tambourine, seemed too personal for group performance; in any case, the Byrds' performance is less than half the length of Dylan's recording of "Mr. Tambourine Man."

The Byrds sing the refrain once more, and the guitar and bass gently fade away.

dramatic light shows, emissions from smoke and fog machines, and other special effects produced their own psychedelic aura, rendering such concerts theatrical events in which music constituted only one of the entertainment elements, and in which the audience was expected to be totally involved. References to drugs, sometimes expressed in code to avoid censorship, became more and more overt: "White Rabbit," performed by Jefferson Airplane, never pretended to be about anything else.

Entertainment in the music

Yet while some acid rock groups, such as The Doors, sang of sex and death and self-destruction, The Grateful Dead, associated with the same movement, remained relatively mild (or at least less violent) in performance. Their members earned credibility by living for a time in the Haight-Ashbury district of San Francisco, sharing the hippie experience they related in their music, and even today these solid rock and blues musicians retain a devoted following.

Psychedelic Blues Two blazingly gifted stars, one a singer, one a guitarist, changed the concept of musical sound and experience in their astonishing performances of psychedelic blues. When Janis Joplin passionately sang of her sad and hopeless life, or Jimi Hendrix set fire to his guitars on stage, the audience literally felt the performers' pain.

Janis Joplin (1943–1970, Figure 98), a white woman inspired by Bessie Smith and Willie Mae "Big Mama" Thornton, imbued every song she sang with the passion and sincerity of the blues. With a voice sometimes described as coarse sandpaper, Joplin became the most powerful female performer of the rock era, expressing with eloquence, but never overcoming, the agony of her sad and hopeless life.

A poor, half African American, half Native American left-handed guitarist from Seattle, **Jimi Hendrix** (1942–1970, Figure 99) captured the spirit of despair and frustration of late-sixties American (and British) youth with his scorching electric guitar. Indulging freely in the drugs he believed enhanced his passion and performance skills, he delivered all the anger and violence of

Figure 98

Janis Joplin. Acid rock was a means of expressing frustration with the values of an older generation. (Wide World Photos.)

the era in his thunderous electric blues, famously dousing his guitar with lighter fluid and setting it on fire at the 1967 Monterey Pop Festival.

Gifted beyond verbal description, Hendrix used his enormous talent to develop guitar techniques beyond the imagination, and the ability, of fellow guitarists. Although solidly rooted in the blues, which Hendrix played to masterful effect, his music forged a new world of previously unheard sounds. To the extreme electronic feedback and distortion being used by other like-minded guitarists, he added his own distinctive vocabulary of riffs, bent notes, scales, and electronic effects, making his music truly personal and in fact inimitable.

Heavy Metal

Heavy Metal The late sixties produced several American groups inspired by the wild, frenzied performances and distorted guitar sounds of the British Led Zeppelin (which developed a huge and nearly fanatical following in the United States) and by the explosive innovations of Jimi Hendrix, whose style became identified as **heavy metal.** The new sound, extremely loud and often electronically distorted, achieved American identity through Blue Cheer, formed in 1966, and Iron Butterfly, whose recording of "In-A-Gadda-Da-Vida" ("In a Garden of Eden"?) added distorted guitar to the sound of an electric organ.

Alice Cooper, as both the musician Vincent Furnier and his band were known, delivered overtly sexual, heavy-metal rock theatrics. Their sensational tactics (Furnier often donned a boa snake) won further acclaim in the early seventies, when theatricality dominated rock performances.

Figure 99
American musician Jimi Hendrix. (Joseph Sia/Archive Photos.)

A Future Unassured

Toward the end of its second decade, rock was being celebrated at major rock festivals across the country, the most notable of which, held at Woodstock, New York, in August of 1969, was attended by more than 400,000 people. But some such festivals spawned violence and tragedy: Four people died at Altamount Speedway near San Francisco, and three were killed at the "Celebration of Life" on the banks of Louisiana's Atchafalaya River. Rockers hardly seemed to know how to celebrate their hard-won recognition; and although rock music had grown strong and varied, its future seemed insecure as the 1970s began.

Terms to Review

rhythm and blues (r&b)   Broadly, black popular music of the 1950s. More specifically, a black popular style in quadruple meter, with strong backbeats and a danceable tempo.

doo-wop   The name given background vocal ensembles accompanying Motown singers, often by singing neutral or nonsense syllables.

rock and roll   A popular music of the mid-fifties to mid-sixties combining characteristics of rhythm-and-blues and country-western music.

vibrato   A slight variation in pitch that adds warmth and intensity to vocal or instrumental sounds.

payola   The acceptance by disc jockeys of money and gifts in return for plugging recordings.

surfing songs   Songs by the Beach Boys and other groups reflecting the easy California lifestyle.

Motown   A highly successful black company that recorded, published, and sponsored black popular music.

soul   A fervent, emotional black style rooted in gospel and the blues.

rock   A collective term encompassing many styles of popular music that evolved from and succeeded rock and roll.

folk rock   The addition of light rock effects to urban folk music.

acid rock   Sometimes called psychedelic rock. Music that attempts to evoke the sensations experienced by a person under the influence of LSD.

heavy metal   A rock style, extremely loud and often electronically distorted, introduced by Jimi Hendrix.

Key Figures

Alan Freed
Bill Haley and His Comets
Elvis Presley
Chuck Berry
Berry Gordy, Jr.
Beatles
Janis Joplin
Jimi Hendrix
Alice Cooper

Suggestions for Further Listening

Atlantic Rhythm and Blues, vols. 1–7
Bill Haley: *Golden Hits*
      Greatest Hits
Elvis Presley: *Golden,* vols. 1–4
Chuck Berry: *Greatest Hits*
Beach Boys: *The Best of the Beach Boys*
Bob Dylan: *Times They Are a-Changin'*
Ray Charles: *Rock Begins,* vol. 1

14

Popular Music since 1970

The year 1970 was one of devastating social and political significance in the United States. Frustrated protests against the war in Vietnam provoked hostility throughout the strata of society, most notably on college campuses around the country. When National Guard troops shot at Kent State University student protesters, killing four and wounding at least nine, student riots broke out but soon succumbed to a despairing sense of demoralization and helplessness. Meanwhile other groups, including women, Native Americans, Chicanos, and gays, inspired by the civil rights movement of the sixties against the conservative "silent majority" caused further unrest in American society.

Rockers were deeply affected by the mood of the time, further darkened by the deaths of several prominent rock figures—Jimi Hendrix (1970) from an overdose of sleeping pills, Janis Joplin (1970) from an overdose of heroin, and Jim Morrison of The Doors (1971) from a heart attack. Musical innovation temporarily lessened as rockers absorbed these shocks and looked ahead; and some groups, for whom the sound engineer had become an essential partner in performance, abandoned live performance entirely.

Nevertheless, solo singers, many of whom wrote their own songs, acquired significance as the new decade began. Synthesizers and other electronic instruments increasingly varied the sonorities of live and recorded performances, and concerts and recordings achieved new levels of sophistication. At this difficult turning point in the history of American rock, the music of a British group, contemporary with but entirely different from the Beatles, helped bridge the gap from the past to the future of rock.

The Rolling Stones — Bridging the Gap from past to future

We have seen that the Beatles belonged, both in actual time and in style, to the sixties. But the style of the rival British group the **Rolling Stones,** who also began performing in the early sixties, was always closer to the acid rock and punk of the seventies; and unlike the Beatles, the Rolling Stones remain somewhat active to the present day.

From the beginning, the Stones differed from the Beatles in nearly every respect. Their leader, Mick Jagger, came from a comfortable middle-class home, and all of the Stones were relatively well off. Although they identified with the

233

music of poor black Americans and sang in black style, their values were highly materialistic, and they soon developed an insatiable lust for wealth.

Again unlike the Beatles, whose messages were generally hopeful and sometimes pleasantly naive, the Stones sang aggressive songs of revolt and destruction. Their style has evolved over the decades, although always strongly influenced by black music, and they have survived, with occasional changes in personnel, to maintain long-lived, if limited, popularity.

Art Rock

Rockers and jazz musicians increasingly collaborated among themselves while also incorporating effects of the music of other cultures. **Blood, Sweat and Tears,** a rock quartet with a brass section and later with a saxophone as well, produced a sound closer to jazz than rock, whereas the even more popular group **Chicago** included rock musicians who incorporated in their music some elements of jazz. Although rock and classical music seem a less likely combination than the vernacular rock and jazz, the interest in fusion also encouraged collaborative experiments among musicians in those fields, with varying degrees of success. The superficial quoting of themes from familiar classics, as in Ekseption's "The Fifth," based on themes of Beethoven, seems musically insignificant, and most arrangements of classical pieces that use rock instrumentation and rhythms have not proved of much or of lasting interest.

Some ensembles, however—several if not most of them British—have achieved an effective blend of serious concert music and rock, called **art rock.** (The term "art rock" does not imply that other rock styles lack artistic qualities: It is simply a convenient way to describe the combination of rock with concepts of "classical," "concert," or "art" music. Each of those terms is flawed as well, and the conscientious musician uses them with qualification.)

Emerson Lake and Palmer related rock to classical music in several intriguing pieces. The Moody Blues produced an art rock album with the London Festival Orchestra in 1967, and Genesis, King Crimson, Pink Floyd, and Yes are among other English groups who have explored the concept of art rock. A Dutch group, Focus, and a New York ensemble, Ars Nova, also have experimented with this combined style. Leonard Bernstein's Mass, written for the opening of the Kennedy Center for the Performing Arts in Washington, D.C. (1971), represents another approach to the combination of art and rock styles.

Funk

Funk began as a new expression of black consciousness, rooted in soul, often with lyrics referring specifically to interracial issues (see pp. 186–187). When a number of white musicians responded to the lure of funk by copying it, funk formed in a sense a bridge between sympathetic whites and blacks.

Jazz + Rock combination

Rock combined with "classical" "concert," or "art" music

The Moody Blues Pink Floyd

*— new expression of black consciousness
— rooted in soul
— lyrics attaining to interracial issues*

Figure 100
American rock, soul, and
funk group Sly and the
Family Stone.
(Hulton Getty Picture
Archive.)

Although related to the blues in mood and instrumentation, funk follows no prescribed harmonic pattern as guitars and/or keyboards fill in simple, repetitive harmonies above a strong bass-guitar line. Rhythms, often highly complex, are punctuated by an intriguing variety of drums. All four beats in a measure may be accented evenly in striking difference from the strong back-beats characteristic of much rock music.

The 1970 recording of "Thank You (Falettinme Be Mice Elf Agin)" by **Sly Stone** (Figure 100) introduced the bizarre spellings imitated by some later funk musicians. **George Clinton,** leader of the group called Funkadelic, is considered a rigorously pure funk musician, but many other groups participate in funk with less consistency and dedication. Thus **Earth, Wind and Fire** is considered a jazz-funk group, whereas **The Commodores** are a smooth funk band with crossover appeal to the disco audience. The funk music of **Kool and the Gang** includes their 1970 recording "Funky Stuff" and, from later in the seventies, "Celebration."

Disco

Disco, which began as *discothèque* in post–World War II France, may be seen as the result of a romance or a clash between the popular cultures of Europe and America, and between the social elite and the cultural underworld. It is a difficult music to place, having begun in French jazz clubs, turned to rock music in the United States in the sixties, and topped the pop charts in 1975.

Swing and jazz clubs in France, banned by the Germans in wartime because of their American and black and Jewish associations, became symbols of dissent in the French underground, enhancing their aura of illicit excitement and thrill. The first American discothèque, which opened on New Year's Eve 1960, catered to a desire among wealthy jet-setters for an entertainment atmosphere less staid than New York's famous Stork Club and

El Morocco. Soon more clubs opened, in New York and in other American cities, all however retaining highly exclusive requirements, including expensive membership dues.

By the mid-sixties, the discothèque had spawned a multitude of dance crazes, including the Twist, the Jerk, and the Watusi among many others, and the role of the disc jockey evolved from the anonymous one of simply playing records to sensing and directing the mood of a crowd throughout the evening. Discothèques of the late sixties offered enormous dance floors, multiple rock bands playing live music (instead of records), huge rotating mirrored light balls, and extreme sonic overload, all inducing virtual hallucinogenic states. But as the role of discothèque attendees altered from frenzied dancer to passive observer, the discothèque phenomenon seemed about to fade away.

In the seventies, however, it was dramatically reanimated by gay men, blacks, Hispanics, and other urban contingents suppressed during the sixties and reveling in their newly liberated position. Thus relaunched, and rechristened *disco,* the popular dance phenomenon maintained a highly visible presence throughout the new decade (Figure 101). Much of the disco culture concerned drugs and sex, and the hedonistic philosophy that nothing is wrong if it feels right (or as Mae West once said, "Too much of a good thing may be a great thing") remained at the core of disco culture; but it also produced the first distinctive disco music. Dissatisfied with short rock singles not primarily intended for dancing, disco deejays and dancers of the seventies sought extended pieces with continuous danceable rhythms based on the black r&b roots of pop music. The early seventies produced several hit disco songs, and in 1975 Van McCoy and "The Hustle" went to the top of the pop charts, signifying the mainstreaming of a culture that had prided itself on various kinds of exclusivity, from the wealthy elite to black and gay men.

The new crowds attending Studio 54, which opened in New York in 1977, still had to pass the "entrance requirements" of the club's owners; but at the end of that year, the astounding success of the film *Saturday Night Fever* further buoyed disco's rising fortunes. The movie's double-album soundtrack eventually became the biggest-selling record of all time (later replaced by Michael Jackson's *Thriller*), and by 1978 40 percent of all the music on *Billboard*'s Hot 100 was disco. The songs of the Bee Gees, biggest of all mainstream disco stars, were on traditional pop music themes having no relationship to the hedonistic, highly sexualized culture of most early disco.

For a time, rock fans felt threatened by disco, which they viewed as synthetic, aristocratic, and fake; but in the end disco provided the common enemy against which rock fans rallied. The Disco Demolition Rally at Chicago's Comiskey Park Stadium in July 1979, in fact, blasted out of control, as rock fans broke up mountains of disco records as well as much of the stadium itself, giving Comiskey much the same role in defeating disco that the bloody Altamont concert had played in ending the sixties counterculture. After Comiskey Park, the disco market crashed, doomed as well by a conservative political wave and the fear of AIDS.

Figure 101
Overhead view of the crowd dancing at Studio 54 in New York City, New York, October 31, 1981. (Tom Gateo/Archive Photos.)

Punk

Rock styles continued to proliferate as America entered the 1980s. A number of new sounds erupted, and important stars altered or adapted their music to suit quickly evolving tastes. Much like the social conditions of the early sixties that spawned the Beatles, the mid-seventies had produced a crop of young Britishers who were poor, unemployed, and highly resentful of social inequities, political hypocrisy, and rich rock stars. By the end of that decade, most rock musicians were admittedly performing more for the sake of money than for art, blatantly adjusting their styles to meet popular demand. Again it was in Britain that an idealistic reaction arose against the betrayal of the essence of rock. To rescue rock from succumbing under the weight of its own success, the British invented **punk.**

Punk had roots on the American side of the Atlantic as well: the self-destructive behavior of Iggy Pop, the combative stance of Detroit's MC5, and the drone of the Velvet Underground's lead singer Lou Reed all presaged the advent of punk rock in the mid-seventies. The first successful (better, notorious) punk group, the Sex Pistols (who were British), spurred the advent of

another British invention that was a protest to the "money hungry" "rock stars."

Figure 102
Influential American glam
rock band, the New York
Dolls.
(Hulton Getty Picture
Archive.)

*the visual aspects
of punk influenced
art + the fashion
world.*

other groups, British and American, whose music contended that nothing short of overturning society could improve the sorry state of the world.

The musical elements associated with punk include a rigid eighth-note rhythmic throb and a vocal range so narrow as to approach a drone; but ultimately of more interest, perhaps, is punk's association with the art world. A significant number of punk musicians attended art school and brought to their music modern art concepts of shock value, performance as art, and fashion, which profoundly affected the music they performed and the manner they performed it. (We have already mentioned Andy Warhol's connection with the movement.) In fact, the striking visual effects of punk dress, hair, and makeup strongly influenced art and fashion around the world.

American society effectively put down punk not with censorship, but with imitation, as fashion models spiked their hair and ostentatiously fastened gaping holes in their trendy clothes with flashy safety pins. Yet America also produced successful punk bands, most notably the **Ramones** and the **New York Dolls**—five men dressed and made up as women (Figure 102). Among the women actually participating in the punk movement, **Patti Smith** sang angry, gutsy vocals with lyrics and a delivery style calculated to shock her audience.

In the nineties, several California punk-rock bands, including the **Offspring, Rancid,** and **Green Day,** brought punk to a mass public, singing of alienation, resentment, and self-destruction to very short, catchy tunes accompanied by speed-strummed guitars and walloping drums. No longer the music of a righteous minority, the humor and tuneful adrenaline of punk play today to a wide audience.

New Wave

The term **new wave** was loosely applied to several sounds of the mid-eighties, some of which reflected certain characteristics of earlier styles. But the term always referred to new or progressive music, conceived with the aid of modern studio and electronic techniques.

New wave groups, neither angry nor political, further defused punk by emulating its manner but not its substance: Adopting punk's unconventional dress and bizarre stage movements, new wave musicians criticized society without resorting to shock tactics. Although new wave music contained some of the elements of punk, it was far broader in concept, in fact constituting more a philosophy of life expressed through music than a distinctive musical style.

Much of the music of one outstanding American new wave group, the **Talking Heads,** is based on the simple harmonies and complex rhythms of some African musics; but the music of other well-known new wave bands, including the **B-52**s, the **Cars,** and especially, the **Police,** respond to different sources of inspiration. A British brand of new wave, called *ska,* combines Jamaican reggae music with a contemporary rock band usually composed of both black and white musicians.

A Multiplicity of Styles

By the mid-1980s, popularity had shifted away from new wave, as many bands and several individuals with distinctive sounds became rich and famous. They were variously identified by a string of labels (*new romantics, blitz, punk-jazz, blue wave, techno-pop,* and *techno-funk,* among others). Prince (known then as "the artist formerly known as Prince"), Michael Jackson, Lionel Richie, Madonna, Cyndi Lauper, and Sting (formerly of the Police), among the best-known names of mainstream rock in the eighties, maintained various degrees of popularity through the nineties. "The Boss" **Bruce Springsteen,** probably the most successful rock star of the late seventies, having pointed rock in a new direction in his 1982 album *Born in the U.S.A.,* further revitalized music in the mid-eighties with his stirring songs on socially relevant topics, whose messages were further implemented by Springsteen and other like-minded rock stars in the rock-sponsored benefits for starving masses in Ethiopia, "We Are the World" and "Live Aid." In 1995, Springsteen commanded new attention and respect with his profoundly moving songs in the film *Philadelphia.*

Teenagers of the nineties, called Generation X by the press, continued to find rock a congenial medium in which to release their own fears and frustrations brought about by economic uncertainty; family instability; violence on TV, the movie screen, and in the streets; gangs; race warfare; and social injustice. Some craved an angry, harsh, aggressive sound reflecting their own disturbed feelings.

Rap

Rap, which began as a means of black self-expression in the mid-seventies and attracted wide attention throughout the next decade, has raised perennial questions about the relationships among art, politics, and public morality. The rapidly spoken patter accompanied by funk-style rhythms evolved partly

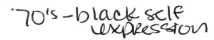
'70's – black self expression

- African chanting
- Muhammad Ali
  and his boasting
  poetry
- Jamaican reggae

from the complex rhythms of African chanting, the boasting poetry of Muhammad Ali, and the message songs (spoken blues) of James Brown in the sixties. Strongest of all was the influence of the Jamaican-based reggae (pp. 207–208).

Rappers deliver rhymed verses addressing topical social and/or political concerns, speaking them extremely rapidly over **hip-hop,** a sound introduced by Jamaican disc jockeys who scratched and otherwise manipulated records spinning on the turntable. The nature of the words more than the style of music renders rap a controversial rock music: Devotees appreciate its fervent expression ranging the gamut of human emotion—anger, passion, love, joy, frustration, even hate—whereas detractors decry the violence inherent in some rap lyrics. Many rappers extol men's domination of women; but Queen Latifah's album *Black Rain* is packed with socially responsible messages about safe sex, relationships, and love; and the female trio **Salt-n-Pepa** (Figure 103) has offered stinging criticism of male promiscuity. Salt-n-Pepa's third album, *Very Necessary,* rhymes the praises of men, however.

Today hip-hop refers to a wide-ranging art form that developed from early rap, music that reports on and reveals the darkest aspects of ghetto life. The language with which Ice-T, Ice Cube, and the Geto Boys, for example, rap about gang warfare and drive-by shootings is offensive to many, but the situations they so blazingly describe certainly exist.

Tupac Shakur, murdered at age twenty-four, rapped about violence, social realism, fate, and pain. Moments of tenderness and compassion in his songs are overwhelmed with fierce black-against-black anger and brutality, and he followed expressions of respectful praise for women with harangues about "bitches" and "ho's." White rapper Eminem, a master of gallows and gross-out humor, gleefully aims cruel jibes at gays, women (including his mother and his wife), and assorted people in real public life; yet he is admired by

Figure 103
Salt-n-Pepa.
(The Bettman Archive, Inc.)

many for his ingenious wordplay, inventive beats, daring candor, and wicked humor. His album *Marshall Mathers,* released in spring 2000, became hip-hop's fastest-selling release ever and the nation's sales leader for eight consecutive weeks.

Scorned and revered, banned and adored, white and black rappers continue to stir controversy and to sell records—in record numbers. Like any other music, rap is a vehicle of expression subject to interpretation by performing musicians and listening audience alike.

Contemporary Black Gospel

Today's black gospel, although deeply rooted in early traditions, sounds very little like the spirituals sung, shouted, and danced in camp meetings over a century ago. Recently, perhaps for the first time, the secular elements of gospel have stirred significant controversy. Electric bass, keyboards, and even a hip-hop flavor bring gospel to rock mainstream airwaves, to the joy of some and the dismay of traditional gospel fans, who see the trend as more toward making money than saving souls.

Certainly the money is rolling in: recently contemporary, or crossover, gospel became America's fifth-largest musical genre, trailing only r&b, alternative, rap, and country on the charts. Gospel's virtuoso instrumentalists blend jazz, rock, country, funk, and hip-hop gestures, and gospel choral singing, full-throated and dramatic, is a thrilling sound. Soloists ignite audiences with the power and range of their voices and with their intricate melodic invention rivaling the improvisations of jazz. Of course the recordings have never sounded better, because of higher production standards.

Kirk Franklin skillfully melds hip-hop and traditional gospel conventions in performances such as his popular hit "Stomp," a collaboration with the group God's Property, featuring the rhythm track to the Funkadelic's funk anthem "One Nation under a Groove" and a guest rap by Salt (Cheryl James) of Salt-n-Pepa. Franklin's explosive vocal presentation has been compared with that of James Brown or Ray Charles—both of whom stood criticism for blending sacred and secular effects.

Traditional gospel continues to thrive as well, most notably perhaps in the person of **Shirley Caesar,** who began her gospel career in the fifties and was recently featured on the soundtrack of the Disney film *The Prince of Egypt.* The crossover trend may be a cyclical phenomenon or simply a natural consequence of the manner in which this important, stimulating sacred/secular music has evolved.

A Promising Future

New technology makes possible an array of sophisticated effects, and acculturation becomes ever more significant as improved communication and expanded travel bring fascinating new sounds to the Western vernacular music experience. Many rockers draw from a wide variety of sources, marrying rap, for example, with punk or other rock musics to achieve vibrant new sounds. On his 1992 album *Body Count,* rapper Ice-T accompanied his angry rhymes about prison, drugs, and police abuse with a heavy metal band, claiming, "It's all rock and roll," and many prominent rockers have followed his influential lead.

In the Northwest, which scored new national attention in the early 1990s with the television programs *Twin Peaks* and *Northern Exposure,* **grunge,** sometimes called the Seattle sound, combined the aggression of heavy metal with a melodic element reminiscent of the Beatles. The pacesetter grunge band **Nirvana** achieved a pop/metal/punk hybrid in songs expressive of the pain and frustration felt by Generation Xers with broken families, dismal economic prospects, and regular exposure to violence on television and in films if not in real life. Pearl Jam followed Nirvana to the top of the chart in 1991, and in 1993, the early grunge band Soundgarden hit the top with *Super-unknown.* The post–baby boomers despair was heightened by the drug over-dose deaths of some grunge soloists and especially the shotgun suicide of **Kurt Cobain,** probably the most important figure in the movement; but grunge con-tinues, through such bands as **Hole** fronted by Cobain's wife **Courtney Love,** to give vent to the anger, frustration, and disillusionment of Generation X much as early rock and roll addressed the needs of the baby boomers.

On the other hand, although social consciousness continues to stir rockers' emotions and stimulate their talents, many rock musicians have returned to their roots: Thus rhythm and blues, rockabilly, soul, and psychedelic music can all be heard today. And so a new generation, representing many cultures, races, and experiences, carries forward the remarkably varied and seemingly durable music we call rock.

Terms to Review

art rock   A blend of rock and symphonic or concert styles.

funk   Rock music rooted in soul but with lyrics expressing interracial concerns.

disco   Commercial dance music popular in the seventies.

punk   A British reaction to flagrantly commercial rock and roll.

new wave   A term encompassing several styles, all conceived within the context of modern studio and electronic techniques.

rap   Rapidly spoken patter derived from reggae performance practices, accompanied by funk-style rhythms.

hip-hop   Sounds accompanying rapped lyrics.

grunge   The Seattle sound, a hybrid of pop, heavy metal, and punk.

Key Figures

Individuals:

Sly Stone
George Clinton
Patti Smith
Bruce Springsteen
Kirk Franklin
Shirley Caesar
Kurt Cobain
Courtney Love

Groups:

Rolling Stones
Blood, Sweat and Tears
Chicago
Earth, Wind and Fire
The Commodores
Kool and the Gang
Ramones

New York Dolls
Offspring
Rancid
Green Day
Talking Heads
B-52s
Cars
Police
Salt-n-Pepa
Nirvana
Hole

Suggestions for Listening

The New York Dolls: "Personality Crisis"
Patti Smith: *Horses; Dream of Life*
The Ramones: *Ramones*
Talking Heads: *Stop Making Sense*
Chicago: *Chicago V*

The form of John Philip Sousa's marches, namely a series of melodic strains, was also the form of ragtime, a written piano music combining black rhythmic effects with European harmony and form. Ragtime pianists play syncopated melodies in the right hand accompanied by a simple duple pattern in the left. By the time of World War I, rags were being widely published by Tin Pan Alley, as the popular music industry was known, and many popular Tin Pan Alley songs had the sound and spirit of ragtime. The great popular songwriters included Irving Berlin, Cole Porter, and George Gershwin, each of whom wrote for Broadway musicals as well as for Tin Pan Alley.

When black musicians combined the forms, harmonies, and timbres of white popular musics with Creole, Caribbean, and black African rhythmic and melodic techniques, they produced a hot new music for dancing and later for listening called jazz. The blues, an early manifestation of jazz, began as a black folk song style but evolved to a sophisticated and influential form of popular music. Boogie-woogie transferred the form and harmonic structure of the blues to the piano.

New Orleans nurtured the first important black combos, in which soloists improvised on a given tune while other combo members backed them up. Later, in Chicago, white Dixieland bands imitated the New Orleans sound. White as well as black teenagers and young adults danced to early jazz, but the white middle-aged public preferred sweet and symphonic jazz during the turbulent depression years. Although not technically jazz at all, these genres introduced the art of the arranger and helped prepare America to swing with the big bands of the 1930s.

In the mid-1930s, jazz reached its peak of popularity, which lasted for about a decade. Big bands played arranged rather than improvised versions of blues and pop tunes, their harmonies more adventurous and their pieces more structured than in earlier jazz styles. Charlie Parker and Dizzy Gillespie led a musicians' rebellion against the commercialism and popularity of big band swing, establishing bebop, a music for listening, not dancing, which ushered in the age of modern jazz. And in the forties, the interest of the general audience and many serious jazz musicians turned away from big bands as singers replaced them in popularity.

Since 1950, jazz musicians have formed alliances with the world of concert music, producing symphonic works with jazzy flavors, jazz pieces in classical forms, and third stream pieces in which jazz and classical music meet, yet retain their independent qualities. Among the individuals particularly influential in the field of concert jazz, Duke Ellington, considered one of America's greatest composers, wrote music for both the concert hall and the church; Dave Brubeck extended the rhythmic concepts of jazz pieces by using unusual meters; and Charles Mingus explored techniques of jazz composition, prescribing a formal framework but no written score for each piece.

Progressive jazz introduced a symphonic approach, and cool jazz added a sensuous element. Free jazz declared independence from most of the preconceived notions about jazz. Fusion melds jazz and rock, and jazz musicians have found many ways to integrate foreign sounds into their music. Today jazz composition is among the most important fields of American concert music.

Country music, rooted in rural and mountain folk traditions, became commercial when Jimmie Rodgers made solo hillbilly songs popular and the Carters brought mountain harmony to the city. First recordings and later radio shows spread country music to an ever wider audience. Country musicians absorbed many influences as they moved to different states, and soon new styles evolved. Texans danced to western swing and listened to honky-tonk; the cowboy songs of western films joined the hillbilly repertoire to produce a new genre, country-western. Bluegrass, an instrumentally dominated revival of mountain folk music, is an exception to the rule that country music consists primarily of song.

In the 1950s, white country-western music combined with elements of black rhythm and blues to produce rock and roll, as the popular music industry responded to the desires and the dollars of American teens. Bill Haley and Elvis Presley, white singers with a black delivery style, made the new music widely popular, and soon cover records of rhythm-and-blues hits were making significant money. Rebelling against this trend, Motown produced records that were popular with whites but earned money for black performers, and soul brought music of a new intensity and sincerity to rock and roll.

Reacting against the overcommercialization of rock and roll, the Beatles revitalized the music in the sixties with their energy and style. Urban folk singers used light rock effects in protest songs on topics of current social interest, whereas acid rock sought to evoke as well as to describe a psychedelic experience.

The Rolling Stones, who came from comfortable English backgrounds, sang of the experience of poor black Americans despite their own highly materialistic values. Later in the 1970s, other British rockers introduced punk in reaction against rich rock stars, although in America punk turned fashionable. Disco faded by the eighties, and new wave defused punk by emulating its manner but not its shock tactics.

Today rap and hip-hop attract record numbers of fans, while gospel also has become a huge music genre, representative of the urge of many to return to the roots of rock.

Part

4

(Photofest.)

Music for Theater and Film

Music and Theater: Historical and Cultural Perspective

Music and drama seem meant for each other, each medium transforming and enhancing the other to form a perfect union immeasurably greater than the sum of its parts. In fact, a close relationship between the two arts dates back in Western history at least as far as the ancient Greeks, who claimed to have achieved the ideal mating of words and music in their magnificent theatrical choruses. Since that time, many have disagreed as to what the Greeks considered this ideal to be, and whether they found the music or the text the most important element in performances combining these arts. But the mutual attraction of music and drama remains as strong and as intriguing today as it was in ancient times.

Music Theater in America   America's earliest professional musical performances (see pp. 44–46), mostly imported from England, proved highly popular in cities large enough and settled enough to indulge in extravagant entertainment. In the nineteenth century, Italian operas drew large and enthusiastic audiences in several southern cities and even in Boston, where puritanical

Alan Jay Lerner

"We are not an aria country. We are a song country."

(Photofest.)

reservations caused nearly every theater to be known, however, as "Museum" or "Athenaeum." French light operas and—especially—the British Gilbert and Sullivan's hilarious operettas aroused tremendous enthusiasm among crowds of Americans, who returned again and again to see the shows.

Early American productions included those based on British ballad operas, incorporating popular songs into melodramatic stage presentations. The first notable American musical, *The Black Crook,* which appeared on Broadway right after the Civil War (1866), was a five-and-a-half hour spectacle of song and ballet. Although so successful as to make its creator (Charles M. Barras) comfortable for life, the show spawned few imitations, and minstrel shows (pp. 67–70) constituted the primary native contributions to the musical stage for the last half of that century. The first American musical comedy is generally considered to be George M. Cohan's *Little Johnny Jones,* produced in 1904 (p. 256).

Broadway Musicals. Much as art and literature reflect the mores and tastes of the era that produces them, Broadway musicals also review and critique the standards of their time. The severe Protestant ethic instilled by the Puritans and practiced in much of American society through the nineteenth century appeared to be crumbling by the turn of the twenti-

eth century, when a looser morality prevailed at least in the large cities: Increased knowledge of sexual hygiene lessened fears of infection; the automobile provided opportunities for courtship away from family observation; movies pictured situations previously inconceivable but highly attractive to the young and inexperienced. As we have seen, provocative Latin dances surpassed the sedate waltz in popularity. Women's dresses became shorter and their underwear less constrictive. And liquor prohibited was certainly more exciting than legal brew.

The Broadway musical stage reflected all of these and other characteristics of American life as well. George Gershwin's *Of Thee I Sing* (1931) was a side-splitting musical satire on American politics, and his opera *Porgy and Bess* (written for the Broadway theater) offered a sympathetic view of Negro life in Charleston. Social commentary pervaded important shows, notably Jerome Kern's *Show Boat* (1927), and more frivolous formats, such as the 1922 revue *Pins and Needles.*

Yet, though the Broadway musical today is the source of admiration and emulation in the very countries that inspired it, the medium indeed is deeply rooted in foreign traditions, and the latter years of the twentieth century experienced a British invasion of the musical stage akin to, perhaps even surpassing, that of pop music in the sixties and beyond. Thus perhaps it is not surprising that although the musical shows of a given period reflect certain styles and mores of their time, the American musical stage cannot be relied upon to provide a cultural snapshot of society. Broadway has been traditionally white and mainstream: jazz, rock, hip-hop, rap, and Latin music have made token appearances, but the overall picture is largely monochromatic.

For economic as well as cultural reasons, the greatest trend in recent years has been to stage revivals of safe (that is, formerly popular) shows: in the 1999–2000 season, only three new shows with an original book and score opened on Broadway. The staggering expense of staging a new musical, and the perceived preference of the contemporary audience for nonchallenging entertainment, have wreaked profound effect upon the development of the Broadway musical.

Opera. Although the line between musical and opera used to be recognizable, if difficult to define, today's musicals and operas are almost interchangeable. Following the example of nineteenth-century European "realistic" (*verismo*) operas, such as Giacomo Puccini's *La Boheme* and *Madama Butterfly,* many American opera composers have based their works on stories of American life or legend (Douglas Moore's *The Ballad of Baby Doe*), or even, more recently, on relatively current events (John Adams's *Nixon in China*). But these—as well as recent musicals by English composers based on popular Italian operas, such as *Rent* (by Jonathan Larson, based on *La Bohème*) and *Miss Saigon* (by Andrew Lloyd Webber, based on *Madama Butterfly*)—have failed to attract the long-lasting devotion of their Italian forebears.

Today, in fact, musicals and operas have drawn so close as to render differences between them not only obscure but largely meaningless. For example, shows Broadway recently addressed to the children's market, including such mammoth Disney productions as *Beauty and the Beast, The Lion King,* and most recently *Seussical,* are largely sung throughout, with little or no spoken dialogue, in the very tradition of classical opera.

Films. When sound came to Hollywood films, music became indispensable to this new form of dramatic entertainment as well. Not only did music evoke emotional response in movies of a dramatic nature; several outstanding Broadway composers took their talents to Hollywood and adapted old or wrote new musicals for film.

Movie musicals have not been prominent lately, although there seems to be a recent gesture in their direction. During the years 2000 and 2001, at least three new Hollywood films—*Dancer in the Dark, O Brother, Where Art Thou?* and *Moulin Rouge*—were billed as musicals, though none of them qualified as original movie musicals in the traditional sense: the first merely quotes numbers from *The Sound of Music,* the second uses music popular in the South during the Depression, and the third draws on popular music from the twentieth century, including the Beatles, Madonna, and such contemporary musicians as Moby, Beck, U2, Massive Attack, and Fatboy Slim. However, music undeniably plays a major role in the allure of movies, and we—the audience—succumb to its effects, however subliminal or blatant they may be.

Despite the glut of alternative entertainment available on video, computers, TV, and a multiplicity of home entertainment systems, audiences continue to fill theaters and movie houses and to buy albums of theater music. This portion of our text explores the relationships between music and drama, the history of American musical theater, and the effects music achieves on the silver screen, in the opera house, and on the Broadway stage. ♪

15

Musical Theater

A variety of songs by European and American composers, including selections from popular English ballad operas and tuneful melodies from the Italian opera repertory, occasional art songs, sentimental ballads, and patriotic tunes, enriched early nineteenth-century theatrical performances in America. Although composers had begun to distinguish between music intended for professional performance and music to be sung and played at home, for the general public the differences between popular and classical, or formal and informal, music remained much less distinct than we find them today.

Variety Shows

As prosperity returned after the turbulent Civil War years, theater—especially musical theater—became increasingly popular in America. Then, as now, theater activity centered in New York City, and by the turn of the twentieth century several kinds of musical shows vied for popularity with the Broadway audience. Full-length musical performances imported from abroad enjoyed popularity and critical acclaim, but most American musical shows between the Civil War and World War I had a variety format with little, if any, plot.

Most popular by far of all the musical shows representative of the period leading up to and succeeding the Civil War were minstrel shows (see pp. 67–70); but before the turn of the century *vaudeville* shows vied with minstrelsy for popularity.

Vaudeville
Vaudeville closely resembled minstrel shows and often included blackface acts; but whereas the members of a minstrel troupe remained on stage throughout a performance, each act of a vaudeville show involved different performers. Vaudeville also featured a much wider variety of entertainment than minstrelsy afforded. Circus stunts, jugglers, dog acts, comedy teams, songs, dances—virtually anything conceived to amaze and delight an eager but unsophisticated audience occurred on the vaudeville stage.

Among the most popular performers of the post–Civil War, or indeed of any, age was the zany comedy and song team of Edward Harrigan and Tony Hart. Depicting scenes of everyday American life, including "ethnic" comedy sketches of Irish and German urban immigrants, **Harrigan and Hart** (see

249

Figure 104
Edward Harrigan and
Tony Hart in a comic
scene from a vaudeville
show.
(The Bettmann Archive,
Inc.)

depicting scenes of American life

Figure 104) captured the devotion of New York City vaudeville audiences, who readily related to the topical humor of their shows. (In 1985, a musicalization of the lives of Harrigan and Hart was highly *un*successful for Broadway.)

Burlesque

late 19th century

satire

Striptease performances between acts

Burlesque, another kind of variety show popular in the last half of the nineteenth century, is a form of satire in which something important is ridiculed or, conversely, something silly is treated with mock dignity for humorous effect; the burlesque shows of the late nineteenth century were strings of comic scenes of this type. Striptease performances inserted between the acts, however, often drew more applause than the comedy scenes themselves so that burlesque gradually degenerated from a rather risqué to a fairly crude—although immensely popular—form of entertainment. For a modern example, in *Sugar Babies,* a rollicking remembrance of the best in burlesque that opened on Broadway in 1979, Mickey Rooney and Ann Miller sang and danced their way through an uproarious evening of nonsense that delighted Broadway audiences for more than a thousand performances and then toured until mid-1986.

Revues

musical variety show

all songs had an interrelated theme among them.

A common theme rather than a plot relates the scenes of a **revue,** still another form of musical variety show. The music may be by one composer, or the song lyrics by one lyricist, even though the songs are taken from several different shows; or each scene of the revue may address the same topic, such as love through women's eyes, or relations between the sexes, or married life—with music selected from various sources. In Irving Berlin's revue *As Thousands Cheer,* for example (successfully revived on Broadway in 1998), each sketch or song was supposedly torn from a newspaper headline of 1933, the year the show was produced.

The lavishly staged revues of the early twentieth century featured lovely costumes, extravagant sets, and—especially—beautiful young women, or "girls" as they were called. Such spectacles, titled "Follies" or "Scandals" or

Ziegfeld Follies Song

Composers
Jack Norworth and Nora Bayes

Title
"Shine On, Harvest Moon"

Form
(Modified) verse-chorus

Meter
Four beats to the bar

Tempo
Moderate

Chorus: In lieu of an introduction, the orchestra plays the first two lines (eight bars) of the chorus, its timbres characteristic of 1930s big band music. A violin plays a *countermelody* above the muted trumpet's main melody line, accompanied by a guitar gently strumming each beat and slightly marking the backbeat. The vocalist (Ruth Etting, very well known in the thirties) sings the last two lines of the chorus, lightly accompanied by the orchestra.

Verse: As Etting sings the verse, which places more emphasis on the text than on the tune, the muted trumpet responds good-naturedly to her lament and her plea.

Chorus: Accompanied by the orchestra and a countermelody in the muted trumpet, Etting sings the chorus again in her own expressive manner.

Chorus: With her silky, supple voice, Etting sings improvised embellishments of and alterations to the melody, bringing the song to a simple close with a slight relaxation in tempo (*ritardando*).

Notice that the verse-chorus form is slightly altered here, beginning with the chorus instead of the verse, and giving the first two lines of the first chorus to the orchestra.

"Vanities," staged every year from the early 1900s to the 1930s, provided generous job opportunities for composers, singers, dancers, stage and costume designers, and orchestra musicians.

Most popular of all revues were the **Ziegfeld Follies,** staged by **Florenz Ziegfeld** (1869–1932) nearly every year between 1907 and his death (with three more Ziegfeld Follies produced after that). Extravagantly staged and costumed, these shows, whose theme (popular at the time) was the glorification of the American girl, included wonderful songs, such as "Shine On, Harvest Moon" from the *Follies* of 1908 (Listening Example 56) and "A Pretty

extravagant

Girl Is Like a Melody," written by Irving Berlin for the *Follies* of 1919. (A musical biography of Florenz Ziegfeld, titled *Ziegfeld,* opened on Broadway in 1988 but was not very well received.)

During the Great Depression of the thirties, when soaring budgets made the elaborate Ziegfeld-type spectacles too risky to produce, more intimate revues took over the popular theater. By then social and political commentary was accepted even in the frivolous format of a revue. Thus *Pins and Needles,* a very successful musical entertainment sponsored by the Garment Workers Union and created and performed by amateurs, was basically a propaganda forum for that union, but it included some great songs and became a hit on Broadway. Since then revues have existed in all sizes and shapes, a glorious grab-bag kind of theater, brainier than vaudeville or burlesque, composed of sketches, songs, and dances, and often addressing a common theme with a humorously skeptical point of view.

Operetta

Unlike variety shows, musical **book shows** have an integrated plot—a story told in song, in spoken dialogue, or in some combination of the two. One example of such a show, the European **operetta,** became immensely popular on Broadway before the turn of the twentieth century, providing a vital stimulus for development of American musical stage.

An operetta (sometimes called a **light opera**) is a musical play integrating the songs, dances, and instrumental pieces with a story. Although the music of the great operettas is of a quality and a level of difficulty suitable for trained singers, no effort or experience is required of the audience, who may expect to be thoroughly entertained.

Three national styles of operetta invaded America in the late nineteenth and early twentieth centuries, each destined to become extremely popular and to have important and lasting effects upon the development of an indigenous American music theater. It is difficult to explain the popularity in America of French comic operas, called **opéras bouffes,** especially since they were often performed in the French language; but the beautiful staging and visual spectacle characteristic of French theater contributed much to the charm of the opéras bouffes, and their lilting melodies and lovely chorus and dance scenes richly entertained an audience looking for something between an opera and a minstrel show. The other national styles, one British, one Viennese, captured even more popular attention.

Gilbert and Sullivan   The delightful operettas of **William S. Gilbert** and **Arthur Sullivan** have enjoyed immense popularity in America from the time they first appeared in this country to today. In 1878, the British comic operetta *H. M. S. Pinafore,* with words by Gilbert and music by Sullivan, was performed in Boston, San Francisco, Philadelphia, and finally New York City, breaking all previous records for the popularity of any musical show. Over the next several years, twelve New York theaters staged performances

[handwritten margin note: 30's Great Depression decline in extravagant revenues]

of *Pinafore* (Figure 105), and sometimes as many as three performances were offered simultaneously—the fact that *Pinafore* is in English of course enhancing its popularity in the United States.

Gilbert, a comic poet with a gift for puns, had complete irreverence for every subject under the sun. He ridiculed politics, manners, society—even the British Queen. His **patter songs,** in which ridiculous rhyming multisyllabic words come with amazing rapidity, never fail to delight an audience and have served as models for composers of every kind of humorous musical entertainment.

Although Sullivan was quite a serious composer of music for concert and church, his operetta scores poked musical fun at opera, religious music, virtuosic singing, and every other serious aspect of music. His delightful tunes are unforgettable, and his simple harmonies and attractive orchestration provide a wonderful music experience. The combination of hilarious stories, clever satire, outrageous puns, and above all catchy melodies of the **Gilbert and Sullivan operettas** make them virtually irresistible entertainment.

Viennese Operettas

Last to become popular in the United States, but most influential upon the development of American musical theater, was the **Viennese operetta.** More romantic than comical, these beautiful shows featured exotic settings that lifted the audience from the everyday world to heights of delightful fantasy. The music, too, was Romantic in style, with memorable melodies, rich harmonies, and attractive orchestration; and the complicated love stories, no matter how unlikely or contrived, nearly always ended happily.

Figure 105
A scene from Gilbert and Sullivan's *H. M. S. Pinafore.* (Courtesy *Opera News.*)

humorous entertainment

more romantic than comical

inspiring the waltz to be present in their operettas

Based on European traditions

(Babes in Toyland)

The lilting waltz tunes of the outstanding composer of Viennese operettas, "waltz king" **Johann Strauss, Jr.,** inspired Americans to include many waltzes in their own operettas and early musicals. *The Merry Widow* by Franz Lehar dominated the American musical theater stage from 1907 until World War I, replacing comic opera in the public's affections and precluding the early success of a struggling new form, the Broadway musical comedy.

American Operettas   In the early years of the twentieth century, three musicians recently arrived from Europe became the first composers of **American operettas.** Although based on European traditions and written by composers born and trained abroad, the music of Victor Herbert, Rudolf Friml, and Sigmund Romberg was conceived for an American audience and is valued as a vital part of our American music heritage.

Like their Viennese predecessors, American operettas had foreign or exotic settings and characters who were royal, noble, or secretly wealthy, and often in disguise. Although dated, in the sense that the stories and songs are representative of the late nineteenth and early twentieth centuries, these shows contain a wealth of enchanting music no less appealing today than it was a century ago.

Victor Herbert (1859–1924). **Victor Herbert,** one of the most versatile musicians America has known, was born in Ireland and studied and performed music in Germany and Austria, finally coming to America when his wife (a star of Viennese operetta) was invited to sing with the Metropolitan Opera. A fine cellist, Herbert also conducted bands and orchestras and composed symphonic music and opera. Finally, finding that operettas based on the Viennese style suited him best, he wrote forty operettas in all.

Herbert, who could write any kind of music an occasion required, filled his operettas with lovely waltzes, stirring marches, exciting ensemble scenes, and exhilarating choruses. Some of his shows, including *The Red Mill,* became popular motion pictures, and others, such as *Babes in Toyland,* continue to be revived from time to time.

Naughty Marietta, one of Victor Herbert's most popular shows, exemplifies the best in operetta. Set in exotic eighteenth-century New Orleans during the French occupation, the show gives every opportunity for extravagant staging and costumes. Among the wealth of musical scenes is the "Italian Street Song" (Optional Listening Example), a stunning example of the virtuosic style of singing called *coloratura.*

Rudolf Friml (1879–1972). **Rudolf Friml,** a concert pianist from Bohemia (more recently known as Czechoslovakia), had never composed for musical theater when he was asked to write the music for an operetta under intriguing circumstances: A leading singer under contract to perform in a new show scheduled to be written by Victor Herbert had quarreled with that composer and refused ever to sing Herbert's music again, necessitating the hasty hiring of a new composer! Perhaps to his own surprise, Friml's first operetta (*The Firefly,* 1912) was a great success, and he went on to write several more.

Friml disapproved of the manner in which the new musical comedies, vying for popularity in the 1920s with European and American operettas, interpolated (as we saw in Chapter 7) songs having no connection with the plot of the show. In his own operettas, Friml carefully integrated words and music, writing songs that would further rather than interrupt the drama. His most successful operetta, *Rose-Marie,* had an extremely long run on Broadway and was also performed for several years by four touring companies, becoming one of the most financially successful shows the Broadway theater has known.

he focused on making the plot and music coenside.

Sigmund Romberg (1887–1951). Having studied music in his native Hungary and in Vienna, **Sigmund Romberg** came to the United States thoroughly steeped in the Viennese waltz tradition. Here he readily absorbed ragtime and other American dance rhythms and soon began writing dance tunes and musicals. An incredibly prolific composer, Romberg produced seventeen scores in three years for every kind of musical show on Broadway.

The last of America's great composers of operetta, Romberg was so successful that at one time two of his operettas ran simultaneously on Broadway. One of his best-known shows, *The Student Prince,* made into a movie starring Mario Lanza in the fifties, attracted new generations of devotees to the music of Sigmund Romberg (Listening Example 57).

Musical Comedies

Blessed with a wealth of European and American operettas as well as variety shows ranging from crude burlesques to extravagant revues, the early twentieth-century Broadway audience hardly felt the need for a new form of music theater. Yet despite early resistance, an exciting new genre blending popular entertainment (as in vaudeville) with an integrated plot (as in operettas) emerged just after the turn of the century.

popular music combined with interegrating plot

The earliest **musical comedies,** as the new musical shows were called, were gaudy, boisterous productions barely held together by a thin excuse for a story. Scenery was simply painted on backdrops, and there was little in the way of a stage set. As World War I lessened Americans' enthusiasm for European products, however, we developed a new confidence in our own artistic talents, and the zany entertainment provided by large and talented casts proved irresistible, if unsophisticated, fun.

The eventual great success of the fledgling form was largely assured by the efforts of one brash Irish American who never gave up—George M. Cohan (Figure 106).

George M. Cohan (1878–1942) **George M. Cohan** was born of vaudeville performers and virtually brought up on the vaudeville stage. In fact, by the time he was in his teens, Cohan was providing most of the material for the family's acts. Completely self-taught, he made up the skits, composed the songs, wrote the lyrics, and promoted the shows, in which he acted, sang, and danced.

Operetta

Composer
Sigmund Romberg

Title
"Drinking Song" from *The Student Prince*

Meter
Three beats to the bar (a waltz)

Tempo
Generally fast, but flexible (that is, with *rubato*)

During the *finale* of the first act of *The Student Prince*, members of a student society gather at an inn to find out if the crown prince, recently enrolled at the University of Heidelberg, will join their ranks. During the evening, the prince accepts and is accepted by the students, while he also begins to fall in love with Kathie, a waitress at the inn.

The chorus (of students) enters, singing in a brisk tempo and preserving their jovial mood until, thinking of the girls they love ("Here's a hope that those bright eyes will shine . . ."), they pull back the tempo and express their heightened emotion in a chromatically rising line. The convivial spirit and more tuneful melody return as the tempo picks up, and the chorus and prince (a tenor) join in celebrating their youth and high spirits.

The prince, accompanied by the chorus, again expresses his longing for romantic love. The chorus joins him and the music crescendoes as all return to the celebratory mood.

Notice the orchestra's strong accent on the first beat of each measure ("UM-pah-pah"), heightening the dancelike mood of the music.

Shows had an American theme (Yankee Doodle)

A zealous patriot, Cohan truly Americanized the Broadway theater. His shows, which always had an American theme, were filled with jaunty, flag-waving songs. His first full-length show, *Little Johnny Jones* (1904), usually considered the first real musical comedy, concerned a popular American jockey (whose jaunty character bears unmistakable resemblance to Cohan) who goes to England to win the derby, is accused of throwing the race when he loses, but successfully restores his honor and wins his girl. Although the thin plot hardly holds together, the score is filled with tuneful, high-spirited songs, including "Give My Regards to Broadway" and "Yankee Doodle Boy" (Listening Example 58). (Cohan could not resist claiming, as in the latter song, that he was born on the Fourth of July, although his birthdate was actually July 3.)

Figure 106
George M. Cohan.
(Culver Pictures, Inc.)

Despite competition from highly popular, more sophisticated operettas, Cohan stormed Broadway with show after show that, although not always good, always had catchy tunes and featured American heroes—a reformed gambler, a baseball player, a senator—and rousing patriotic songs. Though to his great regret he was finally replaced in popularity by several more sophisticated composers, Cohan received the highest award our nation can bestow on civilians, the Congressional Medal of Honor, which President Franklin D. Roosevelt delivered to him in person in recognition of Cohan's contribution to national pride and morale during World War I.

James Cagney recreated Cohan's dramatic life in the movie *Yankee Doodle Dandy* (1942), and in 1968 a successful musical, *George M!,* brought the Cohan magic back to Broadway.

Black Musical Theater

Even as minstrel shows waned in popularity, African American musicians continued to be an important influence on Broadway, writing songs for white shows and also writing, directing, and performing in several all-black musicals in the first decade of this century. The earliest all-black musicals closely resembled minstrel shows, which had themselves become more black than white while perpetuating the stereotypical African American characters.

The minstrel reference is apparent in the title of a distinctive black show from 1898: *Clorindy, or the Origin of the Cake-walk.* The composer, **Will Marion Cook** (1869–1944), was a concert violinist who had studied music at Oberlin College in Ohio, in Germany, and later with Dvořák at the National Conservatory of Music. Cook also wrote the music for several other black shows popular during the first decade of this century, including *In Dahomey* (1903), the first all-black musical show to play in a major Broadway theater.

Musical Comedy

Composer
George M. Cohan

Title
"Give My Regards to Broadway" (from *Little Johnny Jones*)

Performer
Al Jolson

Meter
Two beats to the bar (duple)

Tempo
Brisk

Form
Verse-chorus

Orchestral introduction.
Chorus: Eight lines, sung by Jolson. Notice the manner in which his characteristic vocal "slides" add emotional effect to such words as "yearning."
Verse: Four lines, sung by the chorus ("Did you ever see two Yankees part . . .").
Chorus: Eight lines, sung by Jolson.
Chorus: Eight lines, played by the orchestra, which then changes key.
Chorus: Eight lines, sung by Jolson accompanied by the chorus humming and interspersing comments.

The orchestra finishes the piece with two chords, a kind of exclamation point (da-dah!).

Although, as we have seen, the black influence on popular music was particularly strong in the early twentieth century, interest in black musical theater waned for about ten years (from just before until soon after the First World War), even though the musical stage generally was flourishing. Then in 1921 *Shuffle Along,* with music by Eubie Blake and words by **Noble Sissle,** became a Broadway hit. This was one of many shows lying somewhere between a revue and a musical comedy, its loosely integrated plot regularly interrupted by scenes of sheer entertainment. Whites laughed uproariously at the satire, much of which was directed at them, and enthusiastically applauded the stunning chorus line, tap dancing, and singing of the black performance troupe. The cast included **Josephine Baker,** who later became a star in Paris theaters; and the composer William Grant Still (see pp. 334–336) played oboe in the orchestra. One of the songs from the show, "I'm Just Wild about Harry," reappeared as a campaign song for Harry Truman years later.

The 1920s witnessed several other popular shows with all-black casts, although some, including two "Broadway operas" to be discussed in Chapter 17, were written by white composers and lyricists. And the landmark show of the decade, *Show Boat,* written by Jerome Kern (see pp. 121–122), addressed interracial relations with great sympathy and sensitivity.

Jerome Kern's *Show Boat*

Jerome Kern, who worked as a song plugger and a rehearsal pianist for Broadway theaters before he began writing his own shows, in 1927 changed the course of the Broadway musical by writing **Show Boat.** This show, whose unlikely producer was the entrepreneur of girl extravaganzas Flo Ziegfeld (see pp. 251–252), made history in several ways: First, unlike earlier musical comedies—basically collections of songs and variety acts loosely held together by a thin plot—*Show Boat* was based on a novel by an established literary figure, Edna Ferber. Despite *Show Boat*'s success, however, it was a number of years before the revolutionary concept of a literature-based musical became the norm for many if not most musicals (American and otherwise): *South Pacific* based on a novel by James Michener; *Kiss Me Kate* and *West Side Story* on Shakespeare plays; *The King and I* on an autobiography; *Cats* on poems by T. S. Eliot; and *Phantom of the Opera* and *Les Miserables* on French novels, to name just a few.

Further, the story of *Show Boat* addressed highly sensitive social topics, expressing sympathy for the situation of black people in America and even including an interracial love story—astonishing at a time when audiences confidently expected sheer entertainment from a musical show. This too was prophetic in the sense that serious social, political, and even religious messages have been included in many later musicals. After *Show Boat,* the term musical *comedy* would no longer be appropriate for all musical Broadway shows.

Most important of all, Kern wrote sophisticated music of the finest quality for his show. Melodies associated with particular characters recur throughout *Show Boat,* providing musical and dramatic unity, and his lovely melodies and interesting harmonies are as appealing today as they were more than half a century ago. Among them, the classic love song "Why Do I Love You?," the bluesy "Can't Help Lovin' Dat Man of Mine," and the moving "Ol' Man River" seem likely to remain classics in the American song repertoire (see Listening Example 59).

In yet one more way, *Show Boat* proved prophetic of the direction the Broadway musical would pursue: The quality of the music and the serious nature of the plot have caused some to refer to *Show Boat* as an operetta, and indeed the differences among musical, operetta, and opera have become less distinct, and largely meaningless, in recent times.

Music Theater Solo

Composer
Jerome Kern

Title
"Ol' Man River" (from *Show Boat*)

Meter
(Verse) three beats to the bar; (chorus) four beats to the bar

Tempo
Slow

Form
Verse-chorus

Verse: The bass sings the verse, quietly accompanied by the orchestra. The meter is triple (three beats to the bar). The effect, because of the minimal accompaniment and relaxed rhythmic structure, is similar to that of a *recitative* preceding an *aria* in opera. Note the use of *rubato,* adding a pensive air.

Chorus: The meter changes to quadruple. The four lines of the chorus occur in the order **a a′ b a″:** that is, the second and fourth lines are related to the first, while the third phrase differs from them in melody and mood.

> Eight bars **(a)** (beginning, " 'Ol Man River . . ."). The orchestral accompaniment imitates the melodic phrase "Ol' man river. . . ."

> Eight bars **(a′)** ("He don't plant taters . . .").

> Eight bars **(b)** ("You an' me, we sweat and strain . . ."). The chorus sings in the background.

> Eight bars **(a″)** ("I gets weary . . .") The chorus accompanies the soloist. Notice the dramatic crescendo in voices and orchestra.

Throughout the performance, the orchestra supports and enhances the voice part, filling in the ends of lines and greatly adding to the emotional impact of the song. The rich timbre of the bass voice and the dramatically deep tones at emotionally significant points also add to the drama of this famous song.

Golden Age of Broadway Musicals (1930–1955)

Before the 1920s, many great songwriters made their living by writing individual songs to be published by Tin Pan Alley and possibly included in a Broadway musical. Even Irving Berlin, who became involved with the Broadway musical stage while in his teens, was at his best writing individual songs, and his shows often seemed more like revues than like musical comedies. For example, Berlin's *Watch Your Step* (1914) became a hit despite its thin plot because of Berlin's great songs—and also because it featured the famous dance couple **Irene and Vernon Castle** performing the *tango* (Figure 107) and other popular dances of the day.

The Castles helped spark the pre–World War I social dance craze, which in some sense changed American culture. More and more people participated in the new social exercise, often dancing to the music of urban black Americans. And Irene Castle, who remained prominent in public life after her husband's death in 1918, symbolized the newly independent American woman, unencumbered by Victorian restraints.

Like Irving Berlin, George Gershwin had a gift for creating delightful syncopated dance rhythms, and some of his shows included outstanding dance sequences. *Lady Be Good!* (1924) had the wonderful song "Fascinating Rhythm" and featured the famous dance team of **Adele and Fred Astaire.** These and many other early musicals provided vehicles for presenting great songs and dances with little pretence at dramatic unity or integrity.

But during the twenties and especially the thirties, after the economic Crash of 1929, songwriters' incomes from sheet music sales drastically declined. Most people had radios in their homes by then and found it easier and cheaper to listen to the radio than to buy sheet music and pay for lessons to

Figure 107
Irene and Vernon Castle dancing the tango. (© Frank Driggs Collection.)

learn to read it. Yet somehow tickets to Broadway musicals continued to sell; so Kern, Berlin, Porter, Gershwin, and the other great songwriters turned their talents to the Broadway stage, producing an unprecedented quantity of sparkling popular music.

sound movies

After 1929, sound movies (see Chapter 16) gave further stimulus to songwriters' talents and another significant boost to their incomes. Several Broadway musicals were made into sound films that could be shown in any town with a local movie house, and the great songs soon became familiar nationwide. Throughout the thirties and forties, Broadway's amazingly gifted composers and lyricists continued to evolve artistically, producing many shows of lasting quality and beauty.

songwriters

Rodgers and Hart

In a sense, **Richard Rodgers** (1902–1979) had two careers, both of them as a songwriter: Having worked with one lyricist for many years to produce a number of extremely successful musicals, he collaborated on several new shows with a different partner, whose style and character differed markedly from that of the first. Rodgers, who once remarked, "When the lyrics are right, it's easier for me to write a tune than to bend over and tie my shoelaces," effectively adapted the style of his music to suit the words his lyricists provided, thereby greatly furthering the transition from the loosely integrated shows of early musical comedy into unified musical theater.

The lyrics for Richard Rodgers's first outstanding shows were written by **Lorenz Hart** (1895–1943), one of the most talented lyricists Broadway has known. His rhymes—witty, sophisticated, clever, sometimes devilish, and often risqué—typically were unacceptable for the radio stations of his day (which would not play, for example, his famous "Bewitched, Bothered, and Bewildered" until one line was changed from, "Couldn't sleep, and wouldn't sleep, 'til I could sleep where I shouldn't sleep" to " . . . 'til love came and told me I shouldn't sleep").

ballet (dramatic) (dance)

As the Broadway audience developed a strong fondness for classical ballet, this form of dance assumed an ever larger role in musical theater. The Rodgers and Hart musical *On Your Toes* (1936) was remarkable for the manner in which the famous **choreographer** George Balanchine designed the dance steps to be integrated with the drama. One magnificent dance scene in particular, titled "Slaughter on Tenth Avenue," constituted an integral part of the story, advancing rather than interrupting the plot.

Rodgers and Hart's *Pal Joey* (1940), which also included a ballet scene, was remarkable in another way: The main character was an antihero—a two-timing gigolo who took advantage of the innocent to further his own selfish goals. For this reason, in spite of the wonderful music ("Bewitched, Bothered, and Bewildered" is probably the best-known song of the show), the critics hardly knew how to receive it, and the show was much more successful when it was revived twelve years later.

Talented as he was, the erratic Larry Hart finally became impossible to work with, for Rodgers never knew when his lyricist would disappear on an alcoholic binge. Finally, Rodgers turned to **Oscar Hammerstein II** to write the lyrics for his next show, *Oklahoma!*

Rodgers and Hammerstein It was widely assumed that *Oklahoma!* would fail, because it had no opening extravaganza, no chorus line, and no interpolation of songs for the sheer sake of entertainment—all considered requisite in a musical show in the forties. But Rodgers and his new lyricist, Hammerstein—already well known for his lyrics in several important shows, including *Show Boat*—believed that all music and dance should enhance rather than interrupt a musical's plot and accomplished their ideal with magnificent success in *Oklahoma!*.

should enhance rather than interrupt

Like *Show Boat, Oklahoma!* not only was a great success but also is considered a landmark in the history of the Broadway musical. The story was built upon believable characters and situations, and the choreography, by Agnes de Mille (a niece of the movie director Cecil B. de Mille), revealed her gift for the expressive story-dance. Most of all, the songs were simply irresistible. The carefree "Oh, What a Beautiful Mornin'," romantic "Surrey with a Fringe on Top" and "People Will Say We're in Love," comic "Everything's Up to Date in Kansas City" and "I Cain't Say No," and of course the rousing "Oklahoma!" were instant and lasting hits. Critics, audiences, and composers alike realized that *Oklahoma!* had ushered in a new kind of music theater.

'Oklahoma!' landmark in the history of Broadway musical

Rodgers responded to Hammerstein's words, more thoughtful and serious than Hart's, by writing a different kind of music, also more serious and profound than the simple lilting melodies of many Rodgers and Hart collaborations. *Carousel* (1945), like *Oklahoma!*, based on a play, had elements of tragedy and included a beautiful "message" song, "You'll Never Walk Alone." "Hello, Young Lovers" from *The King and I* (1951) is another example of a song more serious than any Rodgers and Hart would have produced. Like Jerome Kern's *Show Boat, South Pacific* (1949) addressed the sensitive subject of interracial marriage. Even *The Sound of Music* (1959), perhaps the frothiest of the Rodgers and Hammerstein shows, concerns real characters involved in difficult situations.

writing more serious songs.

Expansion of the Broadway Musical

In a sense, the revolution Rodgers and Hammerstein implemented in the forties may be said to have finally overtaken them: For as their success faded, other composers and lyricists came to the fore, reflecting in their own manner influences absorbed from the masters of the Golden Age. Classical and popular art again grew close together, as they were before the nineteenth century drew self-conscious distinctions between them, and this too affects current musical theater.

For example, **Frank Loesser** (1910–1969), a composer who previously had written such delightfully entertaining but traditional musicals as *Where's Charley?* and *Guys and Dolls,* produced in 1956 *Most Happy Fella,* which he referred to as "a musical with a lotta music" but which is often called a popular or Broadway opera. It was performed, in fact, by the New York City Opera in 1991, and many felt the show was more at home there than on the Broadway stage; for here Loesser demonstrated his heightened sense of *singing* in the Broadway musical. *Fella* requires highly trained voices and a full orchestra, and like Rodgers and Hammerstein's *Carousel* and Gershwin's *Porgy and Bess* (see pp. 291–293), it probes deeply the emotional lives of its characters. While providing plenty of entertainment and generous comic relief, *Fella* requires more of its performers and audience than did the conventional, earlier style of musical.

Lerner and Loewe The famous Broadway team of **Alan Jay Lerner** (1918–1986) and **Frederick Loewe** (1901–1988) wrote the wonderful shows *Brigadoon, Paint Your Wagon, Gigi, Camelot,* and *My Fair Lady*—the last closely based on George Bernard Shaw's *Pygmalion,* which Rodgers and Hammerstein had considered completely unsuitable for adaptation as a musical play. Their particular contribution to expansion of the musical, in fact, was a heightened sense of the *play,* whose spoken text they preserved as faithfully as its setting to music would allow.

Lyricist Lerner (whose family owned the Lerner women's wear shops) was an American, but the composer, Loewe, came to the United States from Vienna in 1924. His Viennese background is especially apparent in *Camelot* and *My Fair Lady,* which because of their period costumes, graceful and melodic scores, and magnificent sets, are sometimes called modern-day operettas. "I Could Have Danced All Night," "On the Street Where You Live," "I've Grown Accustomed to Her Face," and "If Ever I Would Leave You" are among the great romantic songs from Lerner and Loewe musicals.

Leonard Bernstein (1918–1990) **Leonard Bernstein** (Figure 108) was a pianist, conductor, and composer primarily associated with concert music, although he made significant contributions as well to vernacular music and particularly to the Broadway musical stage. Bernstein adapted his early musical *On the Town* (1944) from a ballet he had written earlier, and the ballet's famous choreographer, Jerome Robbins, participated in directing the new musical, in which the dances were an integral part of the show. *Wonderful Town* in 1953 and *Candide* in 1956 were also successful Bernstein shows, and his Broadway masterpiece, *West Side Story* (1957), further demonstrated Bernstein's heightened sense of *dance* on the musical stage.

Robbins choreographed the wonderful dance scenes of *West Side Story,* effectively working them into the drama, which is a retelling of Shakespeare's *Romeo and Juliet.* The show is set in the streets of mid-twentieth-century uptown New York City, and although this Juliet (Maria in the show) does not die at the end, the aura of tragedy is palpable from the opening moments. The rough language, realistic characters, lyrical music, and stunning dance scenes had an overpowering effect on Broadway and have become familiar to untold numbers of people through the movie version of the show.

One of the most effective kinds of music theater scene is the **ensemble,** in which several characters present their own points of view, singly and then collectively, singing different words and music at the same time. The ensem-

Figure 108
Leonard Bernstein
conducting the New York
Philharmonic.
(© AP/Wide World
Photos.)

ble finale, or final scene, to Act I of *West Side Story* (Listening Example 60)
vividly illustrates the musical and dramatic impact this affords.

The Music of Musicals

Broadway largely ignored jazz in the forties and fifties, and it hasn't encouraged today's hip-hop, rap, and Latin music writers to create new musicals.
The Capeman, with music by Paul Simon, opened in 2000 billed as the first
all-Latino musical, but it was poorly received. *Barrio Babies,* a musical satire
by Luis Santeiro and Fernando Rivas concerning the stereotyping of Latinos
in Hollywood, may or may not find an audience.

Even rock has had only limited effect on musical shows. Although several
shows in the sixties and seventies were based on rock music, they do not
seem to have established a discernible trend; in fact, with the advent of rock
and roll, pop and show music diverged. *Hair* (1967), billed as a rock musical
but more of a revue because it has no integrated plot, addressed concerns of
the youth culture and counterculture of the sixties—drugs, free love, racial
prejudice, the Vietnam War, the burning of draft cards, and more. In one notorious seminude scene, "police" ran through the audience as if raiding the
show, prophetic of the audience involvement that has become characteristic
of many contemporary musicals. The spectacular staging of *Hair* indicated
another important trend in modern musical theater. Although the show

'Hair'— depicting the
rock era

Music Theater Ensemble

Composer

Leonard Bernstein

Title

"Tonight" (Finale from Act I of *West Side Story*)

A gang of assorted Americans, the Jets, have challenged the rival Puerto Rican gang, the Sharks, to a rumble (fight) "tonight." As the finale begins, the Jets and Sharks, each gang singing in unison, make excited threats to destroy each other. Their fast, highly rhythmic song is punctuated by sharp accents in the orchestra.

Anita, girlfriend of the Sharks' leader, enters, singing of her plans for "tonight" to the same music.

Then Tony, the young "Romeo" of the show who is also a leader of the Sharks, sings the love song "Tonight," expressing his fervent wish that the night and his time with his beloved Maria could last forever. Although the underlying pulse of Tony's song is the same as the "rumble" music sung by the gangs and Anita, his soaring melody lines and emotional delivery provide a romantic contrast to the other music.

The gangs begin their threatening lines again, and as they continue, we hear Maria in the distance singing Tony's love song. Tony joins her, and finally Anita completes the ensemble, in which each element (the two gangs, Anita, and the lovers Tony and Maria) express independent and indeed conflicting plans for "tonight." The beautifully written, tightly integrated ensemble achieves an almost unbearable level of dramatic tension.

spawned the hit song "Aquarius" and unabashedly accompanied its many other compelling melodies with the chromatics, rhythms, and word patterns of rock, ultimately *Hair* attracted audiences more with its dramatic stage effects and notorious "nude scene" than with its rock music.

At least two important shows of the sixties/seventies period were based on religious themes, and one of them, *Jesus Christ Superstar,* became a wildly popular rock LP album before the show even went into rehearsal. This show's composer, Andrew Lloyd Webber, is British, but the other, nearly contemporary show based on religious themes was *Godspell,* with music by a New Yorker, Stephen Schwartz (b. 1948). In *Godspell,* more successful than *Jesus Christ Superstar* as a theater piece, a small cast interpreted the Gospel according to St. Matthew in a striking new way, singing

Schwartz's simple, appealing contemporary revival songs, the best known of which is "Day by Day."

Grease (1972), a rollicking hit about the rock-and-roll era, responded to a "nostalgia craze" rampant at that time, as it does when the show is periodically revived. *Grease* enjoyed renewed popularity in its film version as well, but seems to have been a show of a kind, not a precursor of things to come. More recently, another British composer, Jonathan Larson, offered *Rent,* a retelling of the Italian opera *La Bohème* that intriguingly mixes and matches vernacular musics (reggae, gospel, rhythm and blues, hard rock, pop ballads) with classical forms. But again, this highly successful show (which won the 1996 Pulitzer Prize for drama) originated on the other side of the Atlantic. Of course rock has invigorated other shows as well, but in general rock has not been the music of Broadway.

Neither has country music generally been compatible with the musical stage, although the delightful *Big River* (1985) scored a modest success with Roger Miller's appealing country music. (Country singer Garth Brooks is said to be thinking of a musical based on the western movie *Shane,* but currently this remains rumor rather than news.)

Little in the way of black musical theater appeared on Broadway after the 1943 opening (and 1956 revival) of Oscar Hammerstein II's jazzy adaptation of the French opera *Carmen,* which he called *Carmen Jones,* until several black musicals opened in the seventies and eighties. They included a black interpretation of *The Wizard of Oz* called *The Wiz,* an all-black version of *Guys and Dolls,* and the all-black revue *Bubbling Brown Sugar,* featuring fondly remembered melodies by "Fats" Waller, Duke Ellington, and Eubie Blake among others, produced in 1976. *Me and Bessie* (1975), a two-woman show, narrated the tragic history of Bessie Smith and presented the songs she made famous. *Dream Girls,* based on the experiences of The Supremes, had a successful run in 1981. The 1996 all-black show *Bring in 'da Noise, Bring in 'da Funk* tells the history—a version of the history—of African Americans more in dance than in song, with little if any connection between the scenes.

The last thirty years have been difficult for Broadway and disappointing for lovers of musical theater. New York's theater district declined, as the Times Square area became increasingly sleazy and even dangerous for late-night visitors. Economic pressures affected those on both sides of the footlights, inflation causing ticket prices to soar and producers to cut the size of choruses and the lavishness of sets in the effort to control costs. (It cost $360,000 to mount *The King and I* in 1951 and $5.5 million to revive it in 1996—a fifteen-fold increase!)

As the expense of producing a new musical on Broadway shot out of reason, audiences found more and more revivals of old shows opening on the Great White Way. Revivals, in fact (and imports), have kept Broadway alive during an extended period producing few new American musicals. Thus the nineties have witnessed a curious development on Broadway, which has enjoyed an explosion of talent on the musical stage—but in revivals of earlier hits or shows based on the music of earlier times. Frank Loesser's *Guys and*

Dolls and *Most Happy Fella* were warmly received by both critics and audiences. A new show, *Jelly's Last Jam,* was fashioned from vintage Jelly Roll Morton jazz tunes, and *Crazy for You,* another successful new musical, used classic Gershwin tunes, some of which appeared originally in other shows. The 1996 show *State Fair* is a stage version of the 1945 Rodgers and Hammerstein movie.

Musicals on Broadway in 1996 included revivals of *Show Boat* (1927), *The King and I* (1951), *How to Succeed in Business Without Really Trying* (1961), *A Funny Thing Happened on the Way to the Forum* (1962), and *Grease* (1972), with several imports—*Miss Saigon, Les Miserables, Phantom of the Opera, Sunset Boulevard,* and the new rock musical *Rent*—also maintaining strong runs. Despite the wealth of entertainment all these shows afford, the world of American musical theater has suffered from the lack of opportunity to experiment with new ideas. In 1999 *Contact,* billed as a musical, won a Tony Award without a note of original, or even live, music.

Stephen Sondheim (1930–)

One greatly gifted and prolific American composer, **Stephen Sondheim,** has continued to impress viewers and critics with imaginative, creative, often startling shows of endless variety. Having studied with avant-garde composer Milton Babbitt (see pp. 340–341), among others, Sondheim intended to become a composer of concert music, but like Jerome Kern, he was early and lastingly drawn to Broadway. His first experiences with the musical theater involved writing song lyrics, a technique he studied diligently with Oscar Hammerstein II, his troubled family's neighbor, who offered the unhappy young Stephen friendship, a family, advice, and inspiration, indeed becoming the boy's surrogate father. From Hammerstein, Stephen Sondheim learned the importance of emotional and verbal clarity and the necessity to seamlessly intertwine dialogue, melody, and lyrics to further a show's plot and give it dramatic force. Sondheim vividly demonstrated his own gifts in this area by writing the lyrics to Leonard Bernstein's songs in *West Side Story* before going on to become America's premier composer for the musical stage. There he has established and maintained a distinctive voice and style for more than forty years.

After his early collaboration with Leonard Bernstein, Sondheim wrote both the lyrics and the music for many important shows, including *A Funny Thing Happened on the Way to the Forum* (1962), *Company* (1970), *Follies* (1971), *A Little Night Music* (1973), *Pacific Overtures* (1976), *Sweeney Todd* (1979), and *Sunday in the Park with George* (1985). *Funny Thing* and *Follies* were traditional musicals that proved Sondheim could write within the conventions as well as anyone. *Follies,* however, masterfully reveals Sondheim's scorn for the old-time Broadway musical's inability to deal with reality (not necessarily something vintage Broadway composers wanted to do). The show, which parodies the Ziegfeld Follies, includes "One More Kiss," a soaring waltz in the style of Sigmund Romberg only more so—in fact, cloyingly sweet. The lyrics of other songs in the show brutally express the "follies" of trying to live in a rose-colored past, fantasizing about a rose-colored future, or trying to deny death, hardly the traditional stuff of happily ever after musical fare.

The elegant *Night Music* was admired by critics but faulted by audiences for not having enough "good tunes," although it included the lovely "Send in the Clowns." More recent Sondheim shows include *Into the Woods* (1987), *Assassins* (1990), and *Passion* (1994).

Company introduced a new kind of musical, prophetic of many shows to come to Broadway in succeeding years. Its cast is small, the settings modest, and there is no continuous plot. This so-called **concept musical,** which asserts the impossibility of a successful marriage (at least in upper-middle-class, educated New York society), raises questions and confronts issues without resolving them, indicating important new directions that American music theater would follow in the seventies and eighties.

Pacific Overtures succeeded several musicals by other American composers that also reflected a strong Oriental influence, including *South Pacific* (1949), *The King and I* (1951), *Kismet* (1953), *Teahouse of the August Moon* (1953), *Flower Drum Song* (1958), and *The World of Suzie Wong* (1958). But *Pacific Overtures,* which concerned Admiral Perry's opening of Japan to the West as seen from a Japanese perspective, was more serious than the other shows, and it followed Eastern techniques more literally than Broadway was quite prepared to receive. It also made the unwelcome suggestion that Americans erred by imposing Western ways upon the reluctant Japanese. The use of an Asian cast, Oriental musical instruments, and elements of the stylized Japanese theater called *kabuki* provided fascinating and provocative theater, but the show was not popular with audiences.

Sweeney Todd, subtitled *The Demon Barber of Fleet Street,* startled the Broadway audience even more with its melodramatic subject and profoundly serious music. This grisly story of murder and cannibalism, sometimes called a Broadway opera, unlike Gershwin's *Porgy and Bess* and Thomson's *Four Saints in Three Acts* of half a century earlier (see Chapter 17) is virtually unrelieved by conventional entertainment scenes. It has been critically acclaimed as Sondheim's masterpiece, but audiences generally find it dark and depressing.

In 1985, Sondheim won the Pulitzer prize for drama for *Sunday in the Park with George.* More sentimental and optimistic than most of Sondheim's work, this show describes the struggles and triumphs of the pointillist artist Georges Seurat (1859–1891) and later of his great-grandson, who became a modernist sculptor. In one scene, the actors stunningly portray the characters in Seurat's famous painting *Sunday Afternoon on the Island of La Grande Jatte* (Figure 109).

[handwritten margin note: raises questions and confronts issues without resolving them]

Figure 109
Georges Seurat, French,
1859–1891, *Sunday
Afternoon on the Island of
La Grande Jatte.* Oil on
canvas, 1884–1886,
207.6 × 308 cm.
(Helen Birch Bartlett
Memorial Collection,
1926.224. Photograph
© 1992, The Art Institute
of Chicago. All rights
reserved.)

Current Trends

Unlike vaudeville and burlesque, the revue continues to this day a popular
form of entertainment. Many recent revues have been based on the music of
one composer, such as *Side by Side by Sondheim* (1977); *Eubie!* (1978), a
collection of the rag- and jazz-based songs of Eubie Blake; *Ain't Misbehavin'*
(1978), with songs by Fats Waller; and *Sophisticated Ladies* (1981), a dance
extravaganza on the music of Duke Ellington. The all-black revue *Bubbling
Brown Sugar* (1976) featured songs by several great African American writers, including Eubie Blake, Fats Waller, and Duke Ellington.

The 1975 musical *Chicago,* with music by John Kander and lyrics by Fred
Ebb, gloriously, and hilariously, revived and celebrated the vaudeville tradition in American musical comedy. Its authors even originally subtitled the
show *A Musical Vaudeville.* Quite unlike the distant, sentimental, and exotic
worlds of many fifties and sixties shows, *Chicago* brought peppy tunes,
raunchy lyrics, and brassy dances to the Broadway stage. The story, about a
married chorus girl who shoots her lover, goes to trial, learns how to capitalize
on the sentiments of the public, becomes a celebrity, goes free, and ends up as
a popular performer, evoked the snap and crackle of Chicago in the twenties,
but also struck a familiar chord when revived in 1996 for an audience highly
conscious of media-savvy lawyers and connections linking crime, celebrity,
and money. Every song and dance is staged as a kind of number performed on
the vaudeville circuit stage, and the audience comes to feel like members of
the very public to whom the girl plays, and pleads for her life.

In a reverse of the tradition of transferring musicals to film, some films recently have spawned Broadway shows. Perhaps the first such happy turn-

about, *La Cage aux Folles,* with music by Jerry Herman (b. 1933), opened in 1983. In the year 2000, *The Rocky Horror Show* revived the campy stage musical that became a cult film classic, and *The Full Monty* brought to the musical stage the story made popular in a hilarious British film.

The 1996 musical *Big,* based on the 1988 movie starring Tom Hanks, reverts to the traditional language of the Broadway musical—a straight narrative with no overt concept elements or sociopolitical agenda, presented primarily in the prerock idiom of popular music. But *Big* is something of an anomaly in an era when visual impact has assumed more significance than the music in many musicals. Staging is a more significant element of musical theater than ever before, as stage mechanics and scenic effects integrated into the story propel the action instead of providing background for it. Thus although questions of economy encourage the production of small or **chamber musicals,** the more widely popular shows feature large casts and sets extravagant in design and breathtaking in effect. Very few new shows offer memorable, singable songs destined to become standards comparable to the innumerable Kern/Porter/Berlin/Gershwin/Rodgers songs we continue to sing in the shower and singers continue to record. (Webber's "Memory" [from *Cats*] and Sondheim's "Send in the Clowns" [from *A Little Night Music*] are notable exceptions to this rule.)

There is also today increasing interest in **multimedia shows** combining music, dance, drama, and sophisticated special effects. Audience involvement, complex lighting techniques, tape recordings, films, slides, and videos often are part of the modern music theater experience. Some of the most recent lavishly staged musicals on Broadway were foreign imports: Andrew Lloyd Webber's *Cats, Starlight Express,* and *Phantom of the Opera* feature elaborate staging and costumes, as do *Miss Saigon* and *Les Miserables* by the French composer Claude-Michel Schonberg. Roller skates race on ramps behind and over the heads of the audience in *Starlight Express,* a chandelier makes a spectacular fall over spectators at *Phantom of the Opera,* and a helicopter lands on the stage in *Miss Saigon.*

Dance is more important than ever in the Broadway musical: The loose plot of *A Chorus Line* (1975) concerns the manner in which a choreographer selects dancers, and much of that delightful show's entertainment—in both its live and movie versions—is derived from its wonderful dance sequences. The 1978 movie *Saturday Night Fever* reflected in film the same sheer love of dance. The musical *42nd Street* (1980) is an extravaganza of song and dance that continues to have successful runs around the country and abroad, and a recent revival of Rodgers and Hart's *On Your Toes* was very well received. In *Bring in 'da Noise, Bring in 'da Funk,* a dance show conceived by dancer-choreographer Savion Glover, the music seems nearly incidental to the rhythmic patterning of feet to rap, tap, and funk.

Another phenomenon of the current Broadway musical scene is the concern to address children, an audience musicals rarely catered to in the past. *Cats,* introduced as a grownups' musical, turned out to have broad appeal for children; and since then *Beauty and the Beast* and *The Lion King* have drawn

[handwritten margin note: Dance is important]

[handwritten margin note: Broadway appealing to children]

family audiences, happy to be lavishly entertained rather than challenged in the Sondheim way. *Seussical,* based on the books by Dr. Seuss (Theodor Geisel), clearly hopes to tap into the changing demographics of Broadway brought about by our culture's obsession with youth, nostalgia for our own childhood, and the affordability of high-priced family entertainment fueled by a robust economy.

Seussical's composer, Stephen Flaherty (b. 1961), although a Broadway veteran, is much younger than Stephen Sondheim, John Kander, Fred Ebb, or Cy Coleman, collectively the elder statesmen of Broadway musicals. In fact, the 2000–2001 musical season offered the work of several young composers, some new to Broadway, sometimes writing in a comfortable pop vernacular. The beginning of the new millennium seems to propose a return to the cozy relationship Broadway and pop music used to share in the days of Cole Porter, Richard Rodgers, and their contemporaries, as several pop composers, notably Paul Simon (*The Capeman*), Barry Manilow (*Harmony*), and Randy Newman (*Faust*) have written for the Broadway musical stage. (The music for *Faust* bears a mild relationship to punk and grunge rock.) So far none of these composers has been well served by the books for the shows they have written, and it remains to be seen if some of the songs from their shows will become pop hits. The music and lyrics of *Jane Eyre,* based on the Charlotte Brontë novel, are by a pop composer new to the theater, Paul Gordon. The music of some new musicals has achieved more success on CD than in the theater: Thus the young composer Michael John LaChiusa's *Wild Party* (2000) received poor reviews, but on CD the songs, which recreate—or better, reinvent—authentic period songs of the 1920s with a contemporary bite, make a strong effect. Another young composer, Andrew Lippa, wrote a different version of *Wild Party,* mixing everything from rhythm and blues to Latin to swing to produce a highly eclectic contemporary pop score that also works better, perhaps, on record than on the stage.

The "Broadway musical" has become an international phenomenon, with unprecedented creative and technological sophistication and an apparently limitless variety of styles. Certainly the talents of new choreographers, stage designers, and actors offer enormous hope for this indigenous American musical form. Today's Broadway audiences expect the ultimate mating of the arts that used to be considered the sole prerogative of opera, and many contemporary shows are entirely sung, using no spoken dialogue at all. Thus, Broadway has learned what opera lovers have always known—once caught up in the magic of music theater, we readily allow reality to be superseded by art and enjoy the emotional and aesthetic rewards, which are grand.

Terms to Review

vaudeville   A show with acts of every variety, including blackface scenes, dogs, circus stunts, songs, and dance.

burlesque   A variety show featuring satirical humor; later associated with striptease acts.

revue   Originally, a lavishly staged and costumed show with no integrated plot. Later, a series of scenes united by a theme but without a plot.

book shows   Musicals with an integrated plot.

operetta (light opera)   A form of music theater in which the music and dancing are closely integrated with the plot.

opéras bouffes   A French style of operetta, featuring satirical humor and visual spectacle, popular in nineteenth-century America.

patter song   A feature of Gilbert and Sullivan operettas, as well as other forms of music theater, in which humorous words, outrageous puns, and unlikely rhymes are sung very rapidly, with comic effect.

Gilbert and Sullivan operettas   Comic English musicals (words by William S. Gilbert, music by Arthur Sullivan).

Viennese operetta   The style of operetta written by Johann Strauss, Jr., and other nineteenth-century Viennese composers, featuring exotic settings and romantic plots.

American operettas   Musical shows adapted from the Viennese style, written for the Broadway stage.

musical comedy   A play with music, in which the elements of entertainment are connected by a plot.

Show Boat   Landmark musical, by Jerome Kern, based on a literary work and addressing sensitive social issues.

choreographer   Artist who designs the steps and movements of dancers.

Oklahoma!   Landmark musical, by Rodgers and Hammerstein, integrating all elements of entertainment into the drama.

ensemble   In music theater, a group of solo singers simultaneously performing independent words and music.

concept musical   A musical show presenting ideas subject to the audience's interpretation and leaving provocative situations unresolved at the end.

chamber musical   A musical for a small cast, requiring economical resources.

multimedia show   Performances including some combination of music, dance, film, slides, tape recordings, and/or other sound and visual effects.

Key Figures

Harrigan and Hart — *first musicals about american*
Ziegfeld Follies — *no story, string of musical acts, like TV variety show*
Florenz Ziegfeld — *Ziegfeld follies*
William S. Gilbert — *foreign, european, created down operas*
Arthur Sullivan — *comic english musicals*
Johann Strauss, Jr.
Victor Herbert
Rudolf Friml   *brought european knowledge*
Sigmund Romberg
George M. Cohan — *rhythmic tunes, draw on black, great flty*
Will Marion Cook
Noble Sissle — *first all black "Shuffle Along" 1921*
Josephine Baker
Jerome Kern — *brought musical theatre to new level w/ Show Boat*
Irene and Vernon Castle
Adele and Fred Astaire
Richard Rodgers
Lorenz Hart   *Oklahoma, Sound of Music*
Oscar Hammerstein II
Frank Loesser
Alan Jay Lerner
Frederick Loewe
Leonard Bernstein — *virtuoso pianist, West Side Story, conductor, pop*
Stephen Sondheim

Optional Listening Example

Victor Herbert: "Italian Street Song" from *Naughty Marietta*

Suggestions for Further Listening

Excerpts from any of the shows, or by any of the composers, introduced in this chapter.

16

Music for Films

Music, closely associated with and highly important to theatrical performances since well before the ancient Greeks staged their magnificent choral dramas, has been inextricably intertwined with film since the motion picture industry began, about 1895. In fact, as the famous American composer Aaron Copland (pp. 327–331) pointed out, a film score is simply a new form of dramatic music.

Whereas movie musicals, such as *West Side Story* or *A Chorus Line,* and film stories of great composers, such as *Rhapsody in Blue* (Gershwin) or *Amadeus* (Mozart), are *best* known and remembered for their music, audiences seldom pay much attention to the music of documentaries, cartoons, and feature films having no inherent musical content. Yet for these, too, music serves as far more than accessory to the finished product, continually pushing our emotional buttons in subliminal fashion whether we "hear" it or not while accomplishing a number of mundane technical chores as well. Imagine *Gone with the Wind* without "Tara's Theme," *Lawrence of Arabia* without Maurice Jarre's sweeping score, *The Third Man* without its prickly little zither theme—or the shower scene in *Psycho* without Bernard Herrmann's shrill, stabbing strings.

Functions of Music in Film

Film music evokes moods, defines cultures, authenticates historical periods, and reveals personality traits in a manner more subtle but often more telling than that of spoken dialogue. A movie's music, called the **film score,** based as is any work of art upon principles of variety and repetition, builds a sense of continuity throughout the movie while filling "holes" or awkward pauses in action or dialogue. Music alters the pace of action by changes in tempo, and the sense of space by altering the level of volume, while decorating dull scenes and holding shaky ones together. Musically mimicking, or **Mickey Mousing,** a character's actions adds sub- or semiconscious humor to a scene, while suggestive melodic lines or harmonies effectively foretell or reinforce dramatic events. Sometimes music actually *negates* a visual image in ironic denial of what appears or is said on the screen.

Having drawn the viewer from reality into the atmosphere of a film, music subtly identifies the movie's structural units indicating the beginning and conclusion of significant scenes and bringing the film to an effective close. But while the show goes on, by lessening our defenses and increasing our susceptibility to suggestion, a good film score suspends disbelief and allows us to become gloriously immersed in the unreal—the superreal—world of cinema.

film music engages into the world of unreality

Source versus Functional Music

Some film music emanates from a source, such as a radio, phonograph, or musical instrument, apparent to characters and movie audience alike. Such **source** or **diegetic music,** as it is called, often provides a thematic anchor for the images onscreen. In films featuring dance, for example, such as *Saturday Night Fever* (1977), *Fame* (1980), *Flashdance* (1983), *Footloose* (1984), *Dirty Dancing* (1987), and *The Mambo Kings* (1992), recorded music forms the natural accompaniment for the action. The rock-and-roll classics heard as source music in *American Graffiti* (1973) establish period authenticity, and the radio or jukebox songs in *The Last Picture Show* (1971) further suggest specific social values and moral attitudes—country-western music implying purity of character, time-worn tradition, and innocence, while Tin Pan Alley pop tunes suggest corrupting influences (money, greed, power) associated with urban life.

recorded music that occurs with the actions taking place

characters in the play or movie are aware of the music

Movie convention also readily accepts **functional,** or **nondiegetic, music,** heard by the spectators but not by the characters in the film. When director Alfred Hitchcock expressed skepticism that viewers would accept music in his 1944 film *Lifeboat* (which takes place in the middle of the ocean), film composer David Raksin famously retorted, "Show me the source of the camera and I'll show you where the music comes from!"

← characters aren't aware of the music

Relationships between source and nonsource movie music are frequently complex and the differences between them easily blurred; but together they constitute an aural telling of the story parallel to the scenes viewed on the screen.

History of Music in Films

Even before movie theaters were wired for sound, music constituted an essential enhancement of viewing pleasure, and thousands of musicians made their living in movie theater orchestras. Live musical shows performed before the film began, on a scale less lavish than but related to the concept of today's Radio City Music Hall extravaganzas, had much to do with attracting audiences, and a pianist, theater organist, or even a chamber orchestra accompanying silent films not only heightened the dramatic tension, but also disguised the noise of the projector.

Silent Films
Knowing that familiar songs evoke associations with their text, time, and mood, accompanists made frequent references to songs familiar to the audience, thus adding in subliminal fashion the songs' unheard texts to the silent films' emotional and informative content. For smaller theaters

relying on keyboard as opposed to orchestral accompaniment, musicians used stock musical phrases and harmonies to bring to viewers' minds the sounds and emotions associated with railroads, horse chases, love scenes, comic predicaments, and other formulaic situations. A book published in the 1920s titled *Motion Picture Moods* provided keyboard players with numerous pieces evoking images from gruesome to chaotic, humorous, sentimental, or impassioned. Of course this early movie music raised some questionable associations: Women and African Americans often were depicted unfavorably in music, whereas music associated in the public mind with the American Indian was then—as it remained in the lavish golden-era movie westerns and unfortunately often is today—highly stereotypical.

Early Sound Films

Although *The Jazz Singer* (1927), starring Al Jolson, was neither the first major motion picture to use sound nor the first to make notable use of music, its enormous popularity encouraged a rash of imitative efforts, many of which were greeted with resounding enthusiasm only to be almost immediately forgotten by the public. But by 1930, the ways in which music accompanied film were radically varied, some films remaining "silents," some containing a sound track with music but no dialogue, some having intermittent dialogue and sparse music, and some constituting full "talkies" with or without music accompaniment. (The **sound track** includes all of the dialogue, sound effects, and music of a film, whereas the film score refers to the music only.) More and soon most theaters were wired for sound, forcing movie house musicians out of their jobs.

By 1934, major developments in recording technology made it possible to accompany dialogue with background music that immeasurably enhanced the emotional potency of a film without dominating or drowning out the spoken words. Hollywood hired classical composers to write the music, thus bringing the stirring sound of orchestral music to a brand-new, highly appreciative, audience. Most of the classical composers working in Hollywood were Europeans, but two outstanding American composers, better known for their music written for the concert hall or opera stage, also devoted serious attention to writing film scores. The first major American composer of concert music to write for films was Virgil Thomson (see pp. 290–291), who composed the scores for several government-sponsored documentary films, most notably *The Plow That Broke the Plains* (1936). Aaron Copland's film scores include *Quiet City* (1939), *Of Mice and Men* (1939), *Our Town* (1940), *The Red Pony* (1948), and *The Heiress* (1949), which brought him an Academy Award.

Movie musicals, too, became enormously popular, as Hollywood pounded out hundreds of adaptations of Broadway shows and musicals developed specifically for the movie screen. Sound films continued the tradition of sending programmatic messages through familiar tunes: In *Gone with the Wind* (1939), for example, "Dixie" is heard when war is declared and later as the anxious citizens of Atlanta review casualty lists; the defeated Confederates return home accompanied by "When Johnny Comes Marching Home"; "Marching through Georgia" signifies Northern advances; strains of "Dixie,"

[handwritten margin note: 1934 - dialogue combined with background music]

[handwritten margin note: film scores written by classical composers]

"Swanee River," and the somber "Taps" underscore the final shot of the tattered Confederate flag waving in the breeze; and competing phrases of "Dixie" and "The Battle Hymn of the Republic" suggest the military conflict pervading the period of the film.

Although familiar songs provide an audience with a comfortable frame of reference, the introduction of a pleasing *new* song often enhances sales not only of the movie sound track but also of tickets to the film itself. Several films made during the 1930s and 1940s brought Irving Berlin's music to great numbers of people far from Broadway but able to view feature films in their local movie houses: *Holiday Inn* (1942) introduced Berlin's "White Christmas," one of the most popular songs of the twentieth century, and in 1948 *Easter Parade* gave the title song, written by Berlin for a show in 1933, a new lease on life. These and innumerable other movie songs live a healthy and seemingly endless life quite independent of the films that launched or popularized them.

The Hollywood Sound

The Hollywood studio system, contracting thousands of actors and artisans, gave opportunity to vast numbers of composers, conductors, arrangers, and performers who from the 1930s through the 1950s produced film music of both increasing complexity and reliance upon nondiegetic scores. Using the lavishly varied sounds of orchestral instruments, composers drew upon a body of musical conventions to produce what became known as the **classical Hollywood film score.**

Unlike such well-known Broadway composer/songwriters as George Gershwin, Irving Berlin, Jerome Kern, and Richard Rodgers, whose scores supported numerous movie musicals—and unlike such concert music composers as Virgil Thomson, Aaron Copland, and Leonard Bernstein, who also wrote for films—the Hollywood triumvirate of **Alfred Newman, Max Steiner,** and **Erich Korngold** are best remembered for the music they created for Hollywood films of the 1930s and 1940s. They applied the highly romantic European concert music techniques of lush orchestral scoring, rich harmonies, and sweeping melodies to achieve the grandeur characteristic of films of Hollywood's golden era. Largely ignored or taken for granted for years, their film scores now are recognized as dramatic music of a high level of composition and performance. (There even seems to be some relenting of an entrenched prejudice among the serious concert public against the concert music of film composers who produced symphonic music unrelated to their film careers. Erich Korngold [1897–1957], for instance, whose choral, piano, opera, and orchestral music received lavish international praise before the Viennese composer settled in Hollywood, died unforgiven by the establishment for the lush romantic music with which he had captivated the movie audience; but now his symphonic music is receiving belated but respectful attention in recordings and live performances. Korngold's Symphony in F-sharp Major and his rhapsodic Violin Concerto are among numerous compositions he wrote independent of any association with film music.)

[handwritten margin note: 1930's & 1940's]

Figure 110

John Williams's short "shark" motif (Da-da, Da-da), probably the most famous motto in film music history, clearly warns of impending terror in *Jaws*. (The Kobal Collection.)

the music in the film or particular scene coincided with what action was going on, setting the mood and feeling for the audience.

When in the 1950s science fiction spectaculars adopted the large-sounding effects of the full-blown orchestral score enhanced by increasingly sophisticated synthesized sound, the classical Hollywood score soared to new heights of popularity. Especially, **John Williams** returned the romantic sound of the classical film score to popular favor, adapting the symphony orchestra for the modern recording studio in his stunning scores for the disaster films *The Poseidon Adventure* (1972), *The Towering Inferno* (1974), *Earthquake* (1977), and most notably *Jaws* (1975), as well as *Star Wars* and *Close Encounters of the Third Kind* (both 1977), *Superman* (1978), and *Raiders of the Lost Ark* (1981) (see Figure 110). More than any others, the scores for the *Star Wars* films brought about a tidal wave of emotional film scoring that fully returned such overwhelming symphonic film scores to mainstream filmmaking.

The original *Star Wars* score, with its screaming fanfare of an opening and moments of mysterious quiet for young Luke, told the audience what to feel while the visuals showed what was going on. The maniacally mechanical *Empire March* of the second *Star Wars* movie, *The Empire Strikes Back*, was so compelling in its evil it made viewers want to join the dark side! In *Return of the Jedi*, third movie of the series, the musical themes of good and evil collided and resolved. And the fourth movie—Part 1 of the series—perfectly enhances the spoken and visual melodrama of the film. In all four movies,

pyramiding brass signal danger, trumpet fanfares on repeated notes signal battle, percussion points to something strange, or illusory, and hymnlike writing indicates moments of public, civil order or moments of private introspection (see Figure 111).

Pop Scores In contrast to the symphonic Hollywood film scores, about 1950 many composers began to accompany their films with pop music, and soon movie songs were achieving unprecedented popularity. Although Anton Karas's zither theme for *The Third Man* (1949) became a pop instrumental hit, and adaptations of Scott Joplin's rags in *The Sting* (1973) stirred enthusiasm for ragtime among a new generation of listeners, songs are more likely than instrumental pieces to achieve hit status. (By the summer of 1996, the album of songs from *Forrest Gump* had sold more than six million copies worldwide, whereas Alan Silvestri's score album had sold only about 100,000). Sometimes words are even added to an instrumental movie theme for the purpose of popularizing both theme and film: Thus, noticing that audiences were enraptured by the lovely melody David Raksin composed as his theme for *Laura* (1944), studio executives commissioned Johnny Mercer to set lyrics to Raksin's music—whereupon "Laura" soared to the top of the 1944 Hit Parade, attracting new viewers for the film.

By the 1950s, many movie scores included or largely consisted of popular songs, such as "Do Not Forsake Me, Oh My Darlin' " (sung by Tex Ritter in *High Noon*) and the title songs from *Three Coins in the Fountain* (1954), *Love Is a Many-Splendored Thing* (1955), and *Around the World in Eighty*

Figure 111
Luke Skywalker, Princess Leia, and Han Solo in a scene from *Star Wars*. (The Everett Collection.)

Jazz music accompanied films.

Days (1956). Also during the 1950s, jazz accompanied several important films, including *A Streetcar Named Desire* (Alex North, 1951), *The Man with a Golden Arm* (Elmer Bernstein, 1955), *l'Ascenseur pour l'echafaud* (Miles Davis, 1957), and *Anatomy of a Murder* (Duke Ellington, 1959).

Pop scores achieved even more emphasis in the 1960s, attracting the era's younger-than-ever audiences to films whose songs frequently outshone other features of the score and earned more money than the films that introduced them. (Few people today associate Henry Mancini's "Moon River," for example, with *Breakfast at Tiffany's,* the film that introduced it in 1962.) Burt Bacharach's scores epitomized film music of that decade and the next, beginning with *What's New Pussycat?* (1965), continuing with *Alfie* (1966), and attracting unprecedented attention with "Raindrops Keep Fallin' on My Head" in *Butch Cassidy and the Sundance Kid* (1969). Unlike movie songs that seem almost independent of the films that feature them, the pop songs providing the title sequence for James Bond films recur in instrumental as well as sung versions to underpin the drama throughout those movies. John Barry's title song for *Goldfinger* (1964), for example, is heard with lyrics also and is integrated into the instrumental score. Songs included in Paul Simon's score for *The Graduate*—"Sounds of Silence," "Mrs. Robinson," and the English folk song "Scarborough Fair"—subtly suggest and support mood changes and dramatic shifts in the narrative.

Randy Newman, whose uncles Lionel, Alfred, and Emil Newman composed some of the most famous movie scores of the thirties, forties, and fifties, produced several pop albums before establishing his own film-composing career, which finally took off in the 1970s with *Cold Turkey,* and continued with numerous other well-received films, the most recent of which is *Toy Story II.* His beautifully orchestrated film scores typically incorporate echoes of Americana. Stephen Sondheim, apparently not interested in composing a full film score, wrote five songs for Warren Beatty's *Dick Tracy* (1990), effectively capturing the period flavor in his music for the film.

Sometimes the marriage of movie and music is less than ideal, of course, but the sound tracks of two hit films of the nineties found commercial success while effectively expanding the vision of the filmmakers: The sound tracks for Quentin Tarantino's *Pulp Fiction* and Oliver Stone's *Natural Born Killers* used pop music to heighten the claustrophobic atmosphere of murder and chaos in each movie. Further, the sound track for *Pulp Fiction* sprawls from fifties crooning to sixties soul to seventies funk, enhancing the film viewer's shifting sense of reality as we lurch from one decade to another.

the marriage of movies and music

But loose collections of pop songs, packaged by Hollywood for an audience shaped by MTV and Madison Avenue, increasingly displace integrated orchestral scores in motion pictures today. The proliferation of electronic editing and other computer-driven techniques allows many young film composers never to develop the basic musical skills once essential in fashioning a score, to the detriment of the field according to some—to its enhancement, in the view of others.

Electronic Music Today, of course, we take electronic effects for granted in movie (and every other kind of) music; but the eerie sounds of the **theremin,** the earliest electronic musical instrument (invented in 1920 by the Russian physicist Léon Thérémin), aroused unprecedented sensations of suspense. The theremin, a wooden cabinet on legs with antennas that respond to the slightest movement of the hands or body in the surrounding space, had prominent effect in *The Bride of Frankenstein* (1935), in Miklos Rozsa's score for Hitchcock's 1945 film *Spellbound,* and in *The Thing from Another World* (1951)—an effect colored by the very unfamiliarity of the music's timbre.

In the late 1960s, composers began to use analogue techniques, although they were difficult to work with, hard to keep in tune, unreliable, and woefully inconsistent. Nevertheless, Giorgio Moroder's score for *Midnight Express* (1978) proved so effective it became the first electronic film score to win an Academy Award.

With the advent of digital systems in the early 1980s and sampling techniques developed later in that decade, exciting and almost limitless new possibilities appeared, and since then synthesized sounds have enlivened the sound tracks of numberless films. More flexible and less cumbersome than the early machines, the new technologies offered far more than new timbres suggesting otherworldly and futuristic effects. Whereas early keyboards allowed production of only one tone on one keyboard at a time, the new multiple-voice keyboards could be played as pianos or other keyboard instruments. And the new machines afforded extensive editing capabilities, enabling people with less experience as composers to create highly effective film scores. Further, a synthesized music track score, such as the nonacoustic score written by Maurice Jarre for *Fatal Attraction* (1987), needs no performing artist but may be accomplished by an "electronic ensemble" under the control of one individual.

Current Trends

Today all kinds of music, from classical to pop and from full-blown orchestral scores to synthesized sound tracks, accompany feature films. Some film scores raid the classics: The scores of two poignant films (*Elephant Man,* 1980, and *Platoon,* 1986), for example, quoted Samuel Barber's lovely *Adagio for Strings* (in Chapter 19 and Listening Example 69) to accentuate the extreme pathos of those films. Audiences sometimes accept in films "ultramodern" music that they might reject in the concert hall, finding that dissonant harmonies, wide melodic leaps, instrumental timbres stretched beyond normal limits, and other extreme effects (discussed in Chapters 18 and 20) effectively raise their level of tension and emotional involvement. Henry Mancini used **quarter tones**—those lying halfway between the half steps of the major or minor scale—in *Wait Until Dark* (1967) John Williams's modernistic percussion effects in *Images* (1972) greatly strengthened the emotional effect of that score. And the *minimalist* techniques (pp. 353–354) used by Philip Glass in his Hopi-titled films *Koyaanisqatsi* (*Life out of Balance,* 1983) and *Powaqqatsi* (*Life in Transformation,* 1988) coordinated well with the visual effect of nonnarrative, time-lapse photography.

Jazz continues to be a vital component of many movies today, whereas films featuring country-western, either as source or nondiegetic music, include *Nashville* (1975), *Honeysuckle Rose* (1980), *Coal Miner's Daughter* (1980), *Sweet Dreams* (1985), and *The Last Picture Show.* In 1987, *The Big Easy* brought the exuberant sounds of Cajun music to a wide new audience.

Ethnic music often flavors film scores—to more or less legitimate effect. Although the adaptations of North American Indian music in *A Man Called Horse* (1970) and *Dances with Wolves* (1990), for example, pander to familiar, often inaccurate stereotypes, Barry Goldberg's score for *Powwow Highway* (1988) gives a more realistic portrayal of American Indian music. John Williams's score for the powerful Holocaust movie *Schindler's List* (1995) combines classical and folk/ethnic references: A winding, eastern European–flavored tune with a folkdance pulse evokes feelings of sad remembrance, while later thematic fragments accompanying harrowing scenes of genocide acutely express human anguish. Hispanic American and African American music enriches many films, recently including *Girlfight* (2000), accompanied with a distinctive blend of hip-hop, flamenco, and hand clapping. And Hans Zimmer's score for *The Lion King* (1994), which includes several songs by Elton John, combines Hollywood symphonics and African chant in an unlikely but highly effective representation of harmony among all peoples and species.

By the 1980s composers had become highly skillful at integrating premarketed popular songs into a film score. The score of *When Harry Met Sally* (1989) consists entirely of songs, with no orchestral underscore whatsoever. Giorgio Moroder's songs in *Flashdance* (1983) genuinely support the film, and in *Philadelphia* (1995), songs by Bruce Springsteen and Neil Young replace the conventional orchestral scoring to profound effect. During the latter film's opening scene, as the camera roams over the slums of Philadelphia, Springsteen (as a homeless man staring at his reflection in a store window) sings to himself his melancholy and compelling ballad "Streets of Philadelphia:" "Oh brother are you gonna leave me/Wastin' away/On the streets of Philadelphia?" And later in the film, toward the end of a poignant passage in which we view home movies of AIDS-afflicted Tom Hanks as a child, Neil Young sings in a small, cracked voice his moving ballad "Philadelphia," whose lyrics ("I won't be ashamed of love") refer obliquely to the gay lawyer who has been dismissed from his firm.

Rock has been used to accompany films since Bill Haley and the Comets performed "Rock around the Clock" in *Blackboard Jungle* (1955), succeeded by Simon and Garfunkel's songs in *The Graduate* (1968), the Bee Gees's hits for *Saturday Night Fever* (1978), Pink Floyd's music in *The Wall* (1982), and songs by Prince for *Batman* (1989), to name just a few examples. The rock hits in *Forrest Gump* (1995), which surveys four decades of American life from the view of a 1960s rock fan, unify the film by identifying periods and styles: Creedence Clearwater Revival and Jimi Hendrix and the Doors bring to mind the Vietnam years, the Mamas and the Papas praise the hippies in "California Dreamin'," and "Running on Empty" and "On the Road Again" accompany Forrest on his run across America. *Pulp Fiction's* songs (1994) also help identify periods (the 1950s, 1970s) and give telling insight into characters. Here the wail of surf music, normally associated with idyllic California beaches, ironically accompanies scenes of gangster carnage, the incongruity of such juxtaposition strongly heightening the horror.

Recent rock groups have produced scores varying in style from fusion to classical, and rock stars have taken more serious roles now than in earlier films—Sting in *Dune* (1984) and The Byrds and Danny Elfman for Tim Burton's *Pee-wee's Big Adventure* (1985) and *Beetlejuice* (1988) come to mind. The soft rock phenomenon of the 1980s known as **new age** music, providing soothing, repetitious blocks of gentle, unassuming sounds produced by synthesizers or acoustic folk instruments, most notably affected Michael Convertino's score for *Children of a Lesser God* (1986).

Even opera has been welcomed into the broad realm of mainstream feature filmmaking, a number of movies produced during the 1980s and 1990s including entire scenes from famous operas that pack a potent emotional punch on unsuspecting listeners having little or no experience with this grandest form of music theater. *Fatal Attraction, Moonstruck, A Room with a View, The Witches of Eastwick, Someone to Watch Over Me, The Untouchables, Hannah and Her Sisters,* and *Prizzi's Honor* name only a few of the many recent films giving more than token attention to famous opera scenes. More recently, the powerful recording of Maria Callas singing "La Mamma Morta" (from *Andrea Chenier* by Umberto Giordano) heard as source music toward the end of *Philadelphia* nearly overwhelms the viewer as well as the film's afflicted star, played by Tom Hanks; the power and beauty of this serious music offer forceful contrast to Bruce Springsteen's and Neil Young's contemporary, relevant, and highly appealing ballads.

The Composer's Perspective

Arnold Schoenberg (see p. 318) once was asked under what conditions he would work with a movie studio. "I will write music," Schoenberg replied, "and then you will make a motion picture to correspond with it."

Desirable as such an unlikely scenario might appear, composers of film music generally find themselves in the awkward position of writing music hardly intended to be heard. To this end, they read the script, listen to the **temp,** or temporary score (consisting of existing music prepared to demonstrate to the composer the type of music desired for the film) if one is provided, and perhaps scrutinize the film, laboriously determining when and how much music should occur and what sorts of music would serve the specific needs of each scene. Composers vary in their desire to view "dailies"—the

(Photofest.)

Aaron Copland
"Film music is like a small lamp that you place below the screen to warm it."

tonality = a mood
settle in
music

detailed footage shot each day, which can be dull and tedious and thereby inhibit the composer's emotional response to the action—and a preference to wait for the "rough cut," which tells the story from beginning to end with most of its elements in place. (The latter method allows composers to capitalize better on their first emotional reaction to the film, which is likely to mirror that of the eventual viewing audience.) Some composers favor working from a script, some from talking with the director, some work from storyboards; some visit the set and talk with actors; some only begin their composition and orchestration when the film's final edit is complete.

Techniques Film composers have developed a vast repertoire of methods, musical and technical, by which to accomplish their practical and aesthetic goals. They know, for example, that the harmonic system of *tonality* offers nearly unlimited means to create anxiety, expectation, or reassurance. Unresolved harmonies build suspense; unorthodox chord progressions effect surprise; and the change from major (often understood to suggest order or stability) to minor (more chromatic and therefore less stable) commonly darkens the mood. Similarly, tonal ambiguity or the use of foreign, artificial, or unfamiliar scales subconsciously affects listeners quite unaware of the intellectual reasons for their emotional response. As we know, listeners differ in their perception of *dissonance,* which some scholars believe in any case is a learned rather than innate phenomenon; but skillful composers use relationships between consonant and dissonant sounds to profound dramatic advantage. Extreme dissonance, suggesting disorder or instability, for example, may be relieved by consonant resolutions.

Timbre also has potent influence on our sensibilities: Orchestral strings tug our own emotional strings, and a trumpet's proud blare evokes within us ecstasies of patriotic pride. We can hardly imagine these instruments' roles reversed, no matter the melodic or rhythmic content of their music.

Thus, working at least from detailed charts of the length and description of scenes, with reference perhaps to a temp score as well, a film composer writes new music and/or adapts excerpts from existing classical or popular music to be heard as source music or skillfully woven into the fabric of the underscore.

Finally, the finished score is subjected to the indignities of being cut, mixed with dialogue and other sounds, and further altered by the director and assorted editors and sound engineers. Composers have been heard to lament that they scarcely recognize their own work in the finished product! Today's film score composers also often complain of being asked to meet impossible deadlines, of having their music drowned out by deafening sound effects, or—worst of all—of having their scores rejected for entirely capricious reasons.

Film Score Performances and Recordings

Film music sometimes comes to attention independent of the film to which it belongs through live or recorded performance. Discovering during the 1950s and 1960s the degree to which films sold music and vice versa, Hollywood composers avidly entered the recording business, producing sound track or film score recordings including some, most, or all of the music of a film. Also, composers sometimes write a **suite** comprised of significant sections of music from the complete score, such as Leonard Bernstein's suite of dances from *West Side Story* and his symphonic suite from *On the Waterfront.* From his sound track for Spike Lee's *Malcolm X,* which brilliantly documents the popular black music of the era, jazz composer and trumpeter Terence Blanchard excerpted *The Malcolm X Jazz Suite,* integrating the disparate moods of the movie score in eleven segments performed by a quintet of saxophone, piano, drums, bass, and trumpet in a highly effective independent composition.

Recently, movie music—suites, excerpts, or themes from popular films—has become a favorite focus of orchestral pops concerts, and such well-known pieces as John Barry's "Romance for Guitar and Orchestra" from the film *Deadfall* (1968) and Korngold's Cello Concerto from his score to *Deception* (1946) are among several movie compositions sometimes heard on the concert stage. For a more recent example of concert movie music, the director of *The Red Violin,* released in 1999, commissioned John Corigliano to write an original score and then made the movie around it; and Corigliano fashioned a concert piece, *The Red Violin Chaconne,* from the movie music (for which he won an Oscar).

In 1999, Philip Glass achieved a sort of combination film/concert experience by composing an original score to accompany the 1931 horror film classic *Dracula.* (No musical score had ever been written for that early movie, which appeared just as silent films were turning to talkies, when sound technology was in rudimentary stages of development.) Glass's score is performed on stage by the well-known Kronos (string) Quartet while the film is projected on the screen.

Would we listen to the film score of a film we had never seen? Judging from sales of sound track and film score recordings, people do, in considerable numbers; sound track albums are selling at unprecedented rates and dominating sales charts more than ever before. Availability on popular recordings of the beautiful themes for *Chariots of Fire, Dances with Wolves,* and *Out of Africa* greatly enhanced ticket sales to those movies; and Elmer Bernstein's score for *The Magnificent Seven* (1960), which may be the most famous score ever written for a Hollywood western, became a classical crossover best-seller over thirty years later when it was voted best sound track recording of 1994.

Within the last decade, sound track and film score collecting has accelerated among people who, although largely unaware of the music as they viewed a film, discover that the music allows them unlimited opportunity to "re-view" it. Although instrumental scores appear on best-seller lists infrequently, albums from *Apollo 13* and *Braveheart* have done very well; and the sound tracks for *Pulp Fiction* and *Natural Born Killers* (1994), which use pop music to heighten the claustrophobic atmosphere of murder and chaos, reached the Top 40 on the *Billboard* album chart. The number one album of

1998 was the sound track to the movie *City of Angels,* a film that made little impact in theaters, but whose sound track spawned two hit singles ("Uninvited" by Alanis Morissette and "Iris" by the Goo Goo Dolls) and stayed firmly lodged in the Top 40 for months. And the number of sound tracks released in a single year climbed steadily through the nineties: in 1990, sixteen sound tracks appeared on the *Billboard* album chart, and in 1998 there were more than fifty. We may note, however, that some "sound track" albums, exemplified by *Godzilla,* actually have music "inspired by" the film, including songs not heard in the movie at all.

Studies of screen music came to the fore in the 1980s and 1990s with the improving quality and growing popularity of sound track recordings, and today movie music is recognized as a subject worthy of serious musicological consideration. Universities, libraries, and other institutions of higher learning are carefully preserving Hollywood film scores, and anthologies of articles, essays, score analyses, and memoirs about Hollywood film music attract favorable attention from scholars and film buffs alike.

Terms to Review

film score   All of the music accompanying a film.
Mickey Mousing   Musically mimicking or accenting an action.
source or **diagetic music**   Music heard by characters in the film as well as by the film audience.
functional or **nondiagetic music**   Music heard by the audience only.
sound track   All of the dialogue, sound effects, and music of a film.
classical Hollywood film score   Lush orchestral scores particularly associated with films of the 1930s, 1940s, and 1950s.
theremin   The earliest electronic musical instrument.
quarter tones   Tones lying halfway between half steps.
new age   A soft rock style providing soothing, repetitious blocks of gentle, unassuming sounds produced by synthesizers or acoustic folk instruments.
temp   Temporary film score, composed of existing music independent of the film, offered to demonstrate to a film's composer the type of music desired.
suite   Generally, an instrumental composition comprised of several pieces; the suite from a film includes several sections of music from the film score.

Key Figures

Alfred Newman
Max Steiner
Erich Korngold
John Williams

Suggestions for Listening

Source or Diagetic Music:
Saturday Night Fever
Dirty Dancing
American Graffiti
Functional or Nondiagetic Music:
Lifeboat
Documentary:
The Plow That Broke the Plains
Scores by Aaron Copland:
Quiet City
The Heiress
Scores by John Williams:
Jaws
The *Star Wars* films
Pop Music Scores:
High Noon
Butch Cassidy and the Sundance Kid

Pulp Fiction
When Harry Met Sally
Philadelphia
Jazz Scores:
A Streetcar Named Desire
Anatomy of a Murder
Electronic Music Scores:
Spellbound
Midnight Express
Rock Scores:
Blackboard Jungle
The Wall
Beetlejuice

Opera in Film Scores:
Fatal Attraction
Moonstruck
A Room with a View
Philadelphia
Film Score Suites:
Leonard Bernstein: Suite of dances from *West Side Story*
Symphonic Suite from *On the Waterfront*
Terence Blanchard: *The Malcolm X Jazz Suite*
John Corigliano: *The Red Violin Chaconne*

17

American Opera

Almost since the first opera appeared in Italy, early in the seventeenth century, Italians have hummed their favorite opera tunes while strolling down the street. Other Europeans also have long delighted in the emotional intensity and high drama or comedy of many wonderful operas in various styles.

But many Americans until recently considered opera an elite and unlikely form of entertainment, and a characteristic American opera was almost inconceivable. The nineteenth-century American composers William Henry Fry and George Bristow (see pp. 94–95) fully intended their operas to sound Italian. Other well-meaning opera enthusiasts sought to attract an American audience by translating Italian, French, or German operas into English. But neither ploy made the medium accessible or meaningful to most American listeners.

Yet opera, the grandest of all the arts, combines singing, acting, orchestral music, drama, staging, costuming, dance, and lighting effects in a form infinitely greater than the sum of its parts. And although it took a very long time for opera to assume the vital role in American music theater it finally enjoys today, since World War II a significant number of American opera companies have been formed, and performances in the major opera houses around the country are regularly sold out. Saturday afternoon broadcasts of Metropolitan Opera performances have been widely listened to since 1931. During the 1980s, films of two Italian operas by Giuseppe Verdi (1813–1901)—*La Traviata* and *Otello*—were commercially successful at popular American movie theaters; and Chapter 16 names some of the many recent commercial films featuring generous opera scenes. Recently network television has been offering full-length live performances of great operas from many countries and periods.

Finally, then, Americans have discovered that there are as many kinds of opera as there are movies or books. Although the complexity of opera requires more preparation from the audience than any other form of art or entertainment, its combined visual and musical effects offer unparalleled rewards.

Opera

An **opera** is a drama that is sung instead of spoken. Like a play, it may be long or short, comic or serious, grand or modest—good or bad. Because it is, of course, unnatural to sing ordinary conversation, the opera viewer must

drama that's
sung instead of
spoken

abandon or suspend rational thought to become immersed in the art—the magic—that is opera; but this is not as difficult as it sounds, for even skeptical viewers quickly become caught in a great opera's spell and forget to notice that the dialogue is being sung instead of spoken. As noted in Chapter 15, many modern musicals use this same technique, which Broadway audiences have come to expect. After all, it is the role of art to express human feelings at a level *beyond* the limits of ordinary communication. As our emotions become involved and the real world slips away (gets out of the way), the most artificial aspects of art somehow seem more real than reality itself.

Solo and Ensemble Singing

In an opera, the exchange of dialogue occurs through **recitative** (from the same root as "recite"), a style of singing in which the words are expressed clearly and economically so as to move the drama along. The melody of a recitative often resembles the inflection of the words as they would be spoken, and the rhythm, free and flexible, also accommodates the text. As you might expect, recitative involves little repetition of phrases, because its purpose is to further, not delay, the action. *Dry recitative* is accompanied by a keyboard instrument only or, in early operas, by a keyboard and another instrument doubling the bass line. The more expressive *accompanied recitative* has orchestral accompaniment.

An **aria,** usually more melodic and often more expressive than a recitative, constitutes a dramatic soliloquy in song, with the emphasis upon the music rather than the text. Time simply hangs suspended as a character reflects upon and expresses the deepest emotions aroused by situations in the story. Arias fully display the beauty and range of a singer's voice, often allowing the performer to indulge in virtuosic singing, because here the words are less important than the expression of emotion. There also may be considerable repetition of text ("I love you, I *love* you . . .") to enhance the emotional impact.

Unlike recitative, an aria has metered rhythm and is organized according to musical principles of design. The most familiar aria form is called **da capo,** which means "from the beginning" and may be illustrated as **ABA:** The composer writes the first section, **A,** and a contrasting second section, **B,** and then instead of writing out the third part indicates that the first section is to be repeated "from the beginning." Here custom offers further opportunity for vocal display, a singer often improvising elaborate embellishments to the repetition of section **A.**

The orchestra may provide far more than simple support for an aria's vocal line, perhaps playing an introduction and concluding passage as well as interludes between sections or verses. Further, instruments may introduce or imitate the singer's melodic phrases throughout the piece or provide sound effects, such as bird calls or storm sounds, independent of the singer's melodic line. Sometimes the orchestra even assumes a dramatic or psychological role, contradicting the singer's words by making musical reference to conflicting ideas, for example.

Handwritten margin notes:
- slight adjustment happens when we are listening to a dialogue being sung instead of spoken.
- little repetition of phrase so that the dialogue moves along.
- music more than text
- expressing emotions rather than spoken words
- aria follows a ABA pattern

Ensemble scenes add excitement to opera as to all forms of musical theater. The members of an opera **chorus** (a large ensemble with several voices singing each line of music) generally represent characters in the drama, such as guests at a wedding or soldiers returning from battle. And again as in musicals, *solo ensembles*—duets, trios, quartets, quintets, or even larger group of soloists—add thrilling drama as well as magnificent contrapuntal musical effect to the opera stage.

Opera in America

New Orleans intrigued by French Opera

NYC admired German & Italian Operas

Before the present century, the few American opera houses confined their repertoire almost entirely to foreign operas, because, as we know, little was available or would have been accepted of native work. French opera had strong appeal in New Orleans, where many people spoke French, and New York City had a small but enthusiastic audience for German and Italian operas. But besides the Italian-style works of William Henry Fry and George Frederic Bristow, no further American operas were presented for a long time.

Then during the first half of the twentieth century, several American composers sought to establish a national opera style by writing operas with American Indian settings. **Mary Carr Moore** (1873–1957) was among the more successful composers of operas on Indian themes; but the idea, although popular for a time, was short-lived.

Operas on Indian themes

Ragtime composer Scott Joplin wrote at least two operas, one of which, *Treemonisha,* was published in 1911 in what is called a "piano score"—that is, without orchestration. Joplin wrote the words as well as the music of *Treemonisha,* whose story illustrates Joplin's belief that blacks must acquire education in order to improve their social and economic situation. Joplin's opera includes some ragtime and other dance pieces, as well as more conventional operatic arias, concluding with a very effective finale in which the large, brightly costumed cast celebrates the happy ending by dancing a stately "slow drag" (Optional Listening Example).

Scott Joplin (Rag) wrote 2 operas (1911)

So little interest was there during Joplin's lifetime in an opera by a black composer, he was unsuccessful in ever achieving a proper performance of *Treemonisha.* However, in the early 1970s the opera was scored for orchestral instruments by Gunther Schuller, and it has been performed, with Schuller's or other orchestral accompaniments, numerous times since then, live and on public television.

Curiously, two operas by white composers, each with an all-black cast and each performed in Broadway theaters rather than in an opera house, first brought American opera to a broad and appreciative audience.

2 white composers with all-black cast brought American opera to the spotlight.

Virgil Thomson (1896–1989)

Convinced by the time he graduated from Harvard University that concert music had become overly complex, **Virgil Thomson** imposed a refreshing simplicity upon his own compositions, which were often based on the folk songs, hymns, and Civil War songs he had heard as a child in Missouri. While continuing his music education in Paris with the extremely talented and influential teacher Nadia Boulanger (see pp. 326–327), Thomson discovered that the French shared his appreciation for musical simplicity, finding as he did the purpose of music to amuse and entertain rather than to improve the listener. Thomson stayed in this congenial atmosphere for fifteen years, only driven home by the impending catastrophe of World War II.

Among Thomson's most stimulating experiences abroad was his collaboration with **Gertrude Stein** (1874–1946), an American writer who spent most of her life in Paris. Stein used words for their *sounds* rather than their *meanings,* producing attractive, often funny combinations of syllables regardless of their sense or lack of it. Gertrude Stein wrote the words, or **libretto,** and Virgil Thomson wrote the music of *Four Saints in Three Acts,* the first American opera to appeal to the American public.

This stunning show, which actually concerns fifteen saints and has four acts, makes little if any sense but ravishes the eyes and ears with the most delightful entertainment. When the show opened in 1934 in New York City, its enchanting sets elegantly constructed of brightly colored cellophane—to the dismay of the city's fire department—provided a magnificent stage. Thomson's choice of an all-black cast seems curious, because the characters are (apparently) Spanish and have nothing to do with black culture, but simply concern the daily blend of meditative creativity and ordinary socializing experienced in Stein's and Thomson's Parisian life. (Thomson claimed that Stein patterned the opera's leading characters, St. Theresa and St. Ignasius, after herself and James Joyce.) In any case, although Thomson's declaration that he simply admired the appearance and voices of the black singers may seem racist in today's more sensitive environment, Thomson's intentions were artistic and aesthetic, and he would have been astonished to think his genuine esteem might be considered discriminatory.

Thomson beautifully set Stein's nonsensical but appealing libretto to music, although it had been thought that American speech did not lend itself to musical settings; this was, in fact, the first time an American libretto was effectively and idiomatically set to an opera score. This, together with Thomson's folklike melodies, attractive hymn tunes, lovely choruses, colorful sets, and imaginative orchestration won the appreciation of Broadway audiences accustomed to more frivolous entertainment.

Revived on Broadway in 1986, the show—on a Catholic theme, written by a Jew and a Protestant—seemed as fresh and bold as ever. Further, some reviewers recognized it as a direct antecedent of the nonnarrative, minimal music theater practiced now by Robert Wilson, Philip Glass, David Byrne, Laurie Anderson, and John Adams.

George Gershwin's *Porgy and Bess*

The same year that *Four Saints* opened on Broadway, songwriter and symphonic jazz composer George Gershwin read a novel by Du Bose Heyward based on the lives of real people who lived in a black tenement area in Charleston, South Carolina. Profoundly moved by the novel and by the play based on it, Gershwin decided to write an opera on the subject.

In preparation, this New York composer spent a summer in the Charleston area, where he listened to people talk and sing. Then having steeped himself in the sounds of the vegetable sellers' calls, the work songs of the men, the lullabies women sang to their babies, and the shouts and hymns performed at church on Sundays, he returned to New York to write *Porgy and Bess*. The new opera opened on Broadway a year after Thomson's opera—also with an all-black cast.

Porgy begins with an instrumental piece, usually called an **overture** but simply called introduction by Gershwin, who intended his show for a Broadway audience. Like a conventional opera overture, Gershwin's introduction sets the appropriate mood for the show and includes some of its important themes.

Porgy, a poor man so crippled that he gets around only by goat cart, falls deeply in love with Bess, a "loose-living woman" from New York who gives up her "big city ways" to live and love with Porgy. Their story, tender and moving, has flashes of wit and humor and plenty of tense drama. A number of the songs (Gershwin also avoided the term "aria") became so popular that, finally, Americans were humming opera tunes on the streets!

The love duet in which Porgy and Bess eloquently express their devotion to one another is one of the most beautiful in the opera literature of the world (see Figure 112 and Listening Example 61).

Figure 112
A scene from Gershwin's *Porgy and Bess*. (Courtesy of *Opera News*.)

Opera Duet

Composer
George Gershwin

Title

"Bess, You Is My Woman Now" (from *Porgy and Bess*)

Poignant falling figures in the strings introduce this beautiful duet, in which Porgy (*bass voice*) declares his love for Bess and insists that she must "laugh an' dance for two instead of one," because he is physically unable to get around. The strings double Porgy's passionate melody, enhancing the emotional impact of the music. The verse has five lines of text, yet seems superbly balanced.

Bess (*soprano*) responds with her fervent declaration of love for Porgy, declaring she will go nowhere without him. At first her melody is the same as Porgy's, but soon she soars to rapturous high notes, as if overwhelmed with love and joy.

Notice as they sing together that Bess generally carries the melody whereas Porgy's comments add contrapuntal interest and harmony. Also notice the orchestra's contributions, including melodic support, harmony, and independent "commentary." You will hear expressively inflected blue notes throughout, derived as we have seen from black performance practice and associated with blues, jazz, and many styles of black music.

Gian-Carlo Menotti (b. 1911) **Gian-Carlo Menotti,** another composer who has written operas well received by a Broadway audience, reversed the prevalent trend by coming from his native Italy to America to study music. A child prodigy who had written two operas by the time he was thirteen, Menotti arrived in 1928 at the Curtis Institute of Music in Philadelphia, Pennsylvania, where he became a close friend of another famous American composer, Samuel Barber (see pp. 331–333).

In 1947, Menotti wrote a two-act thriller titled *The Medium,* which because of its modest resources—five singers, one dance-mime role, and an orchestra of only fourteen players—may be called a **chamber opera.** (It is also quite brief, Menotti intending it to be performed with another miniature opera of his, titled *The Telephone.*) Broadway audiences found *The Medium*'s eerie mood, memorable melodies, and dramatic libretto, which Menotti wrote himself, moving and exciting indeed.

Menotti's next major work, *The Consul,* opened on Broadway in 1950, had a long, successful run, and won the Pulitzer prize and Drama Critic's Award. The story concerns the frustration and ultimate tragedy of a family desperately trying to escape from their unnamed country but confronted with bureaucratic nonsense in response to their urgent pleas for assistance. *The Consul,* written at the time of the Cold War, specifies neither country nor time, allowing us to relate the drama's events to our own knowledge, experience, or imagination. The moving aria "To This We've Come," eloquently expressing the rage and despair of a woman prevented by bizarre circumstances from saving her doomed family, is an Optional Listening Example.

The next year (1951), the National Broadcasting Company (NBC) commissioned Menotti to write the first opera conceived especially for television. Menotti based the resulting work, *Amahl and the Night Visitors* (Figure 113), on a painting formerly, but no longer, attributed to Hieronymus Bosch and on his own childhood memories. Amahl, whose simple, naive story and lovely music consistently appeal to children and, as Menotti says, to "those who like children" as well, has been performed at Christmastime every year since, often on television, and also by amateurs in church and community settings.

Menotti has written symphonic and choral works as well as several other operas, but he is primarily a man of the theater, whose gifts for melody and drama seem to have been best expressed in his early operas written for the Broadway or television audiences.

Figure 113

A scene from Menotti's *Amahl and the Night Visitors.*
(The Bettmann Archive, Inc.)

The Trend toward Realism

Although traditionally operas have dealt with fiction, fantasy, myth, or ancient history, increasingly opera composers choose topics from recent history and even from everyday life. As early as 1937, Marc Blitzstein addressed the traumas of the Great Depression in a Broadway opera about the straggle for labor rights called *The Cradle Will Rock,* in which much of the music was popular in style and the words reflected the ethnic speech of city streets. (A year 2000 movie, *Cradle Will Rock,* dramatized the formation of the pro-union musical, the attempts to shut it down, and the fascinating manner in which the show finally was performed.) Douglas S. Moore wrote about American pioneer life in *The Devil and Daniel Webster* (1939); and in 1958, he set another opera, *The Ballad of Baby Doe,* in the nineteenth century and included some of the music styles popular then. Aaron Copland's *The Tender Land,* about a midwest American farm family, also appeared during the 1950s. A recent opera by Ulysses Kay, *Between Liberty and Oppression* (1991), concerns the life of Frederick Douglass, a hero in African American history.

Beginning in the 1980s, operas based on more recent or even current social and political events began to appear, sometimes raising controversy among still-living participants in the events. Philip Glass's *Satyagraha* (1980) tells of the early struggles of Mahatma Gandhi; *X,* by Anthony Davis (1986), concerns the black nationalist leader Malcolm X; John Adams's first opera, *Nixon in China* (1987), describes President Nixon's visits to and negotiations with that country (Figure 114); in 1990, an opera called *Manson Family,* about the California mass murderer Charles Manson, was written by John Moran; and in 1991, John Adams presented a new opera, *The Death of*

Some chose topics dealing with historical events.

Figure 114
A scene from John Adams's *Nixon in China.*
(© Andrew Popper/Picture Group.)

Klinghoffer, which describes the 1985 highjacking of the ship *Achille Lauro* and the murder of a wheelchair-bound Jewish American passenger. Still another genre, science-fiction opera, has recently been approached by some composers.

Novels sometimes stimulate the creation of operas as well. Thus composer John Harbison's *Great Gatsby,* based on the novel by F. Scott Fitzgerald, scored some success at the Metropolitan Opera in 1999. *Of Mice and Men,* John Steinbeck's short novel about two itinerant farm workers, is now an opera, with music and libretto by Carlisle Floyd. And the opera *Dead Man Walking* (2000), with music by Jake Heggie and a libretto by the playwright Terrence McNally, is based on Sister Helen Prejean's book of the same name, which also inspired a 1995 movie.

Philip Glass (see pp. 353–354), also in 1995, achieved a kind of "film opera" or "opera film" by composing a score to accompany Jean Cocteau's famous 1946 film *La Belle et La Bête (Beauty and the Beast).* In this entirely new kind of theater presentation, the classic film is projected on the screen without its sound track while live performers on the stage below the screen sing the characters' lines, accompanied by Glass's unorthodox ensemble of musical instruments (described on p. 354). Readily achieving the leap of imagination required to accept this combination of film and live performers, audiences tend to react warmly to the emotional and dramatic impact of the multimedia work, which after all concerns magic and transformation—the magical transformation through love of the Beast into Belle's handsome prince. Immersing the audience in the creative process by which Cocteau and Glass achieved their combined art and the Beast his transformation to Beauty, Glass's music provides a truly enchanted evening.

Opera or Musical: Which Is It?

Today many Broadway and London musicals are sung throughout, while operas by Philip Glass and John Adams, for example, often seem closer to Broadway productions than to opera in the traditional sense. How, then, to distinguish between these forms of music theater? With difficulty, if at all! There are opera singers who sing musicals and music theater performers who sing opera. The old definitions of a *musical* as a play with occasional music, an *opera* as a musical drama with no spoken drama, and an *operetta* as something between the two extremes are largely meaningless, as audiences both on Broadway and in the opera house have come to enjoy grand entertainment on a lavish scale and of unprecedented variety and scope.

Still, some suggest that a significant difference between operas and musicals lies not so much in the music, which has increasingly overlapped, but in the *words.* Whether one understands the language in which an opera is written or not, it is often difficult to understand the words as they are sung. Although many opera composers are famous for their music, the names of few opera librettists come readily to mind, and those who do are remembered more for their stories than for the particular turns of phrase with which they delivered it. The Broadway lyric, on the other hand, full of puns and intricate rhymes, must be clearly understood to be appreciated and in fact assumes a full share of importance together with the music. Great lyricists such as Lorenz Hart, Ira Gershwin, and Oscar Hammerstein II retain their reputations, and we admire the songs of Cole Porter and Stephen Sondheim as much for their words (written by the composers) as for their music.

Others propose the role of the orchestra as defining the critical difference between the two genres; that is, in opera the orchestra often plays a central role in the telling of the story, while in musicals the orchestra generally plays a supportive role. Advocates of this theory suggest that musicals in which the orchestra takes a more central and dramatic role, as in *West Side Story,* move toward opera, whereas the supportive role of Stephen Sondheim's orchestra relegates his works—for all their emotional power and dramatic subtleties—to the world of music theater. The fact that most opera composers orchestrate their works and most composers of musicals do not lends credence to this possible distinction. On the other hand, orchestrator Jonathan Tunick refers to Stephen Sondheim's *Sweeney Todd* as neither opera nor musical but as a successful American musical drama.

Stephen Sondheim himself suggests that the difference between Broadway and opera is in the expectation of the audience, going so far as to say that in *his* opinion, when Menotti's *The Medium* and *The Telephone* were performed on Broadway they were "sung-through" shows, and when they were performed in opera houses—for opera audiences—they were operas. In other words, for him the object changes in terms of how it's viewed.

Beverly Sills, who retired from singing opera to become chair of the Lincoln Center for the Performing Arts, distinguishes between the vocal requirements for singing opera and singing musicals. Broadway theaters are usually about a third the size of an opera house, and even in the smaller theaters Broadway singers often rely on amplification, whereas opera singers are taught to project their voices, at soft or loud levels, for impressive distances over sustained periods of time.

Still another difference between the genres was recently voiced by an editor of musical scores, who described a musical as something made up by many people—designers, producers, directors, actors, orchestrators, choreographers, dancers, and maybe more, besides the composer and lyricist, all having creative input—whereas an opera normally is the product of one controlling consciousness.

American Opera Today

Although tightened budgets have put serious constraints upon the world of opera, whose complex presentations are exceedingly expensive to produce, Americans today are interested in all varieties of opera, old and new, domestic and foreign, funny and sad, short and long, simple and complex. Many

American cities boast an opera house and their own resident opera company, and virtually all Americans have access to live or taped performances on radio or television. Foreign operas often are performed in English translation, or alternatively, English surtitles are projected above the stage to avoid interfering with the visual presentation. Thus the American audience seems finally to have recognized opera as the marvelous form of entertainment it was always intended to be.

Terms to Review

opera   A drama that is sung, usually with orchestral accompaniment.

recitative   A declamatory setting of a text, used in opera and other dramatic vocal works, with rhythms and inflections related to those of speech.

aria   A songlike setting of a text, musically expressive, accompanied by the orchestra.

da capo   "From the beginning." An aria with a three-part design: The composer writes the first section and a contrasting middle section; the performer repeats the first section, adding embellishments.

chorus   A large vocal ensemble, with several voices on each part.

Treemonisha   An opera by Scott Joplin.

libretto   The words of an opera or other dramatic vocal work.

overture   In music theater, an introductory instrumental piece that sets the mood and that may include melodic themes from the opera or show to follow.

chamber opera   An opera for a small number of performers and limited resources.

Key Figures

Mary Carr Moore — *Devil & Dan Webster - Ballad of baby Doe*

Virgil Thomson — *white composer, black production, broadway style*

Gertrude Stein — *writer of Thompson's 4 sts. Saints*

Gian-Carlo Menotti — *Wrote tv opera Amahl for Christmes - 1951*

Optional Listening Examples

Gian-Carlo Menotti: "To This We've Come" from *The Consul*

Scott Joplin: "A Real Slow Drag" from *Treemonisha*

Suggestions for Further Listening

George Gershwin: Overture, "Summertime," "I Got Plenty o' Nothin'," and "It Ain't Necessarily So" from *Porgy and Bess*

Gian-Carlo Menotti: *Amahl and the Night Visitors*

PART 4 SUMMARY

After the Civil War, musical theater became increasingly popular in America, as the minstrel show waned in popularity but vaudeville and burlesque flourished. Revues, more elegant and sophisticated than the other variety shows, continue as a popular form of entertainment today.

European operettas, which have an integrated plot, soon stimulated composers to write operettas for an American audience. Gilbert and Sullivan operettas provided hilarious entertainment; but most influential upon the American music stage was the Viennese operetta, with its romantic stories and make-believe settings. Victor Herbert, Rudolf Friml, and Sigmund Romberg are among the best-loved and revered representatives of the Broadway musical experience.

Early musical comedies combined elements of operetta and variety shows. By writing several shows that had a story but included vaudeville's song, dance, and comedy routines, George M. Cohan was most influential in accustoming the Broadway audience to the new style. Jerome Kern's *Show Boat* proved that a Broadway musical could be based on a literary work and could address serious subjects effectively. *Oklahoma!* by Rodgers and Hammerstein successfully integrated all the entertainment scenes with the drama. Each of these shows had a profound effect upon the development of the Broadway musical stage.

The twenties and thirties are considered the Golden Age of the Broadway musical because so many outstanding shows were produced. Since then, the musical theater has become more complex and more sophisticated. Composers have revealed their heightened sense of singing (Frank Loesser's *Most Happy Fella*), the integrity of the play (Lerner and Loewe), and the importance of dance (Leonard Bernstein), and Bernstein and Stephen Sondheim are among several composers who have applied both classical and popular interests in various ways to the musical stage. Many of today's musicals are multimedia affairs combining technologically complex aural and visual effects.

From the earliest days of commercial films, live music introduced and accompanied a movie; and with the advent of sound films, the film score emerged as a new form of dramatic music. Film music, whether heard by the characters in the film (source or diegetic music) or by the viewing audience alone (functional or nondiegetic music), underpins the movie's emotional effects while serving innumerable practical functions as well.

Classical music, pop, jazz, rock, electronic music, and even opera effectively support feature films, setting a mood, establishing a time period, enhancing characterization, and bridging awkward gaps between scenes. Composers vary widely in their techniques of writing film scores, and all face the inevitability of having their music drastically altered by the director, various editors, and sound engineers. Some, however, compose orchestral suites from portions of their scores, allowing their music to be heard as they conceived it by a concert audience or on a recording.

Opera, too, is newly, but immensely, popular in America today. An opera is a grand combination of literary, visual, and musical arts. Although some composers include spoken words in their operas, traditionally opera dialogue was sung in recitative and emotional reactions expressed in solo arias, duets, and large or small ensembles.

In the 1920s, several American operas were enthusiastically received. Both Virgil Thomson's *Four Saints in Three Acts* and George Gershwin's *Porgy and Bess* succeeded on Broadway, as did Gian-Carlo Menotti's operas nearly three decades later. Thomson sought an elegant simplicity in music, Gershwin spoke in the spirit of jazz, and Menotti represents the Italian tradition of lyrical melodies and good theater. Today's mainstream and progressive composers are producing a wealth of new American operas, and this form of entertainment is increasingly visible on Broadway, in the opera house, and on the television and movie screen.

Part

5

(AP/Wide World Photos.)

Tradition and Innovation in Concert Music

Music for the Concert Hall: Historical and Cultural Perspective

The twentieth century witnessed an unprecedented diversity of concert music styles, as new historical and cultural awareness broadened concepts of timbre, pitch, melody, harmony, and rhythm. The political and social turmoil of much of that century, and the many important new technological resources, all had strong cultural repercussions, as artists in every medium found their way along traditional paths or forged entirely new avenues of expression.

During the 1920s, several talented young Americans set out to make their living as composers of concert music, never before considered a viable profession in this country. Whereas earlier American composers had largely depended on income-producing careers as teachers and/or performing musicians, these young people intended to survive as successful professional composers. They meant to write music not radically different from the masterpieces of the European musical heritage, yet sounding distinctively American and of the twentieth century. We may consider that they took an *evolutionary* approach to furthering the history of music.

Other twentieth-century Americans took a *revolutionary* approach to the composition of music. With the energy, curiosity, and independence characteristic of the pioneering spirit, a number of Americans explored musical sound as never before, so extending the boundaries of the definition of the art as to constitute a veritable revolution in the concept of music.

Interaction between the Arts

Throughout the twentieth century, visual and literary artists continued close interaction, sharing an expanded perception of their own disciplines and an interest in the interrelationships among them all. This close association among the arts—often enhanced by new technology—persists today, resulting sometimes in a kind of collision of artists exulting in their own independence *and* in the collage-like results of the interdependence they share. Some compare this congenial friction, if we can call it that, with the modern urban experience, in which widely disparate elements form a complex, somewhat fragmented whole.

The theater, requiring the services of painters, set designers, writers, musicians, dancers, choreographers, and actors, has always represented a collaborative form of art, and, as we have seen, nineteenth-century artists formed other, less traditional, liaisons as well. But today the visual, literary, and various performance arts influence and interact with music even more than in the past.

Dance, liberated from the expectation that it will tell a story, may or may not be accompanied by or set to music today; but although some dances are entirely independent of music or sound, most choreographers still consider music an inherent and vital dimension of dance. Jazz rhythms and electronically produced sounds as well as other popular and classical music dramatically widen the range of the dance experience.

Literature, too, is affected by the new intimacy among the arts. Several twentieth-century writers chose words for their *sounds,* rather than their meanings. For example, neither Gertrude Stein's libretto for Virgil Thomson's *Four Saints in Three Acts* (p. 291), nor the stream-of-consciousness prose of William Faulkner, attempts to follow the rules of grammar or syntax. Further, poetry may have visual as well as intellectual values, as when *shaped poems* are placed on a page in a manner conceived to visually enhance the meaning of the words. Each of these literary concepts (or conceits) can be related to a painter's subjective choice of colors, regardless of their relation to real visual experience, and to a composer's choice of pitches for their timbre rather than for functional value.

Multimedia Performances. The unprecedented degree of collaboration recently occurring among painters, dancers, poets, playwrights, and musicians has produced a wealth of interdisciplinary performances, awakening a healthy appreciation for the arts among audiences whose previous interest in and exposure to art was minimal. Some performances constitute "happenings" combining live and/or taped music with film, slides, speech, and lighting as well as dance, gestures, or movement of some kind, sometimes with audience participation. Painters and sculptors have combined shapes, colors, and sounds in large "environmental" works.

Because music for tape often requires visual or dramatic interest to sustain audience attention in the absence of live performers, some recent compositions involve a combination of live and taped music. Complex multimedia compositions simultaneously address two or more of the senses, and invite spectators to actively participate in their performance.

Relationships between the Visual Arts and Music.
Shared interests and philosophies of art are revealed
not only in such collaborative efforts, but also are
individually expressed in each medium of art. Much
in the way that *pointillist* painters treat spots of pure
color as entities in themselves, for example, composers sometimes treat particular tones or timbres as
isolated phenomena with independent, as opposed
to interdependent, values. In the machines, adver-
tisements, and commercial objects painted by Andy
Warhol and other pop artists, we see the simplicity
and repetition characteristic of musical *minimalism*
(pp. 352–355), generally considered a part of the art
or concert music experience, but of strong appeal to
listeners more accustomed to popular than to so-
called "serious" music. Visual artists often depict
musical instruments (Figure 115) or, more subjec-
tively, the *experience* of listening to music.

Since the early twentieth century, texture has
been a source of interest and experimentation
throughout the arts. Painters like Romare Bearden
add a third dimension to their work by affixing
pieces of fabric or other foreign objects to their surfaces. Other painters build up their surfaces by applying multiple thick layers of paint. Similarly,
composers may vary musical texture by super-
imposing unrelated timbres or chords, or by combining complex layers of sound. Considering timbre, composers today find sounds of nature, of
machinery, and of computer-generated effects to
offer a virtually unlimited palette of musical sound,
much as sculptors may replace traditional materials
like marble and bronze with plastic or with various
found materials.

The Value of Chance

Artists have long recog-
nized the value of the unintended and the unexpected in the creative process. An ancient Roman
treatise tells of an artist throwing a sponge at his
canvas in a fit of rage and being delighted with the
"effect of nature" resulting in his picture, and a
ninth-century Chinese work describes an artist "who
excelled in splattering ink to paint landscapes."
Even Leonardo da Vinci advised aspiring landscape
painters to visualize landscapes when looking at a
wall spotted with stains.

Figure 115

The Virtuoso, by David Adickes, 1983, 36 feet tall.
This whimsical sculpture, which stands in front of an
office building in downtown Houston, is one of the
countless works of art inspired by musical
instruments.
(Courtesy of David Adickes.)

During the 1950s and 1960s, the concept of leaving significant details of their work to chance attracted many visual artists and musicians. *Op art,*
like the chance music we shall consider in this section of the text, involves active rather than passive
participation, as op artists combine lines and colors
to create optical illusions that "activate" the eye instead of "acting upon it" in the traditional way. Jackson Pollock (1912–1956) led the Abstract Expressionist painters, who developed various means to
achieve random effects: Pollock, for example,
dripped or sprayed paint on a large surface, carefully

Figure 116

Jackson Pollock, *Number 1*, 1948, oil on canvas. Pollock's abstract expressionist paintings, expressive of the energy and rapid tempo of American life in the 1940s, involve imaginative interaction between chance and the artist's creative intent.
(Collection, The Museum of Modern Art, New York, Purchase.)

choosing the colors, direction, and density of his paints but allowing chance, or serendipity, to determine the result of his work (Figure 116). Like many artists intrigued with chance, Pollock considered the act of creating art a spiritual experience, more significant than the result. He did not create his work to be hung on museum walls but considered it to be as ephemeral—perhaps even as spiritual—as Navajo sand paintings.

Sculptors attracted to the idea of (literally) moving art experimented with motors, bands, and pulleys, whereas Alexander Calder (1898–1976), finding such mobiles too predictable, created small, delicate sculptures to hang in space, subject to the whim of the lightest breeze. Because one performance of chance music is never like another, Calder's small mobiles never appear exactly the same from one moment to the next (see Figure 117).

Chance occurs in literature, too, when novels written in *hypertext* allow readers to choose on their computers which subplots they wish to follow, as through a maze, rendering a book's form and even its conclusion indeterminate.

American Concert Music We cannot identify, either in Europe or in America, a unifying Western musical language such as prevailed in the several preceding centuries. Rather, the century we were born into gave us a rich multiplicity of musical tongues, which became ever more diverse as composers mixed the great Western tradition with the sounds of other cultures and other times. Experimental, often deliberately provocative music interested some twentieth-century American composers; others chose to follow more traditional paths.

Figure 117

Untitled, a mobile by the American sculptor Alexander Calder, 1976. Aluminum and steel.
(Gift of the Collectors Committee, © 1992 National Gallery of Art, Washington, D.C., 1976.)

As we enter a new century, we can scarcely imagine what musical riches lie in store. Considering how significantly the music of each preceding era differed from the predominant styles it succeeded, we may expect the music of the twenty-first century to chart numerous new and adventurous courses. ♪

18

Experimental Music: Revolution

Three musical pioneers initated the **experimental** movement in America, one a Connecticut Yankee who explored the manifold characteristics of sound, the second a Californian who discovered new ways to use the piano, and the third a European, who dreamed of new instruments that would create *new* sounds and lived to see his dream come true.

Charles Ives (1874–1954)

Charles Ives (Figure 118) derived his musical inventiveness from his father, George, an amateur musician who taught his son to play several instruments and (more significantly) to be ever curious about music and musical sound. George Ives continually conducted sound experiments in the family barn, to the annoyance of his neighbors and fascination of his son.

His father also taught Charles Ives to value each piece of music for its own sake, and all his life the younger Ives valued Stephen Foster's music as highly as Bach's and a good rag as much as a good symphony, viewing each

Figure 118
Charles Ives.
(The Bettmann Archive, Inc.)

307

piece according to its own particular merits and considering differentiation among *genres* of music in terms of quality a form of musical snobbery.

Ives studied music at Yale under Horatio Parker (see p. 102), whom he respected for his accomplishments but considered dogmatic and incapable of pursuing or appreciating new ideas. Convinced by his college experience that his broad musical concepts exceeded those of his contemporaries, and declaring that he did not intend to let his family starve on his dissonances, Ives devoted his professional life to his own highly successful insurance business. (He is remembered in that industry as the father of estate planning and the author of a training manual, *The Amount to Carry,* still in use in the 1980s.) This left him free to write music only at night, on weekends, and during vacations.

Philosophy of Music

An inveterate romantic, Ives had strong literary interests and expressed himself effectively in words as well as in music. He valued the *substance,* or character, of a piece over its *manner,* as he referred to music's superficial beauty, which to Ives was "like a drug that allows the ears to lie back in an easy chair." Believing that music should be strong and challenging—never "nice," which he equated with weak or superficially polite—he found dissonant sounds "clean and virile" and labeled people who feared them musical cowards.

[handwritten margin note: dissonant sounds were of value to him — music should be a challenge—never "nice"]

Instrumental Compositions

Most of Ives's instrumental compositions are program pieces, many reflecting the New England environment he knew and loved. He dedicated his famous *Concord Sonata* to the transcendentalists, whom he admired and whose ideas he shared; each of the four movements of this substantial piano composition describes the ideas and character of one or more members of the famous group (Ralph Waldo Emerson, Nathaniel Hawthorne, Amos Bronson and Louisa May Alcott, and Henry David Thoreau). Ives prefaced this work with *Four Essays Before a Sonata,* explaining there in words the ideas expressed in the musical composition.

One of Ives's best-known programmatic pieces, "General Putnam's Camp" from *Three Places in New England* (Listening Example 62), depicts a small boy's fantasies as he enjoys a Fourth of July picnic held at a former Revolutionary War campsite. This brash and exuberant piece includes snatches of patriotic tunes that Ives altered in the most imaginative and sometimes amusing ways, a technique characteristic of much of his music. Whereas composers often quote familiar melodies in their own original compositions, Ives had a peculiar manner of distorting tunes and also combining them in layers of sound intriguing and sometimes puzzling to the listener's ear.

Songs

Ives also wrote about 150 songs, covering many subjects, with settings that range from simple to complex. He frequently based his songs, like his instrumental pieces, on familiar tunes, quoting fragments, phrases, or complete melodies from American hymns, rags, marches, patriotic songs, Stephen Foster melodies, and the music of Bach and other composers, altering and/or juxtaposing them into complex layers of sound.

[handwritten margin note: base of his songs were on familiar tunes → altering them into complex, distorted layers.]

Program Music

Composer
Charles Ives

Title
"General Putnam's Camp" (from *Three Places in New England*)

Form
A loose **A B A'**

Texture
Basically polyphonic. The texture is so dense that repeated hearings generally reveal tunes and fragments previously unnoticed or unrecognized. This is *linear polyphony,* in which each melodic line should be heard independently and the resulting combination of tones, which may be quite dissonant, is not considered to produce chordal harmony.

This programmatic work depicts a small boy's fantasies and dreams as he enjoys a Fourth of July picnic at a former Revolutionary War campground site.

The movement opens with a raucous blast (a sound dear to Ives's ears) and continues with a wonderfully virile and highly unorthodox march theme (**A**). Snatches of John Philip Sousa marches and patriotic American tunes emerge from the subsequent confusion, as does a parody of "Yankee Doodle."

The boy wanders off and falls asleep, to dream of the hardship and suffering of the soldiers from long ago (**B**). He imagines that he hears the American General Putnam coming over the hill to save the troops. There is an amazing juxtaposition of two bands (one for strings and woodwinds, the other for piano, drums, and trumpet) that approach and pass each other—as they might in parade—playing different tunes, in different keys and in different meters. (Here the conductor must mark four beats to the measure with one hand and three with the other.)

The boy awakens, hears sounds of celebration, and rejoins his friends at the picnic (**A'**). With a jaunty reference to "The Star Spangled Banner," the piece ends on as raucous a note as it began.

More simply, "At the River" (Listening Example 63) turns a well-known tune into a new composition with its own Ivesian sound.

Other Characteristics of Ives's Music
Consistently delighted by the irregular and unconventional, Ives experimented with unusual tunings of musical instruments, sometimes deliberately achieving the intriguing effect of

unusual tuning of instruments

Original Song Based on a Given Tune

Composer
Charles Ives

Title
"At the River"

Form
Verse-chorus

Tune and Text
By Robert Lowry

Accompaniment
The piano introduction sets a tentative, questioning mood. The piano then accompanies the familiar hymn tune with richly dissonant chords, adding competing melodic interest toward the end of the verse. A brief piano interlude occurs between verse and chorus.

Rhythm
Although the listener clearly feels the *quadruple meter* (four beats to the bar), the rhythm is quite free and flexible, contributing to the "questioning" quality of the piece.

Basically retaining the original tune, Ives alters the end of the verse and the chorus with odd turns of phrase that, together with the imaginative harmonies, enhance the tentative mood of this simple and moving song.

instruments being played slightly out of tune. Although generally respecting the concept of tonality, he considered allegiance to one key at a time confining and occasionally indulged in **bitonality** (two keys at once) **and polytonality** (multiple simultaneous keys). His use of all twelve tones of the chromatic scale in some pieces foreshadowed by some years the *atonal* music of other composers.

Ives also conceived extremely complex rhythmic relationships, frequently combining two or more rhythmic patterns into simultaneous **polyrhythms.** Recognizing the continuum of pitches lying between the half steps of a keyboard instrument, he availed himself of quarter tones and **microtones** in some of his music.

The qualities of sound were a further source of endless fascination for Ives, who made space and the manner in which sound traveled through it a significant element in some of his compositions. He also valued a degree of spontaneity in performance, anticipating what later became known as "chance music." Both timbre and chance play more than the usual role in *The*

Space + how sound travels through it

'The Unanswered Question'

Unanswered Question (Optional Listening Example), a rather mystic, programmatic piece in which a solo trumpet poses "The Perennial Question of Existence." A group of woodwinds, positioned at a distance from the trumpet, attempts to find "The Invisible Answer," while a string ensemble, located off-stage, plays slow, quiet, mysterious music, oblivious of the squabble taking place on stage. Six times the trumpet poses "The Question" and rejects the woodwinds' increasingly agitated replies. Finally, "The Question" is heard once more, to remain unanswered.

In his prefatory instructions for performing this piece, Ives indicated that "The Question" may be posed by any instrument that can play the trumpet's pitches, and the woodwinds may either be all flutes or a combination of instruments from the woodwind family. He also suggested that "The Answers" need not begin at the points where he notated them in the score but could as well come a bit early or late. Thus, *space* (instruments widely separated from each other) and *chance* play a small but significant role in this fascinating piece, which has earned a distinguished place in the American repertoire. The Moody Blues ended their album *Knights in White Satin* (". . . we decide which is right,/And which is an illusion???") with a brief quotation of "The Question." The moving sounds of *The Unanswered Question* have been heard in many media and contexts; for example, the piece was played with haunting significance at President John Kennedy's memorial service, and it is heard to poignant effect on the music track of *The Thin Red Line,* a 1999 war film that hovers between layers of consciousness and leaves many disturbing questions unsolved.

Ives's Place in History Ill health prevented Ives from continuing his musical explorations after the 1920s, but it was twenty years after that before his music came to public attention and high if belated recognition. His Third Symphony, written about 1904 but first performed in 1947, won a Pulitzer Prize; and other Ives pieces have since received similarly prestigious awards. Although many of his innovations have become part of today's normal music experience, the spark of his invention, the verve, the very *nerve* of his style remain fresh and invigorating today.

(AP/Wide World Photos.)

Charles Ives
"Music—that no one knows what it is—and the less he knows he knows what it is the nearer it is to music—probably."

Henry Cowell (1897–1965)

By the time of the birth of **Henry Cowell** (Figure 119), the American frontier had been pushed all the way to the West Coast, where Cowell was born, in San Francisco, into an eclectic environment whose varied influences are reflected in his highly original compositions. Cowell based some programmatic pieces upon Irish folklore absorbed from his own Irish American family; and childhood friends introduced him to Chinese music, beginning a lifelong interest in the music of East Asia. Further musical experience was afforded by an organist friend who allowed the budding young composer to attend his practice sessions, where Cowell absorbed the modal sounds of Roman Catholic church music. Cowell also was attracted to early American hymn

Figure 119
Henry Cowell.
(Bettmann Newsphotos.)

and fuging tunes, using some of them as inspiration for an attractive set of instrumental pieces.

Early Compositions Having decided by the time he was eight years old to become a composer, Cowell taught himself to play the piano his own way, creating sounds he found interesting and eventually using those sounds for imaginative programmatic purposes in his highly original compositions. For example, while still in his teens Cowell wrote a piano piece called "The Tides of Mananaun" (Optional Listening Example), in which the performer uses the flat of the hand or forearm to play large *clusters* of keys in the lower range of the piano, evoking the sounds of the rolling, roaring ocean tides. The extremely dissonant result effectively suggests the deep, unstable, ever-changing sounds he wished to achieve.

Cowell, who believed simply that dissonant combinations evoke strong emotions whereas consonance suggests simplicity, was astonished to learn later that some people tend to hear dissonance and consonance as "bad" or "good" sounds. He and others came to recognize dissonant **tone clusters** as a new kind of chord, built upon seconds rather than the thirds of conventional tonal harmony. Although they later became friends, Cowell and Ives did not know each other's music at the time they both began using clusters, and it was only later that both men discovered they had "invented" the same idea at about the same time.

Piano Experiments Although Cowell wrote many kinds of music, the piano particularly interested him, probably because it was the most readily accessible musical instrument. Desiring to extend the range of sounds the piano could produce, for programmatic reasons or to achieve non-Western effects, he discovered he could do this by playing directly on the strings of the piano as on any other string instrument.

Playing the inside of a piano.

Piano Experiments

Composer
Henry Cowell

Title
"The Banshee" (excerpt)

Program
According to Irish (and Scottish) folklore, a banshee is a *fairy-woman* who foretells death by materializing nearby one doomed to die and wailing her long, howling cry.

Techniques
To achieve just this effect, "The Banshee" requires two performers: one is seated at the piano depressing the damper pedal, and the other stands in the crook of the piano and manipulates the strings. Cowell specified the following techniques, indicating in prefatory notes how they could be read in the score:

1. Sweeping the strings from the lowest note to a specified note with the flesh of the finger.
2. Sweeping the strings up and back.
3. Sweeping the length of one string with the flesh of a finger.
4. Plucking the strings.
5. Sweeping the strings with the back of a fingernail.
6. Sweeping the strings with the flat of the hand.

Cowell wrote several pieces in which the piano strings are to be stroked, strummed, plucked, or struck, each technique producing an entirely different effect. He achieved even further variety of sounds by having the pianist either depress some of the keys while manipulating the strings, or mute (stop) the strings with one hand while playing on the keyboard with the other. The techniques he applied to manipulating the piano strings in "The Banshee" (Listening Example 64) and other pieces are very similar to those indicated in the tablature notation used by Chinese and Japanese players of various string instruments and flutes, indicating what their fingers should *do* in order to produce the required notes, rather than the notes themselves (Figure 120.) These and other piano experiments proved particularly fruitful for other composers, suggesting the possibility of also producing effective new sounds by playing other traditional instruments in nontraditional ways.

Sources of Inspiration
Cowell was among the first Americans to be fascinated with the music of central and eastern Asia and to be gifted in reflecting

3. The Banshee

Henry Cowell
(1925)

Figure 120

For "The Banshee," Cowell modified traditional music notation by the addition of circled letters, each identifying a specific technique for manipulating the piano strings. (Copyright © 1930 by W.A. Quincke & Company, Los Angeles, CA. Copyright Renewed 1958 by Henry Cowell. Copyright Assigned 1959 to Associated Music Publishers, Inc. [BMI] International Copyright Secured. All Rights Reserved. Reprinted by Permission.)

The Banshee
Explanation of Symbols

Figure 120
(Continued)

"The Banshee" is played on the open strings of the piano, the player standing at the crook. Another person must sit at the keyboard and hold down the damper pedal throughout the composition. The whole work should be played an octave lower than written.

R. H. stands for "right hand." L. H. stands for "left hand." Different ways of playing the strings are indicated by a letter over each tone, as follows:

(A) indicates a sweep with the flesh of the finger from the lowest string up to the note given.

(B) sweep lengthwise along the string of the note given with flesh of finger.

(C) sweep up and back from lowest A to highest B-flat given in this composition.

(D) pluck string with flesh of finger, where written, instead of octave lower.

(E) sweep along three notes together, in the same manner as (B).

(F) sweep in the manner of (B) but with the back of fingernail instead of flesh.

(G) when the finger is halfway along the string in the manner of (F), start a sweep along the same string with the flesh of the other finger, thus partly damping the sound.

(H) sweep back and forth in the manner of (C), but start at the same time from both above and below, crossing the sweep in the middle.

(I) sweep along five notes, in the manner of (B).

(J) same as (I) but with back of fingernails instead of flesh of finger.

(K) sweep along in manner of (J) with nails of both hands together, taking in all notes between the two outer limits given.

(L) sweep in manner of (C) with flat of hand instead of single finger.

*fascination of
Asian music
(music of the East)*

the sounds of Persia, Japan, and even Iceland in music that bore the distinction of his own style. The music of the East encouraged Cowell to explore elements he felt had been neglected by Western composers; that is, whereas they had concentrated primarily on *melody* and *harmony,* Cowell and soon many other American and European composers found that *timbre* and *rhythm* offered them many new and stimulating ideas.

Cowell divided rhythms by five, seven, or other numbers as well as by the conventional two, three, or four; and like Ives, he invented complex polyrhythms, difficult to notate and to perform. Cowell even devised a new rhythmic notation in order to write down his sophisticated concepts. In collaboration with Léon Thérémin (inventor of an early electronic instrument that bears his name, see p. 281), Cowell developed a machine called the *rhythmicon,* which made it possible to reproduce rhythms of a complexity beyond the capacity of human performance. Of course the rhythmicon has since been replaced by computers and electronic instruments, but in its time it allowed composers greatly to extend their rhythmic creativity.

Writings   Like Ives, Cowell wrote about his ideas and ideals, beginning with a book called *New Musical Resources* while still a college student. Deploring the manner in which conventional publishers ignored American experimentalists, he founded a quarterly journal, *New Music,* in which he published provocative works (and to which Ives apparently gave anonymous financial support). The term **New Music,** in fact, came to mean music of an advanced or experimental nature. Cowell also edited a collection of essays by important contemporary composers, and he and his wife Sidney Cowell collaborated on a book about Charles Ives, with whom they became friends. Cowell was among the first to bring Ives's music to public attention.

Writer, teacher, lecturer, editor, inventor, theorist, and composer, Henry Cowell contributed immeasurably to the cause of experimentalism and opened many doors to the future of American music. He traveled extensively, seeking instruction from others and also sharing his own ideas. He played his compositions to appreciate audiences in Europe and was the first American to give concerts in the former Soviet Union (1928), thus arousing interest abroad in the new experimental American music.

Edgard Varèse (1883–1965)

Edgard Varèse was born in Paris but settled in New York City to become a part of the American music scene during World War I. Although educated in European traditions and acquainted with many important composers of his day, Varèse was intensely interested in the music of all the Americas. He organized a PanAmerican Society and composed a piece titled *Amériques,* which he said symbolized discovery, adventure, and the unknown.

Philosophy of Music   One of the first composers to think of music simply as organized sound, Varèse believed that *any* sounds—including those called noise—could be used in a musical composition. He spoke of and visualized music as "sound masses moving in space." Varèse considered the potential forms of a composition, formed around a particular idea, to be as limitless as the external forms of a crystal formed around a grain of sand.

Early Compositions

Like Ives and Cowell, Varèse was immensely intrigued with the many qualities of sound; but more than either of them, he craved sounds that had not yet been realized! Making do for a time with what was available, he composed for a wide array of mostly wind and percussion instruments, including besides the more usual drums, cymbals, gongs, bells, and chimes, many of indeterminate pitch and many not traditionally found in a music ensemble, such as anvils and chains, rattles, woodblocks, and sleigh bells. Varèse's *Ionisation,* an Optional Listening Example, was one of the first pieces composed for percussion instruments only. The instruments played by thirteen players in this innovative piece include several Caribbean instruments (bongos, claves, guiro, maracas) and three hand-operated sirens, whose "curving sounds" Varèse particularly liked.

Varèse also achieved varied effects by using instruments in their extreme high and low ranges of pitch, where they normally are not sounded. He liked sustained glissandos, especially when made by sirens soaring dramatically through a wide continuum of pitches. Unlike keyboard instruments, on which the smallest interval is the half step, sirens allowed him to achieve varied "hues" of sound, just as painters achieve subtle hues of color on their palettes.

Used high + low ranged pitches when playing instruments

Sharing Cowell's concern for the need to bring New Music to public and critical attention, Varèse founded a New Symphony Orchestra expressly for this purpose but had to give it up when the public rebelled at his progressive programming. (We should take note that among the works they vigorously resisted were those by Claude Debussy and Béla Bartók, now among the best-known and most-admired twentieth-century composers.) In 1921, Varèse founded the International Composers Guild, also to support New Music.

A Career Interrupted

Having experimented boldly with all the materials available, Varèse simply stopped composing for about fifteen years, apparently having run out of interesting sounds. He predicted that one day new instruments would create sounds at a composer's will and that other machines would reproduce exactly what a composer intended, without relying on a performer for interpretation—prophetic predictions indeed, accurately describing many functions of the electronic synthesizer, electronic tape technique, and computers. And when these in fact became available, Varèse plunged enthusiastically into composing more New Music (see pp. 339–340).

Meanwhile, important new technology made it possible for experimentalists to produce original sounds and rhythms of unprecedented complexity. And as non-Western instruments offered a wealth of possibilities, it became quite usual for even traditional or mainstream composers to include non-Western instruments in their ensembles. Although the twentieth-century orchestra is generally smaller than the orchestra of the late Romantic period, it often includes a larger proportion of percussion instruments, which not only emphasizes the rhythmic qualities of contemporary music but also adds a wide range of exotic timbres.

Concrete Music

During the 1940s, a number of composers of different nationalities working in Paris experimented with recorded musical and nonmusical sounds, which they manipulated to form a new kind of music called **musique concrète,** or, in English, **concrete music.** Having altered the sounds electronically—a process made all the more versatile with the invention of magnetic tape after World War II—they used the products of their manipulations to create musical compositions, rendering the music *concrete* in the sense that it could not be performed or interpreted but existed only on tape.

Five processes are involved in the composition of concrete music:

1. *Selecting* the sounds to be taped. The sounds may include those of traditional instruments, such as piano or voice; sounds of nature, such as raindrops or birdcalls; or sounds of machinery, including a vacuum cleaner or jet plane. Any sound, in fact, may provide the raw material with which the composer works.
2. *Recording* the sounds. In order to alter the sounds and produce a work of art, the composer must have them on tape.
3. *Manipulating* the sounds. Sounds played backward, or faster or slower than normal, may become unrecognizable. Composers use these and other techniques to manipulate sounds as they please.
4. *Mixing* the sounds. This is the step in which the composer combines the sounds he or she has created, much as the traditional composer orchestrates a piece.
5. "Cutting and pasting" the tape—a process called *montage*—to achieve the form of the completed composition.

Twelve-Tone Technique

A principle developed by Austrian composer **Arnold Schoenberg** (1874–1951) offered composers still further means of imposing mathematical and intellectual control upon their work. Schoenberg discovered that by arranging all twelve pitches of the chromatic scale into a series or **row,** each pitch being of equal importance and no tone being repeated until all others had been sounded, he effectively negated the tonal system, in which each tone bears a specific relationship to the all-important tonic. Methodical use of the tone row provides all of the melodic *and* harmonic, or the linear and vertical, material of a twelve-tone composition; that is, *all* the tones must be selected in order from the row governing that piece. But it is important to note that although **twelve-tone** music evolved as an atonal concept, it may be adapted to tonal music as well.

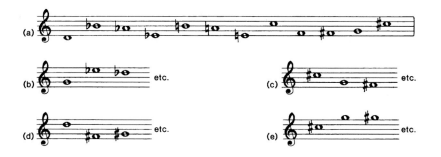

Figure 121
(a) A twelve-tone row.
(b) The row transposed up
a fourth. (c) The retrograde
version (the row
backward). (d) The row
inverted (upside down).
(e) The retrograde inversion
(backward and upside
down).
(Courtesy of Frederick Carl
Gurney.)

Variety is achieved in twelve-tone music by using the tones in reverse order (the *retrograde* version of the row), in *inversion* (a mirror image), or in *retrograde inversion* (backward and upside down) (Figure 121). Further, the tones of the row may be selected from any octave, resulting in the angular or disjunct melody lines characteristic of much twelve-tone music. (This technique, called **octave displacement,** is something we all have probably experienced: When singing a song that includes some notes too high for our voices, we normally jump down an octave to sing those passages, returning to the original pitch levels when it becomes comfortable to do so.)

Although twelve-tone music is so tightly organized, the scheme applied rigidly is too complex for the ear to recognize; and whereas some twelve-tone music certainly is emotionally accessible and intensely moving, some suggests a relentless sameness or, conversely, an effect of unrelieved chaos. Few composers limit themselves to twelve-tone music today; but it made an important impact on American music in the 1950s, and some continue to find it a valuable alternative to traditional systems of organizing music.

John Cage (1912–1992)

Having dutifully sampled and then soon abandoned both the twelve-tone and magnetic tape methods, **John Cage** (Figure 122) (like Varèse) wrote some music for percussion ensembles; and (like Cowell) he extended the timbres of the piano. In fact, this soulmate of Charles Ives tried everything available and invented what was not.

Because Cage studied music theory and composition with Arnold Schoenberg and with Henry Cowell, it is not surprising that he took an unorthodox approach to writing music. But having organized some of his early works according to the twelve-tone technique, Cage soon decided that even that was too rooted in the past to offer a viable path leading music to the future. And having experimented as a young composer with magnetic tape techniques (producing the first American example of concrete music, titled *Imaginary Landscape no. 5,* 1951–1952), he found they also soon ceased to intrigue or satisfy him.

Figure 122

John Cage.
(© Steve Kagan/Photo
Researchers, Inc.)

interest in Eastern music.

Cage, the son of an inventor, consistently addressed his musical dilemmas with an inventor's ingenuity and creativity. Like Cowell, Cage was born on the West Coast and felt less tied to European traditions than did many German-trained composers in New England and New York. Profoundly interested in Oriental philosophies, religions, and music styles, he soon turned from traditional Western instruments to those producing an intriguing variety of sounds similar to the music of the East. Because he wished to use pitches not in the Western chromatic scale, such unusual "instruments" as cowbells, automobile brake drums, and anvils, combined with Japanese temple bells, Chinese gongs, and other exotic non-Western percussion instruments, attracted him and met his early purposes.

Gamelan Music Cage discovered that an elegant Indonesian percussion ensemble called a **gamelan** *(GAH-meh-lahn)* produced many of the sounds and pitches he desired. The gamelan is an orchestra, in the sense that it is a combination of instruments from various families; but unlike the Western string orchestra, the gamelan consists primarily of percussion instruments (Figure 123). These include *metallophones,* which are sets of metal keys suspended over a bronze or wooden frame and struck with a mallet; tuned gongs of various sizes, usually arranged in a semicircle; and drums. The gamelan ensemble also includes a few wind and string instruments that play sustained pitches and add color to the sound. Listening Example 65 gives a brief indication of the delicate and varied sounds of gamelan music.

Although Cage included a gamelan in some of his early compositions, the ensemble—visually as well as aurally stunning—is too expensive to be widely available (although gamelans are in fact becoming increasingly familiar in the West). Therefore, Cage invented a method of altering the grand piano in order to approximate many of a gamelan's sounds.

Figure 123
A Javanese gamelan.
(© George Holton/Photo
Researchers, Inc.)

Listening Example 65

Balinese Gamelan Music

Title
Kebjar Hudjan Mas

Form
A series of variations evolves over relentlessly repeated ostinatos,
which provide stability and seem to anchor the composition.

Timbres
The metallic sounds of gongs and metallophones, dominating the
beginning of the piece, suggest the meaning of "kebjar"—to flash
or flame, as in a burst of light. Soon the full gamelan accompanies
the joyous peals of sound.

Prepared Piano In 1938, Cage was the piano accompanist for the famous
choreographer Merce Cunningham, with whom he continued to collaborate
on many projects throughout his life. Challenged by Cunningham's dance
company to extend the range of timbres in their performance music without
exceeding the limits of their budget, Cage discovered that the grand piano
could be altered or "prepared" so as to change the timbres and pitches it produced. By applying pieces of wood, metal, and rubber to the strings of the
piano, he slowed the rate at which the strings vibrated, slightly changing the
pitch as well as the quality of the sound. His new, or modified, instrument is
called the **prepared piano.**

altering of pianos
traditional sound

These measurements apply to a Steinway, L, M, O, A or B

TONE	MATERIAL	STRINGS (left to right)	DISTANCE from Damper (inches)	MATERIAL	STRINGS (left to right)	DISTANCE from Damper (inches)	TONE
	Rubber	1-2-3	$15/16$*				E
	Rubber	1-2-3	$1 7/16$*				B
	Rubber	1-2-3	$1 7/16$*				E
	Weather Stripping	1-2	1	Screw and Nuts	2-3	$2 1/4$	D
	Rubber (damper to bridge = $4 9/16$; adjust measurements accordingly)	2-3(B♭)-1	$3 3/8$	Screw	2-3	$1 7/16$	B
	Weather Stripping	1-2	$3 3/4$	Bolt and Nuts	2-3	$2 1/4$	A♭
	Weather Stripping	1-2	2	Bolt	2-3	$1 3/4$	E
				Bolt (small)	2-3	4	D♭
	Weather Stripping	1-2	6	Screw and Nuts	2-3	$1 1/2$	B♭
	Weather Stripping	1-2-3	4				A♭
	Weather Stripping	1-2-3	3	Weather Stripping	1-2-3	$3 1/2$	G
	Rubber	1-2-3	5				F♯
	Weather Stripping	1-2-3	$8 1/2$				E
	Bamboo Slit	1-2	$4 7/8$	Bolt	2-3	4	E♭
	Weather Stripping	1-2-3	11				D
	Double Weather Stripping	1-2	13	Screw and Nuts	2-3	12	D♭
	Double Weather Stripping	1-2	7	Screw and Rubber Washer	2-3	$6 3/4$	B♭
	Weather Stripping	1-2-3	$4 1/2$				G
	Bamboo Slit	1-2	$2 1/4$	Bolt	2-3	2	F
	Weather Stripping	1-2	$1/4$	Bolt	2-3	1	D
	Screw and Weather Stripping	1-2	$3 7/8$				F
	Screw and Weather Stripping	1-2	5				D
	Screw and Weather Stripping	1-2	7				B♭
	Screw and Weather Stripping	1-2	14				A♭
	Wood and Cloth	1-1	$2 3/4$				E-F

*Measure from Bridge

Figure 124

The notated tone (left column) indicates the pitch (identified by its letter name in the column on the right) that should be "prepared" by applying the material specified to one or more of its strings at a certain distance from the *dampers* (small pieces of felt-lined wood attached to piano strings).

As most keys on a piano keyboard control three strings each, nuts, bolts, screws, bamboo strips, or other materials may be placed on one of the strings, between any two, or touching all three. A composer indicates precisely which strings of which keys are to be prepared, what foreign materials are to be used, and at what distance from the soundboard they are to be placed (Figure 124). When the hammers strike the prepared strings, timbres and tones similar to those of a gamelan or a Western percussion ensemble are sounded. A wide variety of sounds and pitches may be achieved in this way, all on a readily available instrument and at the control of an individual performer. Further, the pianist may also strike the wooden parts and metal braces of the instrument with the hand or an implement, producing even more varied sound effects. Many musicians were impressed with Cage's several independent compositions for prepared piano (see Listening Example 66), and soon other composers also were writing pieces in which a few, or many, strings were to be prepared.

By the 1950s, John Cage had become the dominant figure of American experimental music, as we shall see in Chapter 20.

Prepared Piano

Composer

John Cage

Title

The Perilous Night

Preparation

At the beginning of the score, Cage indicated the precise manner in which the piano should be prepared. Nuts, bolts, washers, strips of bamboo, and pieces of weatherstripping are placed at measured points between specific strings, creating a variety of wooden, metallic, and indeterminate sounds (see Figure 124).

Form

Suite for prepared piano. The suite consists of six pieces of various character, although all have a muted, delicate effect because of the dampened piano strings.

1. Ostinatos and repeated notes, irregular rhythms, and pitches that lie between half steps suggest certain non-Western musics, including music for the gamelan.
2. This piece, busier than the first, builds in intensity and then tapers off to a quiet close.
3. All the tones of this piece are chosen from the chord outlined at the beginning of the section, emphasizing the economy of pitches characteristic of *The Perilous Night.*
4. The left hand gives the effect of a bass drum pattern, accompanied by a rapid *ostinato* in the right hand.
5. This short piece explores the dynamic ranges of the prepared piano. Although notated as "extremely loud" (*fortississimo,* or *fff*) and "extremely soft" (*pianississimo,* or *ppp*), the range is actually limited by the damping of the strings.
6. The longest and most complex of the pieces builds to an exciting intensity but ends with great simplicity and a sense of repose. The repetitive nature of the music is again reminiscent of music for the gamelan.

Terms to Review

experimental music   Music challenging accepted concepts of musical sound.

bitonality   Two keys at the same time

polytonality   More than two keys at the same time.

polyrhythms   Two or more simultaneous rhythmic patterns.

microtone   Any interval smaller than a half step.

tone cluster   A chord, usually of several tones, built upon seconds. Clusters are often played with the flat of the hand, the arm, or a board cut to a specified length.

New Music   A term used for music of an experimental nature.

musique concrète (concrete music)   Music created by manipulating taped sounds.

row   An arrangement of pitches on which a twelve-tone composition is based.

twelve-tone   A technique of organizing music, developed by Arnold Schoenberg, in which all twelve tones of the octave are of equal significance.

octave displacement   The choice of a note of the same letter name but from a different octave.

gamelan   An Indonesian percussion ensemble.

prepared piano   A grand piano on which some or all the strings have been "prepared" by placing foreign materials on them, thereby altering pitch, timbre, and dynamic level.

Key Figures

Charles Ives · *the most important musician America has produced*

Henry Cowell · *invented rhythmicon — the*

Edgard Varèse · *used non main stream instruments*

~~Arnold Schoenberg.~~

John Cage · *influenced by multi cultural west coast*
Silence for c/min 33 sec

Optional Listening Examples

Charles Ives: *The Unanswered Question*
Henry Cowell: "The Tides of Mananaun"
Edgard Varèse: *Ionisation*

Suggestions for Further Listening

Charles Ives: "*Hallowe'en*" (orchestral)
Ives: "Serenity" (song)
Henry Cowell: *Hymns and Fuging Tunes*
John Cage: *Sonatas and Interludes* (prepared piano)

19

Mainstream Concert Music: Evolution

Unlike their experimentalist colleagues, many twentieth-century composers took an *evolutionary* approach to furthering the development of music. Some, notably William Schuman (1910–1992), found a source for their compositions in American subjects or tunes. Several American composers found jazz and other vernacular sources useful material to tap. Since folk and popular dances have long enlivened European concert music, it seems natural for contemporary classical musicians to draw ideas from popular musics, now more varied and sophisticated than ever; but in the 1920s and 1930s, many Americans found this a novel and intriguing concept. Although some musicologists now dispute the view, until recently it was generally acknowledged that Europeans preceded Americans in recognizing jazz as a source of inspiration and material for concert music. Almost from the start of jazz, such European composers as Darius Milhaud, Béla Bartók, and Maurice Ravel integrated the distinctive rhythms, timbres, and performance techniques of the new American vernacular music in their classical compositions. But in America, Charles Ives's appreciation for good jazz, equal to his appreciation for good symphonic music, struck many as a veritable aberration.

In any case, evolutionary, often nationalistic, works constituted the mainstream of twentieth-century American concert music.

The Paris Scene

Most of the eager young composers of the 1920s and 1930s traveled to Europe to study, as America did not yet offer comparably advanced music training. They turned not to Germany, however, as had the Second New England School composers, but to France, which became the world center of artistic creativity after World War I. Not only musicians but also poets, writers, painters, dancers, and choreographers from all over the world met in Paris, where they shared ideas—disparate but fresh and invigorating—that stimulated each other to reach new heights of creativity.

The young American composers found their study in France a liberating experience indeed, for unlike the German masters who insisted on teaching the "correct" way to compose, the French encouraged them to develop their individuality and explore new ideas. Especially, a young French organist, composer, and highly gifted teacher named **Nadia Boulanger** (1887–1979)

Figure 125
Nadia Boulanger.
(Courtesy of Milton
Babbitt.)

Figure 126
Aaron Copland.
(American Symphony
Orchestra League.)

(Figure 125) offered superb instruction to this and several successive generations of composers, <u>brilliantly teaching skills and technique without inflicting
style upon her students</u>. Recognizing each young composer's distinctive talents, she defined the ways each might reach his or her best potential.

taught without putting on restrictions

The first American to study with Boulanger was a young man destined to
become known as the dean of American composers: Aaron Copland.

Dean of American composers

Aaron Copland (1900–1990)

Aaron Copland (Figure 126), born in Brooklyn, New York, to a family not
particularly interested in music, decided while still in his teens to become a
composer of serious music. To this end, Copland spent three years during his
early twenties studying in Paris with Nadia Boulanger.

To his astonishment, Mlle. Boulanger suggested that Copland borrow jazz
techniques as one means of giving his music a distinctively American sound. In
any case, several of Copland's early pieces, including a suite for small orchestra
titled *Music for the Theater* (1925—the year after Gershwin's *Rhapsody in*

Boulanger encouraged
him to incorporate jazz
in his music.

Inspired more by
· cowboy songs
· american hymns
· mexican folk
    + popular music

Blue) and a concerto for piano and orchestra completed the next year, certainly reflect the rhythms, melodies, harmonies, and timbres of jazz.

Although appreciative of these fresh and nationalistic effects, Copland soon found jazz, as he said, emotionally limited, and he sought inspiration in other American sounds, including cowboy songs and early American hymns. An avid proponent of American music from both north and south of the Mexican border, Copland also effectively captured the flavors and spirit of Mexican folk and popular music. First performed in 1937 in Mexico City, his delightful *El Salón México,* a musical potpourri of Copland's versions and orchestrations of Mexican folk tunes, remains among the favorite Copland works today.

Depression and War Years Determined to develop an American audience interested in hearing music by American composers, Copland and another prominent American composer, Roger Sessions (1896–1985), organized and supported a series of programs from 1928 to 1931 at which American concert music was performed, heard, and reviewed; thus important new American compositions gained public and critical attention at a time before musicians could rely upon recorded music to reach a wide audience. The **Copland-Sessions concerts** had inestimable value in encouraging the development of American music.

20's - 30's

exposing american
concert music

gained public &
    critical attention
before recordings
    came into play

The music Copland wrote just before and after the stock market crashed in 1929 is rather difficult, austere, and uncompromising, although beautifully written and stunning in effect when performed well. Many believe, in fact, that the *Piano Variations* (1929) is his finest composition. But the Great Depression profoundly affected the development of an American repertoire, as it affected every phase of American life: People simply were not able to address new subjects and cultivate new tastes at a time when their energies were absorbed by private and public tragedies. Copland, deeply sympathetic to the conservative attitude of the shocked and saddened American people, urgently wished to communicate with them through his music, on which he deliberately imposed a new simplicity. Thus most of his works from the Depression period through the years of World War II are readily accessible and reflective of Copland's great interest in all of America.

Great Depression &
    music
    ↓
Copland, in response,
simplified the
        music

Intending his music to have practical as well as aesthetic purpose, Copland diligently provided scores for radio, films, schools, amateur musicians, and ballet companies. In 1942, he stirred the wartime audience's patriotic spirit with *Lincoln Portrait,* a musical composition that quotes fragments of Stephen Foster songs and American folk tunes accompanied by the narration of some of Abraham Lincoln's well-known speeches.

A festive **fanfare**—a short, dramatic piece for brass instruments—also written in 1942 has become one of Copland's most famous works. Although a fanfare usually celebrates a royal or state occasion, Copland titled his wartime piece *Fanfare for the Common Man.* Its dramatic theme, based on a rising motive introduced by a solo trumpet, is variously treated by combinations of brass instruments, forcefully punctuated by percussion. Copland's *Fanfare* (Listening Example 67) is frequently played today at events of na-

Fanfare

Composer

Aaron Copland

Title

Fanfare for the Common Man

Copland's *Fanfare,* one of several fanfares written in response to a challenge issued in 1942 by the conductors of the Cincinnati Symphony Orchestra, has become one of the best-recognized and favorite American compositions. It is often performed at occasions of patriotic significance and pride.

Timbres

Brass and percussion. Such instrumentation is characteristic of a fanfare, intended to make a dramatic and emphatic musical statement.

Melody

Bold ascending and descending leaps in the melody line lend strength and drama to the piece.

Key

The *Fanfare* begins in B♭ major and moves through abrupt and startling key changes—which keep the piece harmonically interesting—to end in D major. The dramatic, emotionally uplifting thrust up to the final chord brings the brief composition to a thrilling end.

tional significance, such as the Olympic Games, and to highlight announcements of dramatic American accomplishments and import.

Music for Dance   The interest Americans developed in Broadway musical stage ballet and modern dance during the 1930s and 1940s remained very strong, and Copland's best-known works include his dance compositions, usually called *ballets,* although in fact they represent *modern dance.*

Classical ballet is a formal, stylized dance form in which steps, gestures, and positions, together with mime, describe characters and dramatize a story. Particularly characteristic of classical ballet are the female dancers' positions *en pointe,* or on the points of their toes. (The language of ballet, which evolved in the seventeenth-century French court of Louis XIV, remains French today.) The movements of the dancers (classical or otherwise) are determined by a choreographer, who may set steps to existing music or to music composed especially for a particular dance. Choreography used to be handed

[handwritten margin note: 30's + 40's – broadway popularity / Copland composed famous ballets]

down by tradition only, but methods of notation have been developed—some of them quite recently—that make it possible to preserve a choreographer's ideas accurately. Videotape provides another effective tool for this purpose.

Copland's "ballets," however, are examples of **modern dance,** a twentieth-century American contribution with steps and gestures more varied and less stylized than those of classical ballet (Figure 127). The costumes of modern dance also are simpler, and the dancers perform barefoot rather than in the rigid, tightly laced shoes allowing ballerinas to dance *en pointe.*

Inspired by Copland's attractive versions of traditional American tunes and cowboy songs for two of his effective dance performances, *Billy the Kid* and *Rodeo,* the famous modern dance choreographer **Martha Graham** (1893–1991) commissioned Copland to write for her. Copland, who had no story in mind as he wrote the music, titled his new composition simply *Ballet for Martha.*

But Copland's music, which includes country fiddling and an early American hymn tune, reminded Martha Graham of a poem titled "The Bridge" by the American poet Hart Crane (1899–1932). This very long poem includes one section, "The Dance," in which the phrase, "O Appalachian Spring!" occurs, inspiring Graham to title the dance piece *Appalachian Spring.* A year later (1945), Copland extracted the most musically significant portions of *Appalachian Spring* (Figure 128) and composed an orchestral suite that has become one of his best-known works.

The story of the dance (although not of Hart Crane's poem) concerns a young pioneer bride-to-be and her fiancé, who, as the performance begins, stand in front of their newly built farmhouse soberly anticipating the joys and responsibilities of married life. A revivalist preacher solemnly exhorts the earnest young couple and primly dressed members of his flock to follow the ways of the Lord, while an older woman advises and comforts the young bride. Soon the young couple's irrepressible joy replaces the solemn mood, and they leap with glad excitement.

The most famous section of the dance and of the suite is a set of variations on a well-known American hymn tune, "Simple Gifts" (Listening Example 68).

Figure 128
Erick Hawkins, Martha Graham and Company. In this scene from *Appalachian Spring,* the young husband-to-be dances his joy while his bride seriously contemplates her new responsibilities, primly attended by the preacher and members of his flock. (Graham 1944). (© Arnold Eagle.)

Later Works In the 1950s, Copland wrote two sets of *Old American Songs* and an opera with an American setting called *The Tender Land* (mentioned in Chapter 17). He also surprised many people by writing several works based on progressive principles, including twelve-tone technique, that abandoned traditional concepts of Western music. In fact, throughout his career, Copland demonstrated an unusual variety of tastes and talents, never remaining committed to a consistent trend or direction. Among his large body of works are choral pieces, film scores (including *Our Town,* 1940; *The Red Pony,* 1948; and *The Heiress,* 1949), chamber music, large orchestral works, the opera, and other ballets or dance pieces. He also wrote several very readable books about music.

Samuel Barber (1910–1981)

Beginning in the 1920s, many American composers followed Copland to Paris to study with Nadia Boulanger. Most, like Copland, were basically **traditionalists,** who sought progress of an evolutionary kind. Many were at the same time **neoromantics** ("new romantics"), who organized their compositions according to programmatic rather than to strictly intellectual concepts, emphasizing lyrical melodies and richly dissonant harmonies and imbuing their music with warm emotional expression.

Prominent among the latter was **Samuel Barber** (Figure 129), whose best-known works include several beautiful art songs. One, *Knoxville: Summer of 1915* for soprano and orchestra (Optional Listening Example), is a setting of a beautiful text written by James Agee in 1938 (later placed by Agee's literary executors, after the author's death, as the Prologue to his Pulitzer-Prize-winning novel *A Death in the Family*). Unlike Copland's ballet *Appalachian Spring,* Barber's song is a conscious interpretation by an American composer of an American literary work. So strongly was Barber attracted to song and the singing

neoromatic composers

Music from the Dance

Composer
Aaron Copland

Title
Variations on "Simple Gifts" (from *Appalachian Spring*)

Theme
The folklike hymn tune titled "Simple Gifts," which forms the theme of this section of *Appalachian Spring,* was composed in 1848 by a Shaker named Joseph Brackett. (The Shakers were an offshoot of the Quaker religious sect.) The theme, which is introduced by a solo clarinet over a very simple accompaniment, has two parts: The first begins with a rising inflection, and the second with a descending phrase.

Variation 1: The melody is played in a higher range by an oboe with a slightly faster tempo.

Variation 2: Violas play the theme at half its former tempo (a technique called **augmentation**), punctuated with an ostinato in the harp and piano. The violins and cellos then play phrases of the theme in imitative polyphonic texture.

Variation 3: After a brief transition, trumpets and trombones state the theme at twice the former speed (**diminution**), accompanied by rapid figures in the strings.

Variation 4: Slower and quieter, this variation gives the second part of the theme to the woodwinds.

Variation 5: The full orchestra plays the last variation, which is stately, majestic, slow in tempo, and fortissimo in volume.

Figure 129
Samuel Barber.
(Bettmann Newsphoto.)

Neoromanticism

Composer
Samuel Barber

Title
Adagio for Strings

Form
Arch form. Gently rounded to end much as it begins, the *Adagio* forms an asymmetrical arch, building through most of the piece to its emotional climax and coming soon thereafter to a quiet close.

Melody
The lovely main theme winding gently throughout the piece is long and irregular, unbound by conventional concepts of balance or symmetry. Introduced by the violins, it is repeated *sequentially* (at changing—in this case higher and higher—levels of pitch), to intense emotional effect.

Harmony
Tense dissonances alternate with soft, sensuous harmonic resolutions to raise and release the level of intensity. Notice that the relentless rise in pitch level leading toward the climax of the piece coincides with particularly tense harmonies and a dramatic crescendo; and notice, too, the overwhelming effect of the moment of silence succeeding the climax.

voice that even his instrumental music has lyrical, songlike melodies rendering them among the most accessible and appreciated compositions of this century.

For example, in 1936, noticing that audiences particularly responded to the slow movement (Adagio) of one of his string quartets, Barber arranged that movement to be played by a larger group of string instruments; and as an independent piece in this more sensuous guise, his *Adagio for Strings* has become fondly familiar to the American public. This quietly solemn piece, acknowledging the reality of sadness but offering solace and rest, was played during the radio announcement of Franklin Delano Roosevelt's death in 1945 and has frequently been performed at solemn state occasions since. It was heard in its entirety at the end of the poignant 1980 film *The Elephant Man* and was the musical theme of *Platoon* (Best Picture of the Year, 1986). Some suggest that the long, asymmetrical, rhythmically relaxed melody of this emotionally expressive yet unpretentious piece, clearly unfettered by preconceived rules and measurements, characterizes the American spirit. In any case, Barber's *Adagio for Strings* (Listening Example 69) has become one of the best-loved pieces in the American repertoire.

Harlem Renaissance

The **Harlem Renaissance** applies to a movement of the 1920s in which African American painters, sculptors, poets, playwrights, musicians, novelists, and essayists broke from convention to "promote racial advancement through artistic creativity." Responding to writers Langston Hughes, Zora Neal Hurston, and many others, black artists in every field traveled to Harlem (in uptown New York City), seeking within the heady environment of this unprecedented concentration of African American talent to effect a true renaissance—a rebirth—of black "high art."

Although treated primarily as a literary movement, the Harlem Renaissance inspired visual artists as well to express modern urban life from the African American point of view. And the movement used and was supported and accompanied by music. Among the musicians it attracted to New York, Eubie Blake created *Shuffle Along* on Broadway, W. C. Handy ("father of the blues") established his music publishing house, Fletcher Henderson and especially Duke Ellington drew huge numbers of white people to Harlem to hear jazz, James P. Johnson and Thomas "Fats" Waller virtually created jazz piano, and Bessie Smith sang the blues. These were prominent among many others who introduced, developed, and promoted the black popular music and jazz of the Harlem Renaissance.

Primarily it was in the realm of concert music, however, that Harlem Renaissance musicians sought to develop folk materials from the black cultural heritage into artistic creations commanding the respect of white as well as black artists and intellectuals, Harry T. Burleigh and Robert Nathaniel Dett were among the most successful black composers basing classical compositions on familiar spirituals, and singers Marian Anderson and Paul Robeson brought these eloquent songs to a large and appreciative concert audience. Although the Harlem Renaissance ended (with the onslaught of the Great Depression) before many composers could fully develop their skills, the accomplishments of these and countless others reveal the rich cultural milieu in which black intellectuals made high art in the Harlem Renaissance.

Preeminent among the Harlem Renaissance composers, William Grant Still became the first black composer to have a symphony played by a major symphony orchestra, the first to conduct a major symphony orchestra, and the first to have an opera produced by a major American company.

William Grant Still (1895–1978)

As a child, **William Grant Still** (Figure 130) showed both interest and talent for music, studying violin and listening avidly to his stepfather's opera recordings. But as a young black living in the American south, he found it difficult to be taken seriously as a classical musician.

Nevertheless, Still won a scholarship to the prestigious Oberlin Conservatory of Music in Ohio, and after earning his degree continued his studies with the evolutionary (Second New England School) composer George Chadwick

Figure 130
William Grant Still.
(© Frank Driggs Collection.)

Harlem Renaissance Composition

Composer
William Grant Still

Title
Afro-American Symphony, third movement

Tempo
Animato (animated, rapid)

Form
Variations on a theme

Following a cymbal crash, a brief introduction sets the carefree mood, whereupon the syncopated theme enters, accompanied by a banjo brightly marking the backbeat. This unorthodox orchestral instrument has much to do with the programmatic character of the movement, intended to reflect happier moments in the African American experience. The theme soars to raptures of unalloyed pleasure.

A solo oboe begins the theme again, lightly, delicately, passing it to other instruments, which respond call-and-response fashion. A four-note motive ("dum-te-dum-dum") extracted from the light-hearted theme is tossed sequentially higher and higher, then passed through the ranges of the instruments.

A second theme, bluesy in mood, smooth (*legato*) rather than bouncy, almost—but not quite—of a plaintive tone, momentarily sobers the effect, blue notes heightening the poignancy of this brief passage. But the irrepressible main theme returns shortly with its confident banjo backbeat. The orchestra sounds increasingly jazzy as it accompanies the saucy tune to an entirely satisfying conclusion.

and the revolutionary Edgard Varèse (pp. 316–318). For several years, he played in dance bands and variety shows while working for a popular music publishing company, and before becoming definitively involved with concert music. Then, during his long and successful career, he wrote several operas and ballets, some film scores, and many songs and choral pieces.

Still, whose racial heritage was mixed, had personal interest in American Indian and Spanish American music but identified primarily with black Americans, and it was their experience he wished to express. Declaring his purpose to "elevate Negro musical idioms to a position of dignity and effectiveness in the field of symphonic and operatic music," Still allied himself with the Harlem Renaissance during the pre-Depression years, producing his fine *Afro-American Symphony* in 1930 (Listening Example 70).

[handwritten margin notes:]
- first to have his symphony played by major orchestra
- first to conduct major symphony orchestra
- first to have opera produced by major American company

Many American composers of the late twentieth century, including those discussed in Chapter 21, shared the ideals so eloquently expressed in the music of Copland, Barber, Still, and other early mainstream composers. Indeed, their accomplishments inspire much of today's American music.

Terms to Review

Copland-Sessions concerts   A series of concerts sponsored by Aaron Copland and Roger Sessions from 1928 to 1931 for the purpose of promoting music by American composers.

fanfare   A brief, dramatic piece for brass instruments, with the character of an announcement or celebration.

classical ballet   A formal, stylized dance form that evolved in seventeenth-century France.

modern dance   A contemporary American dance form, less stylized than classical ballet, although today many dancers and choreographers combine the two techniques.

traditionalist   A composer who makes no radical departures from the conceptions of earlier music.

neoromantic   A contemporary composer whose music reveals nineteenth-century melodic, harmonic, and expressive characteristics.

augmentation   A rhythmic variation in which note values are doubled, making a theme twice as slow as the original.

diminution   A rhythmic variation in which note values are halved, making a theme twice as fast as the original.

Harlem Renaissance   A cultural movement centering in Harlem in the 1920s in which African American artists in every field achieved high art.

Key Figures

Nadia Boulanger – *influenced almost all American mainstream composers*
Aaron Copland *exhibits chare. of mainstream not SNES*
~~Martha Graham~~
Samuel Barber – *keyboard*
William Grant Still – *AA draws on AA heritage folktunes, spirituals*

Optional Listening Examples

Samuel Barber: *Knoxville: Summer of 1915*
William Grant Still: *Afro-American Symphony,* first movement

Suggestions for Further Listening

Aaron Copland: *Music for the Theatre*
Copland: *Piano Variations*
Copland: *El Salón México*
Copland: Concerto for Piano and Orchestra
Copland: *Billy the Kid* Suite
Copland: Third Symphony
Samuel Barber: Piano Concerto

20

The Avant-Garde after 1950

Experimentalism, which romantically denies traditional boundaries, abandons established rules of composition, and explores new concepts of the very meaning of music, appeals strongly to Americans, a romantic people, creative, inventive, independent, and accustomed to freedom and space. It is not surprising, then, that Americans have often been in the forefront of the experimental movement in music.

Experimentalists both here and abroad have followed diverse paths, some choosing an intellectual, controlled approach to their music, and other avant-garde composers remaining detached from the compositions they produce, thus leaving important aspects to be decided by the performers, listeners, or simply the vagaries of chance. Some composers of new music include elements of both romantic and classical styles in their work.

Rhythm and Timbre

By the mid-twentieth century, rhythm and timbre had replaced melody and harmony as the elements of primary interest for many American composers. Experimentaists carried forward the work begun earlier in the century by Ives, Cowell, and Varèse, altering traditional instruments, or playing them in new ways in order to produce unusual sounds. Many composers use traditional instruments, including the human voice, to produce sounds—such as whispers, shouts, groans, or teeth clicks—that do not conform to the traditional concept of beauty. Microphones may be placed inside music instruments to amplify the sound, alter or distort the timbre, and/or produce echo effects. Players may be directed to produce breathy, squeaky, or raucous sounds, sometimes but not always for programmatic effect. Several composers have found that the resonant timbres of mallet instruments, such as the marimba, xylophone, or glockenspiel, offer attractive alternatives to traditional orchestral or other Western sounds, whereas the precise rhythmic effects expert players can achieve on mallet instruments further enhance their appeal for many composers today.

In *Voice of the Whale* (scored for three masked musicians playing flute, violoncello, and piano), George Crumb (b. 1929) requires a flute player to hum while playing the instrument, achieving a sound eerily like that of the humpback whale. *Voice of the Whale,* which directs that the performers wear

337

Figure 131

Musical instruments invented by Harry Partch. (AP/Wide World Photos.)

George Crumb = 'Voice of the Whale'

masks to obscure their identity and that the stage be bathed in the deep blue light of the sea, is also a mild example of a **theater score,** which requires performing musicians to act as well as play their instruments and sing. (Crumb's "El niño busca su voz," an Optional Listening Example, also involves unusual vocal and instrumental effects.)

Some composers, of whom **Harry Partch** (1901–1974) is the best known, invented entirely new musical instruments. Known as the hobo composer, because he spent time on the rails, Partch designed and built an amazing array of exotically named instruments, including the kithara, crychord, marimba eroica, and spoils of war among others (see Figure 131).

Tape Music and the Electronic Synthesizer

A few French composers having developed the techniques of *musique concrète* in the 1940s, and some German musicians in the early 1950s experimented with **tape music,** storing electronically generated sound materials on tape and then manipulating them, much as the French had manipulated their prerecorded sounds. They worked with the new **electronic synthesizer** (Figure 132), an instrument of seemingly unlimited capabilities. Composers achieve the *pitch* they desire on the synthesizer by plugging into electronic

Figure 132
Electronic music workstation including sophisticated equipment with which to compose, perform, and record music. (Corbis/Bettmann.)

oscillators. ("Oscillation" is another word for vibration.) A **finger board** allows players to slide through a range of pitches, unhampered by frets or keys. By plugging into other outlets on the synthesizer, one can alter the shape of the **sound wave,** thus determining the timbre of the sound to be produced. Electronic **filters** can select out high and low ranges of a broadly "spread" sound, such as industrial or machinery noise, producing a narrow band of melody of an interesting but nontraditional timbre (Figure 133).

Not only do the synthesizer and other electronic techniques make it possible for composers to achieve sounds never heard before but also composers now can hear their compositions immediately instead of waiting for live performances to be arranged. Further, if the results please them, they can save the sounds on tape. It is not necessary to rehearse a piece and rely upon the abilities of (or pay a salary to) performers, because a composer may at will accomplish all of the sounds of a piece, independent of human assistance.

The new electronic techniques offered a thrilling new range of experience to composers interested in creating new sounds and exercising total control over their performance. Among the American composers enthusiastically participating in tape music experimentation was Edgard Varèse (see pp. 316–318), whose dreams of instruments capable of creating sounds at the composer's will had finally come true. Much as certain contemporary visual artists acknowledge and seek to retain the integrity of the medium (wood, canvas, etc.) with which they work—emphasizing instead of disguising the natural grain or the pattern of weave, for example—Varèse desired to project a sound and then let it take its own course.

In 1957 to 1958 Varèse composed *Poème électronique* specifically for performance at the Brussels World's Fair Pavilion. Mixing sounds from both natural and electronic sources, Varèse here anticipated the mixed-media and

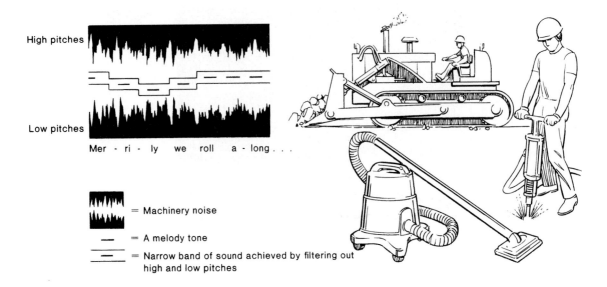

High pitches

Low pitches

Mer - ri - ly   we   roll   a - long . . .

= Machinery noise

— = A melody tone

— = Narrow band of sound achieved by filtering out high and low pitches

Figure 133

On an electronic synthesizer, high and low pitches can be filtered out of machinery noise to produce a narrow band of sound or a melodic line.

environmental works of the 1960s. The concept of the piece was grand indeed: listeners heard the taped piece through 425 loudspeakers arranged throughout the fair's Philips Pavilion, its astonishing array of sounds swirling over and around their heads to dizzying effect.

Today computers aid composers in the process of notating music, rendering the procedure faster, more accurate, and more efficient than in the past. Computers also allow the use of tempos too fast and rhythmic combinations too complex for humans to accomplish live, as well as nontonal intervals very difficult for musicians to hear and reproduce with accuracy. Thus in effect, electronic techniques allow composers total technical control over the performance of their work.

Milton Babbitt (1916–)

Became leader in applying Schoenberg's twelve-tone technique

As a student at New York University, **Milton Babbitt** (Figure 134) discovered that using Schoenberg's twelve-tone technique allowed him to achieve the mathematical precision he desired in his own musical compositions. Soon Babbitt became a leader in the movement to apply Schoenberg's concept of an orderly series of pitches to other aspects of composition as well, arranging patterns of rhythms and durations, for example, into series that also are systematically repeated throughout a composition, an extension of the twelve-tone technique called **total serialism, serialization,** or **serial technique.** In some pieces, the various series are mathematically related to each other; in others, they are independent.

Babbitt = electronic music

Babbitt also was one of the earliest enthusiasts and primary exponents of electronic music, codirecting the establishment of the first electronic synthesizer built in America (1959), a project sponsored by Princeton and Columbia Uni-

Figure 134
Milton Babbitt.
(Courtesy of Milton
Babbitt.)

versities and located at Columbia in New York City. It was several years later
before synthesizers became available to composers in other parts of this country.

Babbitt, who finds rhythm and timbre more interesting to work with than
melody and harmony, uses electronic techniques to achieve the exotic sounds
and complex rhythms he desires. A brilliant man who composes challenging
music and deplores mistakes or misinterpretations by performers, Babbitt
writes pieces that exist only on tape and for which there is no score, knowing
these will always be heard as he intended. Together with the resources of the
electronic synthesizer, computers, and magnetic tape technique, total serialism allows Babbitt to achieve the highly ordered and logical music he prefers.

"Ensembles for Synthesizer" (Listening Example 71) is an early classic of
this kind of electronic music.

[handwritten margin note: Interests are more into Rhythm and timbre than in melody and harmony]

Chance Music

Some musicians turned away from the taut control of twelve-tone and magnetic tape techniques, preferring to leave certain aspects of the performance
of their music to *chance.* They were represented in the visual arts by the Abstract Expressionist painters, led by Jackson Pollock, and by the moving
sculptures of Alexander Calder, among many others. Free jazz musicians
brought chance to the world of vernacular music, and John Cage (see
pp. 319–324), the leading experimentalist of the 1950s and 1960s, led the
movement toward chance, or indeterminacy, in the concert world.

Cage found the lack of spontaneity afforded by twelve-tone and concrete
music profoundly dissatisfying, and his primary interest for many years was
in **chance** or **aleatoric music,** in which significant aspects of each performance are left by the composer to chance. His commitment to Zen Bud-
dhism, less judgmental and dogmatic than Western philosophies and religions, inclined him to resist hierarchical determinations as to what in music is

[handwritten margin note: John Cage led chance movement in 1950's and 1960's]

Concrete Music

Composer
Milton Babbitt

Title
"Ensembles for Synthesizer" (excerpt)

Form
This piece is a mosaic of tiny fragments (ensembles), each distinguished by a characteristic timbre, range of pitch, rhythmic pattern, dynamic level, and texture.

Timbres
Babbitt programmed the synthesizer to produce various metallic, wooden, and mysterious airy sounds, with occasional references to the sound of an electronic organ.

Rhythms
The rhythmic patterns are varied and complex, and are sometimes played at extremely rapid tempos, requiring electronic performance techniques.

Pitches
All twelve tones are used, although not according to Schoenberg's row technique. The ranges of pitch level are extreme.

Because this music is conceived and constructed differently from traditional compositions, it must also be approached differently by the listener. Concentration on and appreciation of the highly sensuous sounds and the fascinating rhythmic techniques yield intense listening pleasure.

proper and desirable. The ancient Greeks determined that division of the octave into seven tones constituted the most satisfactory system of scales; but Cage proposed that the octave might as well be divided by ten, twenty, or any number of intervals at all.

Improvisation is one form of such **indeterminate music** (as chance or aleatoric music is also called), requiring performers to make certain decisions concerning melody, rhythm, and harmony; but aleatory encompasses much more than this. The root of the word *aleatory* comes from the Latin word for dice, and throwing dice is among the ways of determining various aspects of an aleatoric piece—for example, melodic or metric patterns, or the number of repetitions of a phrase or section. Other imaginative techniques used by composers of chance music include graphic notation that may be interpreted in many different ways; performance decisions that are based on the Chinese

Book of Chance, called *I Ching* (pronounced "E Jing"); scores that may be read backward, forward, or upside down; and circular scores that may be read clockwise or counterclockwise. The range of possibilities is limited only by the limits of a composer's imagination.

The degree of possible indeterminacy ranges from minimal, as in Ives's *Unanswered Question,* to **random** music, in which almost all of the composition changes from one performance to another. Thus Cage's *Imaginary Landscape no. 4* (1951) is "scored" for twelve radios, indicating specific positions on the radio dials, dynamic levels, durations, and even the degree of abruptness with which each sound begins and ends; but of course different material will be broadcast at each "performance."

As the meaning of music is being reexamined in our time, respected opinions on the subject of what constitutes music and musical sound vary. Some would argue that Cage's *Imaginary Landscape no. 4* is random *sound* as opposed to *music,* whereas others believe that the piece is clearly "organized sound" and therefore meets the broad definition of music. Still others insist that the *quality* of the sounds determines whether a composition is music or simply a listening experience.

Silence We have seen that composers notate rests, or periods of silence, as carefully as they notate pitches (see Table 1, p. xxii). But Cage discovered that although specific sounds may cease, there are always *other* sounds that continue; thus, true silence is never part of the human experience. Traditionalists would argue that the continuing sounds are "noise" as opposed to "music," but Cage considered *all* sounds worthy of attention and encouraged us to be aware and appreciative of them. In fact, he flatly stated that "silence" is an absurd concept that simply does not exist.

To demonstrate the nonexistence of silence, Cage placed himself in a soundproof chamber, as silent as technicians could make it; but his own bloodstream and nervous system produced clearly audible sounds. Next he wrote a book titled *Silence* (1961) and composed the notorious "4′33″" ("Four Minutes Thirty-Three Seconds") for "any instrument or combination of instruments," the score indicating three movements, each marked *tacet*— the term musicians use to mean "be silent." According to Cage, however, although the instruments make no sound at all, the audience has "a profound listening experience" throughout the duration of the famous noncomposition.

When Cage died, the American Society of Composers, Authors, and Publishers (ASCAP) expressed their profound respect and regret with the full-page black-bordered announcement shown in Figure 135.

Other Composers of Chance Music

During the 1950s, three composers based in New York City became closely associated with John Cage while developing related ideas of their own. Like him, they intended to achieve objectivity in their music by refusing to specify

Figure 135

This full page appearing in the Sunday issue of the *New York Times* the week of Cage's death gave apt and poignant tribute to this influential composer. (Courtesy of American Society of Composers, Authors & Publishers.)

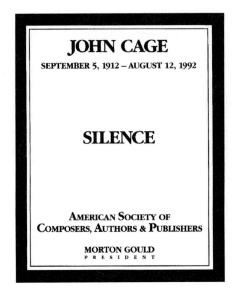

details in the traditional way: In other words, they allowed their music to "come into its own."

Morton Feldman (1926–1987) sometimes used graphic notation to indicate his general intentions, leaving specific pitches and their durations to the determination of the performers. In one piece, he indicated the *notes* but left *rhythms* unspecified, allowing them to evolve within a general tempo established by the conductor at the beginning of each performance. Feldman is among those experimentalists whose imaginative scores sometimes also constitute works of visual art. Feldman's *Projection 2,* for example, is a series of rectangles indicating periods of time, small triangles placed within the rectangles suggesting when to play and how long tones should endure, and the vertical placement of the triangles giving a general idea of approximate levels of pitch.

Earle Brown (b. 1926), another associate of Cage, reflected in his music the mobility of Alexander Calder's sculptures and the spontaneity of Jackson Pollock's paintings, claiming to have composed some pieces so rapidly and spontaneously they represented "performances" rather than "compositions." Brown, too, developed intriguing and attractive graphic notations for his scores, such as *December 1952* (Figure 136), written on one page as a series of vertical and horizontal lines that indicate only in a general way the direction, dynamic level, duration, and pitch of the sounds. A decade later Brown further demonstrated affinity between music and visual art by composing *Calder Piece 1963–1966,* for which Alexander Calder made a large mobile sculpture expressly for use as an instrument in the work.

The third New York associate of John Cage, Christian Wolff (b. 1934), like Feldman wished to "set sounds free," and like Cage was interested in silence as well as sound. His tones sometimes seem suspended in air, surrounded by space that lets them "breathe." Wolff has written some chamber

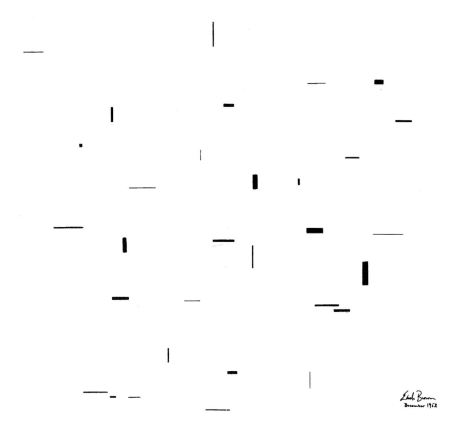

pieces for which neither the instrumentation nor the duration of the tones (which *are* notated) is specified. The score for *1, 2, or 3 People* is a good example of the artistic nature of Wolff's original notation.

Even the ever-adventurous Henry Cowell wrote at least one piece of genuine chance music, the *26 Simultaneous Mosaics* (1963) for clarinet, violin, violoncello, piano, and percussion. The *Mosaics,* brief pieces written for each of the instruments individually, may be played in any order chosen by the players, who also, according to Cowell's instructions, may start and stop playing as they please.

Indeterminacy continues to be significant in today's concert music among so-called mainstream as well as New Music composers. Many who desire a degree of indeterminacy in their largely structured music have devised ingenious techniques for indicating the parameters within which performers are to interpret their compositions.

Lukas Foss (b. 1922) began composing lyrical melodies in **neoclassical** forms (that is, those of earlier periods), but subsequently becoming interested in chance music he developed a kind of compromise between old and new sounds. The members of his Improvisation Chamber Ensemble, established at the University of California in Los Angeles in 1957, learned to improvise

Figure 136

Excerpt from the score for *December 1952* from *FOLIO* by Earle Brown. (Copyright © 1953 [renewed] Associated Music Publishers, Inc. International copyright secured. All rights reserved. Used by permission.)

freely within limits he defined in his own unconventional notation. (Foss finally disbanded the group, however, feeling that its improvisations had become too predictable.)

In spite of his aleatoric inclinations, Foss controls the form of his works, and his German Romantic heritage remains apparent in the lyricism of his melodic lines. *Baroque Variations* (1967) reveals his mixed appreciation for old and new, order and chance: A kind of surrealistic montage of references to music by composers from the Baroque era (Domenico Scarlatti, Handel, and Bach), it yet requires the performers to improvise, and the music has a very contemporary sound.

Notation

Chance musicians such as Morton Feldman, Earle Brown, and John Cage are not the only composers who have created original means of notating their music. Theater scores, for example, often require original methods of notation. Other characteristics of new music necessitating new kinds of notation include unusual techniques of playing on traditional instruments, passages to be sounded so rapidly that composers notate only their start and finish, clusters showing the number and range of tones but not the actual pitches, extremely complex divisions of beats, and extremely long durations better expressed in seconds of time than in quarter, half, and whole notes.

Graphs serve some composers as a means of notating the parameters within which pitches, rhythms, durations, and metric patterns are to be determined. Several composers have devised different means of notation to accommodate the specific demands of each new piece. And visual interest and appeal continue to interest some (see Figure 137).

Pauline Oliveros (1932–)

Pauline Oliveros began composing music in a traditional manner but soon became fascinated with the qualities of all sounds, including those produced by nature (raindrops, wind) and by machinery. She avoids the meter and pulse characteristic of Western music in favor of rhythms that shift, expand, and contract more or less systematically, and her heightened sensitivity to timbre has led her to explore and experiment extensively with vocal and instrumental colors, often to stunning effect.

Oliveros is among the composers who have chosen to give up the idea of individual control over their music. She prefers to guide a group—often of music amateurs—through a mutually creative experience. For example, she once asked the members of a large audience each to sing a pitch of their choice, sustaining it for the length of one breath. Coming to the end of that breath, they were to listen to someone as far away as possible and respond to his or her pitch. For the next fifteen minutes, extraordinary waves of harmony washed over the room, thrilling "composer" and performers alike.

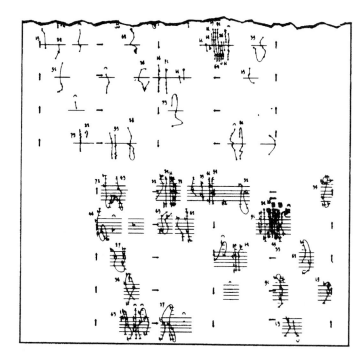

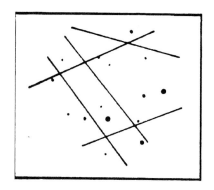

Listening Example 72

Abstract Choral Music

Composer
Pauline Oliveros

Title
Sound Patterns

The score indicates very precise and quite difficult rhythms to be realized by singers improvising pitches within specified ranges. The singers also must produce various sounds, including tongue clicks, whispers, shouts, lip-pops, and finger-snaps. The effect, although entirely the result of human performance, suggests electronic enhancement and is somehow—unaccountably— whimsically humorous.

Figure 137
Nontraditional notation by John Cage.

In Oliveros's *Sound Patterns* (Listening Example 72), a choral work with no text, the voices produce abstract sounds as unrelated to traditional concepts of melody and harmony as are abstract paintings to the shapes and colors of representational art. Using tape and other electronic techniques,

Oliveros creates distinctive pieces of sound imagery, haunting in their seductive sonic beauty.

The composers discussed in this chapter have been in the forefront of those challenging traditional concepts and offering new ideas of the meaning and the sounds of music. Our last chapter will introduce other, more conservative, composers who also have profoundly enriched America's musical landscape.

Terms to Review

theater score   A concert piece that includes visual and dramatic elements as well as music.

tape music   Electronically generated sounds that have been recorded on tape and manipulated to create a music composition.

electronic synthesizer   An electronic sound generator capable of producing, imitating, and altering sounds.

oscillators   The means by which pitch is determined on an electronic synthesizer.

fingerboard   A board on the synthesizer, uninterrupted by keys or frets, allowing a player to slide through a continuum of pitches.

sound wave   The wave by which sound is transmitted, which when altered affects the sound's timbre.

filter   On a synthesizer, electronic instruments that filter high and low pitches from a wide band of sound to produce a narrow band of melody.

total serialism   Also called **serialization** or **serial technique.** Application of twelve-tone concepts to other aspects of a composition (timbres or durations, for example), which, like tones, may be arranged into series and repeated.

aleatory (aleatoric music)   Sometimes referred to as **chance** or **indeterminate** music, aleatoric music leaves significant decisions to the performer of a composition, or to chance. An extreme example of aleatoric music may be called **random** music.

neoclassicism   The preference of some contemporary composers for the smaller ensembles, emotional restraint, and formal designs characteristic of the music of the Baroque and Classical periods.

Key Figures

Harry Partch   _dissatisfied w/tradition, West Coast_
Milton Babbitt   _electronic – dost is meast to be felt_
~~Lukas Foss~~
~~Pauline Oliveros~~

Optional Listening Example

John Cage: *Aria and Fontana Mix* (aleatory)

Suggestions for Further Listening

Harry Partch: "The Letter: A Depression Message from a Hobo Friend" (1943)
Partch: "Plectra and Percussion Dances" (1949–1952)
Milton Babbitt: *Three Compositions for Piano* (serialism)
Lukas Foss: *Baroque Variations*
Foss: *Time Cycle*

21

American Concert Music since 1950

B y the 1950s, Americans enjoyed unprecedented access to a broad range of concert music. They could purchase long-playing records (LPs), listen to many hours of concert music a week on radio stations, and watch live performances on TV. Centers for performing arts were being built around the country, and important music conservatories in several American cities offered music training of the highest quality. All of this music activity stimulated large numbers of American composers to write music intended for concert performance.

The modern American mainstream of music is varied and changing, but its new modes of expression are rooted in the past. Mainstream composers, in fact, are traditionalists who continue the evolution of music in a logical, orderly manner, expressing their ideas in contemporary, yet familiar terms. The elements of music are differently approached than in earlier times: Harmony in recent music is often entirely dissonant, and while a contemporary piece rarely has "no melody"—that is, no meaningful succession of tones forming a musical line—modern melodies often are more angular in contour than the songlike melodies of the nineteenth century. A few composers continue to base their melodies on twelve-tone and serial techniques—no longer considered avant-garde—including the long leaps between tones caused by octave displacement. (To approximate this effect, try playing the first three tones of "Three Blind Mice," for example, choosing each of the tones—say E, D, and C—from a different octave) Some composers simply write melodic contours or "gestures" within a given range but without precise pitch notation; others who specify pitches may choose them from a continuum ranging between extremely high and low tones and including microtones unfamiliar to Western ears. All of these techniques make it difficult for inexperienced ears to follow a melodic line (which is not to say it is not there). On the other hand, a new piece sometimes quotes one or more familiar tunes, such as a patriotic song, a hymn, or a children's tune, bringing comfortable associations to the listener's mind. And some composers simply retain a firm preference for lyricism.

Modern traditionalists, like the experimentalists, often focus on rhythm and timbre rather than on melody and harmony as the elements of primary interest and potential development.

very important composer of 20th century American music.

William Schuman (1910–1992)

William Schuman, a rather conservative composer with strong nationalistic interests, reigned as one of the giants of twentieth-century American music. He began composing while in high school, when he also formed a jazz ensemble (in which he played violin and banjo) and played in the school orchestra. After years of writing popular songs (many with the famous lyricist Frank Loesser, none of them a hit), he finally realized that his real gift lay in the composition of orchestral and other concert literature—often flavored, however, with jazz and with the sounds of American folk traditions. Schuman also had strong executive talents, serving prestigious terms as president of Juilliard, first president of the Lincoln Center for the Performing Arts, and chairman of the MacDowell Colony.

Schuman's orchestral music is mostly for a large orchestra, featuring distinct blocks—as opposed to delicate lines—of color. His long melodies soar over strong rhythmic foundations, giving much of his music an aura of majesty. Among his compositions based on American tunes, the three-movement *New England Triptych* includes sections on two tunes we have studied: William Billings's "When Jesus Wept" and "Chester." Schuman subsequently arranged the "Chester" movement as an *overture* (a one-movement programmatic piece) for symphonic band (Listening Example 73).

Elliott Carter (1908–)

Elliott Carter (Figure 138), who has been particularly interested in new approaches to rhythm, devised a method known as **metric modulation.** Just as harmonies modulate systematically from one key to another, Carter "modulates" rhythms, forming new metric patterns by slowly and methodically altering the value of a basic note. For example, by changing the value of the quarter note from sixty to eighty beats per minute, Carter of course increases the tempo of the music; but if he also uses the new, quicker quarter note as the base value of a new *meter,* we may say he has accomplished metric modulation. The concept of metric modulation is intellectual and the realization complex, but Carter's music is clear and quite accessible to the interested and prepared listener.

Carter's String Quartet no. 2 illustrates this rhythmic technique: The piece's traditional elements include the instrumentation (two violins, viola, and cello) and the four-movement structure; but there is also an Introduction and Conclusion, and the four movements are not separated by pauses but linked by solo cadenzas—one for the cello, one for the viola, and one for the first violin. To enhance their independence still further, Carter suggests that the instruments be placed at some distance from each other on the stage. (Remember Charles Ives's positioning of the instruments in *The Unanswered Question.*) Metric modulation and other complex rhythmic techniques make the piece challenging to performers, but the work, which won the 1960

Concert Overture

Composer
 William Schuman

Title
 "Chester" Overture

Form
 Concert overture. Less formal in design than a piece for orchestra
 might be, this symphonic band overture is a fantasy (although
 Schuman resists the term) on Billings's famous tune.

 It begins slowly and quietly with the melody in the woodwinds.
 Cymbals crash and, with a sudden change of key, a stately second
 verse is played by the brass. Drum rolls and dramatic crescendoes
 enhance the drama.

 The second verse dies away, there is an abrupt change to a fast
 tempo, and the tune returns. The treatment is less literal than at
 first and becomes even more imaginative, as Schuman explores
 keys, timbres, harmonies, tempos, and moods. Fragments of the
 tune are recognizable throughout. Toward the end, the melody
 returns intact, but with new harmonization, and the piece comes
 to a stirring conclusion.

Pulitzer prize in music, is not forbidding from the listener's point of view.
(Elliott Carter's Double Concerto for Harpsichord and Piano with Two
Chamber Ensembles is an Optional Listening Example.)

New Concepts of Form

Some contemporary composers have adapted the symphony, concerto, and
other traditional forms, as Elliott Carter adapted his String Quartet no. 2, to
meet their twentieth-century needs. Many composers view traditional forms,
such as rondo or fugue, however, as formulas too tied to earlier concepts of
symmetry and tonal relationships to stimulate their creativity today. Some in-
vent a new form for each piece they write, believing that the form itself
should be determined by characteristics of the specific piece it organizes.

 Modern concepts of form generally are based on principles of repetition
with variation, rather than on the complex development of motivic ideas
characteristic of music in the Classic style. These formal concepts, as well
as certain rhythmic innovations, bear a relationship to the style called
minimalism.

Figure 138
Composer Elliott Carter.
(AP/Wide World Photos.)

Minimalism

Minimalism began as a kind of "dream music," with simple, restful sonorities changing very slowly over a drone. Changes in melody, harmony, and rhythm also were minimal, and the structure of a composition simply evolved as the music quietly continued. Terry Riley, Philip Glass, and Steve Reich have been particularly involved with minimalist music.

Terry Riley (1935–) Composer/pianist **Terry Riley** pioneered minimalist music in the mid-sixties, writing music reflective of the rhythmic subtleties of the classical music of India, where Riley studied for a time, and also revealing the improvisatory characteristics of jazz. He experimented with tape loops (varying the synchronization of repeated patterns by altering the length of tape, for example). Then, influenced by his experiences with non-Western music, and by the work of another American composer, La Monte Young, he composed a number of pieces in what has come to be called minimalist style.

Riley's composition *In C* (1964) in a sense reinvented the whole process of listening to music. *In C* consists of fifty-three brief motives, each consisting of tones chosen mostly from the octave beginning on middle C. The number or kind of instruments required to perform the piece is not specified, although usually a piano is included in the ensemble. While someone—usually the pianist—marks a pulse by repeatedly playing two very high Cs at the

Figure 139
Philip Glass.
(AP/Wide World Photos.)

same time, the other musicians each play each of the motives, starting to-gether with the first motive and proceeding to the next motives, in order, as they individually choose. Each musician may repeat a motive any number of times (or not), moving to the next motive when ready, regardless of where the other players are in the piece. Each musician chooses how to phrase each mo-tive, where to put the downbeats, and how long to rest between motives, with the piece ending when all musicians finally reach Motive 53. The sound of the music, which has an almost hypnotic effect, has been described as a highly appealing, constantly evolving, tonal tapestry; and certainly it consti-tutes a kind of chance music.

Terry Riley remains an active, creative musician: Carnegie Hall commis-sioned his first orchestral piece, *Jade Palace,* in 1990, and in 2000 he was working on a set of twenty-four pieces for guitar and guitar ensemble. But Riley remains best known today for his pioneering work with minimalist music.

Philip Glass (1937–)
Philip Glass (Figure 139) has been among the leading exponents of minimalism. Having studied traditional composition techniques with Nadia Boulanger and others, he developed a strong interest in sonority, leading him to linger for such long periods on interesting sounds that all sense of pulse became obscured. Impressed by the incredibly sophisti-cated rhythms of the music of Africa and India and thinking he might some-how adapt them to his needs, Glass studied with Ravi Shankar, a famous In-dian sitar player, who interpreted various complex and subtle Indian rhythmic techniques in a manner Glass might apply to his own compositions.

From Indian practice, Glass derived a rhythmic system unlike the Western metric system, which *divides* measured units (see Table 1, p. xxii). Glass's is an *additive* procedure, starting with a simple rhythmic pattern, repeating it for some time, and then altering it *very* gradually by systematically adding or removing units.

Glass, like so many contemporary musicians, finds affinity with colleagues in the visual fields of art. For example, he says the work of certain sculptors, who stripped their works of all superfluous lines to produce figures of extreme simplicity, inspired him to vary the slowly evolving sounds in his minimalist music by occasional abrupt shifts of timbre or harmony.

More interested in the *sound* than in the *form* of a piece, Philip Glass often requires performers of his music to have creative as well as interpretive skills beyond those of the usual ensemble player. Therefore he formed his own Philip Glass Ensemble, consisting of players—for whom some of his music is specifically conceived—who are able and willing to perform in this new and challenging way. The Ensemble, which Glass himself directs, consists of two electric organs, four woodwind players who double on several amplified wind instruments, and a female singer who uses her voice as another, wordless "instrument." Glass often leaves the choice of instrumentation of a piece to the Ensemble members, so that the sound of a particular composition is actually determined at the time of each performance and may differ considerably from one concert to the next.

Although some listeners consider Glass's music monotonous, it has attracted many enthusiasts who find it soothing, easy to follow, and stimulating in a new, even a spiritual, way. Its cosmic sense of ongoing time addresses an increased interest in various non-Western concepts and techniques, including meditation and an unhurried, relaxed, less organized approach to life. The music is controlled but not intellectual, and its simple, naïve effect has been compared with that of popular music.

Steve Reich (1936–)

Steve Reich (pronounced "Rike") also has been associated with minimalist music, but although his music often moves very slowly it usually has a discernible pulse or beat. (Reich's *Drumming* is an Optional Listening Example.) Some of his compositions reflect his serious study of African drumming techniques, their timbres also revealing the influence of non-European percussion instruments, including African mallet instruments (*Six Marimbas,* for example), Indonesian gamelan, and Latin American claves. Both Glass and Reich have strong interest in the rhythms and procedures of progressive jazz as well.

Reich, considering music a continuing *process* whose evolution is of interest in itself, appreciates gradual and systematic change allowing him, as he says, to "hear the process happening." To this purpose, he has worked with loops of tape, playing them over and over so that their sounds have formed repeated cycles. By playing two or more tape loops simultaneously at slightly different speeds, he has created a form based on the gradual unfolding of a simple idea that he refers to as **process music.** Reich also has created process music for live performance: As instrumentalists repeat simple ostinatos, some move gradually ahead of others, producing the same "out of sync" effect that may be achieved with tape loops.

Women in Music

Many women have paved a promising path for others to follow in classical music, as well as in jazz and other vernacular fields. A number of women have served, or continue to serve, in prestigious posts as opera or orchestral conductors, formerly rare positions for women. **Sarah Caldwell** (b. 1924) made her conducting debut in 1976 as the first female conductor at the Metropolitan Opera and since then has led many well-known opera and symphony orchestras. Another well-known woman orchestral conductor, **Marin Alsop,** also has forged a highly successful career.

However, obstacles remain, as perhaps they always will, for a woman choosing to enter the profession of orchestral conducting: discrimination (by employers, players, and audiences alike) persists, and women managing a career and family may find the time and travel demands of an orchestra conductor forbidding. Of course orchestral instrumentalists face many of the same difficulties, if to a slightly lesser degree.

A number of women who are composers, however, have flourished in our time, immeasurably enriching our American music repertoire. An arbitrary, hardly definitive, list of well-known and highly successful composers of recent years would include, besides Pauline Oliveros, Louise Talma (1906–1996), Vivian Fine (1913–2000), Joan Tower (b. 1938), Barbara Kolb (b. 1939), Meredith Monk (b. 1943), and Libby Larsen (b. 1950). So successful have so many women become in this field that a composer's gender seems of increasingly, and refreshingly, less significance every year.

Thus **Ellen Taaffe Zwilich** (b. 1939, Figure 140) numbers among today's outstanding American composers. Having studied with Elliott Carter and Roger Sessions, Zwilich became the first woman to receive a doctoral degree in music composition from Juilliard. Her Symphony No. 1 received the Pulitzer Prize in music—the first ever awarded to a woman—in 1983, and her works have been played by major orchestras in the United States and abroad. Reviews consistently refer to her music as accessible, melodic, warm, appealing, and of outstanding quality.

A Promise of New Sounds

Compared with the years early in the twentieth century or just after World War II, music in recent decades has remained relatively stable. Most of the composers who are widely known and admired today are over fifty, and some are considerably older than that. Economic conditions threaten concert life

Figure 140
Ellen Taaffe Zwilich.
(Lori Wells Braun.)

and the recording industry, and the Internet makes inexpensive, even free, alternative listening experiences widely available, lessening the support available to today's young composers of serious concert music.

Also largely because of prevailing economic conditions, the symphony orchestra has changed relatively little in recent years. Orchestras today rarely can afford to present typical works of the 1970s, which often called for a large number of percussionists playing a variety of exotic instruments, as well as for special staging, electronics, and lighting.

For these and for their own personal reasons, a large number of contemporary American composers have favored a modest and accessible manner, reaching out to audiences rather than (intentionally or not) alienating them. To their considerable advantage is the fact that performance standards have improved significantly in the last quarter century, as performers have become familiar with new instruments and with new techniques applied to conventional musical instruments. And much to the advantage of audiences is the new musical polylingualism, as composers mix the great Western tradition with music of other cultures and times.

The capabilities of recent technology have dramatically altered our perceptions, not just of music, but of the meaning and goals of human life and the role art plays in it. Laws of relativity, for example, replacing comfortably established laws of science and nature have weakened our sense of stability while expanding the range of our imagination. We have come, in fact, to *expect* the unpredictable, for we know that in life (and certainly in art) things are not always as they seem. But we know that the human experience will continue to be explored and reflected in our visual, literary, and performing arts.

We also know that all the arts will continue to explore and reflect the human experience and the wonders of our changing sensibility, to our lasting benefit and joy.

Terms to Review

metric modulation   Elliott Carter's term for the evolution of one metrical pattern to another through the systematic lengthening or shortening of basic units.

minimalism   A style of music based on many repetitions of very simple melodic and rhythmic patterns.

process music   Steve Reich's term for music whose form can be heard to evolve from the repetition of patterns slightly out of synchronization with each other.

Key Figures

William Schuman – *NE triptch based on 3 works of Billing*
Elliott Carter – *metric modulation*
Terry Riley
Philip Glass
Steve Reich
Sarah Caldwell
Marin Alsop
Ellen Taaffe Zwilich – *Pulitzer Prize in Music 1983*
David Del Tredici – tonal melody Alice in Wonderland

Optional Listening Examples

Elliott Carter: Double Concerto for Harpsichord and Piano with Two Chamber Ensembles
George Crumb: "El niño busca su voz" ("The Little Boy Was Looking for His Voice") from *Ancient Voices of Children*
Steve Reich: *Drumming*

Suggestions for Further Listening

William Schuman: *American Festival* Overture
Schuman: *New England Triptych*
Schuman: *William Billings* Overture
Elliott Carter: String Quartet no. 2
Carter: *Holiday* Overture
Philip Glass: *Music in Fifths*
Glass: *Music with Changing Parts*
George Crumb: *Voice of the Whale*
Crumb: *Ancient Voices of Children*

Just as earlier pioneers defied geographic boundaries, some early twentieth-century Americans extended the horizons of music, breaking ground for succeeding generations of experimentalists by exploring and extending the concept of musical sound. Charles Ives, curious about the properties of sound, equated dissonance with strength and composed in a bold, complex, independent style. Scoffing at the musically timid and encouraging adventurous listening, Ives greatly extended the sounds and the meaning of music.

By directly manipulating piano strings, Henry Cowell proved that *conventional* music instruments could produce new timbres. Among the first Western musicians to draw inspiration from the East, Cowell greatly extended the range of rhythmic complexity and actively supported the cause of New Music. Edgard Varèse explored the sounds of *nontraditional* instruments and predicted the invention of instruments that would create new sounds and reproduce a composer's intentions with absolute accuracy.

Many revolutionary *and* evolutionary modern composers have replaced the earlier interest in melody and harmony with more attention to rhythm and timbre, often finding inspiration in the instruments of non-European cultures. Those who prefer music that is highly organized, such as Milton Babbitt, may use the twelve-tone or total serial technique or render their music "concrete" by electronic manipulations recorded on tape. John Cage and other composers of aleatoric music moved in the opposite direction, requiring performers not only to interpret their music but also to share in its creation.

Although the modern American mainstream of music continues to be varied and changing, its new modes of expression are rooted in the past. Most of the first Americans to become professional composers independent of other sources of income studied in Paris with Nadia Boulanger. The earliest of them, dean of American mainstream composers Aaron Copland, based some of his early music on jazz and later used other means (folk, religious, cowboy music, for example) to give his music a nationalistic stamp. Copland sought to please his audience during the trying years of the thirties and forties by writing orchestral, vocal, and dance compositions with tuneful melodies and catchy rhythms; but some of his more challenging later works have yet to become part of the familiar American repertoire. Other mainstream composers include Samuel Barber, whose music is melodically lyrical and warmly expressive; William Grant Still, whose music addressed the black American's experience; and William Schuman, whose interest in American folk traditions and in jazz flavors much of his music. Minimalism, which has been of particular interest to Terry Riley, Philip Glass, and Steve Reich among others, has disappointed some and at the same time has attracted new listeners to the concert hall.

The meaning and concepts of music and art have changed more significantly in the last half century than during the previous three hundred years. As those involved in the visual arts, dance, literature, and music produce an unprecedented variety of individual and multimedia experiences, we enjoy increasingly ready access to the results of their creativity. Meanwhile, technology and the events of social history continue to affect the arts and the role they play in the life of every American.

The Charge

You are now well prepared to enjoy all kinds of American music. You know about the music of the Yankee pioneers, conceived for utility but considered art today. You have learned about our vernacular musics—from Stephen Foster's songs and Sousa's marches through ragtime, jazz, rock, and musicals. You have followed the development of American concert music and have seen how we became leaders in the field of experimentalism. You understand that American music, rooted like the American experience itself in the cultures of Europe, Africa, the Orient, and Latin America, stands now, brave and free, a monument to *our* culture and a source of infinite pleasure and stimulation.

The new and unfamiliar does not intimidate the initiated listener: Of course it is *safe* to listen to a work long acknowledged as a masterpiece, but it is *exhilarating* to hear the first performance of a potential masterpiece of our own culture and day! To condemn a piece for having "no melody" may be as absurd as to condemn a doughnut for having no center, a piece by Mozart for having no electronic synthesizer, or an African dance for not being accompanied by a symphony orchestra.

And so, armed with the experience you have gathered through this course, with a sense of adventure, and in a spirit of curiosity and happy expectation, may you venture forth to join the ranks of adventurous, prepared, receptive, creative listeners absorbing the many musics of today. Enjoy!

Glossary

A

a cappella   Unaccompanied choral music.

acid rock   Sometimes called "psychedelic rock." Music that attempts to evoke the sensations experienced by a person under the influence of LSD.

acoustic instrument   The natural, as opposed to electric, instrument.

alabado   A religious song of praise, belonging to Spanish and Mexican folk traditions.

Alberti bass   An accompaniment pattern consisting of rhythmically regular broken chords.

aleatoric music   Sometimes referred to as **chance** or **indeterminate** music, aleatory is music in which the composer has left significant decisions to the performer or to chance. An extreme example is called **random** music.

alto or **contralto**   The low female voice.

American operettas   Musical shows adapted from the Viennese style, written for the Broadway stage.

answer   The second presentation of the fugue subject, on the dominant.

anthem   A through-composed religious song, usually with a biblical text, for performance by a choir rather than a congregation.

aria   A songlike setting, musically expressive, accompanied by the orchestra.

armonica or **glass harmonica**   A musical instrument invented by Benjamin Franklin, consisting of tuned, wet glasses that were rubbed to produce sound.

arrangement   In jazz, a written musical score that includes most or all of the notes to be played.

art rock   A blend of rock and symphonic or concert styles.

art song   A secular song intended for concert or recital performance.

atonal   With no tonic note or tonal relationships.

augmentation   A rhythmic variation in which note values are doubled, making a theme twice as slow as it was originally.

B

backbeat   Heavy accent on normally weak second and fourth beats of a measure in quadruple meter.

baile   Traditional Spanish social dance, popular in areas of the southwestern United States.

ballad   A folk song, strophic in form, that tells a story.

ballad opera   An English form of musical theater setting comedy and satire to popular tunes.

banjo   A string instrument derived from the African *banjar*.

bass   The low male voice.

bass clef (𝄢)   Usually used to notate lower pitches.

Bay Psalm Book   The first book printed in America, a psalter that first appeared in 1640.

bebop   A complex, highly improvised jazz style, largely developed by Charlie Parker and Dizzy Gillespie.

big bands   Popular dance ensembles of the thirties and forties, consisting of twelve to eighteen players. The bands had brass, reed, and rhythm sections.

bitonality   Two keys at the same time.

blue notes   Flexible notes, usually slightly under normal pitch.

bluegrass   A commercial instrumental style derived from mountain music.

blues   A black vocal folk music.

bomba   Puerto Rican couple dance derived from Africa.

bones   A folk percussion instrument consisting of a pair of castanets tied together and held in one hand.

boogie-woogie or **piano blues**   A popular piano style with the form and harmony of the blues, but a faster tempo and a dance beat.

book shows   Musicals with an integrated plot.

bossa nova   Brazilian rhythm, slower, more subtle than Cuban dances, reflecting the influence of cool and progressive jazz.

break   A dramatic, unstable, strongly rhythmic section, as in a march.

broadside   A written ballad, printed on a large sheet or in a set of sheets called a *songster.*

burlesque   A variety show featuring satirical humor; later associated with striptease acts.

(

cadenza   Solo passage.

Cajun music   A country music of the Cajuns (Acadians), vibrant, light hearted, often with a strong dance beat.

cakewalk   A plantation dance with syncopated melodies, including the *short-LONG-short* figure that became characteristic of ragtime.

call-and-response   A solo voice alternating with a chorus of singers. The effect may be applied to instrumental music as well.

canon   A polyphonic composition in which all of the voices perform the same melody, beginning at different times.

cantata   A relatively short choral work on a religious or secular subject, accompanied by organ or orchestra.

chachacha   A slower version of the mambo, with a double beat added between the last and first beats of each measure.

chamber musical   Musical for a small cast and economical resources.

chamber opera   An opera for a small number of performers.

chamber orchestra   A small orchestra with a few instruments per line of music.

chance music   See **aleatoric music.**

changing meters   A different number of beats to the measure within a piece or section.

chantey   Folk song about sailors and/or the sea.

character piece   A relatively short piano piece, often in ternary form, of a characteristic style or mood.

chord   A meaningful combination of three or more tones.

chordal texture   The texture in which a melodic line is accompanied by chordal harmony. Also called **homophonic texture.**

choreographer   Designs the steps and movements of dancers.

chorus   A large ensemble, with several voices on each part.

chromaticism   Use of tones not belonging in a particular major or minor scale.

classical   A restrained, objective style of art. Spelled with a capital letter, refers to music of the eighteenth-century Classical period.

classical ballet   A formal, stylized dance form that evolved in seventeenth-century France.

classical Hollywood film score   Lush orchestral scores particularly associated with films of the 1930s, 1940s, and 1950s.

clef   A sign placed on the staff that fixes the pitch of each line and space.

coda   Closing section.

combo   A small jazz ensemble.

compound meter   Each beat in a measure is divided by three.

concept musical   A musical show presenting ideas subject to the audience's interpretation and leaving situations unresolved at the end.

concert band   An instrumental ensemble including brass, woodwind, and percussion instruments.

concertina   A kind of accordion or portable reed instrument. Melody and chords are achieved by depressing buttons or keys, and the wind is supplied by a folding bellows.

concerto   A multimovement (usually three-movement) work for orchestra plus solo instrument.

concert grosso   A Baroque composition for orchestra and a small group of solo instruments. The form has been revived by some twentieth-century composers.

conga   Cuban carnival dance-march, performed in a chain, with a heavy kick marking every fourth beat.

conjunto   Ensemble accompanying dance and song in norteño music, north and south of the Mexico-Texas border.

conservatory   A professional music school.

consonance   Musical sounds that seem to be passive or at rest.

contrapuntal   Another term for **polyphonic.**

cool jazz   A style introduced about 1950 for large bands that included some symphonic instruments.

Copland-Sessions concerts   A series of concerts sponsored by Aaron Copland and Roger Sessions from 1928 to 1931 for the purpose of promoting music by American composers.

countermelody   A melody performed together with another melody.

country-western Western music with a country flavor, including western swing, honky-tonk, and cowboy songs.

cover, cover recording A re-recording of a popular record, sometimes intended to appeal to a broader audience than the original recording addressed.

Creole In nineteenth-century New Orleans, a person born in America of a family native to another country. Later the term was used for people of mixed racial heritage.

crossover Music that appeals to more than one kind of audience.

cu-bop Dizzy Gillespie's fusion of Latin rhythms with bebop.

D

da capo "From the beginning." A three-part design. The composer writes the first section and a contrasting middle section of a da capo aria, and the performer repeats the first section with embellishments.

diminution A rhythmic variation in which note values are halved, making a theme twice as fast as it was originally.

disco Commercial dance music popular in the 1970s.

dissonance Musical sounds that imply tension, drive, or activity.

Dixieland A white imitation of New Orleans jazz, introduced in Chicago; faster, more intense than New Orleans jazz.

dominant The fifth tone of the major or minor scale, the tone most closely related to tonic. Often represented by the Roman numeral V.

doo-wop The name given background vocal ensembles that accompanied Motown singers, often by

singing neutral or nonsense syllables.

drone A single tone, sounded continuously or repeated.

dynamic level The level of volume (loudness or softness) of a musical sound.

E

eight-to-the-bar Ostinato that accompanies a boogie. Each of the four counts in a measure is divided into a long and short beat.

electronic synthesizer An electronic sound generator capable of producing, imitating, and altering sounds.

elements of music The basic materials of which music is composed.

ensemble In music theater, a group of solo singers, each performing their own words and music at the same time.

experimental music Music challenging traditional concepts of musical sound.

exposition The first section of a fugue.

F

falsetto The singing voice above the normal (full or chest voice) range.

fanfare A brief, dramatic piece for brass instruments, with the character of an announcement or celebration.

field holler An emotional vocal phase, sung as a long, loud call, developed by blacks as a kind of communication with fellow workers.

fife and drum corps An early band, consisting of fifes and drums,

which performed for military and later for entertainment purposes.

film score All the music accompanying a film.

filters High and low pitches may be filtered electronically from a wide band of sound to produce a narrow band of melody.

finale In music theater, the final scene of an act or of the show.

fingerboard A board on the synthesizer that is uninterrupted by keys or frets, allowing a player to slide through a continuum of pitches.

First New England School America's first composers. Also known as Yankee pioneers and singing school masters, they lived in New England in the late eighteenth century and wrote music for practical purposes.

folk hymn Another name for a white spiritual.

folk music Usually music of unknown origin, transmitted orally and enjoyed by the general population.

folk rock The addition of light rock effects to urban folk music.

form The organization or formal design of a musical composition.

forte Loud.

free jazz A style of free improvisation introduced by Ornette Coleman in 1960.

fuging tune A song in two sections, the first homophonic and the second polyphonic in texture.

fugue A polyphonic composition, originally for keyboard instruments, in which the imitative entrances of the voices alternate between tonic and dominant.

functional or nondiegetic music Film music heard by the audience only.

funk   Rock music rooted in soul but with lyrics that express interracial concerns.

G

gamelan   An Indonesian percussion ensemble.

Gilbert and Sullivan operettas   Comic English musicals (words by Gilbert, music by Sullivan).

glee   A part-song with three or more lines of music, in chordal or homophonic texture, with the melody usually in the top voice.

glissando   An expressive slide between pitches.

gospel   Folklike religious songs. White gospel includes camp-meeting spirituals; black gospel has had far more influence on popular music.

Gregorian chant   Term for Roman Catholic plainchant since the sixth century.

grunge   The Seattle sound, a hybrid of pop, heavy metal, and punk.

H

habanera   Cuban dance, whose rhythm is the basis of the tango.

half step   The smallest interval on a keyboard, and the closest interval in traditional Western music.

Harlem   A black neighborhood in uptown New York City that became an important center for jazz.

Harlem Renaissance   A cultural movement centering in Harlem in the 1920s in which African American artists in every field achieved high art.

harmony   The meaningful combination of two or more different tones.

heavy metal   Loud, heavily electronic music, often with distorted sound.

hillbilly music   A term applied to early country music.

hip-hop   Music (sounds) accompanying rapped lyrics.

homophonic texture   The texture in which a melodic line is accompanied by chordal harmony. Also called **chordal texture.**

honky-tonk   A Texas vocal style with harsh, honest lyrics.

hymn   A religious verse set to music suitable for congregational singing.

I

improvisation   The simultaneous invention and performance of music.

indeterminate music   See **aleatoric music.**

interval   The distance between two tones.

irregular meters   Those other than duple, triple, or quadruple (usually five or seven to the bar).

J

jam   To improvise together informally.

jazz   A means of performing music. There are many moods and styles, but improvisation is an inherent characteristic of jazz.

jazz rock or **fusion**   Rock instrumentation blended with the improvisation and flexible rhythms of jazz.

K

key   The name of the tonic upon which a tonal piece is based; also called **tonality.**

L

legato   Smooth, uninterrupted.

libretto   The words of an opera or other dramatic vocal work.

lining out   Each line of text is sung by a leader and echoed by the congregation.

M

MacDowell Colony   An artists' colony established on the estate of Edward MacDowell in Peterboro, New Hampshire.

major, minor scales   The tonal scales.

mambo   Afro-Cuban form of big band dance music

mariachis   Mexican strolling groups of musicians, including strings and often led by one or more trumpets.

mazurka   A Polish folk dance of varying character, in triple meter.

melody   A meaningful succession of pitches.

meter   The organization of rhythm into patterns of strong and weak beats.

metric modulation   Elliott Carter's term for the evolution of one metrical pattern to another through the systematic lengthening or shortening of basic units.

Mickey Mousing   Musically mimicking or accenting an action.

microtone   Any interval smaller than a half step.

minimalism A style of music based upon many repetitions of simple melodic and rhythmic patterns.

minstrel show An entertainment in which white men performed music and comedy in imitation of stereotypical African Americans.

modern dance A contemporary American dance form, less stylized than classical ballet.

modes Seven-note scales within the range of an octave, including but not limited to the scale patterns we call major and minor.

modulate To change key systematically, usually by using one or more tones common to each key as pivot.

monophonic texture The musical texture consisting of one melodic line.

Moravians Europeans who settled in Pennsylvania and whose music compositions and performances were of a highly professional quality.

motive A short melodic phrase, subject to development.

Motown A highly successful black company that recorded, published, and sponsored black popular music.

multimedia shows Performances including some combination of music, dance, film, slides, tape recordings, and other sound and visual techniques.

musical comedy A play with music, in which the elements of entertainment are connected by a plot.

musique concrète or **concrete music** Music that has been created by manipulating taped sounds. Any sounds may be selected for this purpose.

N

Nashville sound Country music's commercial response to rock and roll, with country themes, pop instrumentation, and a heavy beat.

nationalism A nineteenth-century movement in which artists of many nationalities sought to express the particular characteristics of their own cultures.

neoclassicism The preference of some twentieth-century composers for the small performing ensembles, emotional restraint, and formal designs of the Classical and Baroque periods.

neoromantic A twentieth-century composer whose music reveals nineteenth-century melodic, harmonic, and expressive characteristics.

new age A soft rock style providing soothing, repetitious blocks of gentle, unassuming sounds produced by synthesizers or acoustic folk instruments.

New Music The term used for music of an experimental nature.

New Orleans jazz Virtuosic improvisation by members of a jazz combo on a given melody.

new wave A term encompassing several styles, all conceived within the context of modern studio and electronic techniques.

norteño Texas Mexican-American style of music.

notes The symbols with which music is written down.

O

octave The interval of an eighth.

octave displacement The choice of a note of the same name from a distant octave.

Oklahoma! Landmark musical, by Rodgers and Hammerstein, integrating all elements of entertainment into the drama.

opera A drama that is sung, usually with orchestral accompaniment.

operetta or **light opera** A form of music theater in which the music and dancing are closely integrated with the plot.

opéra bouffe A French style of operetta, featuring satirical humor and visual spectacle.

oratorio A dramatic work based on a religious subject and performed by vocal soloists and chorus with orchestral accompaniment.

oscillators The means by which pitch is determined on the electronic synthesizer.

ostinato A repeated melodic and/or rhythmic pattern.

overture In music theater, an introductory instrumental piece.

P

patter songs A feature of Gilbert and Sullivan operettas (and other forms of music theater) in which humorous words are sung very rapidly, with comic effect.

payola The acceptance by disc jockeys of money and gifts in return for plugging recordings.

pentatonic scale A five-note scale within the range of an octave.

piano roll Perforated paper roll on which pianists recorded their performances.

piano Soft.

pitch The highness or lowness of a sound.

player piano Instrument for playing piano rolls by pumping pedals, forcing air through the holes in a piano roll as it wound over a tracker bar.

polymeters　Two or more meters performed simultaneously.

polyphonic texture　The musical texture in which two or more melodic lines are simultaneously combined.

polyrhythms　Two or more simultaneous rhythmic patterns

polytonality　Multiple simultaneous keys.

powwow　A contemporary pan-Indian gathering for singing, dancing, rodeo, carnival, and other celebrations.

prepared piano　A grand piano on which some or all of the strings have been "prepared" by placing foreign materials on them to alter pitch, timbre, and dynamic level.

process music　Steve Reich's term for music whose form can be heard to evolve from the repetition of patterns slightly out of synchronization with each other.

program, programmatic music　Instrumental music that describes a story, scene, idea, or event.

progressive jazz　A symphonic approach to jazz, introduced by Stan Kenton.

psalm tunes　Tuneful settings of the psalms in versions suitable for congregational singing.

psalms　One hundred fifty inspirational verses found in the Old Testament of the Bible.

psalter　A collection of the psalms in metered and rhymed verse, suitable for setting to simple tunes.

punk　A British reaction to flagrantly commercial rock and roll.

Q

quarter tone　The interval halfway between a half step.

R

race records　The term used before 1949 by the popular music industry for recordings intended for an African American audience. (Later called rhythm and blues.)

ragtime　A written piano music, duple in meter and moderate in tempo. The left hand generally marks the beat and the right hand plays a syncopated melody.

random music　See **aleatoric music.**

rap　Rapid spoken patter accompanied by funk-style rhythms; derived from reggae performance practices.

recitative　A declamatory setting of a text, with rhythms and inflections related to those of speech. Used in opera and other dramatic vocal works.

reed organ (parlor organ, cabinet organ, cottage organ, melodeon)　A keyboard instrument, popular in the nineteenth-century for its relatively small size and price, the variety of sound produced by adjusting stops, and the small amount of maintenance it required.

reeds　Wind instruments in which the player causes small, flexible pieces of material called reeds to vibrate. Clarinets and saxophones are single-reed instruments: oboes and bassoons have double reeds.

refrain　A section of melody and text that recurs at the end of each verse of a strophic song.

reggae　A blend of rock and African Jamaican styles.

rests　Symbols indicating the cessation of musical sound.

revue　Originally, a lavishly staged and costumed show with no integrated plot. Later, a series of scenes united by a theme but without a plot.

rhythm　The arrangement of time in music.

rhythm and blues (r&b)　Broadly, black popular music of the 1950s. More specifically, a black popular style in quadruple meter, with strong backbeats and a danceable tempo.

riff　A repeated rhythmic pattern that provides unity in a jazz composition.

rock　A collective term encompassing many styles of popular music that evolved from and succeeded rock and roll.

rock and roll　A popular music of the mid-fifties to mid-sixties that combined characteristics of rhythm and blues and country-western music.

rockabilly　A close amalgamation of country music and rock and roll.

romanticism　Emotional, subjective approach to art. So romantic was the period from about 1825 to 1900 it is referred to as the Romantic period of music.

rondo　A musical form in which various episodes alternate with the opening material: **A B A C A.**

round　A circular canon, which may be repeated indefinitely.

row　The term for the arrangement of pitches on which a twelve-tone composition is based.

rubato　Flexible rhythm and tempo. The word means "robbing" and refers to stealing from the tempo at some points and roughly repaying the lost time at others.

rumba   Group of Afro-Cuban musical and dance forms, with many variants.

S

The Sacred Harp   A popular nineteenth-century collection of hymns and spiritual songs.

salsa   Popular Cuban dance band music with rhythms derived from African American dances.

samba   Most famous Brazilian song/dance; duple meter.

scale   A stepwise rising or ascending pattern of pitches within the range of an octave.

scatting or **scat singing**   Improvising on nonsense or neutral syllables.

Second New England School   The first American composers to write significant works in all of the large concert forms. Sometimes referred to as the Boston classicists.

shape-note notation   A method that assigns a shape to the notated pitches of *fa, sol, la,* and *mi,* placing them on the staff in normal position.

Show Boat   Landmark musical by Jerome Kern, based on a literary work and addressing sensitive social issues.

simple meter   Each beat in a measure is divided in half.

singing school masters   America's first composers. See **First New England School.**

singing school movement   An effort by music amateurs to teach New Englanders to read music and to sing. The movement began in the early eighteenth century.

song plugger   A music store employee who played popular songs on the piano to demonstrate them for customers.

soprano   The high female voice.

soul   A fervent, emotional black style rooted in gospel and the blues.

sound track   All of the dialogue, sound effects, and music of a film.

sound wave   Longitudinal pressure waves. As the shape of the sound wave is altered, the timbre of the sound changes.

source or **diegetic music**   Music heard by characters in the film as well as by the film audience.

spiritual   A folklike religious song with a simple tune.

staccato   Short, detached tones.

staff   Five lines and four spaces upon which music is notated.

stops   Levers or buttons that allow the player to adjust the timbres produced by certain keyboard instruments.

strain   A melodic section in a rag, march, or other vernacular form of music.

stride piano   A jazz piano style in which the left hand alternates low bass notes (on *one* and *three*) with midrange chords (on *two* and *four*).

strophic form   Most common song form. Two or more verses of text are set to the same melody.

subdominant   The fourth tone of the major or minor scale, represented as IV.

subject   The principal melodic theme of a fugue.

suite   An instrumental work composed of several dances or other semi-independent pieces. The suite from a film includes several sections of music from the film score.

surfing songs   Songs by the Beach Boys and other groups reflecting the easy California lifestyle.

sweet jazz   Music with the sound and flavor of jazz, but arranged so

that playing it requires little improvisation.

swing   A term with many meaning, including *(a)* a mood of lilting spontaneity, or *(b)* a danceable music played by the big bands in the thirties and forties.

symphonic jazz   Concert music that has some of the sounds of jazz.

syncopation   The occurrence of accents in unexpected places.

T

tambourine   A small drum with metal disks that jingle when the instrument is struck or shaken.

tango   Graceful, sensuous Argentinean dance, the first of the Latin rhythms to become popular in the United States.

temp   Temporary film score, composed of existing music, offered to demonstrate to a film's composer the type of music desired for the film.

tempo   The rate of speed at which music is performed.

tenor   The high male voice.

texture   The manner in which melodic lines are used.

theater scores   Concert pieces that include visual and dramatic elements as well as music.

theme and variations   An instrumental form in which a theme or melody recurs to provide unity, but in altered guises for variety.

theremin   The earliest electronic musical instrument.

third stream   As coined by Gunther Schuller, the term refers to the combination, but not the blending, of jazz and classical music. The term is loosely used today to refer to avant-garde jazz styles.

through composed A song form containing new music throughout, as opposed to setting new text to the repetition of music as in strophic form.

timbre The characteristic quality of the sound of a voice or instrument.

Tin Pan Alley The popular music publishing industry from the late nineteenth through the first half of the twentieth centuries. Also, the street(s) in New York where the publishing houses were currently located.

toasting, dubbing A technique developed by Jamaican disc jockeys of rapid patter-talking over the sound of spinning records.

tonality, tonal system The system of harmony that has governed Western music for nearly four centuries.

tone A sound with a specific pitch.

tone cluster A chord, usually of several tones, built upon seconds. Clusters are often played with the flat of the hand, the arm, or a board cut to a particular length.

tonic The first and most important note of a tonal scale, often indicated by the Roman numeral I.

total serialism Also called **serialization or serial technique.** Application of the twelve-tone technique to other aspects of a composition, which may also be arranged into series and repeated systematically.

traditionalist A composer who makes no radical departures from the styles and conceptions of earlier music.

transcription An arrangement of a piece originally composed for a particular instrument or ensemble so that it can be played by a different instrument or combination of instruments.

treble clef (𝄞) Usually used to notate higher pitches.

Treemonisha An opera by Scott Joplin.

triad The most basic chord in the tonal system, consisting of three alternate pitches or two superimposed thirds.

trio A strain that is lighter in texture, softer in dynamic level, and more melodic than the others in a piece.

tune A melody that is easily recognized, memorized, and sung.

twelve-bar blues The classic form of the blues, consisting of three-line stanzas with four bars or measures in each line.

twelve-tone A technique of organizing music in which all twelve tones of the octave are of equal significance.

two-step or fox-trot An American dance derived from ragtime. The meter is duple, the rhythm syncopated, the tempo moderate.

U

unison The same pitch at the same or different octaves.

urban blues Blues pieces written for publication and professional performance.

V

vaudeville A show with acts of every variety, including blackface scenes, dogs, circus stunts, songs, and dance.

vernacular The common language. In music, refers to popular music.

verse-chorus form Common song form in which the *verses* relate the story and a tuneful *chorus,* or refrain, is repeated after each verse.

vibrato A slight variation in pitch that adds warmth and intensity to vocal or instrumental sounds.

Viennese operettas The style of operetta written by Johann Strauss, Jr., and other Viennese composers, featuring exotic settings and romantic plots.

virtuoso A performer who possesses dazzling technical brilliance.

vocables Neutral syllables, sometimes called consonant-vowel clusters.

W

Wa-Wan Press A publishing company established by Arthur Farwell and dedicated to the publication of American music.

walkaround A lively plantation song-and-dance routine often forming the finale of a minstrel show.

walking bass A steadily moving pattern in the plucked string bass that has melodic as well as rhythmic implications.

waltz A ballroom dance in triple meter.

western swing The Texas swing band style, influenced by Mexican and Hawaiian sounds and by jazz.

whole step An interval equal to two half steps.

work song Song sung to relieve tension and to regulate the movements of people working alone or in unison with others.

Y

yodel   A singing technique that involves changing rapidly back and forth between the normal and falsetto voices.

Z

Ziegfeld Follies   Elegant revues produced by Florenz Ziegfeld nearly every year from 1907 to 1932.

zydeco   A rock-flavored black Cajun style of country music.

Index